Adventure Guide to

Vermont

2nd Edition

Elizabeth L. Dugger

HUNTER

Hunter Publishing, Inc.
130 Campus Drive
Edison, NJ 08818-7816©
☎ 732-225-1900 / 800-255-0343 / Fax 732-417-1744
Web site: www.hunterpublishing.com
E-mail: hunterp@bellsouth.net

IN CANADA:
Ulysses Travel Publications
4176 Saint-Denis, Montréal, Québec
Canada H2W 2M5
☎ 514-843-9882 ext. 2232 / fax 514-843-9448

IN THE UNITED KINGDOM:
Windsor Books International
The Boundary, Wheatley Road, Garsington
Oxford, OX44 9EJ England
☎ 01865-361122 / fax 01865-361133

ISBN 1-55650-887-5
© 2000 Hunter Publishing, Inc.

Cover: *Hayrake under sugar maple, Peacham,*© William H. Johnson
Photo of author, page xv: © Jenks Studio, St. Johnsbury, VT
All other photos by Elizabeth L. Dugger

Maps by Lissa K. Dailey, © Hunter Publishing, Inc.
Illustrations by Joe Kohl
Indexing by Nancy Wolff

4   3   2

CONTENTS

MAPS

AREA CODE

The area code for all Vermont telephone numbers is 802.

OCTOBER

by Elizabeth L. Dugger

Before the hard frost strikes, I walk my road
finding wild apples, rose hips
flushing red as autumn in the thickets.
I fill my jacket front,
pouching fruit until the zipper bulges.

After the killing frost, the colors
mute to heather, rust, and cold dark greens.
Clover heads stand prickly brown,
and the mud chills, hardening.

Each night I watch Orion dance.
I watch what the full moon brings to life:
Last night three deer walked up my road
dark eyes looking for fruit.

– First appeared in *Yankee Magazine,* October 1995.

About the Author

Well known regionally for her poetry of Vermont's Northeast Kingdom, Elizabeth L. Dugger is a long-time resident of the state. Reporting for several newspapers takes her around its back roads, as well as into the villages, small towns, and a handful of cities. She and her two sons live "with a lake at my feet and a mountain behind me." They follow a family tradition of seeking adventures throughout New England.

Acknowledgments

Hearty thanks go to staff members at the many Chamber of Commerce offices and state information services around Vermont, and to the Green Mountain National Forest offices. The Green Mountain Club gave much more than just trail information, and I wouldn't have missed the overnight snowshoe trek the club organized! (It took me only two days to recover from the stiff muscles; the exhilaration from the hike, though, lasted and lasted.) The local mail carriers did more than their share in keeping me in touch with a quickly changing landscape of exploration, too. Finally, I am indebted to both Vermont Public Radio and the state's glorious magazine, *Vermont Life*, for alerting me to many a hidden pathway and possibility. Almost every day I've found a fresh adventure calling.

Author's Foreword

In this second edition of *Adventure Guide to Vermont*, I've added some new adventures and extra directions, as well as updating lodgings and restaurants (an endless task that explains why I hike so much, to walk off those good meals!). Two major changes have taken place in Vermont since the first edition of this guide was published. One is the advent of the Internet, so that almost everyone has a Web site or at least e-mail address, and I've added many of these. More are appearing daily, and if you want to contact an inn that doesn't have a Web site listed in this book yet, my suggestion is that you first try entering www.innnametypedhere.com, using, of course, the inn name of the place you're trying to get in touch with. You might also try the many search engines available online, or visit the sites listed for the various chambers of commerce. Many of those have links to area accommodations.

The other notable change is that every Vermont road, be it back road or not, now has a name, a necessity for installing 911 emergency communications. This makes directions a lot easier to give (although you'll still find the country version prominent, such as, "go down about a half-mile until you reach the old house that was the Palmers; if you get to the four-corners, you've gone too far"). But the road-naming project is still a work in progress, with some road names not yet posted and some businesses still using post office boxes or less formal location names. Please bear with us; think of it as a sign that you're really out in the country.

Finally, a thank you to the **Green Mountain Club**, the mostly volunteer group that plans, maintains, and helps others to take exuberant advantage of the trails of the Green Mountains, especially along and around the Long Trail. Without their endless care, the woods would suffer drastically. Volunteer labor also helped Vermont trails to recover from the disastrous ice storm of 1998, which turned the peaks and forests into a lovely but treacherous wonderland of ice and snow, bending and breaking acres of trees and blocking miles of pathways. Visit the club office in Waterbury Center if you have a chance, and consider becoming a member, to get a newsletter that will invite you into more Vermont adventures.

Introduction

Adventure travel makes you feel alive, wakes you up to yourself as well as to your surroundings. That doesn't have to mean hanging from a cliff by your fingernails (although if you're into that, Vermont has plenty of mountains). You don't have to dare death to feel glad you're alive, or awed by what's around you. Just being in Vermont can give you that getaway feeling. But adventure gets the blood flowing, the heart pumping. Walk through an orchard. Climb a mountain trail. Canoe on a lake so silently that the loons don't dive underwater but watch you instead, as they continue their long, sorrowing cries into the dusk.

The adventures in this book provide a range of challenges, some relating to climate or wild terrain, others leading you to fresh perceptions of the natural world. Vermont is a mountainous state, still as green as its French name promised. It is a shelter for wild animals, rare plants, migrating birds. It is also a refuge for writers, artists, and musicians who thrive on beauty and seasonal changes. Life in its highest mountains provides a vivid physical challenge for outdoor enthusiasts. And in the towns and handful of small cities, entertainment flourishes. You can bring your family, your first date, your best friend, or come alone. The point is, you're here for an adventure. You're here to feel alive.

You can look the state over from its two (and that's only two) interstate highways, or from a bicycle on a back road. Climbing a mountain in hiking boots or on a multispeed bike will give you different views; so will savoring the silent grace of a hot-air balloon ride over a valley. You might take advantage of having a llama walk beside you through a wildlife refuge, while your gourmet dinner awaits in the gentle beast's saddlebags. Photograph the llama, or the moose that browses in the swamp, or the bold coloring of the pileated woodpecker. Vermonters have specialized in preserving both land and traditions. There's even a song that crystallizes the romantic allure of these mountain retreats: *Moonlight in Vermont*.

Here in the northwest corner of New England are the roots of independence and stubborn insistence on freedom that made Vermont a republic well before it joined the newly uniting states. Here is also the beauty that inspired conservationists before there was such a word. And here is air clear enough that you want to drink it, space wide enough to reconsider your own life in fresh terms. Whether you come to Vermont for a weekend in a Buddhist retreat or a Sunday of Gregorian chants at a monastery, an evening in an Abenaki ceremony, or a walk along the riverbank, there is a potent refreshment ready for you. A high-speed swoop down a ski slope or a moment watching a deer may touch the very same chord.

Assuming that you are eager to explore the special nature of Vermont, to learn new things about this private corner of the northeast, to get out and do things and see things and sample the days and nights, this book is designed to launch your adventures. It provides the information you need to plan and enjoy your exploring, as well as the details of food and lodging that a tired and hungry wanderer appreciates at the end of the day.

No description of Vermont would be accurate without the savor of its regional cuisine, whether it be maple syrup boiled to a sticky delight and poured over plates of fresh white snow, or elegant dining accented by local specialties like fiddlehead greens, fresh brook trout, or mountain-grown blackberries. The name "cheddar" rings best with the word Vermont in front of it. And don't forget pies: venison pie, or chicken pie, or apple and maple and lemon and cherry and even strawberry-rhubarb, home baked, all lined up on planks, ready to sample at an old-time community supper. Adventuring in Vermont will give you plenty of appetite for these foods, as well as for the subtle seasonings that a well-nourished soul requires. See *Vermont Treats* on page 14, which has descriptions and sources for some of the state's best goodies.

Vermont is credited as the most rural state in the country, despite being barely three hours from Boston or Montreal, and just 4½ from New York City. There are about as many maple sugar makers as lawyers, and you'll fin three one-room schoolhouses still in operation. Something about Vermont has always inspired independence, which may be why so many people feel that coming here is coming home to themselves at last.

History

The Native Americans who lived in this region were mostly **Abenaki,** a tribe of the **Algonquin** nation. These "People of the Dawn" left much of their language as a heritage in Vermont's place names: Winooski means wild onion; Passumpsic is clear running water. Neshobe, who has both a river and a school named for him, was a chief. Today there are few native speakers of the Abenaki language, although ethnic pride is making a comeback, especially in the state's northwestern corner. In summer there are several regional pow-wows where the old traditions are showcased, along with fine handcrafted jewelry and clothing.

The first European known to have explored the region was the French explorer **Samuel de Champlain**, in the summer of 1609. He entered from the north, the Quebec encampments along the St. Lawrence River, allying with the Algonquins in an expedition against their enemies to the west, the Iroquois. He arrived at the lake that now bears his name (and marks Vermont's western boundary) on July 4th. His French tongue was the source of "Vermont," green mountain, and French is also still spoken in parts of the Northeast Kingdom and around Barre, where French Canadian settlers were drawn to farming and later to granite cutting. Several towns host festivals to celebrate the French Canadian heritage (and food!).

Introduction

Vermont

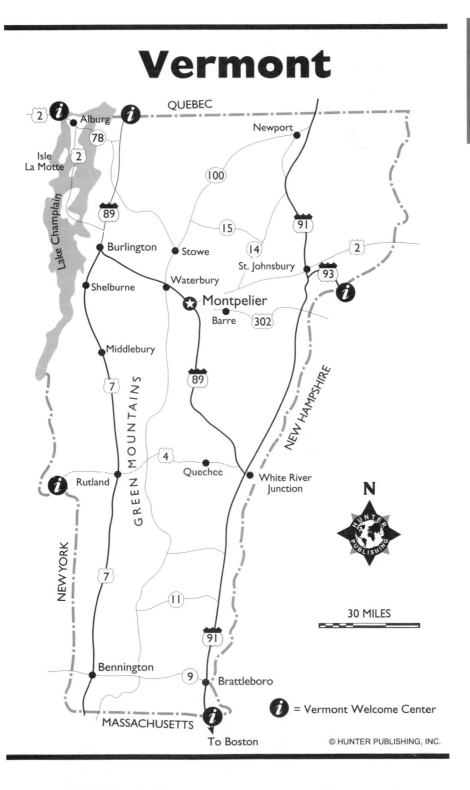

QUEBEC

② Alburg

Newport

78

Isle
La Motte ②

100

89

15

91

Burlington · Stowe

14

St. Johnsbury

②

Shelburne

Waterbury

93

Montpelier

②

Barre

302

Middlebury

89

Lake Champlain

GREEN MOUNTAINS

7

4

Quechee

White River
Junction

Rutland

②

N

NEW HAMPSHIRE

NEW YORK

7

11

30 MILES

91

Bennington

9

Brattleboro

②

MASSACHUSETTS

② = Vermont Welcome Center

To Boston

© HUNTER PUBLISHING, INC.

English settlements moved into the state from the south, starting with **Fort Dummer** near what is now Brattleboro, in 1724. The fort was a defensive outpost in the French and Indian Wars. When peace was made with the French in 1760, settlers from Connecticut and Massachusetts swiftly moved into the region, which was properly called the New Hampshire Grants at the time. Both New York and New Hampshire laid claim to the area. Resistance to those claims gave rise to a local militia, the **Green Mountain Boys,** led by **Col. Ethan Allen** in 1775. Their experience would later give them a significant role in the American Revolution at battles in Hubbardton and outside Bennington in 1777.

American though the land might seem, it was first an independent republic, declared at a meeting held in Westminster on January 17, 1777. The **Republic of Vermont** had its own mint and postal service, and stayed independent until 1791, when the state joined the union as the first "new" member since the original 13. **Thomas Chittenden** became Vermont's first state governor.

Independence has stuck as a habit of mind. Maybe it's in the water – the state is liberally endowed with rivers, streams, and lakes. Although the population now includes nearly as many "flatlanders" as it does those whose families broke the soil in past centuries, newcomers seem to quickly absorb the tendency to defend the woodlands and wetlands, keeping local government in a ferment over how and when to allow development, and how best to protect what people are still coming to savor: the land itself, whether wild or farmed or settled as villages and larger towns.

Geography

 Slicing along the north-south axis of Vermont are the **Green Mountains,** and their imposing presence dominates travel time and conditions. The two interstates only add up to 320 miles. **Interstate 91** is the north-south route, staying close to the Connecticut River, the eastern boundary of the state. About a third of the way up that highway, **Interstate 89** swings west toward the Champlain Valley, with views of some of the most imposing mountains: Mansfield and Camel's Hump, both over 4,000 feet high, and surrounded by peaks of around 3,600 feet. This is the only "easy" way to cut across the state in an east-west direction.

 TIP: *Any travel you do diagonally or from one side of the state to the other is much slower than you'd expect, because the roads are not multi-lane highways, and the terrain rises through mountain passes.*

The scenery is spectacular, like the views from the skiers' heaven of Lincoln Notch, the wilderness of Hazen's Notch to the north, and the hundred-mile view as old Route 9 climbs up Hogback Mountain in the south.

This up-and-down geography makes Vermont seem much larger than its outline on the map. If you travel on Interstate 91, you can easily make it from the south end of the state to the Canadian border in three hours. But it will also take three hours to drive from St. Johnsbury to Rutland, diagonally, even though that's less than half the "crow flying" distance on the map!

Getting Here & Getting Around

■ Southeastern Gateway

This book considers Vermont in terms of how you'll get to the villages and countryside of each area, and what's on hand to do there. Traveling by highway, most people enter the state in the southeast corner, near **Brattleboro,** so that area is known as the Southeastern Gateway. By most people's standards, Brattleboro would be considered a small town, but for Vermont it's close to being a city, full of arts events, a diverse college-oriented population, and dozens of tempting eateries. This is the hub of the region, and on the map you can easily visualize spokes of a quarter-wheel in the handful of highways spreading west and north. From Brattleboro, much as the British settlers did, the visitor can head up these roads that parallel the lesser rivers descending from the mountains to the ocean-bound Connecticut River. Small mountain towns like Jacksonville, Wilmington, Newfane, and Londonderry form a ring around Brattleboro. Within the same arc is the village of **Grafton.** It was a virtual ghost town until 1963, when a benefactor restored the feeling and prosperity of the 1830 sheep-farming community. In this working village, classic cheddar cheese is now made, sheep graze once more, and miles of hiking and skiing trails surround a gracious inn. Grafton captures the roots of the region in a single setting.

■ Bennington & The Vermont Valley

The less accessible southwestern corner is fenced off from Brattleboro by the high spine of the Green Mountains. But the winding rise of Route 9, once a soldiers' route during the Revolution, carries cars up Hogback Mountain for a three-state view, then past Haystack Mountain, and into the wilds of the **Green Mountain National Forest.** A steady descent westward through the wilderness (the southern reaches of the 350,000 acres of national forest) ends up in **Bennington's Historic Region,**

Regions of Vermont

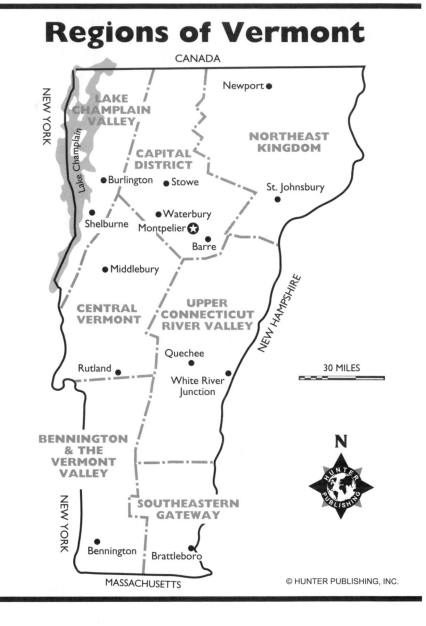

CANADA

NEW YORK

LAKE CHAMPLAIN VALLEY

Newport ●

NORTHEAST KINGDOM

Lake Champlain

CAPITAL DISTRICT

● Burlington ● Stowe

St. Johnsbury ●

● Waterbury

Shelburne ● Montpelier ⊙

Barre ●

NEW HAMPSHIRE

● Middlebury

CENTRAL VERMONT

UPPER CONNECTICUT RIVER VALLEY

Quechee ●

Rutland ●

White River Junction ●

30 MILES

N

BENNINGTON & THE VERMONT VALLEY

NEW YORK

SOUTHEASTERN GATEWAY

Bennington ● Brattleboro ●

MASSACHUSETTS

© HUNTER PUBLISHING, INC.

where there is another chapter of American Revolutionary history laid out in the very walkable college town. This part of Vermont is less like a wheel and more a ladder, heading south to north along the history-rich and scenic **Route 7.** Some of the state's finest fishing is found in the cold, clear rivers and streams of this region, especially along the Battenkill. Watch for canoes and kayaks on the roofs of passing vehicles. Small picturesque villages line Route 7 and make bicycling another popular way to explore. Country bed-and-breakfast homes and elegant inns dating back a century or more give a welcoming feeling to the region. Long before the interstates made American travel swift, "down-country" people discovered the beauty and vibrance of these mountain valleys; the 163-room Equinox Hotel in Manchester spreads its white-columned form against the imposing background of Mount Equinox itself, and dates back to 1769.

■ The Upper Connecticut River Valley

The central part of Vermont is again divided by the ridge of the Green Mountains. The eastern segment has the same characteristic as the Southeastern Gateway: all roads, like all rivers and streams, flow toward the blue ribbon of the Connecticut River and the accompanying travel routes of Interstate 91 and its older, slower shadow, Route 5. Major waterways are the three branches of the White River, and the Abenaki-tongued Ottauquechee and Ompompanoosuc. This is the Upper Connecticut River Valley. The towns and villages closest to the river valley offer pleasant biking and walking. As the land rises up to the west, so do the challenges. A hot-air balloon ride or small plane expedition can give you a soaring view.

DID YOU KNOW?

President Calvin Coolidge, called "Silent Cal," but who was in fact an impressive orator, grew up in the mountains of the Upper Connecticut River Valley.

■ Central Vermont

The section of central Vermont to the west, simply called Central Vermont in this book, is the heart of the state. Here is the valley town of **Middlebury,** with its noted liberal-arts college, and the surrounding hills made famous by poet laureate Robert Frost. **Rutland** is in this section too, a city small enough that as soon as you feel you've had enough of buildings and businesses, you're suddenly back in farmland. An amazing amount of this region is actually national forest, and numerous blazed trails lead to steep waterfalls, spectacular vistas, and cliffs where rare peregrine falcons nest and soar. The **Appalachian Trail,** an adventure in itself, veers eastward through these mountains on its way to Maine; Vermont's own **Long Trail,** which extends the full north-south length of the state, continues to hug the crests of the ancient, rocky peaks. Some of the roads that cross from west to east are narrow mountain passes that close in winter; others are recent multi-lane routes that simply require careful driving on the snowiest days.

VERMONT MILEAGE CHART	Bennington	Brattleboro	Burlington	Montpelier	Rutland	St. Johnsbury	White River Jct.
Bennington		40	123	122	56	155	95
Brattleboro	40		138	115	72	120	60
Burlington	123	138		38	69	77	91
Montpelier	122	115	38		66	39	54
Rutland	56	72	69	66		99	47
St. Johnsbury	155	120	77	39	99		58
White River Jct.	95	60	91	54	47	58	

■ The Capital District

With snow in mind, the next region described here, the Capital District, Stowe, & North, includes some of Vermont's tallest mountains: Mount Mansfield, reaching 4,393 feet, and Camel's Hump at 4083. (Killington, another tall one at 4,135 feet, is farther south.) The best known towns here are **Stowe,** a ski resort, and **Waterbury,** home of Ben & Jerry's Ice Cream and other gastronomical delights, and also the capital, **Montpelier,** where residents have defended their stance as the only state capital without a McDonald's restaurant. (The nearest McDonald's is only five miles away, but there are no golden arches within view of the golden dome of the statehouse!) Hiking and skiing both take advantage of this mountainous region, but so do back-road biking, mountain biking (even in winter!), and photographing the striking scenery. Once an area hard to reach, this stretch of "big hills" is now easily entered from Interstate 89, connecting travelers with the thriving city of Burlington to the northwest and the river-valley railroad town of White River Junction to the southeast. Other roads here are slow to travel, even if the map marks them as being major highways, like Route 108 or the scenic Route 100. Two lanes – one for coming, one for going – encourage drivers to take their time and savor the views.

■ The Lake Champlain Valley

A very different landscape spreads itself to the northwest, along the flat valley of Lake Champlain. Dairy farms thrive even at the edge of **Burlington**, Vermont's most lively city. Life has a coastal flavor, enlivened by frequent celebrations and festivals. Marinas and ferry launches line the lake edge. Even from the farms there are invigorating views of the long lake and the dramatic New York state mountains beyond. This is the Lake Champlain Valley, and although it is Vermont's most heavily populated area (Burlington has nearly 40,000 people, more than double its nearest competitor, Rutland), residential areas seem to bunch in clusters. The rural atmosphere is rarely more than five miles away at any moment. Perhaps this intense contrast feeds the musical and creative side: Burlington is famous for its jazz, and the towns farther north are home to many of the best traditional fiddlers, often French-Canadians spinning out reels for well-attended dances. Another intriguing aspect of the Champlain Valley is the cluster of large sandy islands at the north end of the lake. These are Native American traditional grounds, and they also sheltered rum-runners during Prohibition, much as the towns on the shore were once shelters for runaway slaves at last discovering freedom during the 1800s. The Underground Railway, the chain of homes and supporters that enabled these desperate men, women, and families to reach the safety of Canada during the Civil War, also befriended many arriving travelers and ended up helping them settle into a quiet northern farming and fishing existence without having to leave the United States. There are five state parks in the region now, including secluded island campsites so well protected that you can get there only by boat and with prior reservations. Wildlife sanctuaries also hug the shoreline, havens for flocks of migrating waterfowl.

■ The Northeast Kingdom

Everyone describes the Northeast Kingdom last of Vermont's regions, as it has always been the hardest to reach, the most isolated, and the most stubborn at resisting change. It is no longer hard to reach; Interstate 91 bisects it, a neat north-south passage connecting to the back roads that lead to quiet locations such as Coventry, Charleston, and Brownington. The region's resistance to change isn't complete; there have been plenty of changes, and comfortable lodging, boat and bike rentals, and guided tours abound. Skiers and fishermen enjoy different aspects of the mountains and valleys. But the outstanding effect of its isolation and steadiness is that the wild places in the Northeast Kingdom are preserved. Moose, wild turkeys, and rainbow trout abound; eagles and hawks soar on sunny days. The air is so crisp and clear that it makes you feel your own wings rustle in your chest, waking up urges as potent as the pulse of maple sap in a spring tree trunk. Artists, writers, actors, and people with scraps of poetry in their souls are drawn here, whether to put their strong feelings into words or paintings, or to simply savor the sensations of walking, canoeing, or touring along the winding roads and waterways.

Climate

 The contrast of four distinct seasons means there is plenty of variety in Vermont's climate. Although sunny summer days may reach 90° for a few hours, the 70s are more common; summer evenings cool off to the 50s, and an occasional night in the 40s or even 30s does happen. Spring and fall each have rainy days and sharp winds – exhilarating but also chilly if you don't prepare for the changes. Expect heavy morning dew even in the summer. A spring or glorious autumn day may include a 40° drop in temperature between noon and evening.

Windproof outer clothing and plenty of layers are the secrets of comfort, along with sturdy walking shoes that can take you over damp or wet ground.

Winter temperatures in Vermont average in the 20s, but nights get colder, dropping below zero for a few weeks each year, most likely at the end of January and in February.

AUTHOR TIP

Learn from the residents: listen to local weather forecasts in the evening as you plan your next day's excursion. Pay serious attention if the forecast includes a winter storm watch or warning. Savor the exhilaration of the weather, but do it safely.

Two seasons especially affect road conditions: early spring is known as "mud season," for its glutinous effects on the many unpaved roads. An ounce of caution will save many pounds of stuck-in-the-mud vehicles! And obviously, winter driving is a skill much in demand. For the most part, good planning simply means having plenty of warm clothes with you in your vehicle (or backpack if you're on foot or skis), and when driving winter roads, carrying a shovel in the trunk is always a good idea. See winter driving tips on the following page.

Weather has tremendous importance as you explore and seek adventures in this rural state. Local residents follow detailed weather forecasts, which are found on most radio and television stations, as well as in the regional newspapers. If in doubt, get a highway update by calling ☎ 800-ICYROADS. Vermont has some of the best-prepared and hardest-working state road crews, and there are usually only a few days each year when travel by either road or air is restricted while the crews plow, sand, and salt the surfaces. The contrast of daily weather adds spice to most visits, and encourages snuggling into sweaters, walking briskly to feel your own energy, and sitting peacefully at the side of a toasty woodstove or crackling fire with friends or good books and the warming beverage and tasty meal of your choice.

DRIVING IN SEVERE WINTER WEATHER

These precautions apply mainly to those who are determined to drive in the most difficult winter weather. Actually, Vermont road crews, local and state, take great pride in making sure that ordinary caution and a small decrease in speed will let you travel the winter roads safely and with pleasure. But if you are determined to sample the adrenaline of travel in stormy winter weather, or have chosen to spend time well beyond the reach of plowed roads, here's a quick review of the main points.

■ If you have a choice, get snow tires rather than all-season; it makes a difference if you're doing a lot of snow driving.

■ Always add a gas-line "drying" fluid to your tank if the night temperature is going below zero.

■ Go slowly. Many difficult road conditions can still be managed if you slow down enough.

■ Listen to the weather forecast, the local news and the people at the general stores. If the state police have closed the road or are recommending that people stay home, take it seriously; going off the road on ice makes a trip take much longer and pushes the stress level up to where it's just not fun anymore.

■ If you're going to drive in snow for more than a week or so, put a shovel in the trunk and carry a bag of cat litter; these two simple things will get you out of most common problems. (The cat litter goes on the ground to give your tires traction.)

The only season when insects are pesky in Vermont is late May to early June, called "black fly season" after the tiny biting gnats that hatch in wetland areas at that time. Regular bug spray works well as a defense; some of the most rugged outdoor workers swear by the benefits of Avon's *Skin-So-Soft,* a fragrant body oil. Windy days also disperse the insects. Although tick bites leading to Lyme disease are rare in Vermont, it is a good idea to wear socks and long trousers when walking through high grass, as in uncut pastures.

Foliage Tours

 Long known as the state's most scenic highway, **Route 100** is the traditional north-south foliage touring road. Despite its official-sounding title, the road is mostly a two-lane country journey, passing through small villages and winding alongside riverbeds.

Introduction

*A **Fall Foliage Hotline** operates in fall, beginning September 1, advising travelers about the most colorful displays.* ☎ *802-828-3239 and 800-837-6668.*

The peak weeks of foliage viewing – the last half of September and the first week of October – bring thousands of travelers to the state. And no wonder! The scarlet and gold of the sugar maples flames against the dark backdrop of spruce woods, with birches and poplars delicately outlined in their own softer golden fluttering. So try the back roads, especially the mountain passes. In the south of the state this means **Route 9** over the high ridge of Hogback Mountain, **Route 100** north into the Dorset villages, and driving toward the scenic reservoirs, Harriman and Somerset.

FOLIAGE TOURS BY TRAIN

The **Green Mountain Flyer** is Vermont's famous scenic railroad run, with twice-daily trips through summer and fall from Bellows Falls to Chester and back. Round-trip fares are quite low (adults $11, children $7) for this classic treat, and fall foliage season is a perfect time to enjoy it. The railroad adds sunset trips on the first two weekends of October. For information, contact Green Mountain Railroad Corp., PO Box 498, 54 Depot Street, Bellows Falls, VT 05101; ☎ 463-3069 or 800-707-3530; Web site www.rails-vt.com. Other routes provided by Green Mountain include the Champlain Valley Weekender, from Burlington through Shelburne and Middlebury to Vergennes in the summer (ask about possible autumn trips), and the Manchester to Arlington trip on the *Vermont Valley Flyer*, which gets extended in the fall to North Bennington (closed Tuesdays). Rail cars date from the 1940s and 1950s on the *Vermont Valley Flyer* (and are air conditioned); the *Green Mountain Flyer* cars go back to the 1930s and are pulled by a vintage diesel. Pack a picnic with you, or plan to eat at the other end of the route.

■ Suggested Foliage Routes

Bennington & The Vermont Valley

From Arlington, don't miss the **Kelley Stand Road**, which heads east into the Green Mountain National Forest. Take any of the forest roads leading north and south from the Kelley Stand Road for a glimpse of the wilderness.

Southeastern Gateway

Ski areas offer a special way to savor the foliage; ride an aerial tram or other chairlift to the summit for a breathtaking vista. **Stratton Mountain** in Bondville expects plenty of foliage visitors; so does **Mount Snow**.

Central Vermont

In the central part of the state, head for the mountain passes at Mount Horrid **(Route 73),** Bread Loaf **(Route 125),** and Lincoln **(Route 17).** You are in Robert Frost country here; all the back roads above Middlebury, leading away from Ripton, include bridges and mountain slopes. A stop at the Robert Frost Wayside on Route 125 will remind you of how the poet saw and celebrated the region. A little farther north, take the Mountain Road between Stowe and Smuggler's Notch for a challenge, with its steep stretches and sharp turns.

Capital District

One of the loveliest long drives for foliage viewing is to head north from the Stowe area along **Route 100** to Lowell, where you can drive through Hazen's Notch on **Route 58**. From Montgomery, enjoy **Route 118** and then **Route 109** for the covered bridges and wild country along the way back to **Route 15**, which carries you east along the river to Route 100 again.

Northeast Kingdom

The most remote part of the state is **Essex County,** between Interstate 91 and the New Hampshire border in the far north. Find your way to East Burke, where you can take the old "Toll Road" up **Burke Mountain** and climb the fire tower for incredible views. Return to the center of East Burke and follow **Route 114** north another two miles to the right turn marked Gallup Mills; this gently rising drive will carry you through woods where the deer and moose far outnumber the people. It is about 20 miles to Guildhall, where you can either turn north and drive clear to Canada before heading home again, or head south along the Connecticut River on **Route 102** and then **Route 2**.

Photographers won't want to miss the traditional villages of **Peacham**, **West Barnet**, and **Waterford**, where many an isolated flaming maple in front of a white-clapboarded home says "New England" most clearly. In southern Vermont, satisfy the urge for picturesque villages in Grafton or Chester, and don't miss Newfane, on Route 30 less than half an hour's drive from Brattleboro. These are lovely villages year-round, but the brief spectacle of the changing leaves is part of what Vermonters hold in their hearts to carry them through the long winters ahead.

If you have time for only one short foliage trip, make it along **Darling Hill** north of Lyndonville in the Northeast Kingdom. From the center of town head north and connect with Route 114, as if you were going to East Burke – but instead, a mile north of Lyndonville, just north of the intersection with Route 5, find the left turn clearly marked Darling Hill (and also marked for the Wildflower Inn). Another two miles brings you to the imposing roadside rows of cutleaf maples towering over the fields; the vista to the northwest into Willoughby Gap is especially lovely at sunset, when the fields and the protectively arching trees take on the most tender colors. A walk in the gardens at the Wildflower Inn will add one last drop of pleasure to this elegant drive before you return to Lyndonville, either backtracking along the road you've taken, or continuing north on the Darling Hill Road to the first right (another mile), which descends into the village of East Burke.

Vermont Treats

■ Cheese

Cheddar cheese and Vermont are practically synonyms in New England, and **Cabot Creamery** has taken its blue-ribbon cheeses around the world. But there are many varieties of cheese made from the milk of the mountainside farms, and some of the cheesemakers are still tiny independent home businesses. Tours are often available. Here are a few to start with.

■ Brattleboro: **K.C.'s Kritters**, call for directions, ☎ 257-4595. Kevin Kingsley offers tours of his small goat cheese operation, where he makes four types of fresh cheese in whole-milk and low-fat varieties.

■ Cabot: **Cabot Creamery**, Route 215, ☎ 563-2231. There are tours here throughout the year, and in summer and fall they are offered several times a day. The creamery also has a small theater to show films explaining the cheesemaking process, but most interesting is watching through glass panels as the cheese curd is prepared and cut. In addition to cheddars, Cabot makes Monterey Jack and reduced fat cheeses, plus yogurt.

■ Grafton: **Grafton Village Cheese**, in the center of the village behind the inn, ☎ 472-3866. The cheddars from this modest cheesemaker are favorites among those who like their cheeses

Crowley Cheese, in Healdville.

rich and tangy. There's an outdoor picnic area in which to savor your purchases.

■ Hardwick: **Kingsey Cheese of Vermont**, Routes 14 and 15, ☎ 472-5763. This is the least romantic of the local cheesemakers, set in a practical factory, but the cheeses make it worth a visit, with Vermont Swiss, Monterey Jack, garlic and parsley, jalapeño, and more. Be sure to try the cheese twists, a favorite.

■ Healdville: **Crowley Cheese**, Healdville Road (off Route 103), ☎ 259-2340. This is the oldest New England cheesemaker, working from a modest house at the side of Okemo Mountain. The sharp cheddars are especially flavorful, and the cheese kitchen is so small you're almost part of the process. Smoked and herbed cheeses add to the variety.

■ Milton: **Willow Hill Farm**, 313 Hardscrabble Road, ☎ 893-2963. Here are the certified organic raw milk aged sheep cheeses that are so hard to find. Tours should be arranged by calling ahead.

■ Plymouth: **Plymouth Cheese Corp**., at the Plymouth Notch Historic District off Route 100A, ☎ 672-3650. Tours are given in summer and fall. Watching the old-fashioned "granular curd" cheese being made takes you back into the days of Calvin Coolidge, who grew up nearby.

■ Putney: **Vermont Shepherd**, 915 Patch Road, ☎ 387-4473. Cynthia Major offers tours of the Shepherd cheesemaking operation. Prepare to taste with delight.

■ Shelburne: **Shelburne Farms**, 1611 Harbor Road, ☎ 985-8688. This large working dairy farm on Lake Champlain offers premium farmhouse aged cheddar cheeses.

■ Warren: **Three Shepherds of the Mad River Valley**, call for directions, ☎ 496-3998. Larry and Linda Faillace offer tours of their sheep's milk cheesemaking. Save time to tour the surrounding back roads for grand vistas.

■ Websterville: **Vermont Butter & Cheese Company**, call for directions and hours, ☎ 479-9371. A must for gourmands: creme fraiche, fromage blanc, quark, mascarpone, basil torta, salmon torta, and five goat's-milk cheeses.

■ Chocolate

When Madeleine Kunin was governor of Vermont, she often compared the state to her native country of Switzerland. She was talking about the mountains and dairy farms, but today she might also have fine chocolate in mind. There are more than 20 chocolatiers in the Green Mountain State, and many of them display their kitchens with tours and tastings. Here are some of these sweet places:

■ Brattleboro: **Tom & Sally's Homemade Chocolates**, 6 Harmony Place, ☎ 254-4200 or 800-827-0800. Tom and Sally Fegley offer tours and a chance to see how their famous cow pie candy bars are made. There are also gourmet treats with French and Belgian chocolate, and novelties like chocolate body paint.

■ North Brattleboro: **Chocolate and Gifts Express International**, North Putney Road, ☎ 800-432-3834 or 800-443-8706. Johanna Godfrey uses old family recipes with real butter and cream for her homemade fudge. Tours are offered.

■ Burlington: **Champlain Chocolate Company**, 431 Pine Street, ☎ 800-634-8105. James Lampman calls his delicacies the original chocolates of Vermont. See how the American truffles and the wonderfully rich and sculpted Lake Champlain Chocolates are made, and enjoy a discount on factory seconds.

■ Jacksonville: **Coombs Maple Products**, Maple Lane, ☎ 800-338-1849 and in Vermont 800-464-7305. Arnold Coombs offers tours to show how he makes pure maple candy hand-dipped in imported chocolate, as well as the maple caramel, nut, and chocolate chewies.

■ Manchester Center: **Mother Myrick's Confections**, Route 7A (half a mile south of the center of town), ☎ 362-1560. Ron Mancini's hand-dipped chocolates, buttercrunch, truffles, and fudges are hot competitors at the annual Taste of Vermont competition. As well as tours, there's a café on the premises serving cakes, pastries, and ice cream sundaes.

■ Shaftsbury: **Vermont Confectionery**, call for directions, ☎ 800-545-9243. Bruce Wamsley's viewing room reveals some of the secrets of 20 varieties of truffles and more than 200 seasonal novelty chocolates.

■ Waterbury Center: **Green Mountain Chocolate Co.**, Route 100 (north of Interstate 89), ☎ 244-8356. Be sure to visit the dipping room to see the hand-crafted chocolates and truffles made, and sample the maple candies and fudge.

■ Wells River: **Bread & Chocolate Ltd.**, 1 Cross Street, ☎ 757-2088 or 800-524-6715. Tours take you inside Jonathan M. Rutstein's processes of making Belgian chocolate dessert sauces, flavored cocoas, and white chocolate drink mixes.

■ Maple Syrup

Vermont maple syrup comes in several "grades," which are really descriptions of the color and intensity of flavor. All are delicious, and are made in the same way, by boiling down the sap from maple trees in early spring. Color and flavor are determined by tiny differences in the sap-gathering and heating, and by the effects of weather on the trees. Most sugarmakers will produce and market several grades each year.

Most elegant is the **Vermont Fancy** grade, with its pale amber color, mild maple flavor, and delicate fragrance. **Grade A Medium Amber** is just a bit darker in color and has a more pronounced "bouquet."

Popular among those who like a full flavor is the **Grade A Dark Amber**, which is more robust. Many local folks prefer **Grade B**, though, the strongest and darkest of the table grades; its rich flavor makes it the best for baking, too.

Giant maple syrup can at Maple Grove Farm, St. Johnsbury.

Maple candies and maple cream are made by boiling the sap down even further, and beating it as it begins to crystallize, then letting the product set until cool. Nearly every village has a well-known cook who prepares maple fudge, buttery and rich, often with walnuts added.

Can you drink the plain maple sap as it comes out of the tree? Sure. But don't expect it to taste like candy. It's barely sweet, a fresh cool drink of spring on the way. It takes about 40 gallons of sap to boil down into one gallon of the familiar maple syrup.

TIP: *If you're in Vermont during sugaring season, watch for the community gatherings called* **Sugar on Snow parties,** *where the hot syrup is boiled until it's nearly candy, then poured over a mound of fresh white snow and eaten by twirling the cooled taffy-like threads with a fork, with bites on the side of raised doughnuts or even sour pickles for contrast.*

Border Crossings

The northern border of Vermont is an international one, allowing simple, no-fuss crossings into Canada. In Derby Line you can walk across the bridge and be on foreign soil.

But the border is taken very seriously, with smuggling an international concern. When you prepare to cross it, watch for signs that tell you which Customs office to visit when, and don't joke with the Customs agents; their lack of sense of humor is notorious. Sailing on Lake Memphremagog is also likely to take you across the border; watch for the shoreline Customs offices. There are several ways the two countries monitor crossings, so if you haven't stopped en route, be sure your first stop when you dock is with the Customs folks, within the first few minutes.

If you're an American citizen, you can cross the border easily with your driver's license for identification. But it's a good idea to have a passport or birth certificate as proof of citizenship (which a license doesn't prove), as some entry points are more particular, and airports are especially so.

TIP: *Be sure to notify your car insurance carrier that you're going into Canada, so that you'll have coverage during your visit. It's a good idea to carry a statement from your agent verifying Canadian coverage.*

Regulations prohibit bringing plants, fruits, and vegetables back into the United States; there is also a modest Customs tariff if you've purchased more than a minimal amount of consumer goods in Canada. Alcoholic beverages must be declared as you cross. Traveling north into Canada, the big concern is firearms. If you have good reason to transport them, such as for a gun show or a hunting trip, call the Customs office in St. Albans ahead of time for specific regulations, which change from year to year (☎ 524-6527).

Pets traveling with you should have proof of vaccinations for rabies and be in good health.

AUTHOR TIP

*For the pleasure of crossing the border without any visit to Customs required, visit the **Haskell Free Library and Opera House** in Derby Line, north of Newport. This lovely little showpiece straddles the border and has a thick black stripe painted on the floor to show you where it is! Read a book with your feet in one country and your pages in the other. In the opera house the stage is in Canada and most of the seats are in Vermont.*

How To Use This Book

As outlined on page 6, this book divides Vermont into seven regions. Each chapter starts with a general introduction to the region, which covers the layout of the major roadways and connections among villages, as well as history, celebrations, main sites and activities. The sections on *Touring* present smaller areas, in clusters of villages and activities, as well as general highlights of each major town. Contact numbers to help you plan a trip are found here too, as well as special resources like the state parks and transportation options.

Once you're familiar with the general touring outline, dip into the sections that follow: specific adventures for each location. There are opportunities for independent explorers, as well as for linking up with knowledgeable guides, whether for wildlife, canoe routes, or mountain slopes, summer or winter. Your adventures can be as vigorous and challenging or as simple and harmonious as you like. For example, a visit to Lake Willoughby in the Northeast Kingdom could include fishing, exploring the shorelines, climbing the cliffs of Mount Pisgah or Mount Hor, or exploring the well-worn trails of Wheeler Mountain. On the other hand, photographing the glacial lake and then sampling the nearby Evansville Trading Post, especially at Abenaki powwow time, or the somber history of the Old Stone House in Brownington, may not require more exercise than a relaxing drive along the back roads.

Suggestions for accommodations and dining wrap up each section, along with useful local phone numbers and, when available, e-mail addresses.

The following briefly describes the kinds of activities explored under each of the *Adventure* categories.

■ Adventures On Foot

 You could be looking for an easy scenic stroll to calm your pulse, or a strenuous challenge. Vermont's up-and-down landscape will probably offer you both choices within a five-mile radius. This category will let you know where to go and how to prepare for it: by packing sunscreen and a comfy pair of sneakers, or toting field glasses and a bird book to tell the hawks apart, or gearing up for changeable weather on a

mountain peak. There are hundreds of miles of trails in Vermont, and countless back roads that can be nearly as unpopulated. Those villages richest in historical architecture and events also offer self-guided walking tours.

Best of all, though, is the walking and hiking tradition that has grown up here. It might be stretching it some to call the Revolutionary War soldiers "the first Vermont hikers," but they left sturdy paths across the mountains, such as the Bayley-Hazen Road and the Molly Stark Trail. In 1910, the Green Mountain Club brought 23 members together to "make the Vermont mountains play a larger part in the life of the people." Since then, club members have become the hardworking angels of the trail systems, by mapping, clearing, and preserv-

Woodford trailhead, Appalachian Trail and Long Trail (AT/LT)

ing. The Civilian Conservation Corps used to craft careful approaches to the mountain peaks with stone steps along the steepest stretches. Now the Youth Conservation Corps follows up on that effort. Clearly blazed trails and even small neat markers with trail names and destinations are found even in remote back woods.

GUIDE SERVICES: *An abundance of guide services and outdoor classes will smoothly acquaint you with, say, the best fishing holes on the Battenkill, or the call of a hermit thrush. And with so many spectacular mountains here, area rock climbing supply firms and guide services have years of experience from which to draw.*

Two prominent trails draw long-distance hikers: the **Appalachian Trail,** which cuts across the southern mountains of the state on its way to Maine, and the **Long Trail,** a Green Mountain Club creation following the length of the Green Mountains from the Massachusetts border north to Canada. You can get an idea of how "up and down" this wilderness ridgeline trail is by noting that Interstate 91 takes only 185 miles to go from border to border – the Long Trail takes 265! Side trails and approach trails add up to another 175 miles. About 70 simple overnight shelters and primitive tent camping areas provide convenience for the long-distance walker.

A number of the hikes in this book are short and simple: half-hour approaches to waterfalls or blazingly blue lakes, or soothing rambles along country lanes. Most are mid-range efforts, taking half a day and drawing you up worthwhile climbs that reward with wildlife sightings and stunning views. Lightweight hiking shoes with some ankle support are nice for these, but sturdy walking shoes will also carry you on most day-trips. Do plan on running into patches of mud or wet ground here and there; all those streams and rivers leak now and then, and rain isn't quick to evaporate either!

The Green Mountain Club offers a pocket-size guide to the trails in best condition, *Day Hiker's Guide to Vermont* (see *Information Sources* on page 26). The 200-plus trails in the book are loosely categorized as the Long Trail and Appalachian Trail (serious effort required for hiking this part); other hiking trails; multi-use trails, which in winter are meant for snowmobiles but, when snow-free, are open to hikers; nature trails; a handful of fire-tower trails; and the rapidly growing category of ski-touring trails.

AUTHOR TIP

Bring along some drinking water when you hike; the nuisance parasite Giardia infests many streams and lakes, especially if beavers are in the area, and the color and clarity of the water are not real indicators of safety.

If you're a dedicated rock climber, Vermont is probably not tops on your list of places to travel. Rock formations are weathered and loose, and the best places to climb tend to be on private land with limited access. Rock climbers keep tight-lipped about favorite spots for fear of overloading the already nervous landowners. However, climbing supplies are sold here for trips to the Adirondacks just across Lake Champlain, and to the White Mountains of New Hampshire. This book quietly and discreetly mentions a few places to climb... Sshhh!

Preserving the Trails

Now that hikers and climbers can reach any part of Vermont, even the peaks of the mountains, a sense of courtesy to the land and its residents has become critical. Several regions above the tree line include precious stands of rare alpine plants that may not look so special at first glance.

They also grow tiny, wind-dwarfed trees, where a foot of growth could result from a hundred years of stubborn roots mining nutrients out of the rock and dust. Areas of special concern at this time are the peaks of Mt. Mansfield and Camel's Hump, where 40,000 visitors a year are "loving them to death." The same thing is happening to Mt. Abraham. Please stay on the trails when you are above the tree line, always. Save exploring for the lower, more richly endowed areas.

One more brief concern: Fires are generally not encouraged in the woods, except in designated camping areas. Check for details in each region and for each trail. If you visit Skylight Pond in Central Vermont, you can see firsthand one of the big reasons: continued cutting of trees and shrubs for firewood has made the tender land barren, so its caretakers are outlining protection and restricting the number of campers each night. Silver Lake, also in Central Vermont, has similar problems. The Green Mountain Club, along with state and national park rangers, urges campers to say in the abundant wooden shelters in order to minimize the human impact on the wilderness, or else use designated tenting areas. Your gift of concern and caretaking is a legacy for generations to come. You are also helping to protect rare species of plants and animals from extinction. The successful return of the peregrine falcon to Vermont's crags and cliffs shows what a difference concerned people can make.

A NOTE ABOUT HUNTING

Hunting is a specialized outdoor activity, demanding specific skills and a respect for the land and its inhabitants. Vermont regulates hunting closely in terms of seasons and methods of taking game. Hunting bear, deer, and wild birds takes up much of the autumn and some of the winter. There are other trapping and hunting seasons also. Please obtain state materials if you're interested in hunting (available at most general stores and sports stores, or contact the Vermont Fish & Wildlife Dept., 103 South Main Street, Waterbury, VT 05676; ☎ 241-3700). Many outfitters and guides provide hunting services; they are readily available, so this book does not list them.

One brief caution does apply to nonhunters, however. If you are walking in the woods in the firearm deer season – generally the last half of November – wear light, bright clothing, preferably the "blaze orange" caps and vests offered in most general stores and sports stores. Deer season attracts many newcomers and inexperienced hunters who may mistake your presence for that of the animal they've waited so long to see. Better yet, stay out of the woods entirely during deer season. You will be doing a kindness to yourself, to the hunters, and to the animals, who need no extra disturbance at this time.

■ Adventures With Llamas Or Horses

You know how to throw yourself into a hike with enthusiasm, how to look over the hillside or the trail across the fields and feel the challenge and freshness of it. Your feet itch to move forward and your legs already anticipate the steady swing of a good stride. But have you ever considered taking a gentler, less demanding approach? Slowing down enough to savor the sunlight on the trees, the scent of the forest floor, the gentle movement of falling leaves? Sure, I know. You might never "get there" at a quieter pace. And with a full pack containing water bottle, granola, sandwiches, and spare shoes, you don't want to slow down enough to feel the weight pulling at you!

Here's where trekking with llamas comes in. These gentle, mild hiking companions can easily carry a load of some 75 pounds, provided it's expertly arranged, and still keep pace with you along a hillside. They're not for carrying humans; they're for carrying the incidentals that make a trip pleasant. In fact, many llama trekking expeditions include a gourmet meal, complete with tablecloth, dishes, and sometimes even the table. And the steady stamina of the llama inspires its fellow walkers to keep a similar pace.

Horses, on the other hand, are not a traditional Vermont pack animal in this century. The days of riding to church or to market are long gone. But horses still pull sleighs through the snow and haywagons down back roads. You can also seek out lessons, as well as trail rides and challenging athletic events on horseback. If you bring your own mount, there is at least one inn that still maintains stable space for you. Expect to see fine horse-flesh in many parts of the state. The Morgan horse is a Vermont treasure, sturdy and powerful, and some horse lovers breed and show the Morgans in turn-of-the century elegance.

■ Adventures On Wheels

By Train

Amtrak's Vermonter route, recently re-established, has proved so popular that reservations are suggested in advance. The train also provides great traveling room for bicycles, making it possible for you to tour by walking your bike into the train and walking out again in a new town or region. The Sugarbush route connects Burlington with Middlebury for at least half of the year, and winter routes may expand over time. Train service from Burlington to Rutland is also available. In winter, skis are welcome cargo too.

The Vermonter train recently announced more welcome news to bikers: from April 1 to October 1 you can roll your wheels into a special bike baggage car, rather than having to box them up. Reservations are required for each passenger and each bike (☎ 800-USA-RAIL). The bike fee is nominal.

Boxed bikes are accepted as baggage year-round at those stations that are staffed.

By Car

You don't need a four-wheel-drive jeep to travel in Vermont, not even on the back roads. There are still plenty of dairy farms in the hills, and each small town prides itself on having a road crew that makes sure tank trucks can reach those farms to collect the milk at least once a day. Schoolbuses also demand good roads, and travelers get the benefits! If you plan to tour by car or truck in the winter, though, do look over the tips on *Driving in Severe Winter Weather* on page 10 to refresh your memory with (or get acquainted with) some of the standard precautions. With the exception of a half-dozen mountain passes, Vermont is open to cars year-round.

Bicycling

Mountain biking has become a sport that hotels and bed-and-breakfast homes encourage, to make the most of the terrain and already existing trails. These can be hiking trails or the fine snow trails maintained by the Vermont Association of Snow Travelers for snowmobiles to use in the winter months and all comers during the rest of the year. Where trails cross private land, please do stop and ask permission to use them; this courtesy goes a long way toward encouraging landowners to keep their land open, not posted. The high-tech, multi-speed bikes with their rugged tires are a perfect fit for even the less active rider, easing the way your legs pump along the rising terrain. And for those who appreciate the unusual, mountain biking on snow is increasingly popular, with local bike shops stocking studded tires and those equipped with chains for traction.

Back road biking offers a wider range of challenges. Visitors devoted to just relaxing can enjoy pedaling along tree-lined byways, gazing at old country homes, surprising a grazing deer in a nearby pasture, or even meeting one around the corner of a dirt road. Many villages offer bike loops, and larger towns often have bicycle trails, like the well-kept one along the Burlington waterfront. There are also guided bicycle tours for families, groups, or individuals, where your host not only helps if you get a flat, but fills you in on the history or wildlife of the region, and eventually fills you up with a good meal, either brought along or waiting for you at a relaxing country inn.

This book mentions most of the specific bike trails and some especially scenic routes to take among the villages. For more suggestions, plenty of cycling lovers have listed their favorite routes in *25 Bicycle Tours in Vermont* (see *Information Sources*, page 31). The book has been recently updated, and gives detailed directions, whether you are a "caterpillar" to whom each hill looks like a mountain, or a "butterfly" ready to float over the peaks. Northern Cartographic also includes good routes in its *Vermont Road Atlas and Guide*. Another great source is the *Vermont Life Bicycle Vermont Map & Guide*. The state has been a welcoming host for cyclists for years, but now the sport is supported by specialty shops, which are rarely more than 15 miles apart.

Naturally, you'll want a helmet for bicycling. This is especially important, because even a small hill can get your wheels spinning fast enough to carry you into a tree trunk and cause some real damage, if a stone in the road happens to send you off course. The other common sense reminders also apply: dress for the changes in weather, especially temperature; wear bright colors; carry water with you; and hug the right side of the road.

Finally, only the Lake Champlain Islands are going to give you reliably flat cycling. Look to the hills not only for challenges, but for scenic views, for fresh perspectives, and for discoveries about yourself.

■ Adventures On Water

Boating

Several regions of Vermont are downright crowded with lakes, from the 10-mile-wide stretches of Lake Champlain to the deep glacial gouge of Willoughby, where the cliffs rise high above the dark water and there are rumors of a deep underground channel to the more northern waters. Streams run everywhere; wetlands abound. Rivers are swift until midsummer, and water releases from power and flood control dams add extra spice to riding the action.

Loosely speaking, Vermont waters are divided into flat water (lakes) and rivers. Canoes and kayaks can take you into real wilderness, and the awkward stance of a blue heron can surprise you at the corner of many a lake. You can come so close to a loon that you'll see the blank glitter of its beady black eyes (although if it's nesting season, please stay farther back). On Memphremagog or Willoughby, Bomoseen or Fairlee, Morey or Dunmore, there are wide spaces for sailing, motoring and, of course, board sailing, that intensely personal interaction with wind and water.

The Appalachian Mountain Club puts out a *River Guide* (see *Information Sources* on page 33) to both Vermont and New Hampshire in a single volume, a good notion since the Connecticut River is shared by the two states. Local boating newspapers like Burlington's *Harbor Watch* give tips and updates. State and national parks generally have boats available, and facilities may range from heavy launches that ferry campers to isolated islands, to trim fishing boats on Seyon Pond, where the only allowed activity is fly-fishing (and it's great!). Increasing numbers of paddlewheelers are found on the large lakes and even on the southern reaches of the Connecticut River, and allow guests to get away from shore without effort. The Burlington area offers several touring boat services that dabble in fishing, sightseeing, or dining and dancing with a stunning view of the fabled Lake Champlain sunsets (sometimes called the world's second finest!).

BOATERS TAKE NOTE: *the state is desperately trying to contain the spread of zebra mussels, a non-native pest that fouls boats, boat engines, and beaches, clogs water intake pipes, and alters native ecology. Before you move a boat from one water body to the next, remove and place in the trash all plant material and attached mussels; drain all water from the boat, engine, and other equipment; and rinse the boat and gear with tap water, preferably hot, or leave the boat out in the sun for two days.*

Fishing

Fishing is a big part of lakeshore life, as can be seen in the general stores closest to boat accesses. Often a special refrigerator is set aside for neat stacks of capped containers, each labeled "worms"! In winter, live bait means minnows, and some shops have their own tanks where you can scoop out a netful. Fly-fishing is a separate art; watch for the occasional roadside sign of a fly-tying pro.

FISHING LICENSES: *If you're 15 or older, you need a license to fish in Vermont; it's not expensive (from $7 to $35 for nonresidents), and the money goes to the excellent cause of taking care of the lakes, rivers, and streams. Licenses are available at many general stores, as well as outdoor specialty shops and town offices. Only landowners have the privilege of fishing their own lands without licenses.*

Swimming & Diving

Vermont waters are safe for swimming almost all the time. Lifeguards are found only at designated patrolled beaches, but most of the lakes have long shallow sections, making family swimming a treat. Scuba diving is mostly confined to Lake Champlain, although Willoughby and Memphremagog have occasional dives. Classes and equipment outfitters are listed in this book. If you've never "skinny dipped," a secluded backwoods pond can bring you this experience, which is less and less likely in other locations! The related sports of tubing and water-skiing are mentioned with boating discussions.

■ Adventures On Snow & Ice

 The old Vermont saying is, "We've got 10 months of winter and two months of poor sledding." It's not really true: only the most northern mountains suffer the problems of snow in June or August! But the reliability of long, cold winters brings skiers, both downhill (alpine) and cross-country (Nordic), as early as mid-October to the resorts where snow is encouraged by spray rigs. Spring skiing in April is a treat on the last peaks to thaw out.

Good snowcover made by nature settles in a bit later in the season. By Thanksgiving there's usually a coating of white, and Christmas, New Year's, and the months of January and February are downhill skiing delights.

Skiing

Cross-country skiers, who can enjoy the sport with even a few inches of cover, make the most of the long frozen season. After the cloudy days of No-vember and early December, the sky opens out blazingly blue, and sun on the snow and ice recreates a world of glory. The prints of wild animals track across every field and along each woods trail; signs of foxes and squirrels are everywhere, and deer hoofprints line the back roads. Ruffed grouse, known locally as partridges, burst out of snowy sanctuary and explode in sound; crows, bluejays, and chickadees chatter. If you're lucky, you'll see a snowy owl perched on a fencepost, or the swift, supple slide of an otter diving over a snowbank toward the partly open water of a cold stream.

Skiers headed into the lodge, Burke Mountain.

Many of the country inns and bed-and-breakfast homes and farms re-alize how entrancing the country-side is to Nordic skiers, and have made an effort to establish their own trail networks. Some have been laid out by Olympic ski coaches and athletes; others follow traditional paths through evergreen stands, around thick-trunked maple trees, and across open pastures where the wind sculpts the thick snow into drifts and sweeps.

Taking advantage of all these trail networks, as well as snowmobile trails, old logging roads, and public trails, the 280-mile **Catamount Trail** gives Nordic skiers a chance to glide pretty much the length of the state. Accessi-

Introduction

ble to those of all abilities, the trail, which is relatively new, is open for skiing along about 90% of its route from the Massachusetts border to near Readsboro, Vermont, to the last stretch north of Jay Peak to reach the Canada line. Where the trail system enters a privately owned ski center, you may be asked to pay a trail fee; a membership in the Catamount Trail Association (PO Box 1235, Burlington, VT 05402; ☎ 864-5794) can give you discounts or even a chance to pass through for free. You don't have to ski the whole trail to feel good about this winter corridor: *The Catamount Trail Guidebook* (see *Information Sources,* page 33) breaks down the course into 26 single-day tours. If you choose to spend more time, wonderful country inns lie close to the route and you can more or less ski from one to the next.

Other Winter Sports

Other snow sports include **snowboarding,** usually done at the downhill ski slopes, **snowmobiling** (there are guided tours, as well as rentals), and the ice specialties of **skating** and **fishing** (done through a hole in lake ice, which may be a foot or more thick). There are several outfitters who teach the far-northern art of **dogsledding**, as well as host dogsledding competitions. On Lake Champlain, ice boats reach high speeds, propelled by wild winds. And in the mountains, rock climbers delight in the strenuous challenges of **ice climbing**, which is also taught in groups by some of the year-round adventure specialists.

The listings for each region give the established downhill ski slopes and the classic cross-country trail networks. Back roads, especially the ones known as "logging roads" where no wheeled traffic enters in winter, can be as glorious to ski as a resort. Maps of snowmobile trails and of the numerous national forest trails are readily available.

Remember that weather shifts can be extreme, and going into unmarked mountain wilderness regions without proper guidance and equipment is dangerous. Bear in mind that frostbite happens even at relatively mild temperatures, as long as the wind is blowing; your best advice may come from the morning's weather forecasts, which can be extensive and will warn of frostbite, wind changes, and severe temperature drops.

Even for the snowbunny who best loves the fireplace and a good book, getting a sense of what's happening outside will enhance each day's pleasure. Winter can be Vermont's most picturesque season, and is surely the traditional hallmark of New England.

■ Adventures In The Air

Although Burlington is home to Vermont's only major airport, there are a number of small year-round state and private airfields. **Helicopters** and **small planes** offer a fresh view of the mountain scenery. **Hot-air balloons** do the same, but with a sweet slowness and near silence that provide a new experience of air and height. Mountains and sharp drops create excellent conditions for **paragliding** and **hang gliding.** Lessons and rentals are found in almost every region of the state.

■ Eco-Travel & Cultural Excursions

Almost any hike in Vermont can be an ecological investigation. A number of the guide and tour services offer special focus on wildlife and plants. Primitive bogs and plenty of wetlands shelter varied bird communities. In the following chapters, listings of these tours and guide services are followed by historical and cultural walking tours and points of interest.

"Cheap Art Store," Bread & Puppet, Glover, VT

■ Where To Stay & Where To Eat

Country inns and bed-and-breakfast homes line every major route through Vermont, and many have gourmet cuisine prepared by extraordinary chefs. Regional listings offer some of the highlights, and give you resources for tracking down more.

In each region there are also tips for sampling some of the less obvious eateries, like tearooms, bakeries, and unusual restaurants. Searching for a good meal can be an enticing adventure; however, if you've been exploring some vigorous sport or even just on the road for several hours, it's nice to have a good place marked out for dinner and for the night.

Vermont's resort hotels often date back to the 1800s, but have been restored or remodeled with modern conveniences. The finest of these are listed in each region, along with a handful of comfortable, country lodgings. Almost all lodgings have at least breakfast available, and most have restaurants nearby. Listings of bed-and-breakfast homes and of farms open to guests change frequently, so this book has some of the more established places and "where to look" to find more in each region.

ACCOMMODATIONS PRICE KEY

Prices are per person, per night, double occupancy, for hotels and resorts. For bed and breakfasts prices are usually per room, per night. Ask when you make your reservations.

$.	Up to $50
$$.	$50 to $100
$$$.	$101 to $175
$$$$.	$176 and up

■ Camping

For the outdoor-bound, Vermont has plenty of state campgrounds and the shelters of the national forest. These may range from the gracious fly-fishing lodge at Seyon Lake to lean-to shelters to tent sites. Some campgrounds are on lakeshores; others are high in the mountains; and there are even some islands in Lake Champlain that can be reached only by boat and require advance reservations with the state park rangers. Reservations will soon be possible by e-mail; call the appropriate campground for e-mail addresses.

Private campgrounds usually offer more family orientation, and some are geared for longer term residence in cottages or recreational vehicles. Local information is available at nearly every general store, and the state Department of Tourism posts weatherproof bulletin boards of lodgings and attractions.

Information Sources

Tourist Boards & Chambers of Commerce

(Area Code 802)

■ **Vermont Department of Tourism and Marketing** (134 State Street, Montpelier, VT 05601-1471, ☎ 828-3237 or 800-VERMONT; Web site www.travel-vermont.com) offers free publications about the state, including winter and summer event guidebooks and guides to campgrounds, country inns, fishing and hunting, and historic sites. Information is also available by fax through an automated fax service; call ☎ 800-833-9756, and follow the voice prompts.

■ **Vermont Chamber of Commerce** (PO Box 37, Montpelier, VT 05601, ☎ 223-3443, Web site www.vtchamber.com, e-mail info@vtchambr.com) offers a regularly updated listing of country inns and bed-and-breakfast homes.

■ **Arlington Chamber of Commerce**, PO Box 245, Arlington, VT 05250, ☎ 375-2800, Web site www.arlingtonvt.com.

■ **Bennington Chamber of Commerce**, on Route 7 (North Street) north of the center of town, ☎ 447-3311, Web site www. bennington.com.

■ **Brattleboro Chamber of Commerce**, 180 Main Street, Brattleboro, VT 05301, ☎ 254-4565, Web site www.sover.net/ ~bratchmb/recreate.html.

■ **Central Vermont Chamber of Commerce** (for Barre-Montpelier area), PO Box 336, Barre, VT 05641, ☎ 229-5711, Web site www.central-vt.com.

■ **Chester Area Chamber of Commerce**, PO Box 623, Chester, VT 05143, ☎ 875-2939, Web site www.chester-vt.com.

■ **Dorset Chamber of Commerce**, PO Box 121, Dorset, VT 05251, ☎ 867-2450, Web site www.dorsetvt.com.

■ **Manchester & the Mountains Chamber of Commerce**, 5046 Main St., Ste. 1, Manchester Center, VT 05255, ☎ 362-2100, Web site www.manchesterandmtns.com.

■ **Mount Snow Valley Chamber of Commerce**, ☎ 877-VT-SOUTH, Web site www.visitvermont.com.

■ **Northeast Kingdom Chamber of Commerce**, 30 Western Avenue, St. Johnsbury, VT 05819, ☎ 748-3678 or 800-639-6379, Web site www.vermontnekchamber.org.

■ **Randolph Area Chamber of Commerce**, ☎ 728-9027, Web site www.randolph-chamber.com.

■ **Southern Vermont Chamber of Commerce**, PO Box 364, Arlington, VT 05201, ☎ 877-SO-VERMONT, Web site www. SoVermont.com.

■ **Stowe Area Association**, Main Street, Stowe, VT 05672, ☎ 253-7321 or 800-24-STOWE, Web site www.stowe.com.

> **ACCESSIBLE ADVENTURES:** *If you've been an "armchair traveler," just reading about adventures but not pursuing them, and your armchair is a wheelchair, start making a list of where you want to go. **Accessible Adventures** provides a 29-passenger motor coach with ADA lift and modular seating to accommodate wheelchairs, and plans tours that go for a day or longer. Contact them at Route 100, Village Square, Waitsfield, VT 05673-0888; ☎ 496-2252 or 888-880-0222. Check out their Web site www. accessibleadventures.com). Also, see the description of the **Golden Stage Inn** in Ludlow, page 149. Note that many Vermont state parks provide wheelchair access for fishing. More changes are coming, and can be followed at the state parks Web site listed below.*

Parks, Forests, Environmental Organizations

■ **Vermont State Parks**, 103 South Main Street, Waterbury, VT 05671-0603 (better to write than to visit this office), ☎ 241-3655 or 800-VERMONT, Web site www.vtstateparks.com.

■ Maps and information, mostly at no charge, are available from the **Green Mountain National Forest** (231 N. Main Street, Rutland, VT 05701-2417; ☎ 747-6700, TTY 747-6765). Better yet, visit one of the three local offices and talk with **Forest Service rangers** in **Manchester** (Routes 11 and 30, ☎ 362-2307), **Middlebury** (Route 7 just south of town, ☎ 388-4362), and **Rochester** (Route 100 south of the village, ☎ 767-4261).

■ **Vermont Department of Fish and Wildlife**, ☎ 800-VERMONT, Web site www.anr.state.vt.us/fw/fwhome.

■ **Green Hotels** in the Green Mountain State (designated lodgings that show a commitment to preserving Vermont's natural resources), Web site www.anr.state.vt.us/dec/ead/eadhome.htm.

■ Guides for outdoor adventures abound in Vermont, some with general services and others specializing in fields like wildlife photography, paragliding, dog sledding, and moonlight sailing. **Adventure Guides of Vermont** (not connected with this book) is a statewide registry that offers a listing of guides pre-screened for expertise and safety, including first-aid and rescue skills. Gray Stevens, president of the guide association and its linked travel agency division, proposes to "turn Vermont into an outdoor classroom." Reach him at Adventure Guides of Vermont, Inc., PO Box 3, North Ferrisburgh, VT 05473; ☎ 425-6211, 800-425-TRIP, fax 425-6218. E-mail and a Web site are in progress; call for details.

Lodging Services

■ Vermont has a statewide lodging reservations bureau: **Vermont Lodging & Restaurant Association**, Three Main Street, Suite 106, Burlington, VT 05401, ☎ 660-9001; Web site www. visitvt.com.

■ **Sugarbush Lodging**, ☎ 800-53-SUGAR, www.sugarbush.com.

Other Information

■ **Enchanted Weddings** (serves all of Vermont with wedding planning), 155 Warm Brook Road, Arlington, VT 05250, ☎ 375-6865 or 800-733-5125, Web site www.enchantedweddings.com.

■ **Vermont Antiques Dealers' Association**, Yellow House Antiques, 88 Reading Farms Road, Reading, VT 05062, ☎ 484-7799, Web site www.antweb.com/vada (brochure of member shops available if you send a self-addressed stamped #10 envelope).

■ On the Internet, check out **www.vtguides.com**, where you can find the *Vermont Traveler's Guidebook* on-line.

Recommended Reading

Several guidebooks are mentioned often in this guide, and can be found at most local bookshops or ordered from the publishers, as follows:

Day Hiker's Guide to Vermont, Green Mountain Club, Route 100, RR1, Box 650, Waterbury Center, VT 05677; ☎ 244-7037.

Long Trail Guide, Green Mountain Club, Route 100, RR1, Box 650, Waterbury Center, VT 05677; ☎ 244-7037.

25 Bicycle Tours in Vermont, by John Freidin, Backcountry Publications, The Countryman Press, PO Box 175, Woodstock, VT 05091-0175.

Vermont Road Atlas and Guide (contains topographic and street maps), Northern Cartographic, Inc., 4050 Williston Road, South Burlington, VT 05403.

Appalachian Mountain Club River Guide, New Hampshire, Vermont, Appalachian Mountain Club Books, 5 Joy Street, Boston, MA 02108.

Catamount Trail Guidebook, Catamount Trail Association, PO Box 1235, Burlington, VT 05402; ☎ 864-5794.

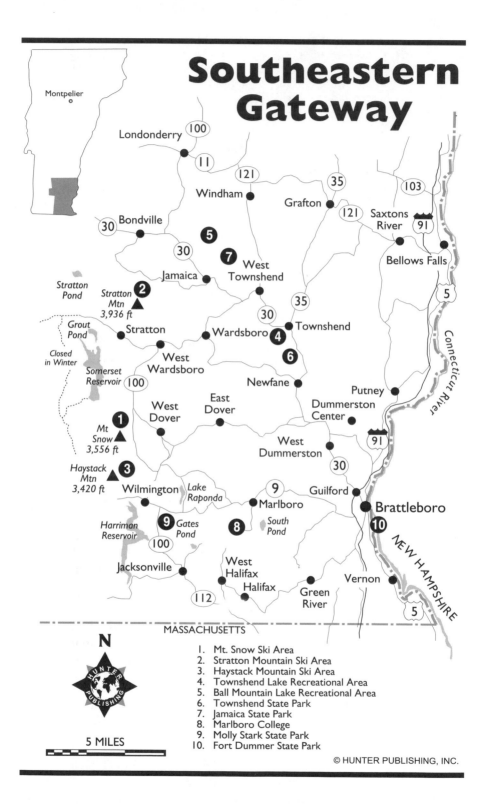

Southeastern Gateway

Montpelier

Londonderry ⑩⓪
⑪

Windham

Grafton

⑫①

Saxtons River

⑩③

⑨①

Bellows Falls

⑤

⑦ West Townshend

Bondville ③⓪

③⓪

Jamaica

Stratton Pond

Stratton Mtn 3,936 ft ②

Grout Pond

Closed in Winter

Somerset Reservoir ⑩⓪

Stratton

West Wardsboro

Wardsboro ④ Townshend

③⓪ ③⑤

⑥

Newfane

Putney

Dummerston Center

West Dover

East Dover

Mt Snow 3,556 ft ①

West Dummerston

③⓪

Haystack Mtn 3,420 ft ③

Wilmington

Lake Raponda

⑨ Guilford

Brattleboro

Harriman Reservoir

⑨ Gates Pond

⑧

Marlboro

South Pond

⑩

⑩⓪

Jacksonville

West Halifax

Halifax

Green River

Vernon

NEW HAMPSHIRE

Connecticut River

⑨①

⑤

⑤

⑪②

MASSACHUSETTS

N

HUNTER PUBLISHING

5 MILES

1. Mt. Snow Ski Area
2. Stratton Mountain Ski Area
3. Haystack Mountain Ski Area
4. Townshend Lake Recreational Area
5. Ball Mountain Lake Recreational Area
6. Townshend State Park
7. Jamaica State Park
8. Marlboro College
9. Molly Stark State Park
10. Fort Dummer State Park

© HUNTER PUBLISHING, INC.

The Southeastern Gateway

The Southeastern Gateway to Vermont puts year-round energy into entertainment, with festivals for all seasons, music and art events dotting the calendar, and a wealth of rivers and mountains, excitement and relaxation. Most visitors arrive here on Interstate 91, after driving through the final flattened out rolling hills of Massachusetts, and find an official Welcome Center just beyond the state line. If you happen to enter on the older parallel highway, Route 5, you'll pass through the village of Guilford, where a number of crafts businesses operate. Here you'll also see signs pointing toward Vermont's only nuclear power plant.

Getting Here & Getting Around

The first three interstate exits are for districts of **Brattleboro,** a city by local standards but nationally known as the fifth-best small town in America (Norman Crampton's assessment from his book, *The 100 Best Small Towns in America*). Nestled between the West and Connecticut Rivers, the town occupies a strategic entry position that was first held by the British in the 1700s with Fort Dummer, intended to control Indian forays as the settlers moved northward.

Roads out of Brattleboro follow the rivers up into the surrounding mountains. Two major ski resorts are within an hour's drive, and two more are scheduled to open at the end of 1997. Between Brattleboro and these highest peaks are rapidly rising hills and picturesque villages. Nearby Marlboro is home to a noted arts college and an equally noted music festival. A winery draws visitors to Jacksonville. The villages of Newfane and Grafton, to the north, preserve the charm of earlier centuries. The roadsides are lined with farms, comfortable old homes, and plenty of inns and bed-and-breakfast lodgings.

At the western edge of this region, the **Green Mountain National Forest** begins, a mysteriously captivating wilderness of long-used trails and plenty of wildlife, from birds to bears to foxes and the occasional bobcat. Two large lakes, the Harriman and Somerset Reservoirs, offer flat-water canoeing and kayaking in wooded surroundings. The Green, West, and Saxtons Rivers are lively whitewater canoe challenges, particularly in spring, and periodic water releases at Ball Mountain Dam in Jamaica turn the West River into a "whitewater rodeo."

The eastern edge of the region borders the wide, meandering Connecticut River, where boating ranges from cruise boats to canoes, kayaks, and sailboats. Fishing catch includes freshwater salmon, which can also be seen at several of the power stations along the river, as the determined fish climb fish ladders to more northern stretches of water. The towns along the Connecticut River offer encouragement and support to bicyclists and hikers year-round, and friendly innkeepers make equipment available. From the railroad town of Bellows Falls, you can still ride a train into the hills in summer and fall. Deer, wild turkeys, and Canada geese come close to "civilization" here too, perhaps drawn by the lush farmland and heavily bearing apple orchards.

Touring

Touring in the Southeastern Gateway begins in Brattleboro. From there, head directly north on Interstate 91 or its slower, more down-to-earth shadow, Route 5, to follow the Connecticut River valley. Or take one of the spokes out from the hub of Brattleboro to reach Marlboro, Jacksonville, and Wilmington to the west, starting on Route 9; Route 30 out to Newfane, Townshend, and the ski country that starts in Bondville and Londonderry, with the water adventures of Jamaica nearby; or meander off Route 30 on the back roads that reach Grafton, one of Vermont's two most dramatic historic preservation efforts.

■ Brattleboro

This small gateway city is a wonderful hodgepodge of history and cultures. It's been called a "college town without a college" because of the casual atmosphere and the abundance of small eateries like bakeries, cafés, delicatessens, and exquisite chef-managed dining. Sports suppliers, tour guides, and outdoor recreation line up next to galleries, films, and musical events. The nearby Center for International Living and the small but notable Marlboro College, where so many artists, musicians, and writers have lived, have drawn diverse ethnic groups and their dining pleasures to the area as well.

A GREENHOUSE ON THE INTERSTATE?

The **Vermont Welcome Center**, where you cross from Massachusetts on Interstate 91, is the busiest in the state. It baffles many a visitor to see greenhouses at the site. Actually the plant habitats are part of an elaborate "Living Machine" that treats wastewater on the spot, first changing it into a fertile sludge and then allowing carefully balanced plant and aquatic communities to use the waste and convert the nutrients in it. It's designed to handle 4,300 visitors a day using the bathrooms, an impressive new approach to protecting the environment. Sorry, visitors can't get tour the system at the Welcome Center, but for more information, check out the **Living Technologies** Web site at www. livingmachines.com (☎ 865-4460).

The Downtown Area

Driving around Brattleboro can be frustrating because the town roads barely cope with traffic at commuter times and the lunch hour. But there's plenty of parking in municipal lots at the center of town, so a walking tour is a pleasure. Stop at the **Chamber of Commerce,** well marked at 180 Main Street, to pick up a leaflet describing a historic walking tour among the widely differing architectural gems. From the 1890 **Wells Fountain** at the north end of Main Street, to the former railroad station now the Brattleboro Museum and Art Center at the southern end of Main Street, the tour is a casual half-hour walk. Midway along the route is the **Latchis Hotel,** 50 Main Street (☎ 254-6300). You won't want to miss the Latchis: it's listed on the National Historic Register of Places, one of only two prime Art Deco-style buildings in Vermont. There are terrazzo floors and chrome fixtures, a restaurant, a pub grille with its own brewery (Windham Brewery, featuring honest ales, porters, and lagers; tours available by calling ahead; see page 73 for more information), and a wide-screen movie theater that blends first-run movies and independent film showings. The 60 hotel rooms are up above.

Although Brattleboro's roots date back to Fort Dummer in 1724 (and before that, to Native American cultures), the current downtown is only 100 to 150 years old. There are dramatically elegant church buildings, and the overhanging roof cornices of the present business buildings vary from copper to brick to clay relief patterns. The Main Street clock, circa 1908, is made of cast iron and tops a Corinthian column with sculpted acacia leaves. This is small-town America at its most decorative!

Southeastern Gateway

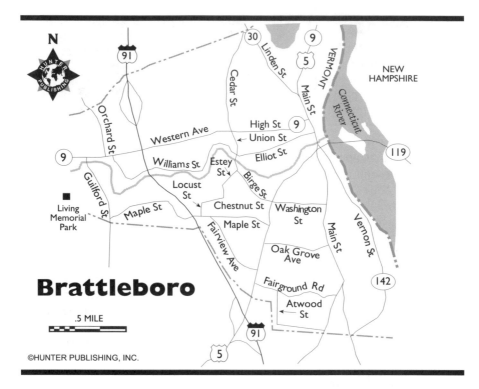

Brattleboro

.5 MILE

©HUNTER PUBLISHING, INC.

FOR HISTORY BUFFS: *The Brattleboro Historical Society has a room on the third floor of the Municipal Building, an impressive Victorian Gothic building with mansard roof at the north end of Main Street. The society houses a collection of artifacts and documents; contact the society in advance to get access (PO Box 6392, Brattleboro, VT 05302-6392; ☎ 254-4957). You can usually count on it being open on Thursday afternoons, 1 to 4 p.m.*

The **Brattleboro Museum and Art Center** (Canal and Bridge Streets; ☎ 257-0124) is open from mid-May to early November. The museum, housed in a former railroad station built of local quartzite rubble, owns a permanent collection of Estey organs, once made in the town. There are also changing exhibits of art, local history, and regional fine craft work. The town has at least 10 more galleries, one within a bookstore and another within a chocolate factory – ask at the Chamber of Commerce for the "gallery walk" listing. All are either on or within a minute's stroll of Main Street.

Your walk from the Chamber of Commerce to the museum may take a casual half-hour, but only if you are immune from distractions, especially the scent of good food. Small luncheonettes cater to the town's business crowd, and there's a fresh-air espresso stand on Main Street during mild weather. There are also the heady aromas of at least three Brattleboro bakeries.

Another downtown road to explore is **Elliott Street,** where the town's second brewery is open seven days a week. **McNeill's Brewery** (☎ 254-2553) at 90 Elliott Street, was called "one of the top 10 beer places in the world" by *Yankee Brew News;* games and food are also available, and the cozy pub welcomes families. Down the road at number 55 is another "food factory," **Tom and Sally's Handmade Chocolates** (☎ 258-3065), which has picture windows at the front and back of the building to let you watch the chocolates being made. (This is the home of a noted Vermont product, Vermont Cow Pies, which are pure chocolate, "no doo-doo.")

PLANS FOR A RIVER VIEW

Over the next few years, Brattleboro residents hope to open the downtown area directly to the Connecticut River by removing an old building from the east side of Main Street, creating waterfront access through a park and food court. If you run into construction in this town of ordinarily trying traffic, think of it as a gift for the future, and take a look at how the project is coming along. It should be a great change.

Outlying Areas

Head north along Route 5, known here as the **Putney Road,** and discover two very different regions of the city. The first is anchored around the Marina Restaurant, on the left, and Connecticut River Safari on the right. These "on the water" businesses take advantage of the Connecticut River to launch visitors into adventure. **The Marina** (☎ 254-1263) is the home of the *Belle of Brattleboro,* a handsome, mahogany-trimmed river boat that heads out for tours. Music, lunch, brunch, and sunset cruises are offered; charters can be reserved too. But if you long to paddle your own canoe, take the other side of the highway and slip into **Connecticut River Safari** (☎ 257-5008). Not only are there canoes and kayaks for rent, there are also river touring and waterway adventure packages for individuals, couples, families, and groups, including overnight trips that involve either camping out or staying at an inn. A canoe shuttle makes life easy. The canoe touring center also offers repairs, paddling advice, and complimentary car racks.

Farther up the Putney Road (Route 5) is a strip of chain stores, restaurants, and entertainment businesses, which would look much like any other business area except for some interesting eateries tucked into the mix. See *Where To Eat* on page 72 for details.

Another northbound road out of the center of Brattleboro is **Route 30**, which leads to some of the state's most picturesque villages. Before it gets

Southeastern Gateway

far from the center of town, it passes the rolling meadows and imposing stone tower that are part of the **Brattleboro Retreat,** one of the oldest psychiatric hospitals in the United States (founded in 1834). The tower is surrounded by pleasant walking trails. You can park on Route 30 by Linden Lodge and walk the marked path to the tower in the daytime.

If you head south instead, go all the way to Vernon on **Route 142** to find the **Connecticut River fish ladder** at the New England Power Company station. American shad and Atlantic salmon negotiate the elevation of 35 feet along a 984-foot fish ladder in a series of 51 pools. The best viewing is from mid-May to mid-July, and it is open at no charge seven days a week. For group tours and special arrangements, speak with Ken Alton at ☎ 603-443-9232. In the same block of town is the imposing office of the **Holstein Association,** a national organization of owners of the black and white dairy cattle that are seen over much of Vermont's landscape.

If you stick with Route 5 instead, south of the downtown area is **Canal Street,** with a mix of pizzerias, small restaurants, car washes, and car dealers. Just as it reaches Interstate 91, there is a small outlet center featuring 11 name-brand clothing and accessory outlets.

Festivals

Festivals are traditional in Brattleboro, and are regularly scheduled to celebrate the seasons. In mid-February there is the **Harris Hill Ski Jump;** a winter carnival follows at the end of the month; and after a classic "home and recreation show" in April, the town turns to a giant block party called **May Magic.** The **Fourth of July** is a big holiday, as are **Village Days** at the end of July (don't miss the river cruises). Autumn includes **Apple Days** (late September). **Holly Days** open December, and **Last Night,** with sleigh rides, free skiing and skating, and a fireworks finale, closes the year. **The Brattleboro Area Chamber of Commerce** (☎ 254-4565) has dates as they are set. Other local gatherings also are listed by the Chamber, including the Earth Spirit Festival of workshops, entertainment, and a spiritual fair.

There are music festivals, too, organized by the **Brattleboro Music Center** (☎ 257-4523). Most noted is the **Bach Festival** each autumn; there is also a winter chamber series, a spring festival, and a summer jazz festival. Call for dates and locations of these festivals and of the chamber concerts presented in fall, winter, and spring.

■ Marlboro

Talk of music leads directly to Marlboro, a village eight miles west of Brattleboro on Route 9. Two miles south of the village center is **Marlboro College,** a four-year private college of arts and sciences with tremendous programs in music and drama. The college has been a leader in innovative, individualized college education. Each summer a series of 15 chamber concerts is held at the college; Pablo Casals and Rudolph Serkin helped establish the music festival. Call for tickets (☎ 254-2394); they can also be ordered by mail: in spring, Marlboro Music Festival, 135 South 18th Street, Philadelphia, PA 19103, and in summer (after June 6), Marlboro Music Festival, Marlboro, VT 05344. By May, some performances are already sold out, but extra seats may be available in the porch adjacent to the college auditorium.

The village of Marlboro itself is quiet in winter, but blossoms into a peaceful rural retreat of mountain views, fishing waters, antique shops, and crafts studios. The **Marlboro Historical Society** in the village is open on summer Saturdays. A relative newcomer to Marlboro is the **Living History Association Museum,** on Route 9. With lively performances and history-laden presentations, the museum brings distant times and events as close as the costumed characters walking into the room. Programs for tour groups interweave folklore and fact, with topics like Colonial Courtesies, and Dulcimer Daze (a Civil War music approach). Write ahead to check availability, especially for groups: Living History Association, PO Box 1389, Wilmington, VT 05363 (don't let the mailing address confuse you; thc museum is in the town of Marlboro). Summer hours are 10 to 5 on Thursday through Saturday; fall hours extend to seven days a week during the last week of September and the month of October. There is no admission charge.

■ Jacksonville

Two miles west of Marlboro is the left (south) turn for Jacksonville. Take Route 112 six miles south of Wilmington and you'll reach this small village, where the **North River Winery** (☎ 368-7557) is open year-round for tours and tastings at its 1850s farmstead. In winter they are open on weekends only; from June through December the winery is open daily. The specialties are fruit wines like apple, cranberry apple, and other blends.

■ Wilmington

Twenty miles west of Brattleboro on Route 9 is the village of Wilmington. This little collection of shops, inns, and historic buildings is a gateway town itself, for the Mount Snow-Haystack ski areas just north and for picturesque Route 100, which winds along river valleys all the way north through the state. The nearby ski areas have had a tremendous impact on the region, encouraging four-season sports and adventuring that ranges from extreme mountain biking competitions to sleigh rides, llama treks, and miles of hiking and snowmobile trails.

Wilmington centers on the crossroads of the two highways, Routes 9 and 100. There's an information booth open in active seasons (closed, for instance, in late October between foliage and skiing!), where there are listings of lodgings and dining, as well as a walking tour leaflet that details town history. Wilmington dates back to the 1700s, a settlement formed around grist mills on the Deerfield River. Just west of town is **Lake Whit-**

ingham, also known as the Harriman Reservoir, where divers can examine the old foundations of the "drowned" town of Mountain Mills. A small paddlewheel tour ship cruises the lake.

Slipping six miles south of town on Route 100 takes you to Jacksonville, noted for its winery and crafts studios. Leaving town leads almost immediately into ski country: take Route 9 about 1.2 miles west to reach the right turn for Haystack Mountain Ski Area, or go seven miles north on Route 100 to Mount Snow. The two resorts are owned by one company, and share passes and connecting trails. Mountain biking trails here are among the finest in New England. In addition, the Merrell Hiking Center keeps the resorts busy in "green" weather.

Recommended spots to visit to soak up the beauty of the Wilmington area are the **Wheeler Farm**, just north of Wilmington on Route 100 (cows graze in front of ancient maples) and the **Adams Farm,** off Route 100 (also north of town) on Higley Hill Road. For views, drive down Route 100 to half a mile south of the Route 9 intersection, and turn left onto Boyd Hill Road. The horse farms along this route are especially lovely. When the road reaches a 'T' after about four miles, a right turn takes you to **Lake Whitingham,** where there are several swimming and picnicking areas. The shoreline is owned by the New England Power Company, which cares for the eight-mile-long lake and keeps it immune from development.

■ Dover, West & East

Dover was once a single village, about five miles north of Wilmington just off Route 100, but Dover Hill has always divided west from east. West Dover developed around an early mill complex, and buildings in the district date from 1805 to 1885, including the old school, church, village store, and a Greek Revival-style inn. West Dover, actually on Route 100, is now primarily focused around the pair of ski resorts, Haystack and Mount Snow. Mount Snow is just west of the center of town. From the Mount Snow turnoff, take Handle Road south toward Haystack to see one of the oldest summer colonies in New England, where the farmhouses have been restored and maintained with pride and elegance.

■ Newfane

Taking a different path outward from Brattleboro, drive northwest along Route 30 to the village of Newfane. In 1787 Newfane became the shire town, the local term for county seat, and was built around a handsome common, with architectural styles ranging from Federal to Colonial Revival, and especially Greek Revival (love those columns!). The entire village is a National Historic District, and a leaflet provided by the town library details a historic walking tour. This is a classic Vermont village, well worth the visit. One of the village's most noted summer residents, economist John Kenneth Galbraith, helped bring the lodging and dining here to public attention. There are two exquisite inns and, of course, plenty

of bed-and-breakfast lodging too. In warm weather, Newfane hosts a traditional Sunday flea market. There are also two general stores to explore,
and an especially interesting cemetery where the remains of Sir Isaac
Newton (the given name of a local resident!) are buried.

■ Jamaica

Jamaica is another interesting stop on Route 30 as the highway rises toward the higher mountains. The old railyards that once were the center of
the town's economy are now part of **Jamaica State Park** (758 acres),
which has campsites and a great swimming hole. The region is especially
dear to adventurers who paddle wild rivers; the West River here swells to
wild abandon with dam releases that result in a "whitewater rodeo," and
even non-paddlers find the excitement worth watching. The dam is on
Ball Mountain Lake, an 85-acre delight in the wilderness, well provided
with campsites. You can follow the old railroad bed from the state park to
the dam.

■ Bondville

At last, 38 miles from Brattleboro, Route 30 rises to the really exciting terrain: **Stratton Mountain** is 3,936 feet high, and Bondville is the cluster of
houses on Route 30 just before you reach the mountain resort. Four miles
up the Stratton Mountain access road is a forest of condominiums and the
Mountain Market. Then comes the mountain itself, well worth the climb.
There are two distinct areas to it, the original North Face and the sunnier
Sun Bowl. In winter, the resort has "adventure parks" for skiers and
snowboarders. In the summer, visitors find tennis, golf, horseback riding,
outdoor concerts, and especially mountain biking. Special highlights are
the **Sun Bowl Ranch** at the Stratton Mountain Resort (☎ 297-2200), featuring scenic trail rides (donkeys also available!), a top-rated tennis
school, and an extension program with the **Orvis Fly Fishing School,**
one of Manchester's greatest assets. Festivals at Stratton bring great music to the region.

■ Londonderry

The village of South Londonderry has an 1800s-era historic district along
the narrow valley of the West River. Reflected in the old buildings are the
mills and industries that gave the region its economic health in the 19th
century. Londonderry is also home to **Magic Mountain,** (☎ 824-5645) a
ski area tentatively back in business. Nearby cross-country skiing and
mountain biking make the region a healthy challenge for outdoor adventures. The area is also comfortable lodging for the three nearby ski areas:
Stratton Mountain in Bondville; Bromley in Peru (a bit farther west); and
Okemo, to the north outside Ludlow.

■ Putney

The third major pathway outward from Brattleboro is Interstate 91 and its humbler antecedent, Route 5, both continuing all the way north through the state along the Connecticut River, Vermont's boundary with New Hampshire. Putney is the perfect distance away for a northward terminus for bicyclists and paddlers; it's about eight miles. Use Exit 4 from the interstate, or take your time and enjoy the gentle rolling bends of Route 5.

The village of Putney still resembles the early industrial center it was, and there are many Federal style homes to appreciate. At least one Putney resident was noted for being a dissident: John Humphrey Noyes, who founded a utopian religious experiment called "perfectionism." A local uproar in 1847 sent Noyes off to New York State, where he ended up prospering along with the Oneida Community.

Now the town is noted more for its **Yellow Barn Music Festival** (☎ 387-6637 or 800-639-3819) of about 20 chamber concerts each summer, and for the impact of the **West Hill Bike Shop** (☎ 387-5718), which has supported mountain biking as a year-round sport for the entire region. A visit to town also should include a stop at the **Basketville Factory Store** (☎ 387-5509), where tours retrace 150 years of the family business. About five miles north of town on Route 5 is a theme park/playland called **Santa's Land** (☎ 387-5550; 800-726-8299), open from Memorial Day to Christmas, designed mainly for children's fun, but also for marketing holiday ornaments and collectibles. The park includes a "sweet shop" and a family-oriented restaurant. Continue north until Route 5 passes under the interstate and take the first right turn to reach **Brandywine Glassworks,** where craftsman Robert Burch works at the fierce flames of the glass furnace. Call ahead if you'd like to visit (☎ 387-4032).

■ Bellows Falls

This is an old-time railroad town, complete with a touring train ride, the *Green Mountain Flyer* (☎ 463-3069) that goes 13 miles into the mountains during summer and foliage season, and a historic district of commercial and industrial buildings. Bellows Falls is named for the Great Falls of the Connecticut River. It is still a working-class town, and the river and nearby power canal are tapped for power with impressive facilities. A walking tour should include the **Vilas Bridge** and, just below it, a glimpse of Native American petroglyphs above the river bank. There is also a small museum, the **Adams Gristmill Museum,** which is open by appointment (☎ 463-4280). Also call ahead if you want to visit the working fish ladder at the New England Power Company dam (☎ 463-3226); for group tours and special arrangements contact Ken Alton at ☎ 603-443-9232.

Southeastern Gateway

HOME-GROWN DELIGHTS: *It's traditional to stop on Route 5 at **Allen Bros. Family Farm and Orchard** (☎ 800-448-5686), a farmstand that's been around since 1956. After you select from the wide array of locally grown fruits and vegetables, explore the kitchen, bakery and deli section, the Vermont cheeses and, of course, the maple syrup. There's good coffee, too. This is a great place to fill up your day-pack for a hike or to prepare for a picnic.*

■ Grafton

From Bellows Falls, detour away from the Connecticut River along Route 121 and enjoy the drive through superb fishing country. Twelve miles brings you through several small villages and at last to Grafton, a remarkable historical preservation project turned into a living treasure. Founded in 1780, Grafton had become a sheep center by 1850, with over 10,000 of the woolly animals grazing in its meadows. Soapstone quarrying, farming, and milling added to its economy.

The **Phelps Hotel,** a stage stop between Boston and Montreal, housed such distinguished guests as Ulysses S. Grant and Ralph Waldo Emerson. Author Rudyard Kipling also stayed there.

But the village economy faded, reaching a low by 1940. In 1963, philanthropist Dean Mathey founded the **Windham Foundation,** which took on the restoration and maintenance of the town's historic buildings and encouraged residents to pursue new avenues toward prosperity. The Phelps Hotel became the Old Tavern at Grafton, a luxury lodging that reaches out into the community with cross-country ski trails that double as summer walking ways. Agriculture bloomed in an active sheep farm and a cheese factory. Craftspeople and a gallery arrived.

Now Grafton is a picture-perfect sanctuary for visitors, specializing in gracious, cultured hospitality.

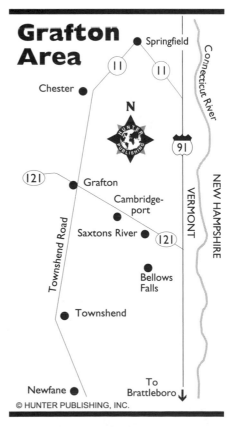

Grafton Area

© HUNTER PUBLISHING, INC.

There are art exhibits, lectures, and historic tours. A visit to the **Grafton Village Cheese Co.** (☎ 843-2348) is both entertaining and tasty. There is a **museum of natural history** (small but dynamic; ☎ 843-2111); an exhibit of Windham Foundation treasures (☎ 843-2211); and collections held by the **Grafton Historical Society** (☎ 843-2564). Bicycles can be rented, and winter brings both cross-country skiing and horse-drawn sleigh rides. Stop at the **Old Tavern** for village maps and more ideas. This can easily be a day's worth of touring, all in one small village.

Adventures

■ On Foot

Brattleboro

Brattleboro's two hiking trails are both easy stretches, a simple river-valley warmup to walking in Vermont. By heading south on South Main Street (which soon becomes Old Guilford Road), two miles of travel takes you to **Fort Dummer State Park.** About a quarter-mile from the park office (where you can get a trail map) is an intersection; the mile-long self-guiding nature trail starts just north of the intersection and meanders for a mile, with two additional loops of about a quarter-mile each. Best part: an overlook on a short spur, from which the vista includes the Connecticut River and Mount Monadnock.

Or, also starting from town, take Route 5 south to the Guilford Country Store, turn right on the Guilford Center Road, bear left after the village onto Sweet Pond Road, and continue 2.5 miles to **Sweet Pond State Park,** on the left. An hour's walk around Sweet Pond is a relaxing ramble, with good possibilities of seeing waterfowl as well as enjoying the scenery.

Take Route 9 west out of Brattleboro for 10 miles to the **Skyline Restaurant** (☎ 464-3536) with its "100-mile views" of the Berkshires from 2,350 feet. The staff will gladly point out a nearby fire tower path for a brisk leg stretch. Another three miles down Route 9 and you'll reach **Molly Stark State Park,** where the trail up 2,415-foot Mount Olga leads to views of three states. When you park at the state facility, do check in with the ranger. Then head for the blue-blazed main trail, which crosses a stream on a wooden bridge, climbs to the east through the woods, and crosses two nice old stone walls before getting steeper. It is 0.8 mile to the summit of Mount Olga. Connecting trails, as detailed in the Green Mountain Club's *Day Hiker's Guide to Vermont,* lead over to the defunct Hogback Mountain Ski Area. When you descend the peak on the blue-blazed trail, there's a turn (also blue blazes) just below the summit that winds around through more stone walls, spending a scenic mile to get back to park headquarters.

Wilmington

Another good "peak vistas" climb is found when you reach Wilmington, the next town west of Brattleboro on Route 9. The center of town is marked by a traffic light for the intersection of Routes 100 and 9; stay on Route 9 another 1.1 miles to a right turn into the Chimney Hills Development, Haystack Road. After another 1.3 miles, make a left onto Chimney Hills Road. Go 1.6 miles more and turn right onto Binney Brook Road to the stop sign. A left onto Upper Dam leads (in another two miles) to the trailhead for the **Haystack Mountain Trail,** marked with a US Forest Service sign. The trail, which follows old hiking, snowmobile, and woods paths, is marked with blue and orange plastic tags; it climbs to the summit in 2.4 miles. Now you can see how Haystack and Mount Snow (originally one of two Mount Pisgahs in the state) are connected by the land ridge. The snowmobile trail ahead of you continues to Haystack Ski Area.

Now that you've gotten this far west, don't miss out on the good hiking around the two reservoirs here, **Somerset** and **Harriman** (also called Lake Whitingham). About 5.3 miles west of the same Wilmington intersection traffic light, look for a right turn onto Somerset Road. It's about six miles to the reservoir, which is a lake more than four miles long. Look for the picnic area just north of the dam; the **East Shore Trail,** a gift of the New England Power Company, begins here and winds along high ground for 4.2 miles. The halfway region is along a slope that has an expansive view of the ridge connecting Mount Snow and Haystack. The trail end, on the other hand, is in low ground at the lake shore, across from Streeter Island. Double yellow blazes are the trail mark. New England Power Company trails are for day use only; no camping or open fires, please.

Measuring again from the Wilmington intersection of Routes 9 and 100, the turnoff for the **Harriman Reservoir Trail** is 2.9 miles west. Turn left and cross the Deerfield River on an iron bridge. Turn left again and follow the gravel road for a mile to the picnic area (check out the view of Haystack here!). At a gate across the road, the trail begins. It follows – in an on-and-off fashion – the former railbed of the Hoosac Tunnel and Wilmington Railroad with views across the lake and into the mountains, plus stone walls and foundations, a "ghost trail" through what was once settled land. The trail isn't blazed; it goes 7.2 miles to the south end of the lake, where another vehicle could be parked to catch you if you want to do only one direction. To reach the south end of the trail, take Route 100 south from Wilmington to Whitingham and go a mile west of the Whitingham post office to the paved Harriman Road. It's nearly two miles to the end of the road and a parking area; the trail access is at a gap in the chain link fence, and when you go through it, head about 60 feet to the left of the main gate to find the trail. If you like predictability, you can get a detailed description, by tenths of a mile, of the rock cuts and landmarks along this trail, in the Green Mountain Club's *Day Hiker's Guide to Vermont*. This is one of the nicest day-length hikes in the area, and ties in well with other local activities like boating and biking.

THE MERRELL HIKING CENTER

There's a relatively recent treat in store at **Mount Snow,** where Vermont's hiking boot manufacturer, Merrell Footwear, has teamed up with the ski resort to provide a new hiking center. The **Merrell Hiking Center** offers guided interpretive hikes, and ones focusing on special interests, such as wildflowers, bird photography, and geology, can also be requested (☎ 464-4130 for details and schedules). There are also self-guided hikes and boot and gear rentals (a nice way to try out the products without big expense). Open from Memorial Day to Columbus Day, the Center also makes available (for a small fee) the chairlift to or from the summit. A two-day getaway package is also offered. The Mount Snow trails may seem overly tame by all this assistance, but there's plenty of wilderness out there, and an elevation of 3,600 feet makes the climb a challenge, no matter how much help you get!

North of Brattleboro

Heading from Brattleboro up Route 30 there are plenty of mountain hikes; **Charles Marchant** of Townshend (☎ 365-7937) offers day hikes with an extra helping of history, and his **4 Seasons Touring** also provides trips three to five days long. He specializes in local history and lore, especially old cemeteries and abandoned farms; moonlight trips are also offered! Charles Marchant also works with **Walking Tours of Southern Vermont** (see *Bennington and Vermont Valley,* page 91).

In **Townshend State Forest** is one of four **Bald Mountains** in Vermont. Take Route 30 north from Townshend to reach the state forest, going two miles to the Townshend Dam. Turn left (west) and take a narrow bridge across the spillway, then left again onto a dirt road and past the **Scott Covered Bridge,** which is the longest single-span covered bridge in the state. (Sure, get out of the car and walk across!) Bear right at the bridge to the park entrance, and pay a small day fee. Pick up your trail map at the park office, or use the Green Mountain Club's *Day Hiker's Guide to Vermont* to check off the landmarks of the 3.1-mile loop, which ascends 1,100 feet to the summit. This is a classic woods trail, full of turns, brooks, and even an old cellar hole.

Townshend is the gateway to the outrageously interesting area of **Jamaica State Park** and **Ball Mountain Lake**, where terrain and water link up to provide high excitement in spring and fall with whitewater canoeing and kayaking. Jamaica State Park has a program of guided hikes. Some 3,000 acres of the West River Valley is now a greenway between Jamaica and Londonderry, owned by the Conservation Society of Southern Vermont.

The **Hamilton Falls Trail** begins in the state park and then enters the greenway. Pick up a trail map at the park office or use the *Day Hiker's Guide*. The trail follows an old railbed for about two miles before ascending to one of the highest and most exhilarating waterfalls in Vermont. Once you get above Cobb Brook, you can take a spur to the base of the falls; then go back to the trail and drop downhill briefly before turning to the left onto a footpath that leads about 250 feet to the top of the falls.

There are caution signs at the top of the falls, as too many risk-takers have actually died playing on this slippery rocky area. Hang on to small children if you've taken them along!

The hike is worth every puff and stretch of the muscles. In summer you may have more company than you like, thanks to the falls being so spectacular; consider climbing on a damp day when less determined walkers stay home, or go early in the season when the water is high but most travelers haven't yet arrived. The hike is actually 3.1 miles long, but takes longer than many trails of the same length due to the steeper section.

Jamaica State Park also offers an **Overlook Trail** that starts near the Hackberry lean-to. Again, pick up a map from the park office. This is a sensitive area to walk, as vegetation has suffered greatly from hikers; you can help by being careful to stay on the trail. There are worthwhile vistas at the summit of

Hiking Vermont's trails in Autumn.

Little Ball Mountain. If you follow the trail downhill, it links with the West River Railroad bed along the Hamilton Falls Trail.

Stratton Mountain

Finally, **Stratton Mountain Ski Area** in Bondville, like the other ski areas, has an active summer program with access to its wide network of trails. The mountain also offers a summer day camp for kids ages six to 12. There are plenty of activities if you want to leave part of the family in different surroundings while you head for the peak; ☎ 297-4051 for kids' programs; 800-STRATTON for the resort and general information. A ride on the gondola lift can add variety to the day's hiking. See the resort office for maps of the trails, as they may change from year to year.

The Stratton, Jamaica, and Wilmington area hikes are all at the edges of the **Green Mountain National Forest**; for hiking and climbing in the national forest, see the Central Vermont chapter.

■ Travel With Llamas Or Horses

Llama Trekking

Llama trekking is a wonderful way to relax as you explore the **Green Mountains.** That's right, llamas thrive in Vermont, where their woolly coats and deep breathing fit right in with mountain weather. Gentle and peaceful as hiking companions, they ease the rigors of the trip by packing the weight, and also slow things down just a bit, to a comfortable walking pace. Rather than fighting your way up slopes until you're breathless, or hurrying along wetlands at a speed that frightens away the wildlife, your pace with llamas is smooth and serene. The guide who accompanies your sweet beast of burden often has stories of history, local events, and natural wonders to enrich your ramble, and a gourmet meal may be among the llama's bundles.

If your taste runs to guided tours, especially ones full of information on animal and plant life, or if you'd just like a break from toting that backpack and making your own trail lunch, consider a llama tour. Centered in Wilmington, **Green Mountain Expeditions** (☎ 368-7147) offers various llama-assisted trips ranging from a three-hour nature hike (with or without lunch) to a day trek to an overnight pack trip in the Green Mountain National Forest. Expeditions can include either camping or a cozy bed and breakfast, complete with gourmet cuisine and four-poster beds.

Horseback Riding

In Vermont, horses are usually rented out only with trail guides, and the four riding stables in this region follow that approach. **West River Lodge** in Brookline (Hill Road, ☎ 365-7745) offers English trail rides, lessons, and stopovers with stables. **Jack's Horse Farm** on the Westminster Road in Putney (☎ 387-2782) adds pony rides and hayrides to the trail rides and lessons. At Stratton Mountain, the warmer weather activities include group trail rides or extended rides by the hour; call the **Stratton Mountain Resort** (☎ 297-2200), located off Route 30 in Bondville. **Flames Stables** (☎ 464-8329) is in Wilmington on Route 100, a mile south of the town's main junction, and provides trail and pony rides in addition to its wagon and sleigh rides.

Hayrides

How about a hayride? The Bailey family operates **Fair Winds Farm** with horse power, rather than tractors, but they'll let the horses off from work to take you riding through the fields and woods (even by starlight!) in a wagon or sleigh full of hay. Reservations are required, and you should call well in advance (☎ 254-9067). Refreshments can also be arranged. The farm is on Upper Dummerston Road, reached from Route 30, just north of Brattleboro. Another farm offering horse-drawn rides is the **Robb Family Farm** (see below).

BACKROAD FARM TOUR

A great backroad tour that takes advantage of spectacular scenery and some family farms can be found by taking Exit 2 from Interstate 91 and heading west on Route 9 to Christy's Store; turn left here onto Greenleaf Street, and bear left at the next fork, to reach Ames Hill Road. On your left will be **Ray's Farm Stand**, where you can buy Ben Bell's freshly grown vegetables. Next is the Thurber family's **Lilac Ridge Farm** with veggies and flowers, as well as maple syrup and Christmas trees (☎ 254-8113). Stay with Ames Hill Road by bearing right at the next fork and find the Country Shop at the **Robb Family Farm**, a dairy farm offering farm tours, farm events, horse-drawn hayrides and sleigh rides (reservations required, ☎ 888-318-9087), maple syrup, and homemade donuts. **Upper Way Farm** comes next, with its apple orchard and fresh-pressed apple cider in fall (☎ 257-1157), and **Moore's Orchard** is at the top of the hill, a place to stop and pick your own apples in September. The entire detour is 1½ miles long, and good fun.

■ On Wheels

Road Biking

Because **Brattleboro** is so close to two state lines, several interesting road bike trips include inter-state wheeling. From the center of town, go to the south end of Main Street by the art museum and turn left onto Bridge Street, then immediately right only Route 142. This relatively quiet road takes you along the Connecticut River, passing the Fort Dummer Monument, and on into Vernon, home of Vermont's only nuclear power plant, **Vermont Yankee.** (The visitor's center is open weekdays; ☎ 257-1416.) Proceed to East Northfield, Mass., and return via a third state, by turning left onto Route 10 and taking it to its intersection with Route 119 in Winchester, New Hampshire; Route 119 returns you to the bridge back into Brattleboro. Or, when you reach East Northfield keep going to the southwestern turnoff for Route 10, to the right, which will intersect with Route 5 in about five miles; turn north on Route 5 and return to Vermont, climbing the moderately steep hills through Guilford on the way back.

As **Route 9** goes farther west from Brattleboro, the terrain gets rough for road biking. Steep climbs, winding roads, and narrow pavement with steady car traffic makes bicycling risky; the summer crowds make it downright hazardous. It is possible to avoid Route 9 by taking back roads south of the highway, south toward Guilford, then across through Halifax to eventually reach the Wilmington area, but again, the quick shifts in elevation make this a tough task.

Putney is truly the bicycling center of this region. It's the home of Vermont's first cycling club, the Putney Bicycle Club, and of the **West Hill Shop** (☎ 387-5718), where road, off-road, and mountain biking are launched as year-round adventures. Most visitors reach Putney on Interstate 91 (Exit 4); the bike shop is on the east side of the Interstate. You'll find rentals, purchases, local information, and plenty of advice, including maps, which are marked for you as you discuss your choices. West Hill also has winter biking tires with studs or chains, to make the most of the well-packed snowmobile trails in the area.

RECOMMENDED BIKE TOUR: *John Freidin, founder of Vermont Bicycle Touring (see* Central Vermont *chapter) and author of* 25 Bicycle Tours in Vermont, *probably knows more about biking here than anyone else. He recommends a 41½-mile loop in the Connecticut River Valley that includes views of the river from both banks, as you cycle through two states. The last stretch of the ride, from the small village of Westminster West back to Putney, is a tough workout, mostly uphill. But think of how good it feels as your blood races freely and with plenty of oxygen afterward!*

Newfane's picturesque village scene is also a good starting location for road biking. For more adventure, **Newfane Off-Road Biking** (☎ 365-7775 or 800-540-4671) plans routes and offers tours (with deluxe picnic lunches!) on abandoned town roads, logging trails, and bridle paths. Rentals are available. The shop is located on the Common at Newfane Market.

Finally, you can't go wrong for road biking if you stick with **Route 5** along the Connecticut River. The hills are mostly moderate, and the scenery is terrific. Sugarhouses, crafts studios, and farmstands line the road; general stores are good places for sandwiches, hot soup and good coffee. Although traffic moves briskly, the pavement is wide enough for a good margin of safety.

Mountain Biking

The rise and roll of the landscape makes for good mountain biking, and there are still plenty of old town roads and logging trails at the edges of **Brattleboro**. The town's two bike shops, **Burrows Specialized Sports** (105 Main Street, ☎ 254-9430 or 257-1017, e-mail buspts@sover.net) and the **Brattleboro Bike Shop** (178 Main Street, ☎ 254-8644), will gladly go over maps and choices. **West Brattleboro,** a little less trafficky, has some even nicer back roads; park by the West Brattleboro Firehouse on Route 9 and cycle west to Christy's Store, taking the left onto Greenleaf St. Bear right onto Abbott Road and continue to Ames Hill, where the road goes steeply uphill. At the top, turn left and catch the view from Moore's Apple Orchard. A left at the next road and bearing left before the house gives you a road that turns to a trail, which will connect to Melchen Road. Bear left on the pavement to get back to West Brattleboro. Or, also from Christy's Store, take the route to Green River: again go left onto Greenleaf Street, but this time follow the paved road for 5.5 miles. When the pavement ends, turn left onto the Green River covered bridge and waterfall. If you exit the bridge to the left and then bear left at the first junction, you'll be following the river. After three miles, go left again across the bridge. Take a stiff climb to the Deer Park wilderness area of Halifax. Enter Halifax village by another left turn. When you reach Stage Road, turn left again back to Green River. This adds up to a 14-mile loop.

Vermont's ski areas have become a strong asset for mountain bikers. First, the many cross-country ski trails became available for off-road biking. Then the downhill ski areas also adapted to the sport. In **West Dover,** north of Wilmington, **Mount Snow Resort** (☎ 464-3333, 800-599-5754, Web site www.mountsnow.com) announces itself as the "mountain bike capital of the East," and has hosted World Cup races and extreme games with dual slalom and dual downhill. The resort's motto: "This is Vermont anyway... if you want flat, go to Kansas." Tours, rentals, competitions, festivals, and a noted mountain bike school add to the 100-mile trail network.

DON'T MISS: *Mount Snow's **Wicked Wild Mountain Bike Festival**, held at the end of July, with downhill, dual slalom, and cross-country competitions. ☎ 464-1100, ext. 4371 for information.*

The town of **Dover** is building a five-mile paved pedestrian and bicycle trail from Mount Snow to the historic village center to the south. The **Valley Trail** is already half done, and funds are pending for the rest of the project.

Stratton Mountain, reached from Route 30, also hosts mountain bikers on its trails in the summer. Call the resort (☎ 800-STRATTON), or visit the resort's Internet site at www.genghis.com/stratton.htm for dates of summer races and the autumn mountain bike jamboree. Rentals are available, as is a mountain bike gondola pass; there's a bike repair shop for tune-ups, too. **Viking Ski Touring Center** (☎ 824-3933) in Londonderry also offers bike rentals and tours on cross-country trails.

■ On Water

 The **Connecticut River** in Brattleboro is wide enough for sailing, but most boaters prefer canoes or kayaks here. There is also a cruise boat (see *Touring*, page 41), which leaves from the Marina Restaurant on the Putney Road (Route 5) north of town. Another boating choice is the **West River,** which forms the "meadows," a grassy mix of water and islands, just before it enters the Connecticut.

Rivers To Run

If you enjoy paddling, a good place to start is the **Vermont Canoe Touring Center** (☎ 257-5008), 451 Putney Road (Route 5) in Brattleboro, across from the Marina Restaurant . Pick up maps of the easiest accesses here. **Connecticut River Safari** (☎ 257-5008) is a canoe touring center that rents (and sells) both canoes and kayaks, along with appropriate equipment. They also provide lessons, group programs, touring and guide service, connections for overnight canoe camping and outdoor experiences in more remote locations. The center also repairs boats (aluminum, fiberglass, wood, and canvas). To make life even more enjoyable, there is a canoe and kayak shuttle service, upriver, downriver, and west to Somerset and Harriman Reservoirs (near Wilmington).

RECOMMENDED READING: *If you plan to paddle Vermont rivers without a guide or tour service showing you the "ropes," the* **Appalachian Mountain Club (AMC) River Guide to New Hampshire and Vermont** *is indispensable. The book is organized by watershed; rivers in the Southeastern Gateway empty into the Connecticut River, so they are in the Upper Connecticut River chapter. Check the listings for the Connecticut River and, heading north, for the West and Saxtons Rivers. One of the nicest treats for paddlers is 14 miles of unobstructed river (no dams) from Bellows Falls south to Vernon, the town south of Brattleboro.*

For the West River and the Saxtons River, as for any river, it is important to check the route before paddling it, to find out where downed trees or decomposing dam structures have created potential life-threatening dangers. Also, remember the 50/50 rule: if the water and air temperature together don't add up to at least 100, it's too cold to paddle without a wetsuit or drysuit.

Accidents do happen, and river drownings are terrible events that occur all too often. Prevent them with these precautions, as well as the obvious others. Always wear a fully protective **flotation jacket** *– never rely on a floating cushion.* **Know how to swim***, and* **don't exceed your skill level** *(be realistic!).*

The best part of the Saxtons River to canoe is from Grafton to the town of Saxtons River; the section that follows, on down to the Connecticut River has too many dams to be really enjoyable. The put-in is at the Route 121 bridge about three-quarters of a mile northwest of the Route 35 intersection in Grafton. There are several choices for taking out, with a simple one being a half-mile before the town of Saxtons River.

The **West River** actually begins in Weston (see *Upper Connecticut River Valley* chapter), but becomes more navigable in Londonderry. A challenging five-mile section of ledges gives way to 6½ miles of easier water before reaching the backwater of the Ball Mountain Dam. There is a pretty tough carry here, up a half-mile to the road. Around the other side of the dam is the famous **West River Run**, an exciting stretch for canoeing and kayaking, thanks to spring and fall water releases at the dam. For this year's dates, check the Jamaica State Park Web site at www.stateparks. com. There is a lot of fun to be had here – it's a true whitewater rodeo, complete with crowds of spectators whooping the racers onward. The take-out is at Salmon Hole, nearly three miles past the dam. After this, there are three simpler sections of the river to run, but ledges and rapids should be carefully studied first.

Be sure to check on release schedules before you even think about running this stretch of the West River; water releases are powerful, fast, and dangerous. Know when they will happen and judge whether your skill level justifies being on the water at the time.

Flatwater Paddling

Lake boating in this region mostly means the **Harriman and Somerset Reservoirs,** near Wilmington. There is enough room here and good winds for sailing and board sailing, too. Harriman is also called Lake Whitingham; it is the largest lake that's held entirely within the state, and was formed by damming the Deerfield River (by hand, a century ago!). It is over eight miles long with 21 miles of shoreline. New England Power Company owns and maintains the shoreline, and provides several access areas. **Wards Cove** is found by taking Route 100 south from Wilmington for a mile to the Flame Stables sign, with a right turn onto a dirt road that leads to the lake. Or, stay with Route 100 south through Jacksonville to Whitingham Center; half a mile past Brown's Store take the right turn with an immediate left to the lake. You might also try the Mountain Mills access, reached by going to the center of Wilmington (where Route 100 turns north) and making a south turn onto Castle Hill Road. Turn quickly right onto Fairview Avenue, following signs to the boat launch, and then take the dirt road to the lake. For the Ox Bow access, stay with Route 9 west out of Wilmington for 1.7 miles to the Green Mountain Flagship business on the right, and pull in on the left. These four areas all have boat launches; there are rentals available at **Green Mountain Flagship** (☎ 464-2975), which also runs a 65-passenger tour boat with historical narration (call for schedules, which vary by season).

Somerset Reservoir is accessed by taking Route 9 for 5.3 miles west of Wilmington to Somerset Road. There is a boat ramp at the dam. The lake is 10 miles long and well framed by the Mount Snow and Haystack peaks on one side and the Green Mountain Forest on the other.

Grout Pond and the **Retreat Meadows** (see next page) also offer relaxed flatwater exploration.

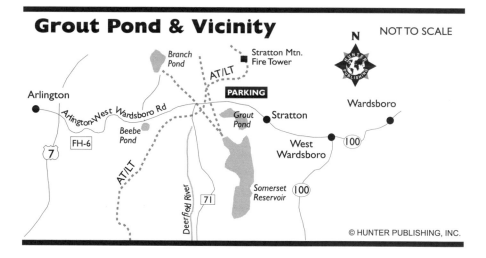

Grout Pond & Vicinity

NOT TO SCALE

N

Branch Pond

Stratton Mtn. Fire Tower

AT/LT

PARKING

Arlington

Arlington-West Wardsboro Rd

Beebe Pond

Grout Pond

Stratton

Wardsboro

West Wardsboro

100

7   FH-6

AT/LT

Deerfield River   71

Somerset Reservoir   100

© HUNTER PUBLISHING, INC.

Fishing

Fishing in the **Harriman** and **Somerset** reservoirs can yield brook trout, smallmouth bass, perch, pickerel, northern pike, and yellow smelt; Harriman also has landlocked salmon. They are especially well known for ice fishing. On the **Connecticut River** there is now shad fishing, as well as brook, rainbow, and brown trout, largemouth and smallmouth bass, walleye, pike, and perch. The **West River** is an especially good trout stream (brook and brown). The **Saxtons River** has rainbow trout as well.

One more pond to take note of is **Grout Pond,** reached from West Wardsboro (located on Route 100). From the center of the village, take the Arlington-West Wardsboro Road west through Stratton to reach the national forest parking area. The pond is also used by canoeists and windsurfers, with a 200-foot portage from the access road. Fish include perch, pickerel, and bass.

The **Retreat Meadows**, reached from Route 30, has a pull-off for parking, and offers bass, bluegill, pike, pickerel and perch. You can fish from the bank.

LOOKING FOR ANGLING GEAR? *Try Sam's Outdoor Outfitters at 74 Main Street in Brattleboro (☎ 254-2933) and on the Square in Bellows Falls (☎ 463-3500).*

FISHING GUIDES & OUTFITTERS

■ **Strictly Trout,** David L. Deen (Orvis-endorsed), RFD3, Box 800, Westminster West, VT 05346; ☎ 869-3116. Three guides, licensed in both Vermont and New Hampshire. Cover all Vermont rivers but have special interest in the Connecticut, especially fly-fishing and American shad (June).

■ **Bass Fishing Charters,** Jim Sweeney, HCR63, Box 16, West Dover, VT 05356; ☎ 464-5485.

■ **Black Mountain Enterprises,** Milt Sherman, RD1, Box 308, Brattleboro, VT 05301; ☎ 254-5184.

■ **Mission Fishin' Sportfishing Charters,** Captain Gary Longley, RR1, Box 1, South Londonderry, VT 05155; ☎ 824-6031 or 297-1213.

Swimming Holes

There are beaches at many state parks, but area residents get a lot of fun from dipping into (unsupervised) swimming holes like the ones off Route 30 in the **West River**, by the Dummerston Bridge and by the Scott covered bridge. There's also a good spot below the **Vermont Dam**, just south of Brattleboro. Look for the cars by the side of the road.

SWIMMING LESSONS

■ **Tyler Swim School,** Colonial Motel & Spa, Putney Road, Brattleboro, VT 05301, ☎ 254-5040, offers lessons for infants to coached masters swimming and water aerobics, year-round in a 75-foot heated indoor lap pool. Jacuzzi and massage services available. Certified by the National Swim School Association.

■ On Snow & Ice

Downhill Skiing

Mount Snow/Haystack might as well be considered one very large ski resort of 540 acres, although there are facilities for each mountain. The **Ridge Touring Trail,** for Nordic skiing only, ties the two peaks together, and both are owned by American Skiing Company. With 130 trails and 24 lifts, this is the most active ski slope in Southern Vermont. Most of the lifts are chairlifts, including a 7,300-foot quad, the Yankee Clipper, as well as a high-speed mile-long quad, the Canyon Quad. Snowboarding is a big priority, with a snowboard park that includes a 400-foot illuminated halfpipe for night riding. Mount Snow offers 137 acres of tree skiing, too. Child care is available for infants on up, and includes kids' activities and camps as well as lessons.

There are three lodges and a Vacation Center at Mount Snow and a pair at Haystack. Snowmaking coverage is nearly complete, making sure there's skiable terrain no matter how erratic the weather gets. The North Face of Mount Snow is the most challenging, with nearly every trail having either a single- or double-diamond rating. The season is sure to open by mid-November and lasts well into April. The site also includes rentals, repairs, a ski shop, cafeterias, restaurant, lounges, and a night club. For information, ☎ 464-3333 or 800-599-5754; Web site www.mountsnow.com.

Stratton Mountain (☎ 800-STRATTON or 787-2886, Web site www.stratton.com) offers over 500 acres of challenging terrain, dropping 2,003 vertical feet, with a high-speed gondola and what the resort calls "the best halfpipe on the planet" for snowboarders. There are adventure parks for skiers and snowboarders, with terrain gardens, woods trails, carving parks, bump terrain, and pocket playgrounds. Twelve lifts operate, including the summit gondola and the six-passenger detachable chairlift. Snowmaking coverage is 75%. Events, races, and celebrations keep the slopes lively. A unique Night Rider Program offers newcomers a chance to learn to ski and snowboard under the lights every Friday and Saturday evening.

The resort includes luxurious accommodations, designer outlet shops, and restaurants, as well as ski and snowboard schools, and child care/camp activities from age six weeks.

Two downhill ski areas in this region are struggling to reopen, and are likely to be less crowded. One, **Maple Valley Ski Area** at Sugar Mountain in West Dummerston (☎ 254-6083), has been closed for renovations. The other is **Magic Mountain** in Londonderry (☎ 824-5645). Call the resorts to find out current status.

Cross-Country Skiing

Cross-country skiing is found at the **Timber Creek Cross Country Ski Center** (☎ 464-0999) across from Mount Snow. It has 16 km of trails, and offers instruction, ski shop, restaurant, and lodging. The **Hermitage Inn** (☎ 464-3511) has 55 km of trails at an elevation of 2,000 feet, and also offers instruction, a ski shop, dining, and lodging. A third Wilmington location for Nordic skiing is the **White House Inn** (☎ 464-2135), which has a 43-km ski touring center; rentals include snowshoes, and there are guided tours as well as lessons, with gracious dining and lodging on site.

Stratton Mountain has its own cross-country trails (20 km); for information, ☎ 297-4063. Instruction, rentals, and repairs are on hand. Also in Londonderry is **Tater Hill** (☎ 824-6578), with 25 km of trails, instruction and rentals; and **Viking Cross-Country Ski Center** (☎ 824-3933), one of the first public ski touring centers in the country, offering 40 km of trails and a range of instruction, ski shop and rentals, and dining and lodging. At Viking, the **Cobble Hill Trail,** a 13-km backcountry loop, is a treat for experienced skiers.

STAY & SKI: *Many inns in this region now offer cross-country skiing in the fields and back roads nearby.* ***The Sitzmark*** *in Wilmington (☎ 464-3384) has 12 km of trails, plus rentals and lessons. In Landgrove, the next town over from Londonderry, there are 26 km of trails and a rental shop and lessons at the* ***Meadow Brook Inn*** *(☎ 824-6444). And in Londonderry itself, the* ***Swiss Inn*** *(☎ 824-3442 or 800-847-9477) created a network of snowshoe trails, woodsy and easily traversed. The Swiss Inn also arranges sleigh rides with a nearby farm, as do many other country inns.*

The Brattleboro area also offers Nordic skiing, but a special attraction there is the **Harris Hill Ski Jump,** a 70-meter Olympic-size jump. There is an international competition here each February, sanctioned by the US Ski Association and sponsored by the **Brattleboro Outing Club,** PO Box 335, Brattleboro, VT 05302; ☎ 257-7345. The club also puts together cross-country events, ski orienteering, weekend snowshoe and ski lessons, and a once-a-year (February) tour of the Harris Hill Ski Jump (details below), when you can actually try the jump yourself. The club maintains its set of Nordic ski trails and a ski hut on Upper Dummerston Road in Brattleboro, and offers information on ski hut and snow conditions (☎ 254-4081); for lessons, call ahead for an appointment (☎ 254-6965). Founded in 1921, BOC is one of the oldest civic outdoor associations in the United States.

Southeastern Gateway

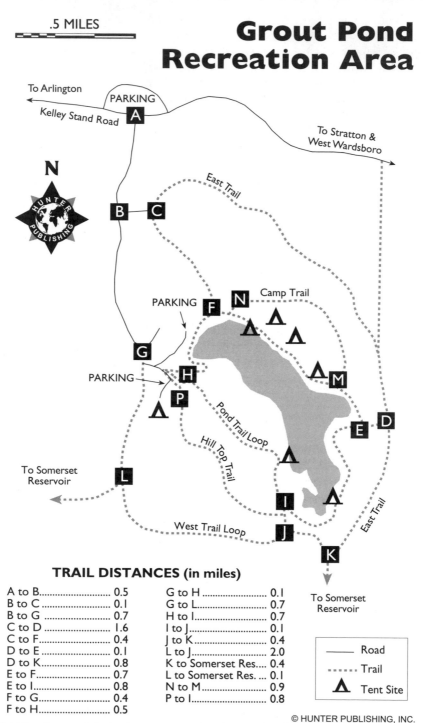

Grout Pond Recreation Area

.5 MILES

N

HUNTER PUBLISHING

To Arlington

PARKING

Kelley Stand Road

To Stratton & West Wardsboro

East Trail

PARKING

Camp Trail

Pond Trail Loop

Hill Top Trail

To Somerset Reservoir

West Trail Loop

East Trail

To Somerset Reservoir

TRAIL DISTANCES (in miles)

A to B	0.5	G to H	0.1
B to C	0.1	G to L	0.7
B to G	0.7	H to I	0.7
C to D	1.6	I to J	0.1
C to F	0.4	J to K	0.4
D to E	0.1	L to J	2.0
D to K	0.8	K to Somerset Res	0.4
E to F	0.7	L to Somerset Res	0.1
E to I	0.8	N to M	0.9
F to G	0.4	P to I	0.8
F to H	0.5		

	Road
····	Trail
▲	Tent Site

THE BOC SKI JUMP COMPETITION

The BOC competition is held on a weekend in mid-February, weather permitting; you can get this year's dates by calling ☎ 254-4565. Tickets are available at the gate and run less than $10 (children get a discount). But come early – it's now a Pepsi Challenge event, world class, and well advertised. Saturday's events include form and distance in three jumps; Sunday wraps up with the Longest Standing Jump, where skiers soar as far as their leap will take them. To get to the Harris Hill Ski Jump from Interstate 91, take Exit 2 to Brattleboro, then follow the signs to Cedar Street.

Grafton's historic village gears up for cross-country skiing at **Grafton Ponds**, with The Old Tavern at Grafton coordinating arrangements. There is a quaint and friendly ski center with instruction and rentals; trails range from easy to intermediate (see map on next page). There is also a skating rink, and skates as well as snowshoes may be rented. Contact the **Grafton Ponds Cross-Country Ski Center,** ☎ 843-2400, or **The Old Tavern** (☎ 843-2231 or 800-843-1801).

Keep in mind that national forest land is open to cross-country skiing. **Grout Pond Recreation Area** (see map on previous page), near West Wardsboro, has ungroomed areas open to the public. Also, the first six sections of the Catamount Trail wind along the mountain peaks from Harriman Reservoir north to Londonderry; each segment is about the right size for a single day's ski touring. *The Catamount Trail Guidebook* gives details of the trails (Catamount Trail Association, PO Box 1235, Burlington, VT 05402; ☎ 864-5794).

Snowmobiling

SNOWMOBILE TOURS

■ **Outpost Snowmobile Rentals and Tours,** c/o Best Western, PO Box 755, West Dover, VT 05356; ☎ 464-5112 or 800-451-4289, with day and night trips on national forest trails.

■ **Wheeler Farm,** HCR 63, Box 9, Wilmington, VT 05363; ☎ 464-5225, a working farm with guided tours; snowmobiles furnished. Please make reservations.

■ **High Country,** PO Box 1565, Wilmington, VT 05363; ☎ 464-2108 or 800-627-7533, provides snowmobile tours and guided trips in the Green Mountain National Forest. Trails start at the log cabin on Route 9, 8½ miles west of Wilmington; reservations are recommended.

■ **Snowmotion Snowmobile,** PO Box 380, West Dover, VT 05356; ☎ 464-5504 or 464-3384, offers tours on a private trail sys-

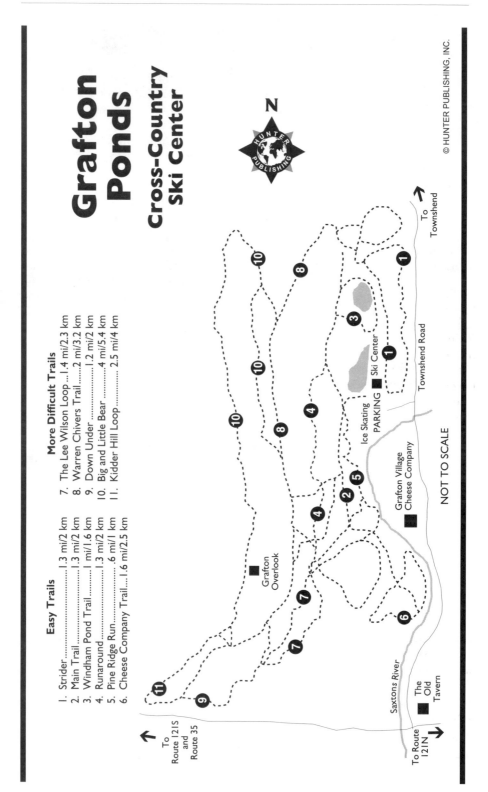

Grafton Ponds
Cross-Country Ski Center

N

HUNTER PUBLISHING

© HUNTER PUBLISHING, INC.

Easy Trails

1. Strider.........................1.3 mi/2 km
2. Main Trail...................1.3 mi/2 km
3. Windham Pond Trail.....1 mi/1.6 km
4. Runaround..................1.3 mi/2 km
5. Pine Ridge Run...............6 mi/1 km
6. Cheese Company Trail...1.6 mi/2.5 km

More Difficult Trails

7. The Lee Wilson Loop ...1.4 mi/2.3 km
8. Warren Chivers Trail.......2 mi/3.2 km
9. Down Under ....1.2 mi/2 km
10. Big and Little Bear ....4 mi/5.4 km
11. Kidder Hill Loop............2.5 mi/4 km

To Townshend

Townshend Road

Ski Center

PARKING

Ice Skating

Grafton Village
Cheese Company

NOT TO SCALE

Grafton
Overlook

Saxtons River

The
Old
Tavern

To Route 121N

To
Route 121S
and
Route 35

tem and in the Green Mountain National Forest, day and night safaris, and adventure tours. Reservations recommended.

■ **Greenduck Snowmobile Tours,** Route 9 East, Wilmington, VT 05363; ☎ 464-3284 or 800-479-3284. Rides start to the west in Woodford.

SNOWMOBILE RENTALS

■ **William Hance,** Emerald Lake Road, East Dorset, VT 05253; ☎ 362-3946.

■ **Stanley Bill's Sales, Service & Rentals,** Route 30, Townshend, VT 05353; ☎ 365-7375.

Sleigh Rides

Many country inns now arrange sleigh rides for their guests, calling on nearby farms. One farm specializing in sleigh rides that sample the delights of snowy days and nights is the **Adams Farm** (☎ 464-3762) in Wilmington. Three double-traverse sleighs are drawn by Belgian draft horses, and accommodate 15-20 passengers each. The romantic ride includes two 45-minute segments with a narrated tour. There is a stop at a log cabin in the woods, which offers an old fashioned woodstove, hot chocolate, and a player piano. Advance reservations are suggested for all sleigh rides.

SLEIGH RIDE CONTACT INFORMATION

■ **Adams Farm,** Higley Road, Wilmington, VT 05363; ☎ 464-3742.

■ **Valley View Horses & Tack Shop,** Box 48A, Northwest Hill Road, Pownal, VT 05261; ☎ 823-4649.

■ **Karl Pfister Sleigh Rides,** RR1, Box 217B, Landgrove, VT 05148; ☎ 824-6320.

Skating

Most ponds and lakes can be skated in December, although it is wise to wait until the ice has been tested for depth by local ice fishermen or by snowmobilers. However, outdoor skating is less pleasant after the first cycle of thaw and storm, when the ice becomes rough and often pocketed with air. Ask locally about safety and public access before going out onto any pond or lake ice.

The wetland known as the **Brattleboro Retreat Meadows**, north of Brattleboro, freezes over each winter and is dotted with fishing shacks.

That's a good sign that the ice is thick enough to skate on, and sometimes there's a cleared area next to the road to make it easy.

Rink skating is available at **Memorial Park Skating Rink** in Brattleboro, ☎ 257-2311; rentals are available.

Eco-Travel & Cultural Excursions

If you are interested in ropes courses, as an individual, family, or group adventure, contact **Project Adventure** about activities at its **Brattleboro** location, on the campus of the Austine School for the Deaf. Project Adventure, PO Box 100, Hamilton, MA 01936; ☎ 800-468-8898.

As you rise up the slope of the Green Mountain range from Brattleboro to Marlboro, you emerge at **Hogback Mountain**, where there's a great view at least a hundred miles long (see *On Foot*, page 46). You'll be 12 miles west of Brattleboro and five miles from Wilmington. Here on the ridge, right by Route 9, is a little museum that started as a sort of home collection of stuffed birds. It has now grown to include 80 dioramas and over 500 species of New England birds and mammals. It's the **Southern Vermont Natural History Museum** (☎ 464-0048), open daily from Memorial Day (end of May) until October, 9-5. Call for winter hours, which vary. Admission is $2 adults, $1 kids.

In **Wilmington,** the **Adams Farm** (15 Higley Hill Road, Wilmington, VT 05363; ☎ 464-3762) offers four seasons of farm activities for guests, ranging from exploring bear caves to gathering eggs and milking goats. In winter they have nostalgic sleigh rides to a log cabin or intimate journeys for two in a one-horse open sleigh. Reservations are recommended.

A list of working farms to visit is available from the **Windham Country Natural Resources Conservation District,** ☎ 254-5323. Some of the most unusual are **Green Mountain Llamas** in Townshend, ☎ 365-7581; **Berry Hill Farm** in Cambridgeport, ☎ 869-2369, with sheep, maple syrup, and hops for the homebrewer; a children's day camp at **Maple Ridge Farm** in Wilmington, ☎ 464-5243, where kids aged six to nine can learn about caring for farm animals and natural resources; **Spirit Hill** in Halifax, ☎ 257-0233, another llama farm, featuring hand spinning of their wool; and a tree farm, **Elysian Hills,** in Brattleboro; ☎ 257-0233. Don't miss the milking at the **Miller Farm** in Vernon, ☎ 254-2657, which has one of the nation's first registered Holstein herds. Call ahead for any of these before visiting.

In **Grafton,** photographer **Neal Landy** (☎ 843-2703) offers fall foliage photo workshops as a fresh way to "see" nature. He prefers small groups and teaches at levels from novice to advanced amateur, providing take-home workshop notes for reviews and reference.

Where To Stay

■ Brattleboro & West Brattleboro

For real historic character and Art Deco at its best, the **Latchis Hotel** (50 Main Street, ☎ 254-6300, $$-$$$) in the heart of downtown Brattleboro can't be beat. The building also includes a restaurant and microbrewery. There are deluxe and standard rooms, as well as suites. Restored to much of its 1938 glory, with terrazzo floors, chrome fixtures, and rooms that have a playful, rural charm, the Latchis also has the modern amenities of private baths, cable TV, telephones, and plenty of parking.

A new bed-and-breakfast inn at the very center of town is perfect if you want to enjoy the weekend exuberance of the town. The **Artist's Loft** is at 103 Main Street in the Amedeo de Angelis/Union Block, which dates to about 1861. De Angelis was an immigrant Italian shoemaker who owned the building in the 1920s and achieved the American Dream through much hard work; he erected an immense bronze plaque on the building as a memorial to himself. If you stay here, your lodging is in a two-room suite that overlooks the Connecticut River, and homemade breakfast is included (☎ 257-5181, Web site www.sover.net/~artguys, $$).

Three inns stand out for the Brattleboro region, one just up the hill from the downtown area: **The Tudor,** a bed-and-breakfast inn, at 76 Western Avenue (☎ 257-4983 or 258-2632, $$-$$$), has rich wood paneling, formal gardens, and six fireplaces. Innkeepers John Penford and Joy Wallens-Penford provide relaxed elegance in a quiet retreat, including breakfast and teatime treats.

40 Putney Road (☎ 254-6268 or 800-941-2413, Web site www.putney.net/40putneyrd, $$) is located to match its name, on the main northbound road out of Brattleboro. But it's as different as could be from the chain motels farther along the road. Here you'll find a French baronial estate full of antiques, with classically landscaped grounds complete with fountains. Breakfast is included, and you can walk to downtown.

The **Meadowlark Inn** on Orchard Street (☎ 257-4582 or 800-757-3389, Web site http://homepages.together.net/~lark, $$-$$$) is just west of Exit 2 of Interstate 91; take the second right onto Orchard Street and go 1.5 miles. Between the main house and the 1870 coachhouse, there are four rooms, each with cozy farmhouse character raised a notch in elegance, and modern comforts. Breakfast is served. The view from the hilltop is truly panoramic, and deer sometimes visit the yard.

Southeastern Gateway

Farther west on Route 9 is the village of West Brattleboro, where **Dalem's Chalet** (16 South Street, ☎ 254-4323, $$) can be seen on the hillside to the left a mile from Interstate 91, Exit 2. European hospitality in an alpine setting makes the lodging attractive. Modern amenities and an outdoor pool complement the setting.

Also in West Brattleboro are the **West Village Motel** (480 Western Avenue, ☎ 254-5610, $) and the **Molly Stark Motel** (Route 9, three miles west of Interstate 91, ☎ 254-2440, $-$$).

The Putney Road, also known as Route 5, heads north out of downtown Brattleboro to a strip of convenient shops, grocery stores, restaurants and snack bars, and lodgings for travelers seeking reliable American motel comforts. The **Quality Inn** (Putney Road, ☎ 254-8701, $$) is five miles from the downtown region, near Exit 3 from Interstate 91. It also offers meeting and banquet facilities. There is a sauna, Jacuzzi, and indoor pool, plus the Steak House Restaurant and lounge.

Also on the Putney Road, half a mile south of Exit 3, is the **Colonial Motel and Spa** (☎ 257-7753 or 800-239-0032, $$), which has an indoor pool and spa plus a restaurant and lounge. There is a **Super 8 Motel** (☎ 254-8889 or 800-800-8000, $$) close to Exit 3, next to McDonald's. This motel has recently been fully refurbished, including complete handicap access.

■ Wilmington

Set on the crest of a high rolling hill and surrounded by formal gardens, the **White House** (Route 9, ☎ 464-2135 or 800-541-2135, $$-$$$) is a Victorian mansion with turn-of-the-century grandeur, yet a welcoming atmosphere. The *Boston Herald* called it "one of the 10 most romantic places in the world." There are 23 guest rooms, beautifully furnished with period pieces; nine have fireplaces, and four have large whirlpool tubs – just the thing for relaxing after hiking or skiing the inn's 45 km of trails. A cross-country ski center on the premises provides instruction and rentals. There is also a 60-foot in-ground pool. The menu features "creative Continental" dishes ranging from baked Brie en croûte to boneless duck stuffed with apples, walnuts, and grapes (for example!).

Wilmington's other elegant country inn is **The Hermitage** (Coldbrook Road; ☎ 464-3511, $$$$), where 29 rooms in several buildings offer New England elegance at its finest. A hobby of the innkeepers is the game bird farm on the premises, which includes peacocks and black swans. There is also a trout pond, and the cross-country ski center has 50 km of trails, plus instruction and rentals. The dining is gracious and exquisite, incorporating game birds in the menu each evening, as well as an award-winning wine list of over 2,000 labels.

The **Nordic Hill Lodge** is a relaxed family spot where there's a hearty country breakfast and an outdoor heated pool, plus fresh popcorn and homemade cookies always available (34 Look Road, ☎ 464-5130 or 800-

326-5130, $$). Or there's the homey feel of the **Misty Mountain Lodge**, a cozy 1803 farmhouse with eight guestrooms, where they serve not just a full breakfast but a full family-style dinner as well, and the host may include you in an evening of song or stories (326 Stowe Hill Road, ☎ 464-3961, Web site http://homepages.together.net/~mistymtn, $$). More interested in peace and quiet and being pampered? Go for the **Whitingham Farm bed & Breakfast**, surrounded by 50 acres at the end of the road, and furnished with antiques, oriental rugs, and private baths; ask about a carriage ride after the gourmet breakfast (742 Abbie Morse Road; ☎ 368-2620 or 800-310-2010, Web site www.whitinghamfarm.com, $$$-$$$$).

■ Mount Snow (West Dover)

From the center of Wilmington, take Route 100 north for 9.7 miles to the **Inn at Mount Snow** (☎ 464-3300 or 800-577-SNOW, $$-$$$$), a country bed and breakfast with 14 guestrooms and breathtaking views of Mount Snow.

The resort at Mount Snow offers condominiums and a lakeside lodge, as well as the **Grand Summit Resort Hotel** (☎ 800-664-6535, Web site www.mountsnow.com, prices range widely). Also close to the slope is the **Lodge at Mount Snow**, with its lounge, massive fieldstone fireplace and mountain views (Route 100, ☎ 464-5112 or 800-451-4289, $$). More intimate is the **Austin Hill Inn**, also on Route 100, where afternoon wine and cheese is a tradition; ask about the Murder Mystery weekends, too (☎ 464-5281 or 800-332-RELAX, Web site www.austinhillinn.com, $$-$$$).

The **Deerfield Valley Inn** is a bed and breakfast on Route 100; many of its rooms have fireplaces and all have private baths (☎ 464-6333 or 800-639-3588; Web site www.deerfieldvalleyinn.com; $$-$$$). For more secluded accommodations, try the **Snow Goose Inn** (call for directions; ☎ 464-3984 or 888-604-7964; Web site www.snowgooseinn.com; $$-$$$). Also popular is the **West Dover Inn** (including Gregory's Restaurant), a quietly luxurious country inn with memorable dining (Route 100, ☎ 464-5207, Web site www.westdoverinn.com; $$$-$$$$).

MOUNT SNOW LODGING ASSISTANCE: *There are many more lodgings at Mount Snow; for more suggestions, and for lodging packages, get in touch with the **Mount Snow Valley Chamber of Commerce** at ☎ 877-VT-SOUTH (Web site www.visitvermont.com).*

Especially suited to skiers is the **Weathervane Lodge** (Dorr Fitch Road, West Dover, ☎ 464-5426 or 800-464-2735, $), which serves breakfast and has 12 rooms. Close to Mount Snow is the **Red Cricket Inn** (Route 100, ☎ 800-733-2742 or 464-8817, $-$$), a family-run lodge with lounge and game room. On Route 9 is the **Horizon Inn** (☎ 464-2131, $$), a blend of a well-run motor lodge with a country inn, specializing in customized tours for senior groups, as well as in housing for Marlboro Music Festival attendees and skiers.

■ Newfane

Located on the village green behind the courthouse, the **Four Columns Inn** (☎ 365-7713 or 800-787-6633, $$$-$$$$) offers gracious lodging. There are 15 rooms and suites, some with fireplaces, and a fine restaurant that serves a distinctive blend of European and New American cuisine. The chef here especially favors fine local foods, creating Green Mountain menus that include game birds, rabbit, and veal. There is a romantic, candlelit dining room. Outside, 150 acres of wooded land behind the inn offer hiking trails, and there is a pool for summer swimming.

The **Inn at South Newfane** (☎ 348-7191, $$-$$$) is reached from Interstate 91 by taking Route 9 east to connect with Route 30 north, going nine miles, then making the right turn by the inn sign. It's another three miles of scenic drive that includes a covered bridge before you reach South Newfane. By this point you've come unexpectedly close to Mount Snow, and the inn encourages guests to take advantage of the resort. There is a private pond for swimming, and the common rooms of the inn encourage informal conviviality in the evenings.

Smaller but full of charm and comfort is the **West River Lodge** (north of Newfane; call for detailed road directions, ☎ 365-7745, $$-$$$), where antique furnishings make the eight guest rooms attractive; breakfasts and dinners are served. Also north of Newfane but on Route 30 is the **River Bend Motel** (☎ 365-7952 or 800-599-7952, $-$$), 20 rooms with privacy and moderate rates and a restaurant next door.

■ Townshend

When you come to sample the adventures of Jamaica State Park and the West River run, there are two very different choices for nearby lodging. The first is the much-photographed **Old Brick Tavern,** on the common in Townshend (☎ 365-4527, $$). There are only three bedrooms, but they are comfortable and the tavern is friendly. Breakfast is available. Or, just south of town, take the turn off Route 30 toward Townshend State Forest and go two miles to **Redwing Farm** (Carol Rees and Joe Scanlon, ☎ 365-4656, $$), a working organic produce farm with three cozy bedrooms upstairs in the 19th-century farmhouse. There's a homemade Continental breakfast.

A third lodging in the area is noted as one of the most romantic and elegant (though also costly): **Windham Hill Inn** at 311 Lawrence Drive in West Townshend (☎ 874-4080 or 800-944-4080, $$$$). The exquisite accommodations look out over the West River Valley, and the dining is superb. Explore their Web site, www.windhamhill.com, for an extensive virtual tour.

Hosts Grigs and Pat Markham have crafted a memorable retreat at their 1825 farmhouse, and the 160 acres around it include a clay tennis court, pool, and the lovely New England rock walls and fields to wander along. There are fireplaces in most rooms, a Jacuzzi, and since your hosts love to hike, they can guide you in selecting activities in the nearby mountains.

■ Jamaica

Three Mountain Inn is an original 1780s Colonial village inn with a hundred acres to ramble and superb mountain views. Guest rooms are generous in size, and some offer queen-size canopy beds and working fireplaces. Charles and Elaine Murray keep their guests busy and happy, offering a choice of menus in the dining room and pub lounge, a swimming pool, and nearby hiking, biking, and skiing (downhill and cross-country). Room rates may include just the full breakfast, or also dinner. The inn is on Main Street, which is also Route 30 (☎ 874-4140, $$-$$$$).

■ Londonderry & South Londonderry

The innkeepers of the **Swiss Inn,** the Donahues, take the seasons and hospitality so deeply to heart that they present their own newsletter of activities. This family-run inn is on Route 11 (☎ 824-3442 or 800-847-9477, e-mail swissinn@sover.net, $$) and has its own Nordic skiing, hiking, and snowshoeing trails; snowshoes are available at the inn. The restaurant menu features predominantly Swiss and German specialties, with treats of cheese and chocolate fondue.

At **Frog's Leap Inn** on Route 100 the maple trees are two centuries old, there's a 52-foot heated pool and a tennis court, and hiking and ski trails wind across the premises. Hosts Kraig and Dorenna Hart love to cook, and their breakfasts show it; they also enjoy gardening, reading, and fishing, all fruitful subjects to share. Arrangements can be made for pets. The Harts formerly worked at the noted Mohonk Mountain House in New York. They are still making renovations at Frog's Leap; check their Web site for the latest news, www.frogsleapinn.com. (☎ 824-3019 or 877-376-4753, $$$-$$$$).

Take Route 100 a bit farther south, into South Londonderry, and on Route 100 you'll find the **Londonderry Inn**, owned by Him and Jean Cavanagh and Esther Fishman since 1981. The 1826 Colonial on nine acres includes a game and billiards room as well as a living room with immense fireplace, a library, and a children's outdoor play area. You'll have views of the West River and of Glebe Mountain (☎ 824-5226, Web site www.bestinns.net/usa/vt/london.html, $-$$$, seasonal rates).

■ Stratton Mountain (Bondville)

The lodgings at the **Stratton Mountain Resort** (☎ 800-STRATTON, $$-$$$$) are interesting and extensive, and this is the first place to consider if you are here to ski. Another option is across the street from the lifts, the **Birkenhaus** (☎ 297-2000, $-$$), where innkeepers Ina and Jan Dlouhy offer their living room, their library, and 18 guest rooms. If the atmosphere reminds you of a Central European hotel, that's just what was intended; dining is Continental, and there is also a bar for after-dinner relaxing.

■ Putney

Traditionally, bikers and other guests have gravitated to the **Putney Inn** (☎ 387-5517 or 800-653-5517, $$-$$$), where even the low red-painted buildings reflect country charm. The inn is located in one of the earliest buildings of the region, with rooms furnished in Queen Anne-style to replicate Colonial warmth. All meals are served, and the village is a short walk away from the Exit 4 location. West Hill Shop, the region's most vital bike center, is just across the road.

Putney also has some comfortable bed-and-breakfast lodges: **Mapleton Farm** (☎ 257-5252 or 800-236-5254, $$) has five guest rooms and a two-room suite in an 1803 farmhouse. It is six miles south on Route 5 from Exit 4 of Interstate 91. **Hickory Ridge House** (Jacquie Walker and Steve Anderson, innkeepers, ☎ 387-5709, $$) is just north of the center of Putney, on Hickory Ridge Road. It offers seven guest rooms, with the breakfast pleasures of fresh eggs and homemade jams, jellies, and baked goods. Also north of the village is the **Putney Summit** (☎ 387-5806, $$), with guest rooms and, in warm weather, guest cottages, plus a restaurant full of New England character and homemade meals.

■ Bellows Falls

John and Linda Maresca and their children welcome guests to the **River Mist Bed and Breakfast**, an 1880 Queen Anne Victorian with charming antique-furnished guest rooms, a formal parlor, wraparound porches for enjoying the evening and, of course, full breakfasts (the house specialty is the banana pancakes, but there are also New England traditionals). Children are welcome, and the Marescas will gladly help you set up a train trip on the Green Mountain Flyer or a riverboat cruise (7 Burt Street, ☎ 463-9023 or 888-463-9023; Web site www.river-mist.com, $$).

■ Grafton

The **Old Tavern at Grafton** (☎ 843-2231 or 800-843-1801, $$-$$$$) is a poet's choice of rural elegance and historical richness. Daniel Webster, Oliver Wendell Holmes, Nathaniel Hawthorne, Ralph Waldo Emerson, and Rudyard Kipling are just a few of the noted guests who have stayed here since 1788. Restored by the Windham Foundation in 1965, the Old Tavern is now equipped with modern conveniences like plumbing and heating, but so discreetly that the elegant mood of a previous century is hardly disturbed. There are 35 rooms in the Main Tavern building and the Windham and Homestead cottages. Another six guest houses sleep from eight to 14 people each. Each room and cottage is distinct in furnishing, and all are comfortable and charming. The dining room at the Old Tavern offers breakfast, lunch, and dinner daily, exalting New England cuisine to culinary elegance. Bikes and cross-country skis are available to use on nearby back roads and trails. There is a stable that houses six horses if you care to bring your mount!

■ Camping

Most Vermont campgrounds are open only from mid-May to mid-October, the best weather of the year, and even so, you may well have ice in the water jug! Plan for black flies and mosquitoes at the early end of the season, and expect wide ranges in temperature; even in summer, an occasional frost happens. But the cool breezes drive the bugs away swiftly, and there are few pests to interfere with having a good time.

Don't judge a campground's location by its address – or its name! The **Brattleboro North KOA** (RD2, Box 560, Putney, VT 05346; ☎ 254-5908 or 800-562-5909) isn't in Brattleboro or Putney, but in Dummerston, on Route 5 between the two towns. A gift shop and cottages add to 42 sites, and there's plenty of room for RV camping too. Hot showers are free, which is one reason this campground has made a hit with hikers and cyclists.

The campground that really *is* in Brattleboro is **Hidden Acres** (Route 5, Box 401A, Brattleboro, VT 05301, ☎ 254-2724 or 800-254-2098). The 37-acre campground has 55 sites, and the ice cream bar adds to summer pleasure.

Moss Hollow Campground (RD#4, Box 723, Brattleboro, VT 05301, ☎ 368-2418) is between Brattleboro and Wilmington, and it's a good idea to call or write for directions so you make the right turns. There are great rustic and private tent sites (50 altogether), hayrides on some weekends, and mountain biking both at the campground and at nearby Mt. Snow.

Camperama Family Campground (Depot Road, Townshend, VT 05353, ☎ 365-4315) is up Route 30, 17 miles northwest of Brattleboro. The 215 sites are well supported with amenities and games. Not far away is **Kenolie Village** (Newfane, VT 05345, ☎ 365-7671), set in the West River Valley and offering 100 sites, both wooded and open. Kenolie stays open to December 1, longer than most.

There are 34 developed campgrounds at Vermont state parks. The ones in this region are at **Fort Dummer State Park** (Brattleboro, ☎ 254-2610), **Jamaica State Park** (Jamaica, ☎ 874-4600), **Molly Stark State Park** (Wilmington, ☎ 464-5460), and **Townshend State Park** (Townshend, ☎ 365-7500). Townshend and Molly Stark are small, with about 30 sites; the other two have around 60 sites each.

Primitive camping is allowed in most regions of the **Green Mountain National Forest**. The forest also has established campgrounds, either to help with support for the camping experience or to protect fragile wildlife and plants in the wilderness and alpine regions.

WISE WORDS

CAMPING TIP: *Only dead and down wood should be used for campfires, and the Forest Service requests that campers practice leaving no signs of their presence when they leave.*

Grout Pond is a national forest recreation area near West Wardsboro. Follow Route 100 north from Wilmington to West Wardsboro and turn left (west) on Forest Highway 6. The parking area is well marked. There are nine campsites around the pond, including an all-season cabin, three open-faced shelters, and tent sites, and several of the facilities (picnic area, outhouse, camping) are barrier-free. Four of the sites are accessible only by canoe!

Where To Eat

In general, the fine dining in Vermont is at the inns. This section mentions other opportunities. If a town is not listed here, take a look in the *Where To Stay* listing for possibilities.

■ Brattleboro

The college town feeling of the downtown area means there are lots of coffee shops and bakery/deli options. For fine dining, consider **Peter Havens,** 32 Elliott Street (☎ 257-3333), elegant cuisine, dinners only. **T.J. Buckley's Uptown Dining** (☎ 257-4922), also on Elliott Street, just past McNeill's Brewery, seats only a few tables in a tiny former railroad car, and the menu is at the discretion of the chef, but it will be excellent and intriguing. A local favorite for regional fare and heavenly desserts is the **Latchis Grille** at the Latchis Hotel, 6 Flat Street (☎ 254-4747), serving lunch, dinner, and Sunday brunch.

A stroll down Main Street gives you a choice of ethnic specialties at **La Sirena** (Mexican, ☎ 257-5234) or soups and sandwiches at **Carol's Main Street Café** (73 Main Street, ☎ 254-8380, closed Sundays). If you are a coffee lover, be sure to stop at **Mocha Joe's Coffeehouse and Market** on Main Street, or duck around the corner to the cafés off the Harmony Place parking lot. My own favorite is the **Backside Café** (☎ 257-5056), where the blackboard specials provide a yummy lunch, and there are always fresh desserts like Naughty Nancy's Chocolate Cake or Indian pudding. Open daily for breakfast and lunch, and on Fridays for dinner. You'll find a combination of bookstore, gallery, and café at 29 High Street in **Collected Works & The Café Beyond** (☎ 258-4900, Web site www.bookweb.org).

North of town, the **Marina Restaurant** on the Putney Road (Route 5) offers an inexpensive menu, fireplace, and gorgeous sunsets over the water. Farther up the Putney Road, skip the chain fast food regulars and duck into **Picnic's** (☎ 254-9675), which promises "real food fast" and comes through with barbecued and rotisserie meats, pastas, deli salads, and fried seafood, opening at 7 a.m. on weekends for breakfast. If you explore beyond the downtown area via Route 9 west, when you get to West Brattleboro try **Dalem's Chalet** (☎ 254-4323) for German, Swiss, and Austrian specialties, dinner only (☎ 254-4323), or the treasure of the area, the **Chelsea Royal Diner** (☎ 254-8399), with its famous hearty and sociable breakfasts, across from the state police barracks.

Brattleboro has two microbreweries: one is the **Windham Brewery** (☎ 254-4747) at the Latchis Grille, 6 Flat Street, brewing "honest ales, porters, and lagers," plus specialty brews to celebrate the seasons. The other is **McNeill's Brewery** (90 Elliott Street, ☎ 254-2553), serving award-winning beer and adding an atmosphere of games, good food, and family fun.

■ Marlboro

The **Skyline Restaurant** (☎ 464-5535) on Route 9 sits on Hogback Mountain and offers a noted 100-mile view. Although the food is middle-of-the road (pancakes are the best bet, and the prime rib dinner buffet is also popular), the view is truly great, and it's a good place to sit with a hot cup of coffee or cocoa while you warm up to face the wind on the ridge.

■ Wilmington, Mount Snow, Haystack

Dining in Wilmington is a high point of its inns, and the **White House** (☎ 464-2135 or 800-541-2135) offers the epitome of romantic candlelight dinging on fine continental cuisine. Other inns also have open dining rooms. Another delightful place is at the **Two Tannery Road Restaurant** (☎ 464-2707), close to Mount Snow, serving continental cuisine in a charming 17th-century home that once belonged to Teddy Roosevelt.

But Wilmington also offers entertaining dining, in the form of **Poncho's Wreck Restaurant**, south of the light in downtown Wilmington, ☎ 464-9320. "Vermont's only known shipwreck" features Mexican food as well as seafood and live entertainment. **The Silo Restaurant** (half a mile south of Mount Snow on Route 100, ☎ 464-2553) also has entertainment, as well as dancing, a game room, and two large fireplaces, to go with its classic American steak-and-seafood and pasta-and-pizza menu.

For a more delicate touch in the kitchen, sample the bistro cuisine and atmosphere at **Julie's Café** on Route 100 in East Dover (☎ 464-2078). The dinner menu changes every two weeks, lunches are unusual, and an espresso bar and luscious desserts complete the picture.

■ Putney

There is a traditional "don't miss this" dining experience in Putney, but it's not haute cuisine. It's the **Putney Diner,** serving fresh homemade food, three meals a day, seven days a week. Three-egg omelets and Belgian waffles are on the breakfast menu; the lunch-time grill includes tempeh burgers and veggie pockets in addition to the tried-and-true burgers and tuna melt; and dinner platters are hearty meals like turkey and gravy with mashed potatoes, or meatloaf, or fisherman's catch. There's even macaroni and cheese. For dessert, there are pies, of course! The diner is on Main Street at the center of the village (☎ 387-5433).

For a memorable outdoor dining experience (warm weather only), stop in at **Curtis' Barbeque** (☎ 387-5474) on Route 5, near Interstate 91; Southern barbeque lunches and dinners are offered Wednesday through Sunday, but call to make sure the weather is right.

Bennington & The Vermont Valley

The Vermont Valley is a scenic pathway up the western side of southern Vermont, centered on a series of winding rivers along Route 7. To the west, massive and majestic, are the Adirondacks of New York State; to the east is the rock-ridged spine of the Green Mountains. In the river valleys there are busy towns with year-round celebrations of human endeavors, from cultural festivals and events to art and craft studios and some of the state's most history-laden homes and byways. Critical moments of the Revolutionary War touched this region. Later, presidents visited when the resorts were born; Abraham Lincoln's son resided in a glorious mansion that is now open to visitors.

This is the entryway to the wildest portions of the **Green Mountain National Forest.** Over 350,000 acres of untamed land with more than 500 miles of trails make this area irresistible to hikers, skiers, mountain bikers, and those who treasure the sight of a herd of white-tailed deer or a family of black bears. Moose browse in the soggy swamps of bogs and beaver ponds; hawks and even eagles circle the crags.

The region is anchored by **Bennington** in the southwest corner, 12 miles from Massachusetts and even closer to New York. Once centered on its river mills, the town is history-laden, with elegant homes, a striking monument to Vermont's participation in the Revolutionary War, and craftspeople like the noted Bennington Potters.

Getting Here & Getting Around

You may reach this region from the Brattleboro area, taking Route 9 westward over Hogback Mountain and Mount Olga and passing close to the **George Aiken Wilderness,** a 5,000-acre untamed plateau of wetlands. The wilderness is named for one of Vermont's noted senators, who led the effort to expand the National Wilderness Preservation System in the eastern United States. Also close to Route 9 are **Prospect Mountain Winter Sports Area** (a cross-country skier's haven) and **Woodford State Park.**

Traveling north from Bennington are the twin Routes, 7 and 7A. Route 7 is a brisk and sometimes divided highway. It connects Bennington with the city of Rutland, and passes through the shopping mecca of Manchester along the way. Route 7A is called "Historic Route 7A" as it rambles through the picturesque villages and clings closely to the river banks – first **Furnace Brook,** then the fishing-famous **Batten Kill,** and at last **Otter Creek,** Vermont's longest river entirely within the state. Covered bridges, grand mansions, and spectacular side drives make the route fascinating and worth taking slowly.

Route 30 crosses Route 7 in Manchester; it heads northwest toward the softly rolling Lake Champlain Valley, first meandering through the noted summer resort area around lake St. Catherine. Heading east from Manchester on Route 30 soon connects with Route 11, which in turn rises into the Green Mountains to where Bromley Mountain offers both a ski area and a summer activity center. Both Routes 30 and 11 cross the mountain ridge into the Southeastern Gateway region.

Touring

Route 9, as it traces the pathway of Revolutionary War soldiers over the southern Green Mountains, is also called the **Molly Stark Trail.** In 1777, Molly Stark's husband, General John Stark, traveled back to Brattleboro with his Hessian troops after a heroic victory at the Battle of Bennington. The villages of Searsburg and Woodford are small and spare, befitting their high elevation on the bony ridge of the mountains, but they also stand at the entryway to impressively wild territory. Even if you don't plan to hike the Long Trail or the Appalachian Trail, pause at the trailhead on Route 9 just west of Woodford. Step far enough along the path to see how carefully this well-used trail has been designed to carry hikers into the Green Mountains, without stealing too much from the very wildness that draws visitors.

■ Bennington

The descent into Bennington leads past numerous inns and restaurants and into the center of town. A good first stop is the **Chamber of Commerce,** just north of town on Route 7A (alias North Street and Veterans Memorial Drive) next to a small park; pick up maps and walking tour brochures to better explore this town. The town has a double nature: a business center in the valley of the Walloomsac River, and a preserved historic district to the west where the land rises into Old Bennington. The roads can be confusing, and congested in summer and foliage season, so detailed

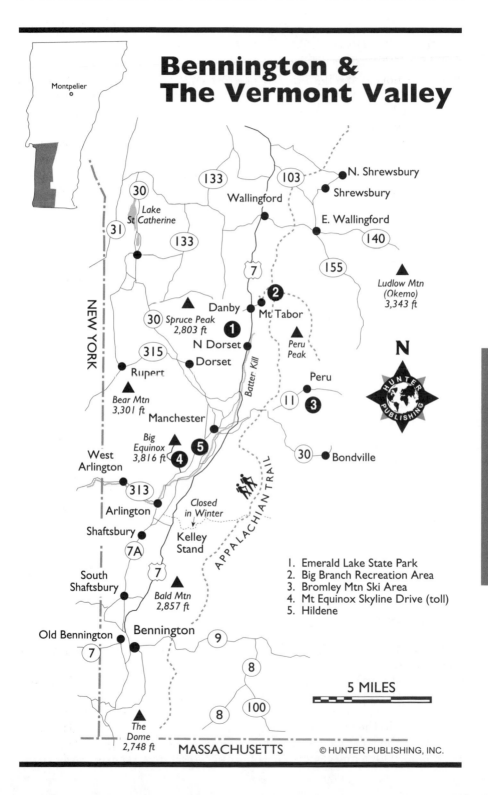

Bennington & The Vermont Valley

Montpelier

NEW YORK

Lake St Catherine

Wallingford

N. Shrewsbury

Shrewsbury

E. Wallingford

Ludlow Mtn (Okemo) 3,343 ft

Spruce Peak 2,803 ft

Danby

Mt Tabor

Peru Peak

N Dorset

Dorset

Rupert

Bear Mtn 3,301 ft

Peru

Manchester

Big Equinox 3,816 ft

West Arlington

Bondville

Batter Kill

APPALACHIAN TRAIL

Closed in Winter

Arlington

Shaftsbury

Kelley Stand

South Shaftsbury

Bald Mtn 2,857 ft

1. Emerald Lake State Park
2. Big Branch Recreation Area
3. Bromley Mtn Ski Area
4. Mt Equinox Skyline Drive (toll)
5. Hildene

Old Bennington

Bennington

5 MILES

The Dome 2,748 ft

MASSACHUSETTS

© HUNTER PUBLISHING, INC.

Bennington & Vermont Valley

maps are a nice advantage. Take note of the **Bennington Brewers** and the **Blue Benn Diner** on Route 9, so you can find them quickly later in the day. Armed with your maps, start south on Route 9 and make the first left onto County Street for a visit to the **Bennington Potters Yard,** famous for early American stoneware and also home to today's fine designers. You'll see early work of the potters at the Bennington Museum (see below).

When you return to Route 7A, keep going south (a left turn) and return to the center of town and Route 9. Go to the Old Bennington hill and find a place to park (this can take some doing on busy summer days!). It is worthwhile walking from Route 9 toward the 306-foot-high battle monument that dominates this part of town. The road, called Monument Avenue, is easy to find. It is lined by spacious homes, some dated 1781, 1790, and 1821. At the top of the hill, in a small park, is the blue limestone spire that resembles a small version of the Washington Monument, three-fifths its size. This is the **Bennington Battle Monument,** in honor of the battle fought here on August 16, 1777. The British were on their way to Bennington to try to capture supplies and ammunition, but instead the armed Vermonters stopped them in North Hoosick, New York, for a victory that helped move the Revolutionary War to a successful conclusion. From mid-April to the end of October, you can climb the monument for a three-state view and a survey of the river valley; there is also an elevator. It's open daily. For information, ☎ 447-0550.

Walk back down Monument Avenue and pause at its foot to explore the **Old First Church,** "Vermont's Colonial Shrine," organized in 1762. New England's most famous poet, Robert Frost, is buried here, along with five Vermont governors and many of the region's pioneers. Across the road is the tumbledown **Walloomsac Inn,** dating to 1796, once a stage stop for such distinguished travelers as James Madison and Thomas Jefferson. The **Joseph Cerniglia Winery** is just around the corner and a mile or so down Route 9. If you continue west on Route 9, you'll come to the **Oldcastle at Bennington Center for the Arts,** home of the noted Oldcastle Theatre Company (mid-April through October, ☎ 447-0564). Three miles west of Bennington is the Hemmings' famous Sunoco station and the home of *Hemmings Motor News,* the bible of old car collectors and lovers; open weekdays year-round (☎ 447-3101).

Go back to the east-west passage of West Main Street and head westward down the hill to visit the **Bennington Museum** (☎ 447-1571). Open year-round, its collections include regional history, glass, pottery, furniture, and the largest public collection of the folk-art paintings of Grandma Moses. These paintings are not just an art treasure; they give a joyful picture of village and rural life that satisfies any lover of New England nostalgia.

The downtown district is a brisk walk away, and the walking tour brochures will lead you along the busy riverfront. Or, if you're ready now to go on to North Bennington, drive back up the hill, turn right up Monument Drive, circle the monument, and turn onto Walloomsac Road, making an almost immediate right onto Fairview Street and another onto Silk Road.

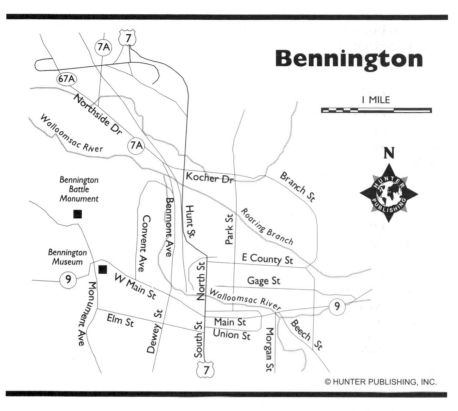

Bennington

I MILE

N

© HUNTER PUBLISHING, INC.

You are now passing through a covered bridge and arriving at Route 67A, with Bennington College just ahead.

Head left on Route 67A for the region's other historical gem, the **Park-McCullough House.** This 35-room French Empire-style mansion was completed in 1865 and was home to two Vermont governors before becoming a public historic site in 1964. Not only are the rooms and grounds elegant and gracious, but Bennington's cultural life, especially concerts, revolves here in the summertime, and there are special programs like croquet and a Victorian Christmas (and yes, you can have a wedding here!). Plan to visit during the warm weather, from late May to late October, or call ahead (☎ 442-5441) for special events.

North Bennington's historic mill on Water Street houses **No B.I.A.S.** (☎ 447-7754), a gallery and forum for art works in all media. The closeness of Bennington College also encourages small restaurants to bloom here.

Follow the signs back to Route 7A and start north to reach the villages of Shaftsbury and North Shaftsbury. The very active historical society here offers a self-guided tour of houses, as well as a drive-it-yourself route to the many cemeteries. This is the town where the oldest Vermont Baptist Society had its meetinghouse. The Greek Revival-style Baptist church is now the historical society's home, open from June to mid-October on Tuesday afternoons. Look for the turreted steeple of the building, on Route 7A in Center Shaftsbury.

SWEET TREATS & MORE: *Chocolate lovers will notice the **Chocolate Barn** (☎ 375-6928) on Route 71. This 1842 sheep barn also holds two floors of antiques, including a wonderful collection of early chocolate molds.*

■ Arlington

Route 7A leads north from Shaftsbury to **Arlington,** a small picturesque village noted for its country inns and covered bridges. This is also where the Batten Kill, the region's most famous trout stream, reaches the north-

The Wagon Wheel fishing access in Arlington.

south route and begins to keep company with travelers. Author Dorothy Canfield Fisher wrote many of her novels here in the 1950s and left the state a legacy of children's literature. Even more closely associated with Arlington was artist Norman Rockwell, creator of years of *Saturday Evening Post* magazine covers; a permanent exhibit of his paintings can be seen at the **Arlington Gallery** in the center of town (☎ 375-6424; open year-round). Another collection to visit is the **Dr. George A. Russell Collection of Vermontiana** (open Tuesdays, ☎ 375-6307), also in the village, behind the Martha Canfield Public Library.

Arlington could practically fill a Vermont history book by itself. Chartered in the name of George III in 1761, it was part of the struggle to decide whether Vermont would be part of New Hampshire or New York or independent, as it soon declared itself. The Green Mountain Boys fought in the Revolutionary War near here; the state's first governor, Thomas Chittenden, had his office in Arlington in 1778. Taverns, stage stops, and country inns multiplied, and the first gristmill in Vermont was built here by Remember Baker. The town also had the state's first fulling mill (for preshrinking and thickening woolen cloth), furnace and foundry, rope factory, chair factory, and marble quarry! Even the state's first medical

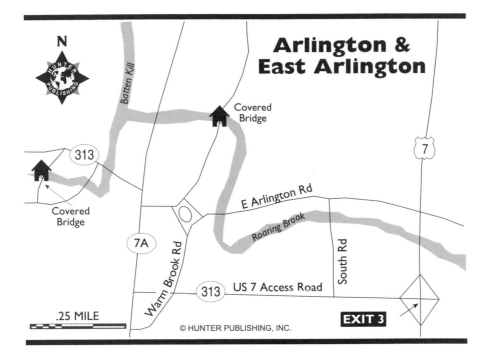

N

Arlington &
East Arlington

Batten Kill

313

7

Covered
Bridge

Covered
Bridge

E Arlington Rd

Roaring Brook

7A

Warm Brook Rd

South Rd

.25 MILE

313 US 7 Access Road

EXIT 3

© HUNTER PUBLISHING, INC.

Bennington & Vermont Valley

school was here in 1790, in a brick house that still stands on Route 7A. Later, Daniel Webster honored the town with one of his famous orations: the Kelley Stand speech. A marker honoring the day is close to where, in 1909, James P. Taylor come up with the idea of a "footpath in the wilderness" that would become the Long Trail, the nation's first long-distance hiking trail. You can take the Kelley Stand Road eastward into the Green Mountain National Forest and connect with the trail, which runs together with the Appalachian Trail all the way north through this region. In memory of so much historical significance, Arlington hosts an annual festival on Father's Day weekend called **Ethan Allen Days.**

Don't miss the detour into East Arlington, where the Roaring Brook cascades down a rocky channel and passes by a cluster of gracious shops and galleries called Candle Mill Village. This is where Remember Baker's gristmill stood; the rushing waters are convincing that the mill belonged here! East Arlington also is the start of the Kelley Stand Road if you want to head east into the forest.

Back on Route 7A, you'll soon pass Batten Kill Canoe, a center of water-oriented activity. Watch for local fly-fishers, too; there's a local business in tying the intricate custom-designed flies for the sport.

The pleasant riverside drive is quiet and scenic. But the classic resort area of Manchester is just ahead. Gracious inns and comfortable bed-and-breakfast homes line the roadside. Watch on the left for the **Equinox Skyline Drive** (as they say in Vermont, "You can't miss it"). It ascends to the top of the 3,816-foot peak, a five-mile climb by car. During foliage season there's a waiting line at the gate, but the view is still worth it, especially if you take the 20-minute ramble from the summit to the lookout; there are hiking trails, too.

When you return to Route 7A, you are only minutes away from **Hildene,** the summer home of Abraham Lincoln's oldest son, Robert Todd Lincoln. One of the charming aspects of this mansion is that the approach road still winds through thick woodlands, screening it so thoroughly from the modern highway that you enter a pocket of time still moored to the turn of the century. You can tour the 24-room mansion (by reservation; ☎ 362-1788) from mid-May through October, and there is also a charming Christmas celebration. The estate has 412 acres of formal gardens and leafy woods with nature trails; cross-country skiers appreciate the trails once snow arrives.

■ Manchester

Manchester was a popular resort for the nation's wealthy and powerful in the mid- and late 1800s, when the grand hotel called the **Equinox** (like the steep and impressive mountain towering over it) thrived. Recently painstakingly restored, the hotel epitomizes luxury vacationing in the Green Mountains. As you drive northward on Route 7A, the Equinox is on your left, and welcomes you to the modern-day resort atmosphere of the town. Outlet stores, designer fashion boutiques, restaurants, and sports shops line the road. On the byways, inns abound; there are also several golf courses and parks.

Although you'll probably lose track of the Batten Kill while you navigate this busy town, one of Manchester's most noted businesses, **The Orvis Company,** grew from the desires of the area's fishing and outdoors enthusiasts. The company, created and staffed by devoted hunters and anglers, has its factory and a large store at the southern edge of Manchester, with a second store in town. Many local and state-wide guides, outfitters, and lodges affiliate with Orvis.

Also in Manchester is the **American Museum of Fly Fishing** (☎ 362-3300), right next door to the Equinox. Open year-round, but closed on winter weekends, the museum displays gear and memorabilia, including those of anglers Cornelia "Fly Rod" Crosby and innovative flytier Carrie Stevens.

Once you travel north of the Equinox, you are in shoppers' paradise (and sometimes traffic purgatory, especially during foliage season). From ice cream shops and bakeries to fine dining, from designer fashions to home furnishings, and from summer sports to snow specialties, Manchester has it all – or at least it seems like it! Most of the shops cluster on Route 7A and on Routes 11 and 30, which come down as a single highway from the high mountains to the east. Take the route eastward some six miles and the two highways divide; Route 11 goes on to Bromley, a family-oriented ski resort

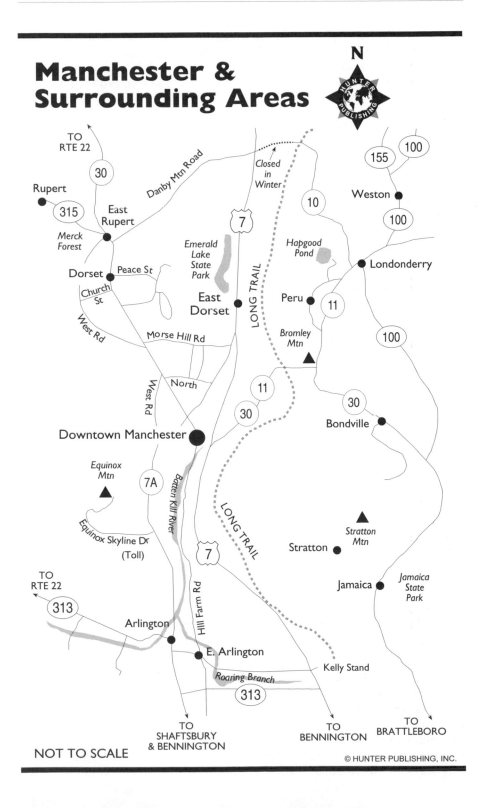

Manchester & Surrounding Areas

N

TO RTE 22

30

Danby Mtn Road

Closed in Winter

155 100

Rupert

100

315

East Rupert

7

Weston

10

Merck Forest

Emerald Lake State Park

Hapgood Pond

Londonderry

Dorset

Peace St

LONG TRAIL

Peru

11

Church St

East Dorset

West Rd

Morse Hill Rd

Bromley Mtn

100

West Rd

North

11

30

30

Downtown Manchester

Bondville

Equinox Mtn

7A

Batten Kill River

Equinox Skyline Dr (Toll)

LONG TRAIL

7

Stratton Mtn

TO RTE 22

Stratton

313

Jamaica

Jamaica State Park

Hill Farm Rd

Arlington

E. Arlington

Kelly Stand

Roaring Branch

313

TO SHAFTSBURY & BENNINGTON

TO BENNINGTON

TO BRATTLEBORO

NOT TO SCALE

© HUNTER PUBLISHING, INC.

Bennington & Vermont Valley

with plenty of summertime activities like motorized go-carts and an alpine slide. Hiking and riding the scenic **Sun Chairlift** (with a five-state view from the observation tower!) are also snow-free activities here, especially during the colorful fall foliage weeks. Route 30 takes you to Stratton, the mountain resort mentioned on page 69 in the Southeastern Gateway section. Spectacular hiking trails and cross-country ski routes branch off both roads, and wilderness is barely a back road away.

Manchester's arts community has always been active, and the region is home to the **Southern Vermont Art Center** (☎ 362-1405, on West Road not far outside the village). Art for the light-hearted is a good description of the **Gremlin Animation Gallery** at 646 Richville Road in Manchester Center, with its collection of Disney, Warner Bros., and Charles Shultz animation art (☎ 362-4766, Web site www.thegremlin.com).

The Vermont Wax Museum (☎ 362-0609) offers family entertainment, not far east on Route 30. And there is an award-winning theater festival that Manchester visitors often come to see, in nearby Dorset, up the westward reach of Route 30. **The Dorset Theatre Festival** is a summer experience (☎ 867-5777), but tickets can be reserved by calling ahead during other seasons also (☎ 867-2223 before May 31).

Manchester's **Chamber of Commerce** and information kiosk are both at the north end of town, on Route 7A; once you pass them, you are headed up a last stretch of "historic" highway and merging with the busy thoroughfare of Route 7 itself. You'll enter East Dorset, which was once the home of Alcoholics Anonymous cofounder Bill Wilson. The **Wilson House** (☎ 362-5524) is still a welcoming center. After East Dorset, you'll pass through the small villages of Danby, Wallingford, and Clarendon. Route 7 is still parallel to the Long Trail/Appalachian Trail, and the rise of mountains to the east is both wild and inviting. **Wallingford** is especially worth a visit, for the tree-canopied back roads and old cemeteries; the Otter Creek winds around the town.

Taking Route 140 east leads to East Wallingford, where Route 103 continues farther east to Healdville; this is the home of **Crowley Cheese,** the state's oldest cheese factory, both a national historic site and a tasty place to visit. To see the cheese being made, be sure to arrive in the morning. Call ahead to double-check the schedule (☎ 259-2340).

From Route 7, the Green Mountain National Forest attractions of **Mount Tabor**, the **Big Branch Wilderness**, and **Peru Peak Wilderness** are close by. Side trips along the scenic smaller routes can include a trip over Route 11 to Peru, with its isolated and quiet single street and old homes; or from Route 7B as it leads north of Wallingford to Pierces Corner, where you can turn southeast (right) onto Route 103 to reach East Clarendon, with its covered bridge. There's also a suspension bridge over Clarendon Gorge, which you can reach by walking a tenth of a mile south on the Long Trail from the trail's parking area on Route 103.

As Route 7 continues north, the busy city of Rutland is just ahead, a temporary but insistent change from rural travel to urban energy.

Adventures

■ On Foot

Bennington

Walking tours of Bennington will give you a feel for the town's history. There are also pleasant trails on Mount Anthony, just west of town. But the real adventures are to the east, where hiking trails connect with old woods roads and create an interesting network with the **Long Trail** (which is also the Appalachian Trail here and throughout this region). Barely a mile out of town, the **Green Mountain Forest** begins. Use the Green Mountain Club's *Day Hiker's Guide to Vermont* for details of these hikes; if you plan to hike the Long Trail for any distance, the Green Mountain Club also has a *Guidebook to the Long Trail,* complete with large map.

One walk begins in town: The comfortable hike to the 2,857-foot summit of **Bald Mountain** is one of the oldest continuously maintained trails in the area, and has good views of the region along the way, then wide interstate views near the top. Check your town map and find Branch Street in the northeast corner, which crosses Route 9 (here called East Main Street). Head north to County Street and bear sharply right, crossing the Roaring Branch Brook before reaching the start of the trail. Some parking is available. The trail goes parallel to the power line up an old woods road and crosses a wider power right-of-way with sweeping views north and south. It soon begins to climb, for a total of four miles to the ridgeline (where it meets the West Ridge Trail) and then another tenth of a mile to the summit. If you're ready for a longer expedition, keep going past the summit to the spring at Bear Wallow, and descend to Route 9, about four miles east of town. You are then only 1.2 miles from the Long Trail.

East of Bennington

For an ambitious ramble along old town roads, woods roads, and even a stage road, try the **Dunville Hollow Trail.** It's reached by heading out Route 9 eastward until you're a mile east of the Route 7 intersection to find Burgess Road, which leads about two miles uphill to a jeep road and then another 1.3 miles to the trailhead. This trail winds through what were once settled areas, and can connect you again with Route 9 about five miles from Bennington, or else continue on the Old Stage Road Trail to the remains of the tiny village (one book calls it a hamlet!) of Heartwellville.

Starting once again on Route 9 and heading east from Bennington, this time for 11 miles, will take you to **Woodford State Park.** The two hiking trails here also include nature trails and a picnic area, and one of the trails winds around Adams Reservoir for a relaxing meander.

Just past Woodford State Park is a US Forest Road, labeled FR74 (look for the brown sign), that is the best access for the **George Aiken Wilderness.** This primitive wetlands area is a treasure of wildlife, harboring deer, beaver, moose, and black bear. The bears are shy and you're not likely to see them (but if you do, always stay well clear of a bear with cubs!); however, you may spot their "scat," tarry and dark with plenty of undigested seeds. Moose scat is in mounds of fat, often golden-brown pellets. Moose browse in the wetlands, like beaver ponds. Do not approach a moose! They are unpredictable. But a browsing moose will often stay still and allow you to get good photos. One more treat from the beaver ponds is the fine trout fishing in this wilderness. Note that the forest trails actually go around the edges of this wilderness, but hikers are welcome to bushwhack through, with compass and map. It's a small enough area that getting truly lost isn't likely.

AUTHOR TIP

Be sure to wear boots that will handle wet soil and swampy regions, and pack bug dope; spring and summer are fierce mosquito and black fly seasons here. Also carry your own drinking water; although the brooks and ponds look lovely and are great for fish, beaver water is notorious for the presence of parasites, especially Giardia, *which gives nasty intestinal symptoms for as long as six weeks.*

North of Bennington

As you head north from Bennington on Route 7A, it's worth pausing near the historic village of Shaftsbury to explore a lovely combination nature and hiking trail in **Shaftsbury State Park.** This park also has a picnic shelter and pleasant sandy beach for summer swimming.

Continuing north on 7A you'll come to Arlington, where the **Kelley Stand Road** (Route 313) leads eastward into the Green Mountain Forest and crosses the Long Trail, which parallels Route 7 about six miles distant. From Route 7, take the Kelley Stand Road 12 miles to the Grout Pond access road and enjoy over 12 miles of blazed year-round trails maintained by the Forest Service, including a loop hike around the 70-acre pond and trails that connect over to Somerset Reservoir (see Southeastern Gateway section). Evidence of nearby Indian camps suggest this valley was used by Native Americans traveling through. Today, there are shelters and picnic sites, mostly on the northeast side of the pond.

Just a tad closer to Route 7, only 7½ miles from Arlington, is one entrance into the **Lye Brook Wilderness.** This 15,680-acre wilderness was heavily logged a century ago, when charcoal kilns were part of the Vermont industrial landscape. Remnants of the kilns, and of the railroad that carried away the charcoal, can still be found. Beaver ponds, meadows, and an area called "The Burning," which was struck by lightning and blazed with flame a century ago, make the area fascinating. There are only two major trails, the **Branch Road Trail** cutting north and the **Lye Brook Trail** at right angles to it; off-trail exploring is encouraged by the Forest Service. Wildlife includes deer, black bears, and – a special treat – wild turkeys. Because the Green Mountain Club notes that this wilderness area is becoming overused, keep your visit short and head on to the others in this region.

WHAT IS A WILDERNESS?

The Forest Service works with this definition: "An area where the earth and its community of life are untrammeled [uncontrolled] by man, where man himself is a visitor who does not remain." Wilderness areas are therefore designated as primitive use only (no motorized or mechanical equipment), with a group limit of 10 people to minimize impact on the resource. You must pack out everything you bring in and, as an extra considerate touch, wear clothing of muted colors to avoid distracting others from the wilderness (except during hunting season, when of course you need to wear blaze orange!). Camping is permitted, but only if you plan to leave no sign of your visit behind.

Manchester Area

When Route 7 leaves Manchester on its way north, it heads through East and then North Dorset and, just before reaching Danby, reaches the Green Mountain National Forest. Travel another 500 feet north past the national forest sign and take the right-hand turn, proceeding less than half a mile to a trailhead parking lot on the left. This is the start of trails to Griffith Lake and Baker Peak. The **Lake Trail** is marked with blue blazes, and reaches a crossing of the McGinn Brook at two miles. Take the trail on the right another 1½ miles for **Griffith Lake,** where there's a shelter at the far end and a summer caretaker to help protect wildlife and plant resources. If you take the left trail at the McGinn Brook crossing, you'll be headed up a one-mile challenge to **Baker Peak,** which has great views of the Otter Creek Valley and mountains to the north. For a variation, from Griffith Lake head north on the Appalachian/Long Trail (white blazes) for 1.8 miles and then meet the **Baker Peak Trail** to come back down to the parking lot. Figure at least five hours to finish this loop.

There are two more Congressionally designated wilderness areas in this region, Peru Peak and Branch Brook. Both are within the **White Rocks National Recreation Area** (NRA), accessed primarily from Peru to the south, and Wallingford to the north. The Forest Service has done an outstanding job of creating access to this mountainous region without turning it into a tame place at all. Hiking ranges from easy rambles to challenging peak and ridgeline hikes. Although you may see more people on the main trails than you really want to in midsummer and during peak foliage viewing, you can always get away from these sections and head out into the wilder woods. Off-trail exploration is encouraged by the Forest Service, although with the warning that you need to know your own skills and limits. You are really on your own, especially in wilderness segments.

ARCHAEOLOGY ON THE TRAIL

At the northwestern corner of White Rocks National Recreational Area, the Long Trail and Appalachian Trail reach **Little Rock Pond**, where there are two overnight shelters. Along the stretch of trail north of the pond, you might spot old bricks, stone foundations, or even glass, ceramic, or iron remnants from long-gone residents. Some time in the 1880s, a mill village called Aldrichville stood here. It lasted for about 20 years, divided into French- and English-speaking segments. Researchers and summertime teenagers at "Relics and Ruins" camp sessions have excavated many of the half-buried traces of daily life of a century past, and some are on display at the US Forest Service office in Rutland (231 Main Street, ☎ 747-6765). You may see some of the investigating crew as you hike by. If you see artifacts that you think mark an unknown site, let the forest archaeologist know, or notify the state archaeologist at the Division for Historic Preservation (☎ 828-3226).

Mount Tabor, 17 miles north of Manchester, stands in the southeastern corner of the White Rocks NRA. It is surrounded by verdant wetlands where beaver and moose thrive; be sure to keep your distance from grazing moose! To the east of Mount Tabor is the **Peru Peak Wilderness,** neatly sliced by the Appalachian and Long Trails as they ramble northward together here. These two major hiking trails head next into the **Branch Brook Wilderness.** The rest of the recreation area has excellent access via trails and woods roads. The forest here is probably the third or fourth to rise from this soil. Logging, farming, and the 1800s trade of charcoal burning all harvested the trees. Once there were 1.6 million sheep grazing in these hills and valleys! Signs of these occupations, as well as of Native American travels across the valleys, make hiking here not only a journey into the forests, but into the past as well. There's an old sawmill village, signs of past forest fires, abandoned farms and cellarholes, and even an old mine with tunnels. Beware of mine shafts at the Homer Stone Brook section of the area, at its northwest corner. Wildlife abounds, from bears to bullfrogs, including some recently released pine martens, members of the weasel family. The Mt. Tabor and Utley Brooks in this region have gravel bottoms that encourage the return of North Atlantic salmon to the adjoining West River Basin.

AUTHOR TIP

Although you are technically on your own when hiking in wilderness areas (and must pay for any search and rescue that could be needed if you are careless), these regions are close to well-used trails and woods roads; if you want privacy, stick to the high peaks. On the other hand, if you're looking for company and for the Forest Service guides and information on wildlife and history, head for the established trails and camp-grounds.

A good basic map of this area is available from the Manchester Ranger District, Routes 11 and 30, RR1, Box 1940, Manchester Center, VT 05255 (☎ 362-2307); ask for the White Rocks information. The Forest Service especially recommends the following trails for day hikes. Off Route 1, the **Lake Trail** to **Baker Peak Trail** (moderate to difficult); parking on FR21 at the southern edge of the area and hiking the Appalachian/Long Trail to **Styles Peak** (short but difficult); and taking the **Green Mountain Trail** along the western edge of the Branch Brook Wilderness, reached from FR10 (moderate to difficult). The wetlands trails are easier walking and are especially rich in bird life – but be sure to wear those waterproof boots! And from May through August, insect repellent is a must. The Green Mountain Club suggests waiting until the end of May, to avoid damaging the muddy trails and fragile plantlife during this wettest period.

AUTHOR TIP

Also remember that temperatures will vary as much as 40° in a day, and more so if you make changes in elevation, so bring layers of clothing, and prepare for rain or heavy dew if you stay overnight.

For a close look at the local phenomenon called the **Ice Beds,** which are 10 to 20° cooler than the surrounding area, there's a hike that starts from the **Wallingford** area, north of White Rocks. From Route 7 in Wallingford, take Route 140 east and drive just over three miles to the **White Rocks Picnic Area,** your parking trailhead. Follow blue blazes for 1.2 miles southeast until you reach the Appalachian/Long Trail (AT/LT), enjoying Bully Brook waterfall along the way. Hike the AT/LT (white blazes) for 0.3 mile to the pile of rocks on your right (west), and turn onto the blue-blazed trail. This is steep and rocky and leads to an overlook, by a final switchback trail that reaches a breathtaking vista of White Rocks. After you've caught your breath, continue on the Ice Beds Trail from the overlook over the embankment and reach the base of White Rocks, which is the area known as the Ice Beds. Anyone got a thermometer? This is a great treat on a hot, sticky summer day!

Now that we've covered the wild and woolly east side of Route 7, let's back-track to Manchester and its shopping highway. Manchester itself rests against the foot of Mount Equinox, another site where trail origins date back into the previous century. These are vista-oriented trails: **Mount Equinox** is 3,825 feet at the peak, **Little Equinox** is 3,315, and the **Burr and Burton/Blue Trail** takes you up there from Seminary Avenue in Manchester.

Above the tree line, every plant struggles for years to reach its full size. A stunted tree a foot tall may already be a hundred years old. Help preserve the fragile alpine plants by staying on the marked trails. Step on the rocks, not the plants.

Check the Green Mountain Club *Day Hiker's Guide to Vermont* for varia-tions on this three-mile route. There are other trails around, and on Mount Equinox; you can pick up a detailed map at the front desk of the Equinox Hotel. The map comes from the **Equinox Preservation Trust,** which seeks volunteers for trail maintenance and support for this alpine ecosys-tem area; if you'd like to help, contact the **Friends of EPT** (☎ 362-4700, ext. 895).

BACK ROAD TOURS: *To experience an ad-venture prepared by local experts, get in touch with* **Backroad Discovery** *(PO Box 49, Man-chester, VT 05254, ☎ 362-4997, Web site www. backroaddiscovery.com). They put together tours that include abandoned marble quarries, water-falls, back roads, and historic and cultural notes. Tours are given daily from noon to 3 p.m.; reservations are required.*

If you take Route 30 northwest from Manchester, there's a less heavily traveled refuge about 10 miles up the road – the **Merck Forest,** more than 2,600 acres of abandoned farmland, now devoted to forestry, education, and recreation. More than 26 miles of old woods roads and trails criss-cross the forest. You can get a map at the parking area, reached by leaving Route 30 in East Rupert for the rise of Route 315 and watching for the gravel road on the left at the Merck Forest sign. There's a barn and mu-seum, and two self-guiding nature trails begin at the upper parking area.

Lake St. Catherine

Farther up Route 30, almost to the New York State border, is Lake St. Catherine. This scenic lake is surrounded by summer cottages, and the **Lake St. Catherine State Park** (☎ 287-9185) lies on its east side. Sandy beaches and nature trails make for pleasant and relaxing walking, especially for younger family groups.

■ Travel With Llamas Or Horses

Llama Trekking

 If you're looking for the simplicity of letting someone else plan your route, enrich your travels with natural history, or even carry the food and gear (on the back of a mild-mannered llama), consider the advantages offered by **Walking Tours of Southern Vermont** (☎ 375-1141 or 800-5-VT-WALK). Based in Arlington, this touring group offers special itineraries full of wildflowers and waterfalls, planning daily strolls of four to seven miles for beginners, and up to nine miles a day for moderate rambles. Tours include the Merck Forest, the Appalachian Trail, and the Batten Kill; extras that make the trip even sweeter include inn-to-inn planning, fine cuisine, and thoughtful discussions of myths and dreams in a romantic landscape.

Horseback Riding

There's a full-service equestrian facility at **Valley View Horses & Tack Shop** (☎ 823-4649), in Pownal, nine miles south of Bennington. Miles of trails surround the farm, and guides offer trail rides seven days a week. Pony rides for children, boarding stables for horse owners, and a well-equipped Western tack shop add to the business.

The elegance of Manchester Village fits perfectly with a horse and carriage, and **Vermont Carriage Tours** (☎ 447-1769) has a top-hatted driver in front of the Equinox in all pleasant weather. Weddings, anniversaries, hayrides, and picnics can also be planned into the excursions.

In Danby, **Mountain View Ranch** offers winter trail rides through woods and farmland, and also through the Danby Marble Quarry. Rides are Monday through Thursday, 9 to 4; reservations are required (☎ 293-5837). Mountain View horses are very gentle, and riders are given time to get acquainted with them. Basic instructions are given to all guests, and the horses respond well to beginners and expert riders alike. Letitia and John Sisters are the hosts of the ranch. (Why no rides on weekends? The horses are giving sleigh rides at Stratton Mountain then.)

In East Dorset, the **Harold Beebe Farm** hosts part of the Vermont Summer Festival of equestrian events; get in touch with them at ☎ 496-4878.

■ On Wheels

Probably the most delightful biking route in this region has already been mapped out by John Freidin in his book, *25 Bicycle Tours in Vermont*. There is the gently rolling terrain of Arlington and North Bennington, pedaling along Routes 313 and 67, enjoying a covered bridge, the rustic beauty of farms and old homes and even an old (but closed) 1784 tavern. Freidin's route is designed to cross into New York State and wind along the Batten Kill, the region's favorite trout stream. An interesting extension, although with some hillier terrain, is to bike over to East Arlington and enjoy the scenic waterways. Don't let the map lure you farther east onto the Kelly Stand Road – cars have taken over at high speed here.

Road Biking

From Arlington to Manchester, bike along the **Batten Kill** on the back roads that connect with various names: Tory Lane and the Depot Road in Arlington, then the River Road as you approach Manchester. Take time out to savor the river and watch the anglers; this is sacred ground for fly-fishing.

Another well-known road biking loop is the one that connects **Middletown Springs** and **Pawlet,** up near Lake St. Catherine. It's about 30 miles of rolling, scenic farmland, amazingly untouched considering how close it is to Rutland and Manchester. If you use John Freidin's route, make sure you include the short extension down into the village of Pawlet; there's a spectacular gorge beneath Mach's General Store, a friendly restaurant in the old station, and a collection of crafts studios and galleries.

Mountain Biking

Mountain bikers can profit from a stop at any of the three bike shops in Bennington, especially the **Cutting Edge,** 160 Benmont Avenue (☎ 442-8664). The staff at these stores are often just back from their own exploring of the trails and back roads. They'll point you toward **Prospect Mountain** (☎ 442-2575), which in winter disguises itself as a cross-country ski touring center, but is a great mountain-biking region. Local stores also stock winter biking gear like tires with studs or chains. Don't let a little snow stop you!

AUTHOR TIP

*While you're at 160 Benmont Avenue, look around for **Off the Wall** (☎ 447-0217), a racquet and fitness club in the same complex. If the weather is making you wait but you're restless for a stretch or a game, stop in. On weekdays the club offers child care.*

At present, mountain biking is not allowed on trails in the Green Mountain National Forest, because it takes such a toll in terms of erosion. Only the forest roads, like FR10 in the **White Rocks National Recreation Area** northeast of Manchester, are legitimate mountain bike terrain. However, the Forest Service has been listening to bikers' requests and intends to include the activity in its next regional plan. Stop at the ranger station in Manchester Center for an update; the forest supervisors hope that mountain biking clubs will get involved on a local basis to establish and maintain trails, much as snowmobilers have already done.

AUTHOR TIP

If you bike in winter on ski trails and snowmobile trails, remember the other sports were there first. Be courteous, and don't expect a high-speed snowmobiler to leave the trail to avoid you; that's your job.

Meanwhile, ski areas, where trail maintenance is already in place, have opened a number of trails for mountain biking. **Bromley Mountain** in Manchester Center (☎ 824-5522) opens its trails in summer for mountain biking, although it doesn't offer lift access. Most cross-country ski resorts (especially when country inns have their own trail networks) are open to the sport. And if you're willing to use standard (but steep) roads for a challenge to your upward mobility, explore Route 315 between East Rupert and West Rupert, the back roads around Peru (up Route 30 to the east), and the hilly byways of Sandgate, reached by heading to West Arlington and taking the turn northward.

BIKING INFORMATION

Suggestions for more back-road and mountainside biking and touring can also be found at **Battenkill Sports** (☎ 362-2734) in Manchester, where Route 11 meets the elevated highway stretch of Route 7. Just follow Route 11 out of the center of Manchester and it will be on the right. Ask here for directions to the **Delaware and Hudson Railroad Trail**, near Dorset, a good mountain biking route. Or head all the way north to Danby, where **Otter Creek Cycles** (☎ 293-6222) is on the village's Main Street.

■ On Water

This region of Vermont has plenty of small rivers and ponds for paddling and angling. But the most striking assets are the **Batten Kill** and **Otter Creek,** both with long stretches for paddling; the Batten Kill is especially noted for its trout. In fact, the **Orvis Company** (☎ 800-548-9548 for orders) in Manchester Center has been designing and building quality fly rods for 138 years. Orvis is also a hunting specialist; the company offers shooting schools at its Battenkill Farm, as well as fishing schools (☎ 800-235-9763 for information). It also provides private and group lessons in casting, on the river and at Equinox Pond (☎ 800-362-3750).

Rivers To Run

Starting in Bennington, a quick look at local rivers shows the Hoosic cutting across the southwestern corner of the region and a handful of smaller streams edging out of town. The **Walloomsac River** is Bennington's center, source of the power that once ran its mills. It's still very paddleable; a nice flatwater run. See the *Appalachian Mountain Club (AMC) River Guide to New Hampshire and Vermont* for details of riffles and dams.

Most serious paddlers are going to head north to Manchester and enjoy the Batten Kill as it heads south to Arlington, or even West Arlington, where the river enters New York State. From Manchester to Arlington is 10½ miles of moderate current, with only two risky spots noted in the *River Guide*. Then there's another seven miles of Batten Kill before it leaves the state to the west. This is one of those easygoing rivers where in summer you can actually learn the terrain on your own, with the *River Guide* as assistant. However, if you are trying the Batten Kill for the first time during high water, be prudent and run it with a friend who's well acquainted with the flow.

For a professional introduction to the river's vagaries, plus some worthwhile enrichment in terms of fishing and natural history, **BattenKill Canoe Ltd.** (☎ 362-2800 or 800-421-5268, e-mail info@battenkill.com) on Route 7A in Arlington is the region's acknowledged expert. The company offers guided and interpreted day trips as well as multi-day inn-to-inn samplers. Walking rambles are also available. More extensive vacations are also preplanned for visitors. This is also the place to rent your equipment (or try a demo) if you're on your own. Canoes, paddles, lifejackets, and waterproof drybags are included with each rental, and a shuttle van makes it easy to get to and from the river.

Flatwater Paddling

For a special water adventure, explore the **Tinmouth Channel Wildlife Management Area,** reached by following Route 140 from its intersection with Route 7 in Wallingford. The area includes 1,148 acres of protected land along the Tinmouth Channel, which is a meandering section of the upper Clarendon River. Canoeists put in at the north end. Take Route 140 to Tinmouth and turn north; after one more mile, bear right as the paved road goes left. Stay with the dirt road, which is North End Road, and at 2½ miles it curves to the right. Another half-mile or so brings you to the bridge over the Clarendon River and the beginning of the Tinmouth Channel. You'll paddle through a shrubby wetland of swamp alders, willows, and buttonbrush, edged by cedar swamp and then softwood forests of white pine and hemlock. There are brown trout and brook trout underneath you; the wetlands around you shelter beavers, deer, wild turkeys, ruffed grouse (locally called partridges), woodcock, and ducks. Bobcats hunt here, although you're not likely to see them; watch for pawprints and scat if you're on land at all. Because the best access to this wild land is by water, there's a lot of privacy and quiet. Slather the insect repellent over you and settle quietly in one spot and wait for the birds, especially at dusk or dawn.

 This area is well hunted on November weekends, so steer clear then, or if you're determined not to miss a visit, wear plenty of "blaze orange" clothing.

Flatwater boating in this region is a treat on the wide expanse of **Lake St. Catherine** (superb bass fishing as well as some nice trout), at the northwest corner of the Lake Champlain Valley. On Route 7 in North Dorset is the islanded gem of **Emerald Lake Pond,** where you can rent paddleboats. Another nice spot is **Hapgood Pond,** part of the Green Mountain National Forest recreation area. From Manchester, take Route 11 east to Peru and turn north; there is good signage for the pond. Trout is stocked at Hapgood, there's a boat launch, and swimmers benefit from a sandy beach (although the water is shallow near the beach). To the east of Bennington, reached from Route 9, is **Woodford State Park,** which has canoes and boats for rent.

Fishing

When you want to get serious about fishing, the Batten Kill is the river for native brook trout and brown trout. Fishing guide **Chuck Kashner** (☎ 800-682-0103, Pawlet) is an Orvis-endorsed guide who specializes in the Batten Kill, as well as the Mettawee and the Otter Creek, farther north. Major hatches on the rivers vary by month, and there's good fishing from May to October.

Battenkill Anglers (☎ 362-3184) is another full-service outfitter that also offers a fly-fishing school with on-stream instruction, private and group lessons, and fly-fishing adventure vacations that include lodging, from exquisite inns to tent camping. Expect to study both the art and the science (entomology, stream ecology, and trout behavior). The schooling is sponsored by noted fly rod maker Thomas & Thomas.

Swimming

In addition to **Hapgood Pond** (see *Canoeing,* above), the beaches at **Lake St. Catherine** are way above average in both beauty and swimming pleasure (although crowded on hot summer weekends). Bennington residents enjoy swimming at **Lake Paran,** in North Bennington.

Bennington & Vermont Valley

■ On Snow & Ice

Downhill Skiing

Bromley is the only major ski area in New England with southern exposure, so its nickname is "Sunny Mountain" – an outlook reflected in the family-friendly atmosphere of the resort. The resort is confusingly located, as it is associated with three town names: **Bromley** is the name that's extinct, **Peru** is the town on the slope of Bromley Mountain where the resort is actually located, and much of its mail goes through nearby **Manchester Center!** Reach the resort from Manchester by heading east on Route 11 for 10 miles; if you're coming from the other side of the state, say up Interstate 91, you'll cross the ridge of the Green Mountains on Route 11 westbound to get there, a short spectacular drive past Londonderry.

Bromley's 39 ski trails shoot down the slope across 300 acres; more difficult trails are toward the east side of the mountain. The vertical drop is 1,334 feet, with a summit elevation of 3,284. The resort has 84% snow-making coverage and nine lifts, including a quad and five doubles. The usual season is mid-November to mid-April, although sunny spring weather can shorten the season. For conditions, ☎ 824-5522; e-mail bromley@sover.net.

Nursery care is available for ages six weeks and up, and kids' activities start at age three years. Bromley also offers special teen programs and prices, and its slopeside lodging is family-style condominiums. At the base lodge is a cafeteria and lounge, cheese and wine shop, and deli bar, as well as the rental shop; group and individual lessons are available.

"SkiWee" children's ski lesson at one of Vermont's many ski areas.

SNOWBOARDERS TAKE NOTE: *Two parks at Bromley are groomed especially for snow-boarding, and there is access to all lifts and other trails. In February the resort hosts the* **Green Mountain Snowboard Series,** *with slalom and Grand Slalom (GS) events. Telemark ski events and competitions also are scheduled.*

Although Bromley's dining and lodging facilities are family-oriented, more elegant inns and restaurants are only a few miles away in Manchester, a lively town with a wide range of cuisine and shopping options. Manchester's designer outlet stores are well known. Traffic there can be heavy, but the town is so picturesque that it's not hard to relax and slow down.

Cross-Country Skiing

There are four Nordic centers close to Manchester. To reach **Wild Wings Ski Touring Center** (☎ 824-6793) go a short distance up Route 11 from the mountain to the village of Peru; take the side road that bears left into the village, and make the left turn at the Peru Church, onto North Road. Again bear left and look for the Wild Wings sign on the left. The 24 km of trails are named for local birds, like the grouse and blue jay, as well as for the snow goose and goshawk; the center is in a "snow pocket" and often has good skiing even when other locations are suffering bare ground. A rental shop and warming room include a shop for extras, and there are group and private lessons.

Hildene (☎ 362-1788), the 24-room mansion just south of Manchester that once belonged to Robert Todd Lincoln (son of Abraham Lincoln), opens its 22 trails (15 km) in mid-December. Gentle woods and meadow outlooks make up most of the trails, but there is a challenging "Cliff Trail" and several other good workouts. Look for the turn from Route 7A; call ahead if in doubt about snow conditions.

The **Equinox,** Manchester's classic hotel, offers its own cross-country trails (☎ 362-4700). A few miles up Route 30 west, between East Rupert and West Rupert, is the **Merck Forest** (☎ 394-7836), where the summer nature trails become winter ones, complete with wild animal tracks to spot (watch especially for fox and rabbit).

To the northeast of Wallingford, in the village of Shrewsbury, is **High Pastures** (Cold River Road, ☎ 773-2087 or 800-584-4738), a bed and breakfast with cross-country skiing on 125 acres.

If you're ready for some skiing in wilder terrain, the **Mountain Valley Trails Association** (a Londonderry group) maintains a set of trails around Landgrove, reached by taking Route 11 to Peru and then taking the left turn onto a town road and traveling another four miles. At the center of Landgrove turn left at the school and pass the Village Inn on the right. Bear left again and park at the next corner, where the trails begin. A detailed trail map is available from the Green Mountain National Forest District Office in Manchester (RR1, Box 1940, Routes 11/30, Manchester Center, VT 05255, ☎ 362-2307).

To the south, near Bennington, **Prospect Mountain** (☎ 442-2575; e-mail xcski@aol.com) in Woodford opens its Nordic center in mid-December. Located on national forest land on Route 9, the ski touring area has 30 km of groomed trails, and offers both skating and classical rentals and lessons. Home cooking is served in the base lodge.

*Another Woodford winter feature is **Twin Brooks Guided Snowmobile Tours** (☎ 442-4054). There's a "sled shed" on Route 9; tours head into the Green Mountain National Forest for picturesque trails and scenic vistas. Guided tours can be booked by the hour, day, or even evening, and kids under 16 ride free.*

Finally, don't forget that many **Green Mountain National Forest** trails are ideal for Nordic skiing; some are groomed by local snowmobile clubs, making the trails even easier. In the **White Rocks National Recreation Area,** which stretches from Mount Tabor north to Wallingford, the **Little Michigan Trail** is earmarked for this, and the **Catamount Trail,** which runs the length of Vermont, cuts across the recreation area. Because of the special challenges of winter weather, though, wilderness areas are probably best saved for expertly equipped expeditions once the snow flies.

Three sections of the **Catamount Trail** are in this region of the state, from Landgrove to Lake Ninevah north of Healdville. Check the trail guide for details. This is a lovely section of the winter corridor, with some glorious mountain views (Catamount Trail Association, PO Box 1235, Burlington, VT 05402, ☎ 864-5784).

EQUIPMENT: *Ski rentals are available not just at the touring centers but also at many area sports shops; one place in particular to note is the **Cutting Edge** in Bennington (160 Benmont Avenue; ☎ 442-8664 for cross-country skis, ☎ 447-7570 for snowboards and skates). Snowshoe rentals are also available here. The staff is passionate about these sports, and full of information.*

SNOWMOBILE RENTALS

■ **William Hance,** Emerald Lake Road, East Dorset, VT 05253 (☎ 362-3946); guide service also available.

SLEIGH RIDES

■ **Karl Pfister Sleigh Rides,** RR1, Box 217B, Landgrove, VT 05148 (☎ 824-6320).

■ **Valley View Horses & Tackle Shop,** Box 48A, Northwest Hill Rd., Pownal, VT 05261 (☎ 823-4649). They also offer wagon rides for snow-free times!

Eco-Travel & Cultural Excursions

Maybe it was the heritage of the Bennington Potters Yard that drew all those artists and craftspeople to the southwestern corner of the state. Or maybe it was the seriousness and enthusiasm with which culture and history are regarded in this college town – concerts, lectures, films, and dance and drama productions make up much of the college atmosphere. Bennington has about two dozen galleries and museums, with more spilling over into North Bennington, and several noted public statues. Pick up the arts map at the Chamber of Commerce on Route 7 (North Street) at the north edge of town; it includes a schedule of events. Especially look for productions by the **Oldcastle Theatre Company,** a professional equity company whose shows range from Shakespeare to musicals, drama, and British comedy.

The Green Mountain National Forest has an office in Manchester Center (☎ 362-2307) at the junction of Routes 7, 11, and 30; stop by to get information on habitat and wildlife, and ask about special events that the rangers may be setting up.

If you're excited by the Long Trail, consider volunteering your help for the endless protection and management needed. This can be a lot of fun, as well as a great way to get in shape and get acquainted with the peak wilderness areas of Vermont. Contact the **Green Mountain Club,** Route 100, RR1, Box 650, Waterbury Center, VT 05677 (☎ 244-7037).

Bennington & Vermont Valley

ARCHAEOLOGY AT THE INTERSTATE?

Prehistory and early history in the Bennington area have left such fascinating archaeological traces that the proposed Bennington Bypass highway system has been held up for years, as a team from the University of Maine uncovers artifacts dating back 4,000 years. Native Americans camped along the banks of the Walloomsac River, and a for a short period of time, some 3,500 to 4,000 years back, they had a village at the site that is now intended to become a highway cloverleaf. There are plenty of stone spearheads and scrapers being found, as well as traces of cooking processes like fire hearths and a roasting pit. You can visit the site daily (9 a.m. to 3 p.m.) and can arrange for tours as well as volunteer opportunities (☎ 447-7391, Web site www.umf.maine. edu/~umfarc). To get to the site, take Route 67A northwest out of Bennington to the interchange ramps and follow signs to the Cloverleaf Site.

Where To Stay

■ Bennington

Most lodging around Bennington is small inns, bed and breakfast homes, or motels. For a touch of elegance, there are three luxurious rooms available at the **Four Chimneys Inn** (☎ 447-3500, $$-$$$) on Route 9 to the west of town; this Georgian estate has a parklike setting and is noted for its fine dining.

At 1067 East Main Street is the **Molly Stark Inn** (☎ 442-9631 or 800-356-3076, Web site www.mollystarkinn.com, $$-$$$), an 1890 country-style inn rich in history and within easy walking distance of both the center of town (where there is plenty of good eating) and the two historic districts, downtown and Old Bennington. There are six cozy guest rooms and a private cottage.

Bennington's **Ramada Inn** (☎ 442-8145 or 800-228-2828, $$-$$$) on Route 7 (north of Route 9) is the only full-service hotel in town, with 104 rooms, restaurant, nightclub, and extras like tennis courts and a heated pool. If you turn south on Route 7, there's the **South Gate Motel** (☎ 447-7525, $$), which in summer offers a picnic area with grill. Another pleasant stop is the **Kirkside Motor Lodge** (☎ 447-7596, $-$$) at 250 West Main Street, close to a group of nice shops and also near the historic monument district.

The **Paradise Motor Inn** (☎ 442-8351, $$-$$$) is in the middle of town at 141 West Main Street and has its own restaurant; you're sure to spot it as you tour Bennington. But you'll have to head north up Route 7A to find the

Harwood Hill Motel (☎ 442-6278, $$) and its "million-dollar view" of Mt. Anthony and the Bennington Monument.

Fresh-cut Christmas trees are a strong local tradition, and Bennington has nine tree farms in and around town (get a list from the Chamber of Commerce or call the Bennington Country Christmas Tree Growers Association, ☎ 447-3311). What's that got to do with lodging? Well, wouldn't you like to go home with your own tree after an early winter visit to the region? Both the **Knotty Pine Motel** (130 Northside Drive, ☎ 442-5487, $-$$) and the **Best Western New Englander Motor Inn** (220 Northside Drive, ☎ 442-6311 or 800-528-1234, $$) will send you home with a fragrant Vermont tree as part of one of their hospitality packages! Both establishments are on Route 7A.

North of town on Route 7A, heading out into the country again, is the **Alexandra Inn**, a bed and breakfast in an 1859 farmhouse with panoramic views of the Green Mountains and the Bennington Monument. Alex Koks and Andra Erickson are experienced innkeepers with decades of local history and enjoy running this smaller scale retreat. They provide guests with a gourmet breakfast (☎ 442-5619 or 888-207-9386, Web site www.AlexandraInn.com, $$-$$$).

Two nearby villages also offer lodging: in Pownal (on Route 7, nine miles south of Bennington), there's the **Ladd Brook Motor Inn** (☎ 823-7341, $$). In Shaftsbury (on Route 7A, eight miles north of Bennington) are the **Iron Kettle Motel** (☎ 442-4316, $$), which also has a Christmas tree package and horseback trail rides, plus listening devices for the speech and hearing impaired, and the **Governor's Rock Motel** (☎ 442-4734, open May through October, $-$$).

■ Arlington

Arlington and East Arlington are richly endowed with country inns that range from the elegant to the cozy. Many line Route 7A, and the most elegant of all is the **Arlington Inn** (☎ 375-6532 or 800-443-9442, $$-$$$$), an 1848 Greek Revival mansion with 18 luxurious rooms and gracious candlelight dinners. The **Ira Allen House** (☎ 362-2284, $$) is also on Route 7A and was built by Ethan Allen's brother; it is a state historic site, a Colonial Revival inn with nine rooms.

To reach the **West Mountain Inn** (☎ 375-6516, $$$-$$$$), take Route 313 west from the center of town and make the second left. The food at this inn is worth almost any trip, and you'll be surrounded by 150 acres to explore, with hiking, cycling, and llamas in residence.

Hill Farm Inn (☎ 375-2269 or 800-882-2545, Web site www.hillfarm-inn.com, $$$) is also outside the village; head north on Route 7A and look for the second right across the Batten Kill. Other favorites are the **Arlington Manor House** (☎ 375-6784, $$-$$$), a bed and breakfast also specializing in antiques, and **Kelan House B&B** (☎ 375-9029, $$-$$$), an

1822 Federal Colonial filled with antiques, situated along the Batten Kill. For more variety, there are housekeeping log cabins at the **Roaring Branch** (☎ 375-6401, weekly rates) in East Arlington, and motels like the **Candlelight** (☎ 375-6647 or 800-348-5294, $-$$) and the **Valhalla** (☎ 375-2212, $-$$).

■ Manchester

There are so many inns and bed-and-breakfast homes in this resort town that it would take a whole chapter to list them! The fine hotel most noted in Manchester is the **Equinox,** a Victorian treasure listed on the National Register of Historic Places. The Equinox achieves a blend of country grand resort style and also traditional charm. There are 154 rooms, and the restaurant and tavern on the premises promise wonderful dining and entertainment. This is also a golfer's haven, with an 18-hole course designed by Walter Travis; the Dormy Grill overlooking the golf course offers lunch and a Lobster Fest. The historic elegance of the hotel is now matched by modern luxuries like a spa program and fitness center. Reservations should be made well in advance (☎ 362-4700 or 800-362-4747, $$$-$$$$).

The **Inn at Willow Pond**, on 20 scenic acres five minutes north on Route 7, is truly a retreat. It has an intimate restaurant that wins acclaim for its Northern Italian cuisine. Baths are marble and tile, and there's an Olympic-size lap pool. Ask for a room with a fireplace. The suites here are an especially good value, with up to four bedrooms, offering a wonderful way to spend a vacation with friends. (☎ 362-4733 or 800-533-3533, Web site innatwillowpond.com, $$$/suites higher.)

Other notable choices include the **Wilburton Inn** (☎ 362-2500 or 800-648-4944, $$-$$$$) with its breathtaking views and Victorian estate; the **1811 House** (☎ 362-1811 or 800-432-1811, $$$-$$$$), a 1770s restored Federal home once the private residence of President Lincoln's granddaughter; and the **Inn at Manchester**, a picture-book New England home with superb breakfasts (☎ 362-1793 or 800-273-1793, Web site www.innatmanchester.com, $$-$$$).

Don't miss the **Reluctant Panther Inn & Restaurant** (☎ 362-2568 or 800-822-2331, $$$-$$$$), even if you just drive by the purple-painted village home; this inn has eight rooms and its own unique pub.

Two romantic hilltop properties specialize in privacy and elegant touches: the **Manchester Highlands Inn** (☎ 362-4565 or 800-743-4565, $$-$$$) in a lovely Victorian home overlooking town, and the **Inn at Ormsby Hill** (☎ 362-1163 or 800-670-2841, $$$-$$$$), a restored 18th-century manor house.

Angling? There's a charming Victorian farmhouse on the banks of the Batten Kill that will get you fishing before or after breakfast. The **Battenkill Inn** (☎ 362-4213 or 800-441-1628, $$$) is located across from Equinox Skyline Drive on Route 7A, about four miles south of Manchester Village.

The historic Equinox Hotel in Manchester.

Croquet on the lawns, ducks in the pond, and comfortable rooms with fireplaces complete the picture.

There are plenty of motels too, like the **Aspen** (☎ 362-2450, $$), a mile north of Manchester; the **Brittany Inn** (☎ 362-1033, $$), three miles south of Manchester Village; the **Weathervane** (☎ 362-2444 or 800-262-1317, $$-$$$), in the heart of Manchester; and the **Palmer House** (☎ 362-3600 or 800-917-6245, $$-$$$), also in town on Route 7A.

ACCOMMODATIONS ASSISTANCE: *There are too many bed and breakfasts to go into detail, but the Chamber of Commerce (☎ 362-2100) at the intersection of Routes 7A, 11, and 30 has up-to-date listings as well as suggestions as to which ones have vacancies.*

■ Peru (Bromley Mountain)

There's a lot of tradition for fun and adventure at **Johnny Seesaw's** (☎ 824-5533, $-$$), a ski lodge and restaurant that also has suites and cottages; the cuisine is Yankee and tasty. An Olympic-sized swimming pool and clay tennis courts add summer fun; the mountain is just down the road for skiing, biking, and hiking. Right next to the resort's Alpine Slide is the **Bromley Sun Lodge** (☎ 824-6941, $$-$$$), a privately owned addition to the Bromley Mountain complex, with 51 rooms, restaurant, bar and lounge, game rooms, and indoor pool. In winter the ski room door of the lodge leads right out to the slopes and lifts.

■ Dorset

Long a haven for artists and writers, this town has a gentle resort ambiance that has encouraged fine inns to prosper. Most noted is the **Dorset Inn** (Church Street, ☎ 867-5500, $$$), a chef-owned, comfortable hostelry with relaxing atmosphere and its own tavern. There is also an exceptional resort at **Barrows House** (☎ 867-4455 or 800-639-1620, $$$-$$$$), an old country inn with 28 rooms and suites. Bike rentals and access to the nearby Dorset Golf Club add to the vacation mood, and the golf club doubles as a cross-country ski location.

For bed and breakfast, try the **Little Lodge at Dorset** (☎ 867-4040, $$), which overlooks a trout pond. The inn is decorated with flowers and antiques. The **Dovetail Inn** (☎ 867-5747 or 800-4-DOVETAIL) is an 1800s bed and breakfast on the green in the village; there are 11 guest rooms, and breakfasts are served by the fireplace. Set high on a hillside among 23 acres of meadow and woodland, the **Eyrie Motel** (☎ 362-1208, $-$$) is in East Dorset on Route 7.

For a special treat, the **Inn at West View Farm**, 2928 Route 30 in Dorset, offers the luxuries of a sitting room with library, closed-in porch, reading room, fine dining in the Auberge Room, and casual fare in the fully licensed tavern. Innkeepers Dorothy and Helmut Stein enjoy conversation, and their interests include history, music, and art, so you can have plenty of stimulus if you just stay inside and relax. But the farmhouse is situated on five acres and is surrounded by mountains that will call you out onto the trails. A full breakfast is included in the room rate (☎ 867-5715 or 800-769-4903; Web site www.vtweb.com/innatwestviewfarm, $$-$$$).

■ Danby

Silas Griffith Inn (☎ 293-5567 or 800-545-1509, $$-$$$) has 17 guest rooms in an 1891 Victorian mansion built for Vermont's first millionaire. There are spectacular mountain views.

Step back in time to a simple, pleasant home with gracious hospitality at the **Quail's Nest Bed & Breakfast** (Main Street, ☎ 293-5099, Web site http://ourworld.compuserve.com/homepages/quails_nest, $$). Six romantic guest rooms feature homemade quilts.

■ Wallingford

The **I. B. Munson House Bed & Breakfast Inn** (☎ 446-2860 or 888-519-3771, $$-$$$) is a classic of 19th-century architecture, complete with Italian motifs and Waverly wallcoverings. There are nine rooms, and the inn serves a full country breakfast by the fireside, as well as afternoon tea.

The **White Rocks Inn** (☎ 446-2077, $$-$$$) is another lovely bed and breakfast on Route 7, featuring canopy beds and four-posters in its four guest rooms. The farmhouse is elegantly furnished, and the landmark barn is spectacular.

■ Poultney (Lake St. Catherine)

Lake St. Catherine has drawn guests for more than a century, and the inns nearby reflect the gracious lifestyle that these early summer visitors enjoyed. Now the inns are open year-round. The **Lake St. Catherine Inn** on Cones Point Road is a country lodge directly on the water, with free use of rowboats, canoes, sailboats, and paddleboats. Hosts Patricia and Raymond Endlich have enjoyed restoring the inn and include a full breakfast and five-course dinner with the room rate. Ask about weekly rates. (☎ 287-9347 or 800-626-LSCI, Web site www.lakestcatherineinn.com, $$-$$$).

Or enjoy a bed and breakfast on the village green at the **Birdhouse Inn**. Host Patricia Birdsell shares her books as well as the fireplace. Continental breakfasts are served. (1430 E. Main Street, which is Route 140; ☎ 287-2405; $$).

Another choice is the **Tower Hall B&B** at 399 Bentley Avenue. Pat Perrine, host, loves to bake as well as to ski and converse, and the house really does have a tower (☎ 287-4004 or 800-894-4004, Web site www.sover.net/~towerhal, $$).

■ Camping

One of the best known campgrounds in southern Vermont is **Greenwood Lodge,** in Woodford only three miles from the Appalachian Trail. The campground contact address is Ed and Ann Shea, Box 246, Bennington, VT 05201 (☎ 442-2547), but it's located out on Route 9 about eight miles east of Bennington. There's a rustic lodge with dormitory or private bedrooms, as well as the camping area (only 20 well-spaced sites, so it's best to call ahead).

In Arlington, there's **Camping on the Battenkill** (RD2, Box 3310, Arlington, VT 05250, ☎ 375-6663), a quarter-mile north of the village on Route 7A, with 100 sites and, of course, fishing and swimming in the Batten Kill.

North of Wallingford in North Clarendon is **Iroquois Land Family Camping** (☎ 773-2832), with 45 open and wooded sites.

State campgrounds in this region include **Woodford State Park** (Woodford, ☎ 447-7149); **Shaftsbury State Park** (Shaftsbury, ☎ 375-9978); **Emerald Lake State Park** (East Dorset, ☎ 362-1655); and **Lake St. Catherine State Park** (Poultney, ☎ 287-9158). All close by mid-October. Woodford and Emerald Lake each have about 100 sites, the other two have about 60 sites each.

The **Green Mountain National Forest** sections here all allow camping: primitive camping in the forests, where campers are asked to leave no trace behind them, and also more traditional camping restricted to designated campgrounds so that the vulnerable plantlife nearby is protected (this is called "site camping"). In the **White Rocks Recreation Area** there are two campgrounds, one at the northeast corner near the Keewaydin Trail and the other in the Big Branch Wilderness. Several shelters are found along other trails. There are no campgrounds in the George Aiken Wilderness, but the **Lye Brook Wilderness** has a campground on the shore of Branch Pond.

CAMPING IN NATIONAL FORESTS

Camping in the national forests, and especially in the wilderness areas, is intended to blend in with the surroundings so that others can enjoy the sense of not being crowded by humans. How do you camp without leaving a trace? Well, for starters, whatever goes in with you, goes back out again. The Forest Service makes the following suggestions for those using national forests:

■ Camp at least 200 feet from water and trails, unless at a designated campsite or shelter.

■ Set up your tent to avoid destroying vegetation. Do not cut branches for bedding.

■ A small, lightweight camp stove is highly recommended for cooking.

■ If you need to build a fire, remove the top 6-8 inches of soil. Use only dead and down wood, and never leave your fire unattended. Before leaving, put your fire out by dousing with water. Leave no signs of your fire.

■ All soaps, even biodegradable ones, pollute the water. Do all washing and dump all waste water at least 200 feet from all water sources, in a small pit. Cover after use.

■ Properly dispose of human waste. Select a spot at least 200 feet from any water or wet areas, and well away from hiking trails. Dig a hole six- to eight-inches deep. If possible, burn toilet paper and tampons, or else carry them out in plastic bags – diapers, too. Replace and lightly pack down the soil after use, and nature will take care of the rest in a few days.

Where To Eat

■ Bennington

For fine dining, there is one outstanding choice: the **Four Chimneys Inn** on Route 9 west of town, where master chef Alex Koks creates elegant cuisine (reservations needed, ☎ 447-3500).

Another local favorite is the **Bennington Station Restaurant** (☎ 447-1080) at 150 Depot Street, in a historic train depot. Steak, chicken, and seafood make up much of the menu, and there are great deli sandwiches. **Carmody's** at 421 Main Street (☎ 447-5748) makes a terrific French onion soup, served in a bread bowl, a hearty start to lunch or dinner. And **Geanneli's** at 520 Main Street (☎ 442-9833) serves breakfast all day, as well as noted homestyle lunch and dinner with daily specials. The buttermilk pancakes are a treat, and the coffee is fresh and good.

Children are welcome at **Jensens's Family Restaurant** (Route 7, ☎ 442-3333), which has a sandwich board and rotisserie specials; take-out is available. The **Publyk House Restaurant** (Route 7A north of town, ☎ 442-8301) is nestled in a remodeled barn among the apple orchards on Harwood Hill.

Ready for informal fun and tasty food in a different atmosphere? Don't miss **Alldays and Onions** (519 Main Street, ☎ 447-0043), for breakfasts, lunches, and dinners enhanced by a bakery, deli, and gourmet pastas; there's outdoor seating in warmer weather, and live entertainment weekly. Or try the **Madison Brewing Co. Brew Pub and Restaurant,** in the middle of town at 428 Main Street (☎ 44BREWS), where six hand-crafted brews are made on site. There's another brewery in town, **Bennington Brewer's Ltd.** at 190 North Street (Route 7, ☎ 447-3510). The firm specializes in ales, and has tours and tastings. Call for seasonal hours. You can also enjoy tastings at the **Joseph Cerniglia Winery** (☎ 442-3531) on Route 9 just west of the monument, where you can sample 11 labels and browse in the food-oriented gift shop.

■ Arlington

Dining means delight at the **West Mountain Inn** (☎ 375-6516) on the River Road in Arlington. Count on wonderful breakfasts and tasty desserts. Dinner is continental cuisine.

Consider **Jonathon's Table** (☎ 375-1021, May to October) for casual and unhurried dining that the restaurant describes as "New England cuisine with a Mediterranean flair." There's a woodsy setting to this location behind the Sugar Shack on Route 7A, and the restaurant serves a special breakfast during March sugaring season; do call ahead.

The Wagon Wheel (☎ 375-9508) is on Route 7A in the Arlington Plaza and has a homey atmosphere, nice for relaxing with the kids.

Remember to take the detour into East Arlington for shopping, scenery, and the **East Arlington Café** (☎ 375-6412), a popular stop for explorers on foot or wheels.

■ Manchester

Northern Italian cuisine at its finest is offered at the restaurant at **The Inn at Willow Pond** (☎ 362-4733 or 800-533-3533) on Route 7A. Appetizers range from polenta to rollatini to grilled medallions of tuna, and the pasta dishes are superb. Fresh seafood and game dishes are featured daily. Classic continental cuisine at its best, with exquisite dining and tableside service, marks the **Chantecleer** (☎ 362-1616) on Route 7A, 3½ miles north of Manchester, actually in East Dorset. Owned by chef Michel Bauman, the restaurant is recommended by many gourmands; reservations are essential. There is also the **Little Rooster Café** (☎ 362-3496) in Manchester Center on Route 7A, offering European café delights, including baguette sandwiches and omelettes.

For good food and good fun, try **Mulligans** (☎ 362-3663) on Route 7A, a steak-and-seafood restaurant with family atmosphere and homemade desserts. **Laney's Restaurant** (☎ 362-4456) is on Route 11 (which is also Route 30) and promotes sports and entertainment celebrities, with its own sports bar. **Candeleros** (362-0836), also on Route 7A, is a lively Mexican restaurant where the guacamole is prepared at the table.

Time for a sweet treat? **Mother Myrick's Confectionery and Ice Cream Parlor** (☎ 362-1560) is on Route 7A just south of the center of town, among the outlet shops. Fresh pies and cakes by the slice, a soda fountain, and fresh fudge are among the delights. Or sample Paula's apple walnut crisp (and Danish, eclairs, and more) at the **Village Fare Café and Bakery** (☎ 362-2544) across from the Equinox.

Of course, the restaurants at the **Equinox Hotel** (☎ 362-4700 or 800-362-4747) serve a wide variety of fine cuisine, and there's a surprise waiting at the Southern Vermont Arts Center on the West Road (☎ 362-1405), where the **Garden Café** offers a nice lunch, and sometimes Sunday brunch; call ahead for hours.

AUTHOR TIP

*A great way to provision for a hike or picnic is to stop at **Al Ducci's Italian pantry** on Elm Street in Manchester Center. There's a full Italian grocery and deli featuring cheeses, pasta, fresh salads, biscotti, and other delights (☎ 362-4449).*

■ Peru (Bromley Mountain)

The casual Yankee dining at **Johnny Seesaw's** (☎ 824-5533) includes prime rib, fresh swordfish and salmon, and pork chops. A game room adds to the fun, especially for children, who get a special menu.

For authentic Chinese cooking, try the **Ginger Tree** at the Wiley Inn (on Route 11, ☎ 824-5500), where master chef Warren Hennikoff offers a different five-course dinner nightly. There's a buffet on Wednesday evenings.

■ Dorset

The **Dorset Inn** (☎ 867-5500) serves "honest American cooking" in a casual, relaxed setting; reservations are recommended. **Barrows House** (☎ 867-4455) offers a more formal approach to regional cuisine, and includes a greenhouse and tavern.

■ Danby

Sitting by the fire in winter or among the flowers in summer are hallmarks of the **White Dog Tavern** (☎ 293-5477), meant for slowing down and savoring the dinners from the often-changed blackboard menu. Ask about the chicken breasts à la Tom!

*While you're in Danby, take time to visit **Vermont Country Bird Houses** on Main Street in the village (☎ 293-5991, open daily). The assortment of avian habitat is amazing, from barns, churches, and even bird villages to old-world traditional forms and replicas of Vermont village homes. Find housing to suite specific songbirds, bluebirds, wrens, nuthatches, chickadees, and more.*

Bennington & Vermont Valley

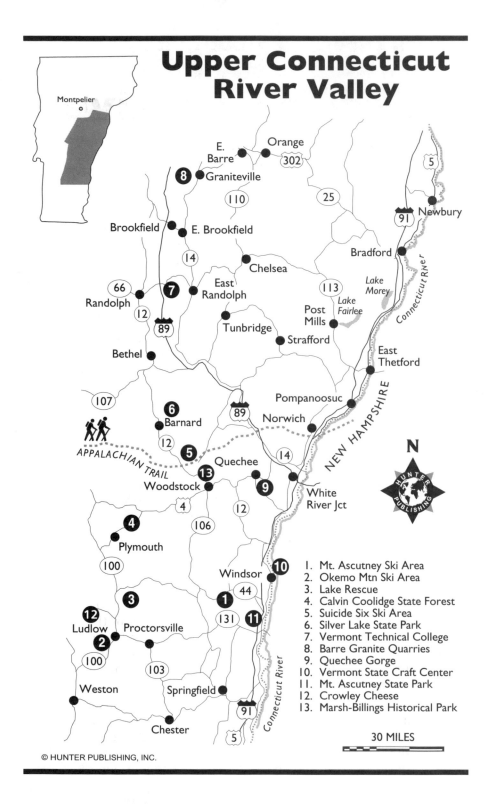

Upper Connecticut River Valley

Montpelier

E. Barre
Orange
302
Graniteville
8
110
Newbury
5
91
Brookfield
E. Brookfield
Bradford
14
Chelsea
66
7
East Randolph
113
Lake Morey
Randolph
12
Lake Fairlee
Post Mills
89
Tunbridge
Strafford
East Thetford
Bethel
107
Pompanoosuc
6
89
Barnard
Norwich
12
NEW HAMPSHIRE
5
Quechee
14
N
13
Woodstock
9
White River Jct
4
12
106
4
Plymouth
100
Windsor
10
1. Mt. Ascutney Ski Area
44
2. Okemo Mtn Ski Area
3. Lake Rescue
3
1
131
4. Calvin Coolidge State Forest
12
11
5. Suicide Six Ski Area
Ludlow
Proctorsville
6. Silver Lake State Park
2
7. Vermont Technical College
100
103
8. Barre Granite Quarries
9. Quechee Gorge
Weston
Springfield
10. Vermont State Craft Center
11. Mt. Ascutney State Park
91
12. Crowley Cheese
Chester
13. Marsh-Billings Historical Park
5

APPALACHIAN TRAIL

Connecticut River

30 MILES

© HUNTER PUBLISHING, INC.

The Upper Connecticut River Valley

The Connecticut River is wide and powerful along the eastern border of Vermont as it passes through the historic industrial centers of Springfield, Windsor, and White River Junction. Further north, the smaller towns of Fairlee and Bradford also meet the river and the railroad, and inventors have been nourished by the atmosphere of commerce along these north-south routes. One of the most noted was Samuel Morey, a lumberman in Fairlee and inventor of the first steamboat, in 1793. This region was also the heart of Vermont's first rebellion, as delegates gathered in Windsor on July 2, 1777, to declare Vermont a "free and independent state."

Getting Here & Getting Around

The path of the Connecticut River is followed by **Interstate 91**, and at **White River Junction** the state's other major route, **Interstate 89**, heads northwest across the heart of the state and through its capitol district, finally reaching Lake Champlain at the city of **Burlington**. Interstate 89 winds alongside the **White River**, whose headwater branches spread out into the countryside as the land rises toward the mountain peaks.

The villages of this region also spread outward from the two major rivers. To the south, **Chester** and **Weston** shelter unusual concentrations of art and cultural events. The **Calvin Coolidge Memorial Highway**, named for Vermont's "strong and silent" US President, leads away from the Connecticut River Valley to **Ludlow**, home of Okemo Mountain Ski Resort.

Then the road continues its mountainous path to **Plymouth**, the former President's boyhood home.

Another ski area lies closer to the Connecticut – Mount Ascutney, which rises in thickly forested slopes outside the railroad town of Windsor. From Ascutney the hilly **Route 106** heads north to **Woodstock**, a town preserved in its rural charm and elegance, thanks to two local families who recognized its rare beauty and took steps to secure it. Woodstock can also be reached from that other traditional railroad town, White River Junction, by passing first through Quechee where the dramatic drop of Quechee Gorge has been a "must see" for generations, probably including generations of Native Americans who hunted and fished these verdant valleys. Over the mountains and the fields hawks hover, and a raptor center in Woodstock celebrates their fierce grace and independence.

Heading up the valley of the White River, the next northwest passage, means a winding route through the college town of **Randolph** (Vermont Technical College) and an open invitation to the picturesque villages around it: Brookfield, Tunbridge, and Chelsea. Time moves more slowly in these pockets; general stores still have oiled wooden floors, country fairs flourish, and communities are made up of many generations of families who have long worked this land and its streams and rivers. South Royalton, birthplace of the Latter-Day Saints (Mormon) prophet Joseph Smith, is also a college town, home of the Vermont Law School.

Incredibly lovely country roads form a network here that includes the horse-loving region of Strafford and the traditional lake resort towns of Post Mills and West Fairlee. Covered bridges and dams abound. Balloons drift by overhead. Each season takes on a poignant tang here, especially summer, savored on wide front porches or from the bow of a canoe on quiet water.

The descent from the hills takes you to **Norwich**, once a college town and now graced with some of the region's finest lodging and dining. Norwich lies close by the Connecticut River and is linked by bridge to Dartmouth College in Hanover, New Hampshire. It's good to get off the Interstate highway here and take its slower shadow route, **Route 5**, along the Connecticut. The riverside terrain is haunting and wild, despite nearby towns, and migrating waterfowl often rest in large flocks here on their way north or south.

The road leads north through Fairlee, then the thriving villages of Bradford and Newbury. The Waits River meets the Connecticut at Bradford, so that Route 25 can work its quiet way northwest along the Waits River's gentle bends. This hilly area is the northern edge of what has been called the Upper Valley, a region reaching across both Vermont and New Hampshire with common industry, commerce, and sometimes schooling. From the height of the land the eastward view of New Hampshire's White Mountains is stunning. Farther north stand the rugged and weather-worn mountains of Vermont's famed Northeast Kingdom, the state's least populated area, where long-legged white-tailed deer are sometimes said to outnumber people.

Touring

■ Springfield

When you think of old-fashioned New England, the Currier & Ives etchings or Grandma Moses paintings probably come to mind: village homes and children in bright clothing against snow-covered slopes, or the spume of snow behind a horse-drawn sleigh, and maybe even moonlight on a silent ridge, where foxes slink under the spruces.

Springfield is an old-fashioned New England town, but it catches a different part of the region's traditions: the eager inventors who fiddled in the barns, back yards and workshops to make new tools, new discoveries, and new comforts for life. The mighty **Comtu Falls** (Native American for "great noise") on the Black River drew potential industrialists here. The Black River's 110-foot drop guaranteed all the power they needed. Access to both the railroad and the Connecticut River meant the town's budding 18th- and 19th-century industries could ship their products to market. Springfield became the birthplace of America's machine tool industry.

Today, the town is still an industrial center, and its nickname was "Precision Valley" long before computer precision arrived. But the gracious homes of the early industrialists, the treasures of art and cultural wealth they amassed, and the recent outpouring of stewardship for the rivers and mountains nearby make Springfield rich in many ways. Orchards surround the town, bringing spring blossom and autumn harvest celebrations.

Old towns mean old roads, and Springfield's geography is a challenge. Driving into town from Interstate 91 takes you right past the **Eureka Schoolhouse,** Vermont's oldest one-room learning center. Open from mid-May to mid-October, the schoolhouse is furnished with period antiques to give visitors a taste of what children (and teachers) managed with more than two centuries ago. A 37-foot-long covered bridge stands nearby.

Continue along Route 11, which is soon named Clinton Street, to Main Street and to a pair of major intersections where half a dozen town roads connect. Park and walk around to get the feel of the town; traffic is frequently congested. Start at the **Park Street Bridge** to get a stunning view of the Black River (Comtu) Falls, which are lit at night. Head slightly uphill away from the center of town to Elm Street, and stop at the Springfield Art and Historical Society Museum's **Miller Art Center** (9 Elm Street, ☎ 885-2415; open early spring through fall), where the locally manufactured dolls and carriages from the early 1800s make a fascinating exhibit. There is also an exceptional group of primitive portraits, an outstanding costume collection, early Bennington pottery, and priceless Richard Lee pewter.

Now go back to Main Street and ramble past the ornate building of the **Spofford Library,** which dates back to 1895, and note the 1835 red-brick **Congregational Church.** Look for the turn for Summer Street, next to the library; three blocks up Summer Street is Orchard Street, and **Hartness House** is at number 30. This impressive mansion is now an inn, but was once the home of Governor James Hartness, better known for his inventions than his politics. He had an amazing gift for machines, and held 120 patents, ranging from turret lathes to safety razors to telescopes. On the grounds of the inn is a highly sophisticated (for its time) telescope; there are evening tours at 6 p.m., except on Sundays (☎ 885-2115).

DID YOU KNOW?

Springfield was considered a strategic target in World War II because of James Hartness' inventions and the town's industries. The breech-loading gun, the steam shovel, and the mop wringer all came from this one town.

■ Chester

Following Route 11 west from Springfield leads to the irresistible town of Chester. Plan to spend at least a day browsing in bookstores and shops, eating well, and walking around the two historic districts. The first is on Main Street, with a lovely village green and stately old homes. The double-porched inn was once the 1920 Chester Inn (and other stagecoach inns preceded that one), and is now the **The Fullerton Inn** (see *Where To Stay*), which stands on the site of four previous hostelries. The inn was recently renamed as the Fullerton, which restored the name that has been here twice before. A favorite with children (and other collectors) is the **Hugging Bear** (☎ 375-2412), which is both an inn and shop and has teddy bears of all sizes (and ages). Across the green is the old brick schoolhouse where the Historical Society and Art Guild portrays Chester's best stories. Don't miss the tale of Clarence Adams, a town citizen who broke into more than 50 homes and businesses in the late 1800s before he was finally caught. Let the museum folks also point out the old town cemetery, with markers dating from the Revolutionary War.

Today this Victorian village is also host to a number of festivals, including **Quilts Around the Town** (third weekend of May), hometown Independence Day and Labor Day weekend celebrations, a **foliage fair** on the weekend before Columbus Day, and an **"overture to Christmas"** on the second weekend of December. Make sure to bring a camera. For specific dates, check with the Chester Area Chamber of Commerce, PO Box 623, Chester, VT 05143, ☎ 875-2939, Web site www.chester-vt.com. Chester also offers antique shops, including the **Stone House Antiques & Craft Center**, a group shop south of the village on Route 103 (☎ 875-4477).

Other unusual shops in Chester include the **Mustard Seed Bakery**, in a little red Cape house just east of the green (☎ 875-4058); an impressive book selection at **Misty Valley Books** on the green, where you'll see shelves marked "Vermont Author" (☎ 875-3400); and an 1871 country store called **Carpenter's Emporium**, also on the green (☎ 875-4466). Take Route 103 south out of town for 1½ miles to the factory shop for **Putney Pasta**, open daily (☎ 875-4500), and keep going into Rockingham to find the second edition of the famous **Vermont Country Store** (☎ 463-2224), where candles, soaps, and shower curtains vie for space with sweaters, gloves, and country kitchen furnishings. Take a catalog home with you if you can't make up your mind!

But let's get back to Chester itself. The village around the green is only part of the story. The other historic district is on Route 103, the **Stone Village,** where there are 10 houses that were built by the Clark Brothers from 1834 onward. These two Canadian-trained native Vermont masons had a passion for gneiss, the rough-hewn, gleaming mica schist quarried from nearby Flamstead Mountain. They probably were part of the underground railway that helped to hide runaway slaves on their way to freedom in Canada before and during the Civil War.

A third section of the town is known as **Chester Depot** and is the northern station for the *Green Mountain Flyer,* the area's scenic excursion railroad. Antique shops and a steepled town hall add to the pleasant atmosphere.

■ Weston

Take Route 11 west from Chester for five miles and watch for the well-marked right-hand turn to Weston. Set high in the mountains, you'd expect this village to be a sleepy one, but there are too many attractions. It lies on Route 100, Vermont's most scenic highway. Centered by a gracious village green with aged, overhanging trees, the village has white churches, homey inns, and the popular Vermont Country Store. The **Weston Playhouse** (☎ 824-8167) is the oldest professional theater in the state, with summer performances, a Christmas production, winter cabaret for the ski season, and other activities ranging from concerts to prestigious craft and antique shows.

The first cluster of buildings to explore is at the north side of the green. The **Farrar Mansur House and Mill Museum** (☎ 824-6630) was built as a tavern in 1797, and now houses a collection of family heirlooms. Next door is the mill, with antique tools and mill equipment (both open summer and fall only). The picturesque **Weston Falls** are behind the mill (this is the West River, a fishing treasure), and it's a very short walk past them to the Playhouse.

At the south end of the green are country stores and galleries. The **Vermont Country Store** (☎ 362-2400) publishes its own catalog, the *Voice of the Mountains,* and tries to create the magic of Christmas year-round, between the penny candy counter, the old-time gifts, and the sturdy country clothing (yes, long johns and wool socks too). The shop is open year-round but closed Sundays; hours are extended during summer and fall. There's a wonderful church on the hill that you can see from the village green, worth a visit to gaze at its four-spired steeple. The church on the main street of the village is the **Old Parish Church,** built in 1816, with a unique bell and clock tower.

Counters full of merchandise at the famous Vermont Country Store.

A drive north of town for about 3½ miles on Route 155 will take you to the **Weston Priory** and **Benedictine monastery.** There's a gift shop here, as well as displays that explain the Brothers' commitment to social justice; do join the daily public prayer, in order to hear (and maybe join in) the Brothers' music, which is simple, harmonious, and thought-provoking.

■ Ludlow

Although Ludlow is a small town in terms of population (2,500), it's full of shops and restaurants, a busy valley town that complements the ski resort on Okemo Mountain (3,343 feet), looming over the town. Sports shops, cafés, and a brew pub keep the village hopping.

Upper Connecticut River Valley

Ludlow's historical claim to fame is that Calvin Coolidge, later to become US President, graduated from Black River Academy here. The school closed in 1938, but is now a museum, open late May through Labor Day and on weekends to Columbus Day.

A wheel of cheese being dipped in wax at Crowley Cheese.

Near the green is the striking Fletcher Library, a small architectural gem from 1900 with an arched ceiling and mosaic floor. On summer Sunday evenings there are concerts and serenades at the bandstand on the village green.

There's an access road to the top of **Okemo Mountain**, reached from Route 100/103 just north of town. If you drive past the resort complex you can reach the summit parking area and take a half-mile trail to the top for a view of five other ski mountains! The Ludlow Tour of the North Hill and East Hill also provides spectacular views. Pick up a brochure at the **Ludlow Chamber of Commerce** (☎ 228-5830) in the building with the clock at the Okemo Marketplace, a small mall opposite the road up to the ski area. Here you can also pick up a schedule for the **Town & Village Bus**, which links several area lodgings with Okemo Mountain and with the nearby picturesque town of Chester (schedules also available by phone, ☎ 722-4770 or 800-869-6287). And a new charter shuttle service, **Moose Caboose**, will take you to the airport, train station, shopping, or just out for the evening (reservations required, ☎ 228-4957), as well as on custom foliage tours that show the best of the mountain scenery.

*The **Ludlow Chamber of Commerce** is rapidly becoming regional and has a lot to offer besides brochures. Check out its blossoming Web site at www.vacationinvermont.com; or e-mail the chamber at heartofvt@ludl.tds.net.*

Just outside town are some interesting shops that lure you into Vermont life. **Crowley Cheese**, Vermont's oldest cheese factory, is a tiny family business north of town on Route 103. You'll see the roadside stand on the left (open summer and fall only), followed by the left turn to Healdville, where the little brown house stands that shelters the cheese-making operation. Watch the cheese curd get raked in the big vats; see a wheel of cheese get dipped into wax to form its protective shell. Above all, taste! And enjoy the vintage visit to an earlier time. Factory hours are Monday-Friday, 8-4, although cheese is most often made in the mornings. Call ahead, ☎ 259-2340.

Also on Route 103 is **Song of the Wolves Gift Shop**, a collection of American Indian items located inside **Ralph & Joan's Bait & Tackle Shop** (☎ 259-2261, closed Wednesdays and sometimes Thursdays), four miles up the road from Ludlow. And the **Green Mountain Sugar House**, a family business focused on everything sweet (the fudge is mouth-watering), is also four miles from town, but you'll have to take the right turn from Route 103 north onto Route 100 to get there (open daily, 9-6, ☎ 228-7151).

One more treat in Ludlow awaits at the old depot, where the **Green Mountain Railroad** stops. Call for schedules and tickets (☎ 463-3069).

■ Plymouth

Step back into a turn-of-the-century Vermont village for a day as you explore the **Plymouth Notch Historic District.** It's reached from Plymouth on Route 100A, a steep climb into the sturdy hills where the 30th US President was born and raised. Calvin Coolidge's boyhood home is here, as well as **Cilley's Store,** where the small space above the store served as the summer White House back in 1924. The Wilder barn displays 19th-century farm implements and horse-drawn vehicles, and there's a coffee shop and restaurant in the Wilder House nearby. A one-room schoolhouse, a perennial garden, the old Union Christian Church, and the **Plymouth Cheese Factory** are among the other buildings here. The cheese factory is operating and samples can be purchased. The entire site can easily occupy a day of pleasant walking and touring, including the pre-1800 cemetery. It's open daily from late May to mid-October. Hours are 9:30 to 5:30 daily; call ahead if you like (☎ 672-3773).

Appreciate microbreweries? From Plymouth, take Route 100A north for six miles to Bridgewater Corners and the intersection with Route 4. Here is the **Long Trail Brewing Co.** (☎ 672-5011), where there are complimentary samples of traditional-style beers, daily from noon to 5 p.m.

■ Windsor

You can't say Windsor in Vermont without putting "historic" in front of its name. The state's constitutional status as a republic was forged here by 72 delegates meeting at the Elijah West Tavern from July 2 to July 8, 1777: the first to give the right to vote to all men, whether or not they were property owners. This document gave standing to the newly declared Republic of Vermont (for many residents, that moment hasn't worn off), established public schools, and also prohibited slavery. The tavern has since been moved to North Main Street and is now the **Old Constitution House Museum** (☎ 672-3773), open mid-May to mid-October.

Machine tools became another claim to fame for the Connecticut River town, which was, like its downriver neighbor Springfield, endowed with more than its share of inventors. When the local Robbins, Kendall & Lawrence Armory exhibited its mass-produced rifles at the 1851 Crystal Palace Industrial Exhibition in London, it garnered both awards and orders from the very impressed British, who began to call this amazing manufacturing technique "the American System." The Armory now houses the **American Precision Museum** (☎ 674-5781), a collection of machinery and power tools, and innovations by Thomas Edison and Henry Ford. Favorites are the gun collection and the scale model collection. Even if you've never thought machines would be interesting, these may intrigue you with their intricacy and cleverness. The museum is open from Memorial Day to November 1, and often adds special short-term exhibits. Find the museum at the south end of town.

THE MACHINE TOOL TRAIL

Windsor's inventiveness seemed contagious, both from the past to the present and from one village to other towns nearby. The **American Precision Museum** offers a brochure describing "The Machine Tool Trail" that features, among other places, the **Inn at Windsor**, former home of industrialist Rowell H. Lamson; the **Windsor-Mt. Ascutney train station**, with its exhibit on the history of railroading in the state; **Cone Blanchard Corporation**, a modern machine tool shop in town making the largest grinders in the world; and in nearby Springfield, **Hartness House Inn**, where the founder of another machine tool company once lived and where today there is a great collection centered around the history of the telescope. So, for a rainy day when you want a fresh way to think about things, take the tour and reflect on the New England approach to making do and finding another way to use every scrap they had. Sites along the "trail" have brochures and maps to make it easier, or you can call the museum and ask for them (☎ 674-5781).

North of town, in the so-called **Industrial Park**, are today's great crafts-people of the region. A year-round pleasure in Windsor is the chance to see teams of glassblowers making pitchers, cake stands, mugs, and more, at a flaming furnace using classic tools of forged steel and water-soaked cherrywood. You can stand on the catwalk at **Simon Pearce's Windsor Glassworks** and sense the heat just enough to feel included in the traditional craft process. The glassworks also includes a retail store and a pottery; it's open year-round, but check for seasonal changes in hours (☎ 674-6280).

MAXFIELD PARRISH PAINTING AT THE BANK?

If you're acquainted with the lovely moody paintings of **Maxfield Parrish**, who lived across the Connecticut River in Plainfield, NH, in the late 19th century, you might think it's odd to go searching for his work at the Vermont National Bank in Windsor. But here's the story: Parrish, like many of the artists in the Cornish Colony at the time, would cross the river to Windsor to do his banking business on a regular basis. The tellers then were as friendly and helpful as they are today – they helped Parrish balance his checkbook and included him in the spirit of the community. He called them his "girls." At the time, that was a term of warm friendship. One day in the early 1950s, he said to them, "Here's a painting for you." What he offered was a work that had already become famous under the title "Summer in New Hampshire," and was later retitled "New Hampshire: Thy Templed Hills." Townspeople treasured it and enjoyed it.

In 1999, as a bank merger took place, someone in management decided that the painting should be sold to the Currier Gallery of Art in Manchester, New Hampshire. Employees discovered the pending sale by accident, the day before it was to close, and in outrage they protested. Fortunately, someone had a copy of a letter that Parrish's son had written in 1967, a year after the artist died, saying, "Dad intended this picture to stay where it is, no matter whether Vermont National Bank and all its merged branches get absorbed by J. P. Morgan or not." The letter was delivered to the local police, who conducted an investigation of who owned the picture. Faced with an enlarging community reaction of shock and anger, bank officials quickly corrected their position and pledged to keep the painting in Windsor after all.

Now retired employees of the bank support the painting with a charitable trust to ensure its future. It stays in Windsor, where Maxfield Parrish gave it to his "girls" at the bank.

In the center of the village is the **Vermont State Craft Center** at Windsor House (☎ 674-6729), a building that first served as an inn in 1840; it was one of the best hotels on the stage route from Montreal to Boston and back. Preserved from the wrecking ball by a last-minute coalition of passionate neighbors, the building now houses the works of Vermont's finest juried artisans. It is open Monday-Saturday year-round, and from June to January it's also open on Sunday. Some classes are offered, and there's a small museum.

■ Mt. Ascutney (Brownsville)

Here's another of the place-name confusions that abound in the countryside. Right where you would expect West Windsor to be (and that has been the local name too) is the town of Brownsville, which includes both **Ascutney State Park** and **Mt. Ascutney** – despite the fact that the town of Ascutney itself is actually farther south down Route 5!

From Windsor, drive south on Route 5 and look for Route 44A, which will be a hard right turn. From Route 44A, the well-marked paved road into the state park leads about four miles to a parking area and lookout located about three-fourths of a mile from the summit. This mountain is called a monadnock, the rock-hard unremovable remains of a much larger mountain. There are several challenging hiking trails here that double as Nordic ski trails in winter.

If you return to Route 44A and continue northwest, you reach Route 44 (of course, you can get here more quickly by taking Route 44 from the southern edge of Windsor if you don't want to visit the state park). Another 1½ miles along Route 44 brings you to the **Ascutney Mountain Resort** (☎ 484-7771 or 800-243-0011), noted as a family ski resort but also a year-round activity center with hiking, biking, tennis, and a fitness center. If you think winter here is gorgeous, come back and see the bright green of the summer ski slopes, or the flames of autumn painted over the treeline.

■ Woodstock

There are several ways to reach Woodstock; the road from the Mt. Ascutney area is especially scenic, as Route 106 rises and falls with the landscape. Or, from Interstate 91, turn north onto Interstate 89 and then immediately exit onto Route 4. The two routes meet at Woodstock's oval green, a genteel, tree-shaded island where strolling townspeople and visitors alike pause to say hello or sit on a bench and savor the peace in the midst of the busy town. The luxurious and elegant 146-room **Woodstock Inn** (see page 151) faces one long side of the green and adds its abundant flower gardens to the ambiance.

This is a town where beauty is relished. Even the foods are extra appetizing in the delicatessens, bakeries, and cafés. There are galleries, bookshops and charming boutiques. Well-preserved historic buildings house sophisticated shops, and *The New York Times* is as readily available as the local paper.

During the summer and fall the **Chamber of Commerce** maintains a kiosk on the green; its winter and spring address is 18 Central Street (☎ 457-3555). Do stop and collect some of the information, especially the numbered map of historic houses. A ramble along Elm Street and Central Street will include many of these sites, as well as a handful of galleries and shops. About a block up Elm Street at number 26 is the **Dana House Museum** (☎ 457-1822), home of the local historical society. Behind its starched white front are collections of decorative arts, toys, costumes, paintings, and a taste of the prosperous life in the 1800s.

WOODSTOCK HISTORY

Credit for the preservation of the town in such elegant state goes to two men who devoted their attention and some of their personal fortunes to the area. The first was a lawyer and railroad magnate, **Frederick Billings**. He bought and preserved land, and encouraged the reforesting of the hill called Mount Tom, which had suffered from logging and fires over the years. When his granddaughter, Mary French, married another philanthropist, **Laurance S. Rockefeller**, the new family member continued to shoulder the task of caring for the town and surroundings, as well as for the Woodstock Inn.

Frederick Billings was also an agricultural experimenter, importing cattle from the Isle of Jersey and keeping scrupulous records of milk production and breeding to improve his herd. His ideas of ecology and reforestation are said to date from those of conservationist George Perkins Marsh, an earlier resident of the farm. The dairy is still operating, reached by heading north from town on Route 12, and is open to the public from May through October. The **Billings Farm & Museum** (☎ 457-2355, e-mail billings.farm@valley.net) includes a museum and shop, dairy bar, and picnic area. In May it features a plowing competition, and in summer the vegetables and herbs of the heirloom garden are a treat to see and smell. During weekends in December, and daily between Christmas and New Year's, the farm opens again to feature a decorated farmhouse and sleigh rides.

Vermont's first national park surrounds the Billings Farm. Newly opened in 1999, despite many aspects still under construction, the **Marsh-Billings National Historic Park** focuses on conservation history and American care for the land. The new park is actually a gift to Americans from Laurance S. and Mary F. Rockefeller and features the couple's mansion and surrounding buildings, with an impressive art collection, as well as landscaped grounds, plus 550 acres of forest on the slopes of Mount Tom. Even here the touch of Billings shows, since in the 1870s he began to preserve the forest, with its tree plantations and networks of trails and carriage roads. Eleven of the original Billings tree plantations still survive. Marsh, Billings, Rockefeller... the line of thoughtful conservationists stretches over two centuries now. A Conservation Study Institute will join the National Park Service in studying this history and advancing conservation in the future. Expect to pay about $7 for adult admission to the park, which is open the same hours as the Billings Farm, May 1 to October 31, 10 to 5 daily (☎ 457-3368). It is less than a mile from downtown Woodstock, on Route 12, and is well marked on the right side of the road. To access the walking trails directly, continue north on Route 12 for another 2.7 miles and turn left onto Prosper Road, at the sign for West Woodstock. When you've gone 0.7 mile you should see a red barn on the right, and a parking lot on the left just after it, where the trails begin.

For such a busy town, it is surprising how quickly Woodstock turns into countryside. If you drive around the green to the southwestern end, where St. James Episcopal Church stands in its fieldstone sturdiness, the farther road is Church Hill Road. Go 1½ miles along Church Hill Road to the **Vermont Raptor Center** (see page 145) to see what wild really means. Here in outdoor flight habitats are 24 species of unreleasable birds of prey, sheltered by the Vermont Institute of Natural Science. "Unreleasable" means the birds would not survive in the wild – many were rescued from accidents.

Woodstock's serene location is part of the shelter of the Ottauquechee River Valley. The spectacular gorge farther down the river is part of the allure of the next town over, Quechee.

■ Quechee

If you travel alongside the Ottauquechee River for the four miles from Woodstock to Quechee, you probably won't expect what the river does next. Just at the western edge of the town of Quechee, it turns abruptly from its eastward flow and shoots southward, plunging into a narrow rocky cleft called **Quechee Gorge,** 165 feet deep and over a mile in length. The gorge is part of a state recreation area, with a campground and picnic area as well as a steep rocky trail into the gorge. Rock climbers will be disappointed to know that climbing here isn't allowed – there have been too many costly and dangerous rescues already. But the gorge trail is interesting, especially on a day when there aren't too many tourists to clutter the view. There are other trails here too, leading to the mill pond where the waterfall flows harmlessly.

HOW THE QUECHEE GORGE WAS FORMED

The impressive cut of the Quechee Gorge is the result of a geological story dating back 100,000 years, to the ice sheet that overrode and froze New England, and then to 13,000 years ago when the river began to flow again into a huge glacial lake. When the gravel dam of Glacial Lake Hitchcock collapsed, the lake drained rapidly into the sea, and the Ottauquechee collided with the path of a migrating waterfall. The river gnawed relentlessly at the hard rock underneath until Vermont's most spectacular river gorge had formed.

After passing the gorge, watch for the left turn off Route 4 into Quechee Village, where the highlight is the mill complex restored and occupied by **Simon Pearce** (☎ 295-2711). It has glassblowing and pottery workshops and an elegant award-winning restaurant serving lunch and dinner (reservations advised; ☎ 295-1470). Be sure to climb down the steps behind the glassworks and see the whirlpool at the base of the falls; some of the hydropower is now harnessed for the glassworks. Inside the workshop there's a catwalk around the glassblowing area, enabling visitors to stand close enough to the furnaces to feel and see the fierce flames as the molten glass is collected and worked. Teams of artisans, many of them with the European background that Irishman Simon Pearce himself brought to the area, share the handcrafting tasks to produce clear glass pitchers, mugs, cake plates, and more. There is also a pottery on the premises, where you can see impressively large pieces hand thrown on the wheel.

Summer entertainment in Quechee includes Saturday **polo matches** on a field near the center of the village and a **balloon festival** for three days in mid-June; for dates call the **Chamber of Commerce** (☎ 295-7900).

■ White River Junction

Welcome to River City, a railroad town that had its true birth on June 26, 1848, when the rails reached town to connect it with Bethel and the rest of the Central Vermont Railway. When the tracks made their critical connection with Burlington and Windsor, White River Junction become the most important railroad town in New England.

When that happened, in 1849, retired riverboat captain Colonel Samuel Nutt decided the town should have first-class hotel accommodations, and he moved the **Grafton House** from New Hampshire to White River Junction. The hostelry soon changed hands, went through consolidation and then a fire, was rebuilt in 1879, and by the turn of the century housed guests brought by five railways with 50 daily passenger trains. Heroes' welcomes, fairs, and performers from the Gates Opera House next door all frequented the hotel, by then called the Junction House. Records show the hotel hosted more than 38,000 guests per year. In 1920, the guests included silent movie star Lillian Gish and the famous director D. W. Griffith, filming ice scenes for *Way Down East*. In 1924, the hotel was renamed the **Hotel Coolidge** in honor of the owner's friend, Colonel John Calvin Coolidge, father of President Calvin Coolidge and frequent guest as the hotel.

The Hotel Coolidge still stands in White River Junction, and the Briggs Opera house is in the same block. Restaurants ranging from elegant to country classic are nearby, and the railroad station is still at the heart of the town, although the trains are now laden with skiers and bicyclists, as well as business travelers.

The **train station** at White River Junction is a hit with kids. who climb the old locomotive at the parking lot. At least once a year there's a **railroad festival** in town; for this year's dates, call the White River Chamber of Commerce (☎ 295-0035).

The town twists around the Connecticut River and almost separates in two; the southern section of it includes the bus depot and several more modern hotels and eateries, but lacks the railroad town character.

■ South Royalton

From White River Junction the most interesting road up into the heart of the state is Route 14, which winds along the White River, a fine trout stream in its own right (although the headwater branches, still ahead, are better). Thirteen miles of relaxed driving brings you to Sharon, and then it's another five miles to the right turn for the **Joseph Smith Memorial.** Joseph Smith was the founder and first prophet of the Church of Jesus Christ of Latter-Day Saints; this wooded site has a historical exhibit about his life and the church, as well as a 38-foot commemorative granite obelisk. Paintings, sculpture, and films enliven the exhibit. There is also a picnic area with a fine view of the mountains.

South Royalton's other claim to fame is **Vermont Law School,** established here in 1972 and now known for its status in the specialized field of environmental law. Vermont has its own environmental law court to administer some of the thorny problems of balancing development with the landscape's beauty and history. There's a cluster of village shops, and a nice green with gazebo for an afternoon picnic.

■ Bethel

From South Royalton, another mile north on Route 14 leads to the left turn onto Route 107 to Bethel, a classic mill town nestled between the river and the mountains. There is good fly-fishing in this area. Also, the **Bethel National Fish Hatchery** (on Route 12 about two miles south of town) raises more than a million salmon smolts per year, which go toward restockingthe Connecticut River with this sturdy game fish. Bethel is also the gateway to the Randolph area; head north on Route 12.

■ Randolph

Here's a former railroad town rediscovering itself as a friendly village for browsers and nibblers. If you enter town from Route 12, you'll want to go all the way down Main Street and bear right onto Central to find the Chamber of Commerce; if it's closed, keep going up the hill (also called Route 66) to the top of the long rise, where there's an information kiosk on the left in the gas station parking lot. Randolph has put a lot of energy into making good information available for cyclists and skiers, as well as those looking for a good place to dine or lodge.

The center of town is compact and easily walked. Park near the railroad and wander along the trackside, where there is a café and pleasant shops. The police department building houses the **Historical Society Museum,** open Sundays in summer and fall and by appointment (☎ 728-5398). On the south side of the tracks is the **Playhouse Movie Theatre,** the oldest operating one in Vermont (dates to 1919, with a curved cinema interior). When you walk the other direction down Main Street away from the railroad, you'll probably be lured by the smell of fresh breads in the entryway at **Lupines Restaurant and Bread Market. Cover to Cover Books** offers new and used plus good regional information, especially guides to hiking, fishing, and boating. Another two blocks takes you to the **Chandler Music Hall and Gallery** (☎ 728-9878), an acoustically outstanding little music hall with a steady run of theatrical performances and music and opera festivals, and a weekend gallery of photography and arts.

Drive up Main Street and take the right turn onto busy Central Street. As the road starts uphill, look for the **Porter Music Box Company** (☎ 635-1938) on the right, where large disc-style music boxes are made. There's a museum open to the public, and a video and tour of the workshop. This little company sells to connoisseurs in Japan and Europe as well as nationally, and the museum collection of classic and antique music boxes includes pieces from the collections of Louis Hoone and Ruth Bornand.

*For more information and seasonal updates, contact the **Randolph Area Chamber of Commerce** (☎ 728-9027, Web site www.randolph-chamber.com).*

It's worth driving the rest of the way up **Sunset Hill** (this steep rise of Route 66) to take a look at the whale sculpture in the little "peace park" on the right. Then drive across Interstate 89 to the very top of the ridge, where **Vermont Technical College** includes an ultra-modern dairy farm (no formal tours, but explore on your own and, between 3 and 4 p.m., visit the automated milking parlor; ☎ 728-1000). There are seasonal farm activities too, like apple picking and maple sugaring. The road that runs north and south in front of the college is Ridge Road; turning northward on it leads you to Brookfield.

■ Brookfield

The nicest way to arrive in Brookfield is from Randolph on the Ridge Road, with its stunning views of mountain ridges to the west. You can also get there from Interstate 89, though, by taking the Northfield exit, Exit 5, and going south on Stone Road, which parallels the Interstate to its east.

Either way, Brookfield is worth the visit; it's a village of unpaved rural roads, white-painted homes with green shutters, and an amazing floating bridge over Sunset Lake. Strolling around the village is pleasant. Bicycling and cross-country skiing are encouraged by the local inns. The lovely **Green Trails Inn** (☎ 276-3412) has an unusual collection of antique clocks.

Take courage and drive across the floating bridge to reach **Allis State Park,** where there is camping as well as picnicking, and a hiking trail with exceptional views and plenty of birdlife.

From the center of Brookfield, Route 65 leads east along the Sunset Brook to reach East Brookfield; turn right on Route 14 and then immediately left to pick up the Chelsea Road, a hill-climbing woodsy cut that takes nine miles to reach Route 110. Take a left (north) on Route 110 to find, in another mile, the "shire town" of Chelsea.

■ Chelsea

Although it is a "shire town," or county seat, Chelsea has escaped many of the changes of the 20th century. The village has not one but two greens, or commons, the south one with the school and courthouse and the north one with the church; there are some Federal-era homes and a turreted town hall. Two brick general stores anchor the center of town. Try the homemade ice cream at **Will's Store,** still owned by Will Gilman after 14 years. Stroll past the southern common to look at the brick **Shire Inn,** which has a granite post fence and fanlight doorway; this home was lived in by five generations of the local Davis family. There is good fishing in the river beyond, which is the "First Branch" of the White River headwaters.

■ Tunbridge

Between Chelsea and Tunbridge there are three covered bridges, all off to the east side of Route 110, crossing the First Branch of the White River. Horse lovers take trail rides through the bridges, and farmers still pull wagons of hay through them. These are good places to sit and ponder, take life slowly, reflect on the ways of life that once called for the wooden bridges with their peaked protective roofs.

Tunbridge is famous for its **"World's Fair,"** held for four days each September. The fair may indeed date back to 1761, when the town's charter was granted and included the right to hold two fairs each year. The Union Agricultural Society first started sponsoring it in 1867, and it is a true agricultural fair, with livestock displays, fiddle contest, midway, horse pulls, and dancing. Check with the Town Clerk (☎ 889-5521) for each year's dates. If you're in the village when it's not fair time, there's still a nice old store to visit, and you can ramble through the fairgrounds and the town's Mill Street covered bridge. If you want a driving adventure, head through the Mill Street bridge and bear left on the unpaved road, passing a cemetery, horses, and an octagonal house. After some rolling hills, the road begins to climb steeply; when you reach a "T," turn left and take the long winding descent to East Randolph, staying with the main road each time there's a split. When you reach the paved road in East Randolph, turn right and find Vermont Technical College and the turn for Interstate 89.

■ Norwich

Three miles north of White River Junction is Norwich, a gracious old college town whose college has moved on but whose noted inn, bookshops, and restaurants promise a delightful visit. There's a maple-lined green and a good bakery. The **Norwich Inn** (see page 153) dates back to 1797, when Colonel Jasper Murdock finished building his elegant mansion and allowed stagecoach travelers to stop by. Although fire destroyed the original building, a Victorian "grand hotel" replaced it, and the present innkeeper, Sally Wilson, has lovingly restored the Victorian features. "America's smallest brewery," **Jasper Murdock's Alehouse,** was added to the inn in 1993.

FOR BOOK LOVERS: *Norwich has an unexpectedly ample bookshop, the* **Norwich Bookstore** *(291 Main Street, ☎ 649-1114). It has two stories, with cubbies and corners that hold a lot of great reading matter. Book-related events take place year-round here, and tend to be crowded.*

South of the village are two unusual places to visit: a science museum and a bakers' supply shop. The **Montshire Science Museum** (☎ 649-2200) is quite near Interstate 91, but set back into a riverside world of a hundred acres of woodlands, wetlands, and wildlife. Walking trails explore the natural features. Inside the turreted museum building are dinosaur displays, aquaria full of fish and walking wildlife, and exhibits that show the wonders of space, nature, and technology, many of them hands-on and geared for both children and curious adults.

The **King Arthur Flour Company** (☎ 649-3361) has its store on Route 5, half a mile south of Exit 13 from Interstate 91. Their large and delightful shop of flours, baking pans, specialty foods and, of course, cookbooks, is open year-round. There is an especially fine supply of chocolate! Their bakery offers freshly made breads and pastries, as well as hands-on classes.

■ Strafford & Post Mills

From Norwich, several back roads lead up into the hills. The villages of Strafford and Post Mills each offer a different sort of life, especially nice to visit in the summer and fall.

Strafford is a horse town and a bicyclist's heaven. The green fields and white fences of **Huntington Farms** provide the perfect background for elegant thoroughbred horseflesh, and the graceful animals are often trained in equitation and jumping exercises in the paddocks near the road. Also in Strafford is the **Justin Morrill Homestead,** a National Historic Landmark open in summer and fall. This 1853 17-room Gothic Revival mansion is filled with period furnishings, with hand-painted scenes on the windows. Morrill was a congressman and US senator for 44 years, and left an immense legacy in the form of the land-grant system of colleges, which opened higher learning to the public. His village is still well preserved, including his father's stone blacksmith shop behind the tall 1799 Town House. The red brick building on the green, where Morrill had his first job, is now a bicycling shop offering good advice for touring.

Post Mills is part of the established summer resort community around Lake Fairlee, where second homes and summer camps line the shore interspersed with gentle woods and wetlands and a state-maintained boating access. Post Mills itself is best known for its tiny airport. Small planes and balloons use the airport year-round, and a row of tiny cabins houses overnight air travelers in simple shelter.

■ The Valley Towns

Thetford, Fairlee, Bradford, Newbury, and Wells River are the towns that rest peacefully in the flat bottom land along the Connecticut River. You can take Route 5 through them all, or visit from the exits of Interstate 91, which neglect only Newbury (possibly the loveliest village of them all).

Each village has its own downtown, with small shops and galleries. There are family-run restaurants and hiking trails and places to buy barn boots. **Thetford** is a collection of five villages and has nice back roads for biking, as well as a scenic picnic area at the Union Village Dam. A good way to start a dull day is with breakfast at the **Fairlee Diner,** (see *Where To Eat,* page 160) followed by a long browse through the used books (creatively catalogued) at **Chapman's Store** (☎ 333-9709), once an old-time pharmacy and now a general store with quirky, interesting twists. Outside Fairlee are the Hulburt Outdoor Center and Coyote Hill Mountain Bike Camp.

Between Fairlee and Wells River is the village of **Newbury**, where a **fiddlers' contest** on the green on the last July weekend is the summer highlight (confirm the date with the Town Clerk, ☎ 866-5521). It's nice to stroll around the green and appreciate the stately village homes; the general store is friendly and well stocked.

The southern part of **Bradford** village is a collection of gas stations, casual eateries, and a plant nursery, but do slip down to the river crossing and visit the **Farm-Way** store, where rugged jeans, jackets, and boots jostle for space. The main village is the northern part, featuring some great restaurants and a good crafts shop. Bradford is also known for its **wild game supper,** held in November and featuring unusual fare like moose and pheasant. Reservations are accepted only after the middle of October; write to Game Supper Committee, Bradford, VT 05033.

Wells River is the businesslike northernmost of this collection of river valley towns; its claim to fame is three good local restaurants, described on page 160, including the 24-hour P&H Truck Stop by Exit 17 of Interstate 91. It is also the gateway into the old granite-cutting towns in the center of the state.

Adventures

■ On Foot

Springfield

About five miles out of Springfield on Route 106, the highway turns abruptly north and you make the right turn with it. Almost immediately you'll see Reservoir Road on the right, which leads into the 70-acre **Springweather Nature Area** overlooking North Springfield Lake. This is a nice relaxed walking place, available for environmental learning in cooperation with the local Audubon group. There are fields, shallow lakes, forests, brooks, and flood plains; bring your wildflower identification book and listen for bird calls.

For a short but interesting bog exploration, try the **North Springfield Bog** (10,000 years old), reached from the center of Springfield by taking Route 11 north. Stay with Route 11 to the left as it splits away from Route 106; cross the Black River and take the next right onto Fairground Road. When you see Riverside Middle School, start measuring 2½ miles; you want the left turn at the southern end of the gravel pit. The area is open for nature study.

Ludlow

In Ludlow, **Okemo Mountain** offers hiking possibilities for summer trail walking, right along the ski corridors. For a more challenging hike, drive on Route 103 around the mountain to the village of Healdville, taking the first road into town. Just before the village center, on the left, is a recreation trail that heads up Okemo Mountain's undeveloped west side. All mountain trails meet near the summit in a loop that wraps a mile of views into one comprehensive packet. Guided hikes are available from **Northern Excursions** in Ludlow, with reservations (☎ 228-4957).

Plymouth

Plymouth offers a wide range of hiking options, from the loop around Echo Lake at **Camp Plymouth State Park,** to a five-mile trail to Reading Pond through the **Calvin Coolidge State Forest** (☎ 672-3612). The Green Mountain Club *Day Hiker's Guide to Vermont* lists a 6.4-mile hike passing near the summit of Slack Hill. The forest manager's station at the entrance of the forest, on Route 100A, supplies trail maps.

Woodstock

Part of the preservation efforts in Woodstock led to lovely walking trails, European-style with benches, on Mount Tom and Mount Peg, which are really just nice hills promoted in stature (Mount Tom is 1,250 feet at the summit and 1,357 at North Peak; Mount Peg is 1,060 feet). The vistas are pleasant, and you'll relax and have enough breath to keep a good conversation going. Pick up your map at the Woodstock Inn (☎ 457-1100).

Windsor

Hiking near Windsor means **Mt. Ascutney**. One hike is actually in the town of Ascutney, south of Windsor on Route 5, at **Wilgus State Park.** It's called the **Pinnacle Trail** and begins on Route 5 across the road from the park entrance. (Arrange to leave your car at the park; see the manager.) The blue-blazed trail follows an old woods road for easy grades to start with, then gets steeper so that at the half-mile point you have a lookout just below the wooded summit. The trail then rises over the crest and loops back down to the highway, a quarter-mile north of where you parked.

A second Ascutney choice is to head for **Ascutney State Park,** on Route 44A. There are four trails, all meeting near the summit. Check the *Day Hiker's Guide* for each of the trailheads, or ask the park manager. Points of interest include a former granite quarry, two springs, and the Cascade Falls on the Weathersfield Trail, where the Ascutney Brook shoots 84 feet down a sheer cliff. These are all good climbs, with plenty of vistas to reward the effort.

Quechee

Although the trail at **Quechee Gorge** isn't long enough to make you tired, it does call for agile and careful footwork as it descends into the 165-foot rock cleft on sometimes slippery steep stone paths. Find the recreation area, about halfway between Woodstock and White River Junction, and pay the small day fee; then start the blue-blazed trail from the central clearing of the camping area. It's a little more than a half-mile down to the river bank; then the trail works its way back upstream to show the increasingly high walls of the gorge. There's a junction where the blazed trail heads back to the camping area, for a total of 1.1 miles; or take the road that lies straight ahead at the junction, and see the old railroad bridge and another view of the gorge before going back.

Bridgewater & Pomfret

A section of the **Appalachian Trail** runs through Bridgewater and Pomfret, just north of Woodstock. Route 12 leads north from Woodstock to the trail, just over five miles from the center of town and immediately after passing through the hamlet of Prosper. If you take the trail west you can climb the Pinnacle, where the summit (not quite reached by the trail) is 2,558 feet; if you go east instead, you'll find a short steep trail up Dana Hill and then Breakneck Hill, passing the Suicide Six Ski Area along the way.

Also in Pomfret is **Amity Pond Waterfowl Area.** The hiking trail here is a 2.7-mile loop; combine it with some serious birdwatching, especially in the early morning when waterfowl are feeding. A good map, like the *Vermont Road Atlas and Guide,* will help you feel more confident about getting to Amity Pond, as it isn't on the regular state road maps at all; you head out of Woodstock on Route 12 north, take the South Pomfret turn, and in South Pomfret go right to reach Pomfret village, which you pass through in order to reach the hamlet of Hewitts Corners. Stay with the paved road as it swings to the right, then take the first left onto a gravel road; the Amity Pond parking area is another two miles up, at the height of the land. Here you'll find the trail, which is not hard to follow; for a rundown of landmarks, check the *Day Hiker's Guide.*

Randolph

In the Randolph area, one of the nicest networks of hiking trails is actually part of the **Three Stallion Inn,** (see *Where to Stay,* page 152) located on the ridge above town just off Route 66. You'll need to check in as a guest if you want to take advantage of the 20 miles of trails on 1,300 acres – but there are so many other pluses to the inn's Sports Center that you might well want to do this anyway! Of course, the back roads around Randolph are great to ramble, especially if you start from Randolph Center and head toward Brookfield; some of these are detailed in the *On Wheels* section on page 136.

Norwich

A perfect short hike, ideal for a day when you have other things to do or to give young children a chance to enjoy a mountaintop, is the **Tower Trail** up Gile Mountain in **Norwich.** The center of Norwich is just half a mile from Interstate 91 (Exit 13). Go right through town, passing Dan & Whit's General Store and measuring another half-mile past the store to Turnpike

Road on the left. Take Turnpike Road for 5.3 miles (it turns to gravel after 1.8 miles), and watch for the small Gile Mountain Trail & Tower Parking sign on the right. The little parking lot is on the left, and the trail is well marked. It's just about a mile long, and there are chipmunk burrows to notice, red squirrels endlessly chattering, warblers in the trees, and rocks and logs to walk along. If you're bringing the kids, point out the water bars – logs or rocks set into the earth across the trail, to direct water off the path and prevent erosion. This trail is maintained by an ardent group of town volunteers. At the top of the small mountain is a 75-foot-tall fire tower, still in good shape. Climb its seven flights of wooden stairs and rise above the bugs, the trees, and finally the surrounding hills, to get a 360° view of the foothills of both the Green and White Mountains.

Walking Tours

If you're ready for back-road walking with an itinerary in hand, a van to take you to the trailhead, and gourmet meals at the end of each day's rambling, consider **Walking Inn Vermont,** a special inn-to-inn program that does all the hard work for you, leaving you free to savor the countryside. There's even luggage transport from inn to inn, and tips on where to look for, say, antiques and swimming holes. Walking Inn Vermont is coupled with Cycle Inn Vermont; the address is PO Box 243, Ludlow, VT 05149-0243, ☎ 228-8799.

Hiking Holidays (☎ 800-537-3850) also has a tour that includes the Calvin Coolidge National Historic Site and the villages if Weston and Woodstock, plus vistas from Mt. Ascutney and evenings in gracious inns; this experienced vacation leader is based in Bristol and is willing to develop custom and private holidays too.

NATURE WALKS: *Both the **Vermont Raptor Center** outside Woodstock and the **Montshire Science Museum** in Norwich have gentle nature rambles through wetlands and rolling meadows. They do get overpopulated in summer, so try these on a less tourist-friendly day.*

■ On Horseback

Ever dreamed of a horseback riding vacation? Say, traveling from inn to inn on back roads and through woods with a local guide who knows the turns and the sweet streams for cool refreshment for you and your mount? **Kedron Valley Stables** in South Woodstock knows that dream and makes it come true. Paul and Barbara Kendall have put together weekend inn-to-inn riding tours, as well as six-day ones, for strong intermediate and advanced riders. Woodside trails, stone walls, and pre-colonial ruins add to the flavor of the trip. Trail rides by the hour are also available, and they also offer lessons, horse schooling, and boarding. There are horse-drawn rides in a surrey, carriage, wagon, and sleigh. Head south from Woodstock on Route 106 for five miles, and the stables will be on the right. The Kendalls also offer a homestead for rent by the week, weekend, or month. Contact them at PO Box 368, South Woodstock, VT 05071; ☎ 457-2734. Riding packages are available from May to November.

Between Springfield and Ludlow is the small town of Proctorsville. From Route 103, turn onto Route 131 east and take the second left onto 20 Mile Stream Road, heading out another 4½ miles to find **Cavendish Trail Horse Rides** (☎ 226-7821), which offers guided rides on scenic trails (Western saddles). It's best to call ahead and reserve , but walk-ins are also welcome.

If you're riding in the area, it's worth knowing about **The Tiniest Shop in Chester**, a harness and saddlery repair shop that's actually closer to Chester Depot, on Route 103. Look for the gingerbread man at the top of the hill, just south of the railroad station. The shop is open Friday-Sunday (9-5) in winter, and in spring, summer, and fall Wednesday through Friday (9-5).

In Plymouth, **Hawk Inn and Mountain Resort** (Route 100, ☎ 672-3811) offers hourly guided scenic trail rides for all abilities.

■ On Wheels

Road Biking

Road biking in the valley towns won't bore you a bit: the landscape is rolling, not flat, and side trips explore bridges and waterfalls. But for mountain biking, you'll probably want to follow one of the northwest routes to higher ground before you start pedaling.

Ride the train to Vermont with your bicycle and wheel it out onto the platform, ready to pedal into any of the railroad towns that line the Connecticut River. **Windsor** is a good place to get off; from the railroad station turn right onto Main Street (Route 5) and follow it through the village and north past Simon Pearce Glass Company. Half a mile past the Interstate 91 interchange, take the right turn for a quick side trip to the Martins Mill covered bridge. When you get back to Route 5, another half-mile north brings you to Route 12, where you turn left for the 1½-mile trip to Hartland Four Corners. Watch for the post office, and turn left again onto Brownsville Road past Skunk Hollow Tavern. Now the roads lose their shoulder, so pedal cautiously. Your next left (less than a mile later) is onto Country Road, which you take for about four miles to the Juniper Hill Road. Left again (you can tell you've made a loop, can't you?), and finish the last mile as you arrive back at Route 5. Turn right to get to the station. (An alternative way to use part of this route is to take it north but not turn onto Route 12; just keep going up Route 5 to White River Junction, the next railroad terminus.) If you want to head south by bike, stay with Route 5 to Bellows

Falls, where there are actually two trains to board: the regular Vermonter, or the *Green Mountain Flyer* Scenic Train Ride.

Interested in a longer, more challenging bicycle tour? There's a two-day, 74-mile version in John Freidin's *25 Bicycle Tours in Vermont* that starts in **Plymouth** at Calvin Coolidge State Park and loops through Woodstock, Barnard, Bethel, Stockbridge, and Sherburne. Freidin also offers a more relaxed 25-mile tour of Woodstock and Quechee and the surrounding farms.

Local cycle repair services include the **Cyclery Plus** (☎ 457-3377) in West Woodstock and **Woodstock Sports** (☎ 457-1568) on Central Street in Woodstock.

INN-TO-INN BICYCLE TOURS

■ There's an inn at Fairlee that rents road bikes and sets up inn-to-inn tours; the program is called **Balloon Inn Vermont Vacations** (RR1, Box 8, Silver Maple Lodge, Fairlee, VT 05045, ☎ 333-4326 and 800-666-1946). Obviously they're into ballooning here, too, but that's another story (see page 144).

■ If you like your routes pre-planned, supplemented with some chef-prepared food, van rides over the boring parts, and nights in small, comfortable country inns, **Cycle Inn Vermont** might be your answer. The professional planners are also cyclists, and they have a good feel for what a nice stretch of the muscles will be. They also rent 10-speed touring bikes and helmets; you need advance reservations, though. Contact Cycle Inn Vermont, PO Box 243, Ludlow, VT 05149-0243, ☎ 228-8799.

■ **Bike Vermont** also puts together inn-to-inn bicycle tours, but these range all over the state. Some classic five- and six-day sessions offered have been to Manchester and southern Vermont, the Northeast Kingdom's villages, and Northfield and Woodstock; weekend tours focus around a particular inn. The company recently celebrated 20 years of business. Their tours do extend just over the New Hampshire border when they're sampling the pleasures of the Connecticut River Valley, but otherwise they travel only in the state. Tours change from year to year; dates are early May to mid-October. Contact them at PO Box 207, Woodstock, VT 05091, ☎ 800-257-2226, Web site www.bikevt.com, e-mail bikevt@bikevt.com.

Upper Connecticut River Valley

CUSTOMIZED BIKE TOURS: *In Ludlow, Vermont Cycle Adventure provides tours that originate at whatever lodge you're staying in, as well as weekend specials that include lodging. Owner David Tyson has mapped out five routes in the area of different challenge levels, and he provides food along the way, as well as a map and a support vehicle. He suggests tours from 25 to 100 miles in length, always customized to a group's or individual's needs. Get in touch by mail or phone (PO Box 456, Ludlow, VT 05149; ☎ 228-5174).*

The **Quechee Inn** (☎ 295-7620) has a wilderness trails program that includes mountain bike rentals and touring, but also couples the sport with canoeing – you can rent one or the other or both! The inn provides 21-speed bikes in children's and adult sizes. They have maps and self-guided tours ready. The Quechee Inn is a mile from the Gorge, down Clubhouse Road.

When you get to **White River Junction**, skip over the urge to mountain bike on the Appalachian Trail – there are too many hikers, some handicapped, and the bikes aren't welcome. But there are some great road loops here, especially if you head up Route 14 along the banks of the White River through Hartford and West Hartford and on to Sharon (stop at Brooksie's Diner for a good local meal). Take Route 14 back to West Hartford and cross the river, connecting with the River Road after 1.2 miles; the River Road goes all the way down to a bridge to Hartford, where Route 14 leads you back to White River Junction. There are more bike routes and trails available from the **White River Chamber of Commerce** (PO Box 697, White River Junction, VT 05001, ☎ 295-6200). **Morris Brothers Mountain Bikes** (☎ 296-2331) at 20 Bridge Street opposite the Grand Union is your White River Junction support resource.

The "don't miss this" trip in **Randolph** is the one that goes to the Brookfield floating bridge and back again. There are several routes to try, but one of the smoothest is to head away from the railroad station on Main Street and make the right turn onto Route 66 (Central Street). After 1.7 miles on Route 66, take a left onto Hebard Hill Road, which is unpaved. In 2.8 miles it meets Howard Road and you swing right for half a mile to the left onto Ridge Road; you're now on the other side of Interstate 89, running parallel to it. It's 4.5 miles to Brookfield Village, which is worth a leisurely exploration itself. Return the same way, or else pedal across the floating bridge over Sunset Lake (roll your pants cuffs), which descends nicely over a four-mile stretch to Route 12, which, as you already guessed, leads south back into Randolph.

Cycling around **Strafford** is for folks who like to feel the burn as they head uphill; there are long stretches of winding back roads, many of them unpaved, and swift ups and downs. Try to include a covered bridge or two on your route, just to savor the Vermont feeling – plan your route with help from Richard Montague at **Brick Store Bicycles** (☎ 765-4441), on the green in Strafford. He also has accessories and does repairs.

From **Norwich** north through the valley towns, the gently rolling roads along the river make a good ride. Leave time to wander across the grassy strip between the road and river and watch the powerful waterway. This close to Hanover, home of Dartmouth College, you may well see some oarsmen out sculling, their long sweeps taking them upstream nearly as quickly as your wheels would.

AUTHOR TIP

RECOMMENDED ROUTES: *The **Woodstock Inn** offers a cycling map that loops among Sharon, Bethel, Barnard, and South Woodstock, with some nice unpaved roads; call the inn (☎ 457-1100) or stop by. Rentals are available here too. I like the roads north of Woodstock especially, pedaling past March-Billings National Park on **Route 12 north** and heading along the back roads of South Pomfret and Pomfret, through quiet farmland with gently rolling terrain.*

Mountain Biking

The very best mountain biking in this region is around **Randolph**, where **Bicycle Express** (6 Park Street, ☎ 728-5568) has rentals and tours available, plus trail maps and good conversation of where the best and most challenging routes are. The sports store not only organizes tours (including a great sunset trip), it encourages mountain bike races and supports a local wheel club. The shop switches over to Nordic skis once the snow falls, although they have winter bike clothing on hand. They close during January and February. You can also get the trail maps of the White River Valley Trails Association here, covering dozens of adventures in Orange, Windsor, and Washington counties. After establishing and mapping 242 miles of trails and 15 loops, the association seems to be worn out, and the group said they were folding in autumn of 1999. However, its efforts were tremendous and can be appreciated when you stop at Bicycle Express to do your own route planning over those trails.

Future bike events in the area are likely to continue at **Three Stallion Inn** (☎ 728-5575), another good place to contact about seasonal and annual races and biking festivals.

Mountain biking has its own specialized camps at **Coyote Hill Farm** in Fairlee, where teenagers and almost-teens can pick basic skills or race-oriented techniques. In July the camp has daily rides with repairs, slalom, and bike rodeos, as well as swimming. Adults can catch a touring and technique weekend, or settle in for race training or personal instruction. Send for the summer brochure from Coyote Hill Mountain Bike Camps, PO Box 312, Fairlee, VT 05045 (☎ 222-5133).

■ On Water

Rivers To Run

 If your concern is just to paddle without a rod in your hands, the **White River** system offers about a hundred miles of good canoeing. Scan the descriptions in the *AMC River Guide* first; then either walk the river before putting in, or take your first trip with someone who has just paddled it, as blowdowns and other obstructions happen regularly. There's no sense in being surprised by a deadly or boat-damaging area without warning.

Other rivers entering the Connecticut along this stretch are the Black, the Ottauquechee, the Ompompanoosuc, the Waits, and the Wells. Skip the Wells for canoeing, and try the **Waits** instead, especially during high water, for the run from Waits River to Bradford (be sure to take out well before the dam). The **Ompompanoosuc** is a problem above the Union Village Dam, but then becomes very runnable in all seasons from the dam to the Connecticut. The upper part of the **Ottauquechee** is a good run during April and May; past Woodstock it gets complicated by rapids, a dam, and Quechee Gorge.

Of the White River branches, the **Second Branch** is known for its covered bridges and the **First Branch** for downright pretty scenery and more covered bridges. Watch out especially for snowmobile bridges that may have sagged during the warm seasons.

> To run the **Black River**, you'll need to find out when releases are scheduled at the dams, especially the North Springfield flood control dam. Look over the River Guide's *cautions carefully before deciding to try this one; it's a challenge.*

Of course the **Connecticut River** itself is a good place for boats. From East Ryegate (just north of Wells River) to Hanover (across the river from Norwich) the Connecticut is increasingly wider and more picturesque. There's a chance to see a bald eagle or an osprey, especially in spring and early summer. Near Newbury there are even boat launching ramps and picnic areas. The section after Hanover is controlled by the dam at Wilder, and most of it is high risk, due to water releases and the complications of the dam and portage. Again, once you've studied the *AMC River Guide*, if you're determined to sample this section, take an experienced buddy the first time and be sure you've checked with the Wilder Dam for release timing. An experienced guide to the Connecticut River can be found at

Fiddlehead Boatworks in Bradford (☎ 257-5008), where expeditions and inn-to-inn tours are planned.

Canoeing and kayaking around Ludlow? Rentals are available through **Northern Excursions** (☎ 228-4957), which will also help work out where to go and how. Shuttles are available in their 14-passenger van from Rob Maccri, who also offers float tubes and other outdoor adventure support.

Flatwater Paddling

Flatwater boating is best on **Lakes Fairlee** and **Morey**, especially if you're looking for wind. But keep in mind the small lakes near Plymouth. Lake Rescue, Echo Lake, and Amherst Lake are connected, and Woodward Reservoir isn't far north. Another sweet spot for canoeing is the **Dewey's Mill Pond** in Quechee, where the waterfowl sanctuary is home to great blue herons, kingfishers, and sometimes ospreys.

TOURS: *One easy way to explore the Dewey's Mill waterfowl sanctuary is to let the **Quechee Inn** (Clubhouse Road, ☎ 295-7620) set you up with a rental canoe and gear. The inn also offers a Connecticut River float trip, which is self-guided and downstream, taking a half-day. Re cently added are kayak trips on the White, Ottau-quechee, and Connecticut Rivers.*

Fishing

Welcome to trout fishing on the three branches of the **White River.** If you're a fly-fisher, you're going to get spoiled rotten. These three separate headwater streams are some of the best trout waters around. You don't have to be an expert to find the good spots, either; start where any other brook or small river enters, and reap the benefits.

The branches of the White River are also exciting trout waters, and **Trout on the Fly** offers guided fly fishing for anglers eager for rainbow, brown, and brook trout. Fish 14 to 18 inches long are common; some are over 20 inches. This guide service designs customized trips (expect to pay about $200 per day, or $275 for two anglers), and provides all equipment. Contact Brad Yoder and Tamara Hutzler, ☎ 763-7576, Web site www.trouton-thefly.com). Of course you can angle on your own, and might enjoy starting in **Sharon**, where the general stores stock extra gear and you can get some ideas for river access. Staying at the **Shire Inn** in Chelsea (see the Randolph Area in *Where To Stay*) will also get you started.

TROPHY FISHING ALONG THE BLACK RIVER

The Black River of Central Vermont (there's another one farther north) flows through Plymouth, Ludlow, and Cavendish. In spring it swells with snowmelt from nearby Okemo Mountain, and is heavily stocked with brook trout and rainbows, as well as Atlantic salmon. The primary fishing area is from Cavendish to Downers, and it's not unusual to catch rainbows in the 17- to 19-inch class, and brookies well over 20 inches. Nightcrawlers will do, but spinning lures may be more successful.

Start at the junction of Routes 100 and 103 in Ludlow, where the Black River meets the Branch Brook. Head southeast to the junction of Routes 103 and 131 at Proctorsville, and follow Route 131 along the Black River, where there are plenty of spots to park and access the river bank. The river heads east to where Routes 131 and 106 meet in Downers. There's also good fishing in the next stretch, along Route 106 as far as Perkinsville. Note the two-trout daily limit in the trophy area from the Howard Hill Bridge in Cavendish to the Downers covered bridge on Upper Falls Road.

Aim for the early season, before the heat of the end of June, or else try the waters in September.

The Quechee Inn on Clubhouse Road (☎ 295-7620, see *Where To Stay*), an attractive country inn with restaurant, is also Marshland Farm, home of the **Vermont Fly Fishing School.** Martin Banak has 15 years of experience guiding and instructing, and offers on-stream instruction on casting techniques, equipment use, and basic entomology, with fine quality equipment provided as part of the package. Special interests are the Ottauquechee (in front of the inn) and the White River. There is also outstanding fishing for smallmouth bass on the nearby Connecticut (20-30 bass of about two-plus pounds on each half-day trip, and rainbow trout average 18 inches). One-day courses start in May and run through late October; contact Martin Banak at the Vermont Fly Fishing School at the Marshland Farm, Quechee, VT 05059 (☎ 295-7620).

If fishing near **Springfield** interests you, contact **Black River Outfitters**, where Bill Drude is an experienced angling guide (☎ 886-2683). In **Ludlow**, get in touch with fishing guide **Kevin Ladden**, at 64 Tucker Road (☎ 228-5195).

Swimming

Just interested in swimming? **Windsor's Mill Pond** has a nice swimming beach; so does **Silver Lake State Park** in Barnard, about eight miles north of Woodstock on Route 12, and **Camp Plymouth State Park** south of Plymouth. **Lake Fairlee** has a public beach, and there are swimming holes on the Ompompanoosuc River at both Union Village and Thetford

Cove of Lake Fairlee.

Center. In **Ludlow** there's the **West Hill Recreation Area,** with life-guard and picnic facilities.

A FAVORITE SWIMMING HOLE

Discover where the locals go for a quiet swim or a little twilight fishing. Take Route 103 out of Ludlow as if you were heading for Rutland – but you're just going a little way past the junction with Route 100, staying on Route 103. Watch on the right for the turn onto Buttermilk Falls Road (by the VFW building). Take the turn and go to the end of the road, park, and wander down the footpath to the falls.

■ On Snow & Ice

Downhill Skiing

There's a ski slope for every taste in this region. **Okemo Mountain** in **Ludlow** (☎ 228-4041; for lodging, 800-78-OKEMO), with its 2,150-foot vertical rise, has 87 trails, 95% snowmaking coverage, and a sophisticated and merry resort atmosphere. Look for snow-boarding (park and halfpipe; one of the Masters races was held here recently), ski school, and 13 lifts including two high-speed detachable quads. Child care is available for children ages six weeks and up. Youngsters age four to 12 can get season passes that include instruction and care plus plenty of snowy fun. There are even introductions to skiing for three-year-olds!

AUTHOR TIP *Get an advance ticket for Okemo Mountain in the village at the **Jackson Gore Discovery Center** at 196 Main Street, next to the post office, for the next day's ski runs. You'll avoid waiting in ticket lines on the mountain.*

Ascutney Mountain Resort (Brownsville, VT 05037, ☎ 484-7771; for lodging, 800-243-0011) is a little smaller at first glance, with a vertical drop of 1,530 feet and 31 trails (four lifts), and certainly less surrounded by restaurants – but the complex has put amazing energy and skill into producing a family resort, with 100% slopeside lodging, and programs and packages for all ages and skill levels. The resort is adding a quad chair to the summit and expanded snowmaking coverage to reach 80%. The emphasis on family has made Ascutney one of the top US destinations for beginners. There are also special programs like the women's Wednesday ski series in mid-winter, and ski team race camps.

APRES SKI PAMPERING: *South of Ludlow at 303 Route 100 South is **Knight Tubs**, a spa located in a restored mill building. Private rooms and ample hot tubs (plus an outdoor tub in a cedar gazebo) let you soak your ski muscles to silk again. It's open from Thanksgiving to April 1, Thursday-Saturday, 3 p.m. to 11 p.m. (☎ 228-2260).*

Woodstock believes that "small is beautiful," and **Suicide Six** (☎ 457-1666; for lodging, 800-448-7900) lives up to the name, adding a touch of elegance as well. Although the vertical rise is just 650 feet, there are 22 trails and three lifts, and the slope is just plain fun for visitors to the area, especially those staying at the Woodstock Inn nearby. The longest run is exactly a mile long; snowmaking covers 50% of the acreage.

Cross-Country Skiing

Nordic skiing thrives in this region, especially around the picturesque country inns that specialize in opening access to the Vermont woods and fields. The **Green Trails Inn** at **Brookfield** (☎ 276-3412 or 800-243-3412), by the famous floating bridge, has 35 km of cross-country trails; the **Woodstock Inn** (☎ 457-1100 or 800-448-7900) has 60 km, of which 20 are skating lanes. **Three Stallion Inn** at **Randolph** (☎ 728-5575 or 800-424-5575) offers 50 km with 20 km of skating lanes, plus snowshoeing on 1,300 acres. All of the inns open their Nordic trails to the public, and their resident guests have free use.

In **Quechee** at the Quechee Inn, the **Wilderness Trails Nordic Ski School** (☎ 295-7620) offers 18 km of trails, rents skis or snowshoes, and has even mapped trails into the Quechee State Park from the 24-room inn. There's also a pond with ice skate rentals available. The **Woodstock Ski Touring Center** (☎ 457-2114) is operated by the Woodstock Inn, located where the country club is in summer on Route 106; there are 60 km of trails – 31 km on Mount Peg and 29 km on Mount Tom – and plenty of rentals.

Lake Morey Inn (☎ 333-4311 or 800-424-1211; Web site www.lake-moreyinn.com) has 12 km of trails and adds the pleasures of snowshoeing and ice fishing. There are also groomed snowmobile trails starting at the inn's front door; rent one of the inn's machines or bring your own. Sleigh rides, tobogganing, and snowsledding add to the fun, and children's activities include all sports plus winter bonfires, a special treat. Ask about their special winter theme weeks and weekends for learning to ski, snowmobiling, and even country dancing.

Okemo Valley Nordic Center at 77 Okemo Ridge Road (☎ 228-8871, Web site www.okemo.com), at the intersection of Routes 103 and 100, has 20 km, all groomed for skating lanes, plus an après-ski lounge and restaurant.

Of course, there's plenty of cross-country skiing and snowshoeing at the state parks in the region. **Calvin Coolidge State Forest** and **Camp Plymouth State Park** in Plymouth are open to winter sports; so are **Allis State Park** in Brookfield and **Ascutney State Park** outside Windsor. Around the **Amity Pond Waterfowl Area** north of Pomfret there's Nordic skiing on the Sky Line Trail.

Other Winter Sports

Ever had a yen to drive a team of sled dogs? This rare opportunity is available through the **Shire Inn** (in Chelsea, ☎ 685-3031), which will call Michelle and Scott Giroux at nearby **Beacon Hill Adventures** for you and set up lessons, or just a chance for you to ride along. If you're not staying at the inn (what a shame to miss it, though), you can call Beacon Hill yourself (☎ 685-4316); dog trips are December through March, depending on snowfall.

SLEIGH RIDE & SNOWMOBILE INFORMATION

SLEIGH RIDES

■ **Kedron Valley Stables,** Paul Kendall, Jr., PO Box 368, South Woodstock, VT 05071; ☎ 457-1480. Sleighs hold up to 12 passengers.

■ **Billings Farm & Museum,** David Yeats, PO Box 489, Woodstock, VT 05091; ☎ 457-2221. Draft horses pull the 18-passenger bobsleighs through farm fields and along the Ottauquechee River.

■ **Janice Nadeau,** 78 Quechee-Hartland Road, RR1, Box 224, White River Junction, VT 05001; ☎ 295-2910. Farm sleigh pulled through woods and fields for up to 14 passengers; wool blankets provided.

SNOWMOBILE TOURS

■ **Okemo Snowmobile Tours,** Route 100, nine miles north of Ludlow; call for reservations, ☎ 800-328-8725.

■ **Snow Country Snowmobile Tours and Rentals,** Route 103 in Proctorsville; ☎ 226-7529.

■ In The Air

 Thanks to the appeal of the tiny Post Mills Airport, there are some wonderful treats in the air in this region. Brian Boland of **Boland Balloon** owns the airstrip and buildings, including a set of tiny rustic cabins (no facilities) where he lets fliers camp out overnight. With over 25 years of ballooning experience, he flies seven days a week, weather permitting, and takes on passengers for the 7 a.m. and 4:30 p.m. departures. Each flight is an hour or more, and he has 50 different baskets to accommodate party sizes up to 12 passengers.

Boland Balloon also offers a school where budding balloonists design, build, and learn to fly their own custom versions. There is no brochure; call and talk with Brian (☎ 333-9254) to swap details so he can create an approach to your own ride or desire to learn.

The **Lake Morey Inn Resort** (Fairlee, ☎ 333-4311 or 800-423-1211), not far down the road from the Post Mills Airport, also arranges balloon flights for its guests, complete with champagne celebration at landing. **Silver Maple Lodge and Cottages** (also in Fairlee, ☎ 333-4326) has a similar program.

Although Burlington is Vermont's only major airport, some flights can be found landing at **Lebanon**, New Hampshire; this shopping city is just across the Connecticut River from White River Junction, so it may be handy for visitors to this part of Vermont.

The tiny airport at Post Mills.

Eco-Travel & Cultural Excursions

Naturalists in this region are extra enthusiastic; look how much they have to share! The **Springweather Nature Area** (take Route 105 north from Springfield to the Reservoir Road) has 70 acres of fields, shallow lakes, forest, brooks, and flood plains around North Springfield Lake. There's no parking in winter, but the foot trails are open year-round.

At the **Woodstock Inn & Resort** the guests and public are invited to the Tuesday and Friday morning (9 a.m. at the inn) "walks on the wild side," guided educational climbs through the forests on Mount Tom. Sign up by calling the concierge desk at the Woodstock Inn (☎ 457-1100, ext. 156).

The **Vermont Raptor Center** (☎ 457-2779, open year-round) shelters 24 species of birds of prey – they receive a lot of wounded birds, and only hold onto the unreleasable ones that could no longer survive in the wild. But their fierce gaze is far from settled down, and the museum staff gives "bird on hand" demonstrations that let you get close to the sharp beaks and talons of these flying hunters. Come be glared at by an owl. From the southwest end of the Woodstock green, take the Church Hill Road 1½ miles to the center, turn by the Vermont Institute of Natural Science, which also offers exhibits and bird-on-the-hand demonstrations.

KID-FRIENDLY

Nature trails make great rambles, especially in summer. The Vermont Raptor Center is a good place for kids to be able to run and climb trees.

There are also nature trails at the **Montshire Museum of Science** in Norwich (from Interstate 91, take Exit 13, turn east, and immediately turn right onto the Montshire Road; ☎ 649-2200), and the museum staff posts notes about changes to look for. The 100-acre wooded site along the Connecticut River is full of bird life and unusual plants. The museum itself is packed with exhibits on space, nature, and technology. The live exhibits are great fun and often touchable, with fish, turtles, and snakes.

Interested in a organized programs for ecology, team challenges, rock climbing, and canoeing? The **Hulburt Outdoor Center** (RR1, Box 91A, Fairlee, VT 05045, ☎ 333-3405) encourages individuals "to enrich and change their lives and the communities in which they live, work, and play through experiential programs." This is where you find wilderness first responder and search and rescue training programs, too. There are family ropes days, riverfests, and teen camps. But it is all organized for groups or specific trainings, so do write ahead and look over the brochures; this is not a drop-in center.

When you've had enough rugged adventuring and want to nourish another part of your soul, consider the **Briggs Opera House** in White River Junction (☎ 295-5432), where music, concerts, and theater are regularly scheduled. The opera house is a gem, and draws good performers.

Another theater treat is the **Weston Playhouse** (Weston, ☎ 824-8167). It hosts mostly summer and fall events, especially Broadway hits and musical revues (there's a lounge and restaurant). For Christmas the Playhouse has a holiday production, and during ski season in February there are cabaret productions twice a week. This is the oldest professional theater in Vermont, and set in an irresistibly lovely village enriched by country stores plus arts and antiques.

Nourish your creativity with a stay at the **Fletcher Farm School for the Arts and Crafts** (611 Route 103 South, Ludlow, VT 05149, ☎ 228-8770). This well-established school, located just east of the center of Ludlow, offers courses in basketry, decorative arts, early American decoration, fiber arts, quilting, needlework, fine arts, wood carving, stained glass, and more. Classes run from June through August and are small, so you'll need to preregister; boarding is on campus.

While you're in the Ludlow area, you can visit **Black River Produce** (☎ 800-228-5481), the wholesale purveyor of local fruits and veggies to many a Vermont store. There's a modest retail outlet now too, on Route 103 in Proctorsville, close to the intersection with Route 131. Open Monday-

Saturday, 8:30-6, and Sunday, 10-5, this is a great place to savor the variety of farm harvests available, and an especially good place to do some explaining if your kids think fresh produce comes from a store shelf.

AUTHOR TIP

Longing to explore the wilderness with a guide who can show you where the coyotes and bobcats are and help you see signs of other wildlife? Contact Rob Maccri at **Northern Excursions** *in Ludlow (☎ 228-4957).*

ARCHEOLOGICAL AND GEOLOGICAL SITES

Do you like to dig into the past, literally? Check out the **talc cliffs** off Route 103, south of Proctorsville Gulf in the village of Gassetts, and ask about the nearby area where garnets can be found. Or head for the old **gold mine** at Camp Plymouth State Park (where you can pan for gold!), the **Indian stones** in Reading on Route 106, or **Comtu Falls** in Springfield (Park Street, ☎ 885-2779). And north of Springfield on Fairgrounds Road there's a **bog** easily 10,000 years old (☎ 885-2779).

Where To Stay

■ Springfield

Even if you don't stay at **Hartness House** (☎ 885-2115, $$-$$$) in Springfield, make time for a visit. The 32-acre turn-of-the-century estate is gracious and elegant, and lodging and dining (in the Victorian dining room) are superb. After all, Charles Lindbergh was a guest here; why not you? Choose his room to sleep in, or the room of Governor Hartness, the town's inventor extraordinaire (see page 114), whose telescope and observatory are still at the estate. Nature trails, outdoor pool, and clay tennis courts can be found here as well. Hartness House is near the center of town: from Main Street, take Route 143 to the first left turn, Orchard Street.

For a Springfield bed-and-breakfast home, try the **Baker Road Inn** (29 Baker Road, ☎ 886-2304, $), which has four guest rooms and is ideal for families. Springfield also has a **Holiday Inn** (☎ 885-4516 or 800-HOLIDAY, $$) on the Charlestown Road, visible as you exit from Interstate 91.

A pair of comfortable inns can be found five miles north of Springfield on Route 106, in the village of Perkinsville. **Gwendolyn's Bed & Breakfast Inn** (☎ 263-5248, $$) is housed in a Victorian mansion and its five guest rooms have period furnishings. Gourmet breakfast in the grand dining room is elegant. The **Inn at Weathersfield** (☎ 263-9217 and 800-477-

4828, $$-$$$$) offers guest rooms and suites inspired by the greatest love stories of all time, blending music, poetry, and romance into a very different ambiance.

■ Chester

The **Fullerton Inn** (previously Inn at Long Last) at the center of Chester has seen many changes, most recently a return to the name it's been known by twice before at its time-honored location at 40 The Common (Route 103, ☎ 875-2444, Web site www.fullertoninn.com; $$$). Jerry and Robin Szawerda, who owned a restaurant in Connecticut before moving to Vermont in 1994, love the 1923 Colonial and maintain its 21 guest rooms and suites full of character, both decorative and literary. Country quilts, lace curtains, and personal touches add to the old-fashioned feeling. Yet the inn's acclaimed dining room is absolutely up to date in elegance and cuisine, and there's a bar and lounge with weekend entertainment. Children age 12 and up are welcome. The inn will also connect you with local rentals of canoes and kayaks, give directions to outlet shopping or castle tours and, of course, send you skiing at Okemo, Stratton, and Bromley, or Nordic skiing at Grafton.

Chester has numerous bed-and-breakfast homes, among them **Night with a Native** (☎ 875-2616, $$), where the bedrooms have hand stenciling and lovely antiques; the **Greenleaf Inn** (on Depot Street, ☎ 875-3171, $$), a quiet and romantic guest house with affiliated restaurant on the green; and the **Chester House** (☎ 875-2205, Web site www.chesterhouseinn.com, $$-$$$), on the village green. Other choices include the **Quail Hollow Inn** (☎ 875-2467, $$), the **Stone Hearth Inn** (☎ 875-2525, $$), and the **Motel in the Meadow** (☎ 875-2626, $$). Two inns have special themes: the **Hugging Bear Inn and Shoppe** (☎ 875-2412 or 800-325-0519, Web site www.huggingbear.com, $$) on Main Street, with its teddies of every size and personality, and the **Inn Victoria and Tea Pot Shoppe** (☎ 875-4288 or 800-732-4288, $$-$$$) on the green, offering "indulgent pleasures of a bygone era," such as fireplaces and afternoon tea. For tranquillity that draws as much from the land as from the Early American furnishings, **Henry Farm Inn** (☎ 875-2674; $$-$$$) on Green Mountain Turnpike is ideal.

■ Weston

On the road from Chester to Weston you'll pass through the small village of Andover, where the **Inn at High View** (☎ 875-2724, Web site www.innathighview.com, $$-$$$) offers romantic comfort and imaginative cuisine to go with its 72 scenic acres of year-round hiking and Nordic ski trails.

After you browse around the common in Weston, you'll easily find the **Inn at Weston** (☎ 824-5804, $$-$$$), an 1848 country inn with comfortable lodging and fine dining. Other choices are the **Darling Family Inn**

(☎ 824-3223, $$) and the **Wilder Homestead Inn** (☎ 824-8172 or 800-771-8271, Web site www.wilderhomestead.com, $$-$$$). There's also the **Colonial House Inn and Motel** (☎ 824-6286 or 800-639-5033, Web site www.cohoinn.com, $-$$), a casual and relaxed country inn half a mile south of Weston village.

■ Proctorsville

If you're going to Ludlow and Okemo Mountain from the south or east, you'll pass through the town of Proctorsville on the way. Here is **The Castle** (☎ 226-7222 or 800-697-7222, $$$), a spectacular and lavishly furnished English manor with 10 guest rooms and supreme dining.

ACCESSIBLE ACCOMMODATIONS

If you or someone in your family has special needs, you'll appreciate the extra miles that the **Golden Stage Inn** has gone to make you welcome. Not only are all public rooms and one guest room accessible to those with physical challenges, but there is a TTY for the deaf community, and the safety alarms are strobe-lighted for those who can't hear them. This lovely inn is well worth visiting for all, though, with its antique-filled interior, sun-filled solarium, candlelit dinners, and welcoming parlor. The inn has a connection with writer Cornelia Otis Skinner, and was a safe house for freedom-seeking slaves in the 1800s. Some of the rooms are drenched in history; others are newer and more spacious. It's a wonderful place to stay in any season, but summer is a special treat with the gardens, orchards, swimming pool, and birds bursting into song. There is also an inn dog and a pair of inn sheep. Innkeepers are Micki Smith and Paul Darnauer. The Golden Stage is in Proctorsville, just outside Ludlow (1 Depot Street, Proctorsville, ☎ 226-7744 or 800-253-8226; TTY for the deaf, 226-7136; fax 226-7882, $$$).

■ Ludlow

Ludlow promises all the lodging options of a classic ski resort town. A good start for selecting lodging is to contact the **Okemo Valley Hospitality Association** (PO Box 9, VWG, Ludlow, VT 05149, ☎ 802-228-8834, Web site: www.vtlodging.com) for listings and package information, or the **Okemo Mountain Area Lodging Service** (☎ 800-78-OKEMO), a reservation and lodging referral service that includes condominiums and private homes as well as the usual choices.

Much of Ludlow's lodging consists of small inns with eight to a dozen rooms, and all are charming. That said, there are two that stand out: the **Combes Family Inn** (953 E. Lake Rd., Ludlow, VT 05149, ☎ 228-8799,

Web site www.combesfamilyinn.com, $$-$$$), on a quiet back road with hearty family-style meals, and the **Okemo Inn** (at the junction of Routes 103 and 100N; ☎ 228-8834, $$-$$$), with outdoor pool, sauna, and fireside lounge. Both participate in the Cycle Inn Vermont and Walking Inn Vermont programs (see pages 133 and 135), so book your lodging well ahead of time and consider joining the fun. The **Andrie Rose** (13 Pleasant St., Ludlow, VT 05149, ☎ 228-4846 or 800-223-4846, $$-$$$$) is an elegant small inn nestled at the foot of Okemo Mountain, with new luxury suites that include fireplace and oversized whirlpool tubs. Hikers and cyclists appreciate the American Youth Hostel and group discounts at the **Trojan Horse Lodge** (44 Andover St., Ludow, VT 05149, ☎ 228-5244 or 800-547-7475, $), where the 100-year-old carriage lodge has bunk beds, shared baths, hot showers, and a kitchen.

■ Plymouth

Plymouth's contribution to family lodging and activities is the **Hawk Inn and Mountain Resort** on Route 100, where biking, hiking, horseback riding, swimming, sailing, and fishing are balanced by the relaxation of an indoor spa. Dining is available at the River Tavern next door. Winter activities include skating, Nordic skiing in the nearby state parks, and sleigh rides (☎ 800-685-HAWK, Web site www.hawkresort.com, $$$-$$$$).

Or try the comfortable and clean **Plymouth Towne Inn** on Route 100, with its full home-cooked breakfasts, living room with fireplace, and spectacular mountain views (☎ 672-3059, $$).

■ Windsor & Mt. Ascutney

Windsor's **Juniper Hill Inn** (153 Pembroke Road, Windsor, VT 05089, ☎ 674-5273 or 800-359-2541, Web site www.juniperhill.com, $$-$$$$) is a 28-room mansion with warm hospitality, including gathering for meals around the immense dining table that seats 20 (or you can choose to dine alone). If you're intrigued by mystery and history, explore the **Inn at Windsor** (10 Main Street, ☎ 674-5670 or 800-754-8668, Web site www.bb-online.com, $$-$$$), where the central open courtyard is surrounded by original 18th-century buildings, underground stone chambers, and messages from the past; there are also elegant fireplaced bedrooms and sumptuous breakfasts.

Lodging at Mt. Ascutney is likely to be slopeside and both comfortable and energized at the **Ascutney Mountain Resort** (☎ 484-7711 or 800-243-0011, $$$), but if you're looking for other options consider the **Burton Farm Lodge** (RFD#1, Box 558, Windsor, VT 05037; ☎ 484-3300, $$) three miles north of Brownsville. It's a lovingly kept bed and breakfast close to biking and hiking as well as the ski slopes. Other bed-and-breakfast homes nearby are the **Pond House** (PO Box 234, Brownsville, VT 05037,

☎ 484-0011, $$) and the **Mill Brook** (Route 44, PO Box 410, Brownsville, VT 05091-1298, ☎ 484-7283, $$).

■ Woodstock

The luxury of the **Woodstock Inn & Resort** (The Green, Woodstock, VT 05091-1298, ☎ 457-1100 or 800-448-7900, $$$-$$$$) is incomparable. Even afternoon tea is an elegant occasion, and the cuisine is superb. Rooms are simply and attractively furnished, the common rooms have a quiet elegance and air of quality, and the staff provides warm hospitality. Activities at the resort allow you to be energetic in any of the four seasons, then relax in front of the fireplaces or in the indoor pool. The inn's hospitality dates back to 1793, and the present building to 1969, blending in beautifully with the groomed and preserved town. The inn offers year-round sports facilities, including a health and fitness center, a country club with an 18-hole course designed by Robert Trent Jones, Sr., a ski touring center, and the Suicide Six Ski Area. In addition, the inn has croquet, racquetball, squash, massage room, and business facilities.

Local inns and bed-and-breakfast homes include the **1830 Shire Town Inn** (☎ 457-1830, $$-$$$), the **Carriage House of Woodstock B&B** (☎ 457-4322, $$-$$$), the **Lincoln Inn at the Covered Bridge** (☎ 457-3312, $$-$$$), and many more. Don't forget the **Kedron Valley Inn** in South Woodstock (☎ 457-1473 or 800-836-1193, Web site www.information.com/vt/kedron, $$-$$$$), where the nearby stables add trail and sleigh rides to your options. The **Woodstock Motel** (☎ 457-2500, $$), at the east edge of the village, is a modest alternative.

■ Quechee

Quechee is close enough to also be a lodging option for Woodstock visits. Most actively involved in providing mountain biking, fly-fishing, canoeing, Nordic skiing, snowshoeing, and ice skating for guests is the **Quechee Inn** (☎ 295-3133 or 800-235-3133, $$$-$$$$). This 24-room 1793 country inn overlooks the Ottauquechee River and is the home of Martin Banak, director of the Vermont Fly Fishing School. Other choices include the **Parker House Inn** (☎ 295-6077, $$$), and **Quechee Bed & Breakfast** (☎ 295-1776 or 800-628-8610, $$$). There is a **Quality Inn** on Route 4 (☎ 295-7600 or 800-732-4376, $$$).

Don and Shelley Hardner have turned an 1810 Federal home into a lovely bed and breakfast at the center of Quechee, nestled between the community church and the library. It's called **Country Garden B&B**, and the gardens are indeed lovely; so is the antique pool. There's an exercise room, a pool table, a video collection – all you need for rainy-day entertainment. On nice days, golf, tennis, skiing, and a health club are nearby. Expect a full three-course breakfast, as well as afternoon cookies and evening sherry (37 Main Street, ☎ 295-3023, Web site www.country-garden-inn.com, $$$).

■ White River Junction

The best sense of railroad town history can still be found at the **Hotel Coolidge** (PO Box 515, White River Junction, VT 05001, ☎ 295-3118 or 800-622-1124, $$) at the heart of the downtown area. The place isn't fancy but it's comfortable, with 96 rooms, and a trace of the grandeur it had when President Coolidge's father was a regular guest. Don't miss the Vermont Room Mural, painted by Peter Michael Gish. White River Junction also has a **Comfort Inn** (☎ 800-228-5150, $$), **Holiday Inn** (☎ 295-3000 or 800-621-7822, $$), and **Best Western** (☎ 295-3015 or 800-528-1234, $$) as well as the **Coach 'N Four Motel** (☎ 295-2210, $$) and a **Super 8 Motel** (☎ 295-7577 or 800-800-8000, $$).

■ Bethel

The biggest house in town is the **Greenhurst Inn**, a Queen Anne Victorian on the National Register of Historic Places. Lyle and Claire Wolf host the inn as a bed-and-breakfast, and offer 13 rooms. Ask Claire if she'll play the piano for you in the evening. Children and friendly dogs are welcome. This is an ideal spot for river access, as the great trout of the White River are about 200 yards from the front door. It's on River Street (☎ 234-9474 or 800-510-2553, Web site www.bbchannel.com/bbc/p202552.asp, $-$$).

■ Randolph Area

Randolph's most lovely and well-endowed lodging is the **Three Stallion Inn** (RFD2, Stock Farm Rd., Randolph, VT 05060, ☎ 728-5575 or 800-424-5575, $$-$$$), with dining and accommodations in the fine New England innkeeping tradition. Located on 1,300 acres, the inn offers tennis, biking, a fitness center, 20 miles of hiking trails, swimming and fishing (in the Third Branch of the White River), horseback riding, and cross-country skiing (50 km of groomed trails). An 18-hole golf course adjoins the property. A pub and chef-prepared meals add to the comforts.

Other Randolph lodgings include **Foggy Bottom Farm B&B**, which offers afternoon teas and wildflower walks, and welcomes horses (☎ 728-9201, $$), and **Placidia Farm Bed & Breakfast** (☎ 728-9883, $$). Both these inns have trails for hiking and Nordic skiing. There is also **Emerson's Bed & Breakfast** (☎ 728-4972, $$).

When you reach Randolph's neighboring town, **Brookfield**, do visit the **Green Trails Inn** (☎ 276-3412 or 800-243-3412, www.quest-net.com/GTI, $$-$$$) by the floating bridge across Sunset Lake. The inn is actually a complex of two historic homes on 17 acres, with 30 km of trails for hiking or Nordic skiing. The inn will arrange ski, snowshoe, and mountain bike rentals for its guests, with advice on route planning, too. They offer a canoe for guests to explore Sunset Lake. Plan on gourmet breakfasts in the cozy common room; there's a terrific collection of antique clocks to spark your curiosity.

Other Brookfield lodgings include the **Brookfield Guest House** (☎ 276-3146, $$) and the **Pimlico Pines Studio Cottage** with one cottage tucked into the pines (☎ 276-3513, $-$$).

If you stay at the **Shire Inn** in **Chelsea** (Main Street, Chelsea, VT 05038, ☎ 685-3031 or 800-441-6908, Web site www.shireinn.com, $$-$$$$) you may never want to go home again. The bedrooms are comfortable and furnished with antiques; five-course dinners are served in a gracious dining room; and you can fish in the First Branch of the White River, relax in an Adirondack chair by the stream, and wander the deer trails among the apple trees and woods. There are books in the parlor and a soul-deep sense of peace and pleasure. Ski cross-country or sled down the slope, or hike into the hills (if you want a challenge, Beacon Hill is close by). Mountain bikes and skis are available at no charge; sleds too.

■ Norwich

Retreat into history at the **Norwich Inn** (225 Main Street, Norwich, VT 05055, ☎ 649-1143, $$-$$$$), a lovingly restored Victorian landmark with charming guest rooms and an elegant dining room; in the old feed barn there's a microbrewery, claimed to be the smallest in the state. Catch up on the story of this traditional hostelry, which was rebuilt in 1889 but dates back in tradition to 1797 as a tavern and rest stop on the coach road from Boston. While you stay, step across the road to the **Lilac Hedge Bookshop** (☎ 649-2921) for a wonderful collection of old, rare, unusual, and entertaining books.

■ Valley Towns

When you reach the old-fashioned summer haven of Lake Fairlee and Lake Morey, the **Lake Morey Inn Resort** (Lake Morey Rd., Fairlee, VT 05045, ☎ 333-4311 or 800-423-1211, Web site www.lakemoreyinn. com, $$-$$$) has a wonderful array of summer and winter recreation, ranging from balloon rides to swimming, boating, and fishing, and in snowy weather to the slip and slide

View from covered bridge, Thetford Center.

of skis, snowshoes, skates, toboggans, and sleighs – plus snowmobile rentals. The inn offers special theme weeks and weekends too, like a getaway for mothers, an Elvis mystery, and a learn-to-ski weekend. A smaller country inn nearby is the **Silver Maple Lodge and Cottages** (☎ 333-4326 or 800-666-1946, Web site www.silvermaplelodge.com, $$).

A very special setting is found in **North Thetford**, where the **Stone House Inn** (North Thetford, VT 05054; ☎ 333-9124, $$-$$$) sits close to the meadows and wetlands of the Connecticut River. Peace and comfort fill the farmhouse; waterfowl come close by. If you get a chance, ask for a room with a view of the water.

■ Camping

There are a handful of private campgrounds in this region, most open from early or mid-May to mid-October. **Sugar House Campground** in **Plymouth** (Rt. 100, Box 44, Plymouth, VT 05046; ☎ 672-5043) is an exception, staying open year-round with 45 maple grove and winterized sites.

From **Chester**, there's a seven-mile out-of-town drive to reach **Hidden Valley Campgrounds** (☎ 886-2497), with 36 sites, swimming, fishing, and horseshoes. Reservations are recommended. Hideaway **"Squirrel Hill"** Campgrounds is only 1½ miles outside **Ludlow** (Box 176, Ludlow, VT 05149; ☎ 228-8800) and has just 24 sites; it's about two miles from Okemo Mountain Resort.

Another campground close to a ski slope is **Getaway Mountain & Camping** (Box 372, Ascutney, VT 05030; ☎ 674-2812), near Ascutney Mountain Resort.

There's a campground in **Gayesville** on Route 107, eight miles southwest of Royalton and Interstate 89, called **White River Valley Camping** (Rt. 107, Gayesville, VT 05746; ☎ 234-9115). As you might guess, it's on the White River and handy for fishing. The campground specializes in nice touches like morning coffee and offers local hiking maps.

Perkinsville is just a few miles north of Springfield, so **Crown Point Camping Area** (Frank Bishop, RR1, Box 505, Perkinsville, VT 05151; ☎ 263-5555) is handy when you visit that area, and is close enough to Ascutney to be a base for there, too. Most of the 122 sites are for travel trailers, but 18 are for either tents or trailers. The campground is on the bank above Stoughton Pond, so there's swimming, boating, and fishing.

The two campgrounds in **White River Junction** aren't exactly in the back woods, but they're close to local attractions. **Maple Leaf Motel and Campground** (406N Hartland Road, White River Junction, VT 05001-3815; ☎ 295-2817) on Route 5 has 20 sites, and **Pine Valley RV Resort** (400 Woodstock Road, White River Junction, VT 05001; ☎ 296-6711) has 74 sites, plus boat and canoe rentals.

CONNECTICUT RIVER PRIMITIVE CAMPSITES

The dividing line between Vermont and New Hampshire is the low water mark on the west side of the Connecticut River – which means that most of the river itself belongs in New Hampshire, not Vermont. That may explain why a New Hampshire group, the **Upper Valley Land Trust**, has coordinated establishing a system of primitive campsites along the water, even though half of them are in the Green Mountain state. Anyway, the important part is, they're available to folks who paddle the river, and most of them are not accessible by car at all, so you get true privacy. The drawback (for some) is that you've got to be really careful with this land. It needs endless protection from litter and the signs of human use. Also, noise carries easily at night by water, so campers are asked to be pretty quiet. Bring your own drinking water, be sure to do any washing well away from the river, and plan to cook on a portable stove rather than a campfire. If such low-impact camping floats your boat, these sites are perfect, and there's no charge for use (except for a state park site in Weathersfield), although the Land Trust asks you to register in order to help monitor usage.

Working from south to north and staying on the Vermont side (west bank), there's a site that's part of **Wilgus State Park** in Weathersfield, about a mile below the Ascutney Bridge (fee charged). Then in Windsor, three miles above the covered bridge and Windsor village, there's the **Burnham Meadow** site at Bashan Brook. You'll notice the **Gilman Island** site between Wilder and Norwich, at the south end of the island (owned and managed by New England Power Co.). In **Thetford**, a mile before the stone bridge of North Thetford, camp midway along the straight stretch of wooded shoreline, opposite a white frame house on the New Hampshire side (watch out for poison ivy here). When you reach the outlet from Lake Morey, you'll come to **Birch Meadow**, just above the marshland; there are private camps farther up the river, too. Paddle into the Waits River by Bradford to find **Bugbee Landing**, where you'll find water, toilets, and stores in the village. And finally, north of Bradford but still a mile before the massive stone abutments that once held the Bedell Bridge, the **Vaughan Meadow** campsite is set on a broad wooded bank above a curving beach.

For a complete list that includes the New Hampshire sites as well, with a simple sketched map, write to the Upper Valley Land Trust, 19 Buck Road, Hanover, NH 03755 (☎ 603-643-6626).

Farther north, in **Thetford Center**, you'll need to take Exit 14 from Interstate 91 and then go east on Route 1143 to Latham Road to find the **Rest 'N Nest Campground** (Box 258, Latham Rd., Thetford Center, VT 05075; ☎ 785-2997). It opens at the beginning of April and has 90 sites.

More like a resort is the **Lake Champagne Campground** (Box C, Randolph Center, VT 05061; ☎ 728-5293) in Randolph, with 122 acres, 132 sites, and a private lake. There are game fields, a rec hall and, of course, swimming.

State parks offering campsites in this region are **Wilgus State Park** in Ascutney (29 sites; ☎ 674-5422); **Camp Plymouth State Park** in Tyson, just south of Plymouth Union (☎ 228-2025); **Calvin Coolidge State Park** in Plymouth (☎ 672-3612); **Quechee Gorge State Park** (☎ 295-2990); **Thetford Hill State Park** in Thetford (☎ 785-2266); and, in Randolph, **Allis State Park** (☎ 276-3175).

Where To Eat

■ Springfield

Springfield has an old-fashioned downtown, good for walking and browsing among eateries. For fine dining, try the **Hartness House Inn** (30 Orchard Street; ☎ 885-2115) for chef-prepared meals with gracious elegance. A local favorite is **Penelope's** on the square (☎ 885-9186), a casual lunch and dinner spot. For nibbling, the **Springfield Bakery** (☎ 885-3504) boasts the best doughnuts in town; you'll find them near the bridge over the Black River Falls.

■ Chester

Chester's finest dining may be at **Ye Olde Bradford Tavern**, which is the restaurant at the Fullerton Inn (40 The Common, ☎ 875-2444). For a terrific lunch, hearty, flavorful, and with great variety, try **Raspberries and Tyme** (☎ 875-4486), a deceptively small place on the green with a long and creative list of sandwiches as well as abundant baked delights. Another local favorite is the **Depot Deli & Pizza** on Route 103 at North and Church streets (☎ 875-6599) with its option of take-home family dinners. Chester is also home to the justly famous **Baba A Louis Bakery** (☎ 875-4666), a mile west of the center of town on Main Street (Route 11). The croissants are a specialty. Open Tuesday through Saturday, 7 a.m. to 6 p.m. East of the village, by the junction of Routes 11 and 103, is the **Country Girl Diner** (☎ 875-2650).

■ Proctorsville

Proctorsville is an easy ride from Ludlow or Springfield, and worth it to dine at **The Castle** (Routes 103 and 131; ☎ 226-7222 and 800-697-7222), where the elegant cuisine includes Vermont game as well as changing vegetarian selections. Desserts are scrumptious.

Another Proctorsville treat is the **Joseph Cerniglia Winery** (☎ 226-7575). Be sure to try the Woodchuck Draft Cider.

■ Ludlow

In Ludlow there's a truly enjoyable restaurant called **Nikki's** (☎ 228-7797), at the base of the Okemo Mountain Resort, where the highly praised menu includes fresh pastas, Maine lobster, Black Angus beef, mixed grill, and broiled New England scallops. The atmosphere is always lively, and the chef has been a regular winner in the "Taste of Vermont" contests. Cafés and a sports bar add to the casual options. For just plain fun, try the **Pot Belly Pub & Restaurant** (☎ 229-8989) at 130 Main Street, where there's often live entertainment.

Other "downtown" favorites are **Wicked Good Pizza** at 117 Main Street (☎ 228-4131, free delivery) and the **Ludlow Cooking Company** at 29 Main Street (☎ 228-3080), a restaurant that also does catering and takeout. It's a good place to stock up for a day's excursion, too. Look around for the **Black River Brewing Company** (☎ 228-3100), a brewer of English-style ales. At last report, the brewery was looking for a new location. And to just plain relax, especially around breakfast or brunch, or as an après-ski treat, slip out to the **Okemo Marketplace** (that little mall north of town, opposite the road to the ski resort), and visit **A State of Bean**. Fresh pastries, good coffee, plenty of choices for tea, and hearty soups are among the satisfying offerings (☎ 228-BEAN; open 7 a.m.-11 p.m. in winter, 7 a.m.-10 p.m. in summer).

■ Windsor & Okemo Mountain

When you ramble around the railroad town of Windsor, dinner at the **Windsor Station Restaurant** (Depot Avenue; ☎ 674-2052) fits right in, complete with Station Master's filet mignon or some of the traditional dining car specialties like chicken Kiev. Teddy Roosevelt and Calvin Coolidge dined here, too!

For an unusual treat in Windsor, try the **Book Room,** between Main Street and the railroad station. This cozy nook is a coffee and tea sanctuary with books, books, and more books, and a flower shop connected next door.

Okemo Mountain offers plenty of slopeside eateries, ranging from the **Harvest Inn Restaurant** in the Resort Hotel, to **Biscotti's Café,** to a base lodge Suicide Six Ski Areateria.

For fun and entertainment, try **Bennett's 1815 House** in **Reading** at Routes 44 and 106 (☎ 484-1815) or **Destiny** (Route 5, Ascutney, ☎ 674-6671), a nightclub with dancing.

For fine dining you might drive to Woodstock and enjoy the Prince & the Pauper for French and American regional cuisine, or to Quechee for the restaurant at Simon Pearce Glass (see listings below).

■ Woodstock

Woodstock's fine dining opportunities are numerous, and so good that it's hardly fair to single one out. There's the **Woodstock Inn** (on the Green, ☎ 457-1100), and the **Kedron Valley Inn** (Route 106, ☎ 457-1473) in South Woodstock. The **Prince & the Pauper** (24 Elm Street, ☎ 457-1818) announces handcrafted contemporary French and American regional cuisine and wins awards as well as much attention in fine dining magazines. Stroll around town and select a casual eatery, and be sure to stop at **Mountain Creamery** (33 Central Street, ☎ 457-1715) for some of the handmade ice cream and delicious pastries that have made it a local favorite. Another sweet spot to visit is the **Chocolate Cow** at 24 Elm Street in the center of the village (☎ 457-9151 or 800-truffle), for gourmet chocolate and homemade fudge. Nearby, at 16 Elm Street, is Vermont's oldest general store, **F. H. Gillingham & Sons** (☎ 457-2100); call for a free catalog.

■ Quechee

Gracious dining in Quechee can be found at the **Parker House** (Main Street, ☎ 295-6077) and the **Quechee Inn** (Clubhouse Rd., ☎ 295-3133). The restaurant at **Simon Pearce Glass** serves homemade breads and soups "to die for," as well as seafood and roast duck. During summer and fall, stop for lunch at Quechee Gorge at the **Ott Dog** and get a generous ice cream sundae. There's a nice family restaurant called **Wildflowers** (☎ 295-7051), with breakfast served until 3 p.m. and a friendly coffee shop.

■ White River Junction

White River Junction has a surprising variety of eateries, starting with the traditional **Polka Dot Diner** (☎ 295-9722) at 1 Main Street, open from 5 a.m. to 7 p.m., Tuesday through Sunday, closing at 2 p.m. on Mondays. **Taste of Africa's Karibu Tulé** is a definite anomaly in this quaint railroad town, but owners Mel and Demaris Hall, who met in Kenya, serve such delicious and different food that the area has adopted the restaurant with delight. "Karibu Tulé" is a Swahili invitation meaning "let's dine," and the food ranges from West African banana-chili fritters to Kenyan vegetable and meat samosas, and to various curry dishes and terrific vegetable "sides" like Nigerian spiced boiled yams or Ethiopian spinach. The fruit drinks are a good foil to the zingy flavors. Save room for desserts like cheesecake or sweet potato pone with whipped cream and sliced fruits. On weekends you definitely need a reservation (☎ 296-3756, e-mail Taste.africa@Valley.Net).

■ Randolph Area

In Randolph for the evening? Drive north of town to dine at the **Three Stallion Inn** (☎ 728-5575) on shrimp, scallops, crabcakes, chicken, pastas, or steak. Lunch in town is casual and tasty at **Lupine's** (Main Street; ☎ 728-6062), a very local spot that changes hands regularly but always seems to do okay.

Call ahead to the **Shire Inn** in **Chelsea** (on Route 110, ☎ 685-3031) to find out whether they have room for extras at their exquisite five-course dinners. Another option (but not for winter!) is to drive south of Randolph on Route 12 about 4.6 miles to **Onion Flats** (☎ 234-5169), a popular local roadside spot with sandwiches and ice cream. Or detour down into **Pomfret** to the **Suicide Six Ski Area** restaurant in winter to sample organic coffees and vegetarian cuisine, where even the milk and butter are local and organically produced.

Stafford visitors may want to call ahead with dinner plans, as **Stone Soup Restaurant** is small (☎ 765-4301). When you reach the village, look for the house on the green with a white fence around it. It's an elegant little hideaway that's a pleasure to discover. Only dinner is served, and only Thursdays through Sundays, 6 to 9 p.m. Maple country spare ribs and roast Cornish game hen are likely to appear among the daily blackboard specials.

■ Norwich

Fine dining in Norwich can be found at the **Norwich Inn** (225 Main Street, ☎ 649-1143), a landmark Victorian hostelry with its own microbrewery. Dinners may include pan-seared sea bass, grilled lamb chops, or rosemary-marinated grilled quail. For a lighter meal, don't miss **Alice's Café and Bakery** on Elm Street (☎ 649-2846), where sandwiches are hearty and desserts are wonderful. The rustic country breads are formed by hand and baked in an authentic French bread oven. Cakes so rich that you'll need a party to share them are found in the cooler, along with delicate pasta treats and other ideas that the chefs have prepared that week. No breakfast, though, so head here for brunch or lunch or plan a glorious takeout for a picnic or hike. While you're in town, explore **Dan & Whit's General Store**, where the ordinary necessities of life bump shoulders with more baked goods from other local bakeries.

■ Valley Towns

The small town of **Fairlee** offers some pleasant eateries: **Leda's** (☎ 333-4773), just south of the village on Route 5, serves lunch and dinner six days a week, with food that's a mix of Greek, Italian and American; it's a family restaurant, owned and run by Leda and Kostas Amatidis, who welcome other families. At the north edge of the village is the **Fairlee Diner,** (Route 5; ☎ 333-3569) immaculate and usually full of local people who know what a good meal they'll get; look for breakfast and lunch to be generous and tasty (open daily from 5:30 a.m. to 2 p.m., and on Thursday and Friday until 8 p.m. for supper). Carol and Ray Gilman have been in the business for two decades and love what they do; you can tell.

In **Bradford**, unexpectedly for the New England neighborhood, there's a really good Italian restaurant, the **Colatina Exit** (☎ 222-9008). It's on Main Street, with a lounge upstairs, and caters to families out for a rollicking good meal and an evening of fun. The pizzas are rich and garlicky; the entrées large, and the pastas tender. Also in Bradford is an epicure's delight: the tiny **Peyton Place**, owned by Jim, Heidi, Sophronia, and Seamus Peyton. Look for the warm lobster and feta salad with blood oranges; another treat is the coconut scallops tempura. Dinner is served Thursday through Sunday, and in summer on Wednesdays as well. Be sure to make reservations (☎ 222-5462).

Wells River has three family restaurants. In town, near the Connecticut River, is the **Happy Hour Restaurant** (☎ 757-3466), pine-paneled and friendly; it's a nice stop for a casual meal. Close to Interstate 91 (Exit 17) on the east side of the highway is **Warner's Gallery Restaurant** (☎ 429-2120), where the salad bar includes shrimp, and the desserts are New England classics. Just west of the Interstate 91 exit is the **P&H Truck Stop** (☎ 429-2144), a 24-hour restaurant with hearty meals and generous slices of pie.

Central Vermont

The rough spine of the Green Mountains runs north to south, creating the state's most exciting hiking and skiing terrain and sheltering acres of wilderness among the high peaks. To the west of the mountains the land settles abruptly into rolling fields and small towns. In this quieter landscape lie the two very different cities of **Rutland** and **Middlebury.** To the southwest is a long-time summer haven around **Lake Bomoseen** – there's plenty of open water for boating, and warm-weather visitors have added humor and zest to the community.

Because of the mountain ridge, access to this region is easiest in a north and south direction; east-west travel takes easily twice as long, as the roads strain upward and swoop back down. The highest of Vermont's mountains are around 4,000 feet in elevation. Although the main roads over the mountains are kept well plowed in winter, icy conditions require caution; on summer nights, the mountain passes are also likely to be challenging as thick fog blankets the routes.

Getting Here & Getting Around

 We explore this region first from the north, as many travelers will arrive from Burlington, either at the airport there, or by car, having traveled first along Interstate 91 and then diagonally across the state on Interstate 89. Visitors arriving from Canada are also likely to come through Burlington.

So, from the Burlington area we choose to travel south on Route 7, saving the lakeshore town of Shelburne to consider in the Lake Champlain Valley region. **Vergennes**, its French name proclaiming Vermont's closeness to French Canada, is the first town to thoroughly investigate; **Bristol's** rocky cliffs are a "must"; then **Middlebury** and the surrounding horse country, a look at **Brandon**'s historical riches, and on into the lively city of

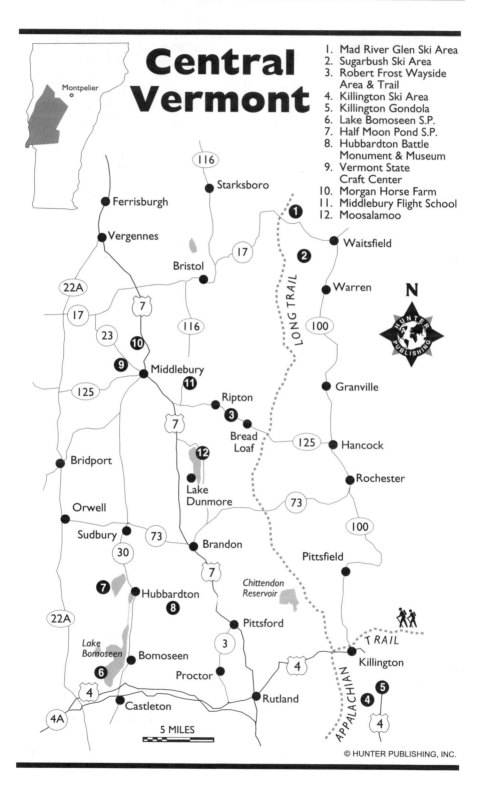

Central Vermont

Montpelier

1. Mad River Glen Ski Area
2. Sugarbush Ski Area
3. Robert Frost Wayside Area & Trail
4. Killington Ski Area
5. Killington Gondola
6. Lake Bomoseen S.P.
7. Half Moon Pond S.P.
8. Hubbardton Battle Monument & Museum
9. Vermont State Craft Center
10. Morgan Horse Farm
11. Middlebury Flight School
12. Moosalamoo

Starksboro

Ferrisburgh

Vergennes

Bristol

Waitsfield

Warren

N

HUNTER PUBLISHING

Middlebury

Granville

Ripton

Bread Loaf

Hancock

Bridport

Rochester

Lake Dunmore

Orwell

Sudbury

Brandon

Pittsfield

Hubbardton

Chittendon Reservoir

Lake Bomoseen

Bomoseen

Pittsford

Proctor

TRAIL

Killington

Castleton

Rutland

APPALACHIAN

5 MILES

© HUNTER PUBLISHING, INC.

Rutland itself. A detour to the resort area around **Lake Bomoseen** is either restful or entertaining.

So reach deep for mountain-tackling energy: hunger to see new vistas, enthusiasm for brisk hikes and challenging cycling, and eagerness for the great ski and hiking slopes of Killington and Pico. From these slopes the curious traveler is likely to drive or cycle north on **Route 100**. Long considered Vermont's most scenic highway, it is only two lanes wide, so that the villages along it are protected from high-speed wear and tear. Slow down with the road and savor the trip from Sherburne Center through Talcville, Rochester, Hancock, and Granville, taking frequent sidetrips into the heights of the **Green Mountain National Forest**. Are you ready to look for peregrine falcons teaching their young?

This stretch of Route 100 is also called the **White River Travelway**, and the Green Mountain National Forest supports activities and research along it. The ecological relationships are intricate. The route also has ancient travel history; as early as 10,000 BC it was used intermittently or seasonally by Paleo Indians, who were rugged nomadic hunters. By 5000 BC the Archaic Culture had moved in, a small group living in balance with the ecosystem and using the White River Travelway for its fish, game, and wild plant foods. When the Woodland Culture arose around 1500 BC, it brought bows and arrows, gardening, pottery, and settled villages. By 1500 AD Euro-Americans were replacing the native cultures, and the region developed agriculture, mining, timbering, and railroads; log drives changed the river bed. The Forest Service sees restoration of the White River ecosystem as one of its long-term goals.

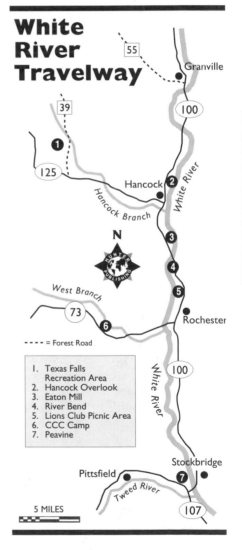

North of Granville, Route 100 enters the **Mad River Valley**, a richly endowed mountain resort area supporting the ski slopes of Sugarbush, Sugarbush North, and Mad River

Glen. In Warren and Waitsfield you can take flight on skis or in a glider; waterfalls, birds of prey, and white-tailed deer are waiting ahead.

Touring

■ Vergennes

Vergennes is officially the oldest of Vermont's cities, although the distinction rests on the slim differences between "town" and "city" governments in the state. It was founded in 1764, and Ethan Allen himself later named the town after the Count de Vergenne, the French minister of foreign affairs, who was strongly supporting the American Revolution. Established as a city in 1788, its population of only 2,600 makes it the smallest city in the United States. Vergennes quickly became a strategic port; being only seven miles from Lake Champlain it was an easy shelter for building a fleet of gunboats and the 734-ton, 26-gun *Saratoga,* critical in American defense during the War of 1812. Today the town still has an old feel to it, with all roads spilling downhill toward the port. **Otter Creek** is the river that's pouring toward the "sixth Great Lake" – it cascades in 40-foot falls at the base of Main Street.

Water power generated the wealth that drove the area's growth. There is now a historic district in town that includes 80 significant buildings constructed between 1825 and 1900, including the Stevens House, the Bixby Memorial Library, and the Ryan commercial block.

Find your bearings by first making the right turn from southbound Route 7 onto Route 22A. At this intersection is the **Kennedy Brothers factory and mall;** the woodenware manufacturing has moved into new premises, and the sturdy red brick factory is divided into small market stalls of antiques, Vermont foods, and regional crafts. Keep going along Route 22A, and just before you reach the center of town the Victorian homes begin. Look for the 1848 **Stevens Mansion** with its cupola and steps of local marble. As you keep going down Main Street, you'll find the **Bixby Library** on the right, a Greek Revival creation worth a look for the unusual interior dome made of stained glass. Route 22A is Main Street here; as it crosses the river it heads the final five miles to Basin Harbor on the shore of Lake Champlain, where the **Basin Harbor Club** (☎ 457-2311) is the region's most noted historic resort. It is perched among wetlands, where migratory birds rest on their travels. **Button Bay State Park** is nearby. Follow signs to the **Lake Champlain Maritime Museum** (☎ 475-2022), which includes a nautical archaeology center, working forge, and active boatbuilding on the lakeside. It's open from May to mid-October.

■ Ferrisburgh

If you can resist the lure of the lake, head back through town to Route 7. Civil War and folk history buffs should slip north three miles on Route 7 to visit **Rokeby House,** home of the Robinson family, Quakers and abolitionists involved with the Underground Railroad. Rowland Robinson's dialect-filled stories of that era are folk classics, and Rokeby is a memorial to his writing and his family's efforts. The museum (☎ 877-3406) is open mid-May to mid-October, Thursdays through Sundays.

■ Bristol

Now head directly down Route 7. In five miles, at New Haven Junction, you may want to take another side trip, this time to Bristol, where the **Bristol Cliffs Wilderness Area** is protected as part of the Green Mountain National Forest. There are cliffs to climb and ponds to explore; in the small town of Bristol itself is a good bakery, as well as several casual eateries. If you take Route 17 through the village, at the far edge of town on the right is a boulder carved with the Lord's Prayer, a good spot to stop and think. Farther up Route 17 is the noted restaurant, Mary's at Baldwin Creek (see *Where To Eat*, page 206).

■ Middlebury

Middlebury is eight miles down Route 7 from New Haven Junction. Before you reach town you'll pass the Dog Team Tavern turnoff on the right. You enter Middlebury by two imposing churches, and take the right turn into town to explore. This is the home of **Middlebury College**, at the far side of town. Shops reflect sophisticated taste, and the historic **Marble District** is also a shopping area. Park near the green and enjoy strolling the walkways. The green was not always a happy place. Gamaliel Painter, "Father of the Town" for his share of Middlebury's commercial development, placed stocks and a whipping post where the village green is now, adjacent to his mills. If you walk across the top of the common and up Merchant's Row you'll find Painter's own house, where the **Addison County Chamber of Commerce** has its office today (2 Court Street, Middlebury, VT 05753; ☎ 388-7951 or 800-SEE-VERMONT; e-mail accoc@sover.net). Pick up the self-guided walking tour leaflet for a good look at the town through the past century. Vermont's marble industry came to life here, as did the Morgan horse, and the town was the home of John Deere, who invented the plow that made farming the Great Plains possible. Also at 2 Court Street is the **Vermont Folklife Center** (☎ 388-4964, open Monday through Saturday, from late May to October 30); folk arts are exhibited here, along with videotapes, workshops, and lectures.

Near the white Congregational Church with its unusual steeple, note the monument to **Emma Willard,** founder of the first American college for women here from 1814 to 1819; Middlebury College itself was established in 1800. Another monument, across the green, commemorates Civil War veterans.

Walk downhill along Main Street and get a good look at the falls of Otter Creek as you cross it. Just beyond the bridge a right turn leads down into Frog Hollow, where the **Vermont State Crafts Center** displays the work of juried Vermont artists and crafters. There is also a stone mill further down the road, now housing a café and shops. If you turn up Park Street you'll find the **Sheldon Museum** (☎ 388-2117), which is open for guided tours late May to October; self-guided tours, a research center and gift shop are available year-round. The museum houses a permanent exhibit of a 19th-century home and its furnishings. When you finish admiring the elegance and style of the home, return to Mill Street and keep going to the pedestrian bridge that crosses to the **Marble District,** nine white marble buildings dating back to the turn of the century, now filled with small shops.

A second green, called **Cannon Green,** displays the Civil War cannon given to the town in 1910. After this green, head uphill to the right and explore the elegant campus of **Middlebury College,** with its tall stone buildings, wide parklike greens, and imposing vistas. The college's Starr Library holds amazing collections of literature, fine art, and rare books, as well as a fine reference library for students and professors; there are often rare book exhibits to enjoy in the atrium of the library. Also worth noting is the college Center for the Arts, with recital hall, dance and studio theaters, and significant art and anthropological exhibits, including permanent collections of 19th- and 20th-century painting and sculpture at the **Museum of Art** (☎ 443-5007; open year-round except during college holidays and Christmas vacation).

Middlebury's interest in the Morgan horse dates back to Colonel Joseph Battell, who began breeding Morgans on his farm in the 1870s. The Colonel's responsibility for Middlebury's success was immense, and he contributed greatly to its college; it is only an accident of geography that the University of Vermont **Morgan Horse Farm** is just across the town line into Weybridge. But you get there from Middlebury anyway. From the downtown area, cross Otter Creek and drive past Cannon Green to the right-hand turn toward the college. Immediately bear right again onto Route 23 and go three-fourths of a mile. Signs direct you to the spectacular multi-story horse barn and training hall, with gift shop, video, and paddocks full of beautiful horses. The Morgan Horse Farm (☎ 388-2011) is open all year, although guided tours are given only from May through October. Excite the budding horse breeder or trainer in you or your group by asking about the farm's apprenticeship programs.

It's worth noting the extra travel access to Middlebury in summer and fall; **Vermont Rail Excursions** runs the *Sugarbush Vermont Express* between Burlington and Middlebury, with stops in Vergennes and Shelburne, and there's free public transit from a dozen places around town (including the Morgan Horse Farm) to the train station. Ask at the Chamber of Commerce for the schedule.

Vermont photos often feature snowy mountainsides and green-clothed gorges. For a taste of a very different landscape and a tender, rich sense of light, explore the small 19th-century villages to the southwest of Middlebury. Leave town on Route 30 south, passing through Cornwall and Whiting. When you reach Sudbury, turn west on Route 73 to Orwell, and head north on Route 22A. This passes through Shoreham before reaching Bridport, where Route 125 east returns you to Middlebury. The open flatlands of the Champlain Valley seem to have more cows than people; these wide fields are lush and rich. Driving time is an hour or a bit longer, depending on how slowly you like to savor the surroundings. There are some truly spectacular sunsets here, but the sultry heat of a summer afternoon also brings out the best colors in this farming haven.

■ Ripton & Bread Loaf

Robert Frost was Vermont's poet laureate, and he had a strong bond with the Middlebury area. He lived for a time in Ripton, reached by taking Route 7 to East Middlebury and then heading up Bread Loaf Mountain on Route 125. When you pass the village of Ripton, start watching on the right for the **Robert Frost Wayside Area and Trail,** where a walking path toward Frost's old cabin is enhanced by his poems on plaques. Farther still up Route 125 is the Bread Loaf Campus of Middlebury College, where the college's famous summer English school is held, as well as the writer's conference founded by Louis Untermeyer, attended by so many of today's writers of fine literature. The **Snow Bowl**, Middlebury's ski slope, is also on Route 125 at the top of Middlebury Gap.

■ Brandon & Pittsford

From East Middlebury it's a gentle three miles to the turn for **Lake Dunmore,** a summer haven for boaters and hikers. The best trails are on the far side of the lake; for an interesting drive, take the lake turn past the fish hatchery and stay left at the junction, Passing Kampersville, and bearing right to go all the way down the east shore, noting trailheads and boat accesses. This is **Branbury State Park,** the western part of the Moosalamoo Recreation Area. The Long Trail, Vermont's end-to-end hiking trail, is less than six miles away. In between are lakes, hiking and ski trails, waterfalls, and the national forest's main mountain biking trails. If you manage to drive past this entryway into the wilderness, you'll arrive at the south end of Lake Dunmore and head back toward Route 7 – just in time, because in another seven miles the town of Brandon opens before you.

Brandon's two greens sit at bends in the road, one on either side of the Neshobe River, and are the centers of its unusual town layout. Over its 200-year history, fires, floods, remodeling, and demolition have taken place, but some 243 significant buildings remain, and almost the entire village has been listed on the National Register of Historic Places. A walking tour is available as shown in a leaflet provided by the **Brandon Chamber of Commerce** (PO Box 267, Brandon, VT 05733; ☎ 247-6401). Greek Revival homes, places that were once used for carriage shops or by cabinet makers, mansard roofs and Queen Anne porches – the village is a feast of architectural history.

*In Brandon you can see the work of America's best-known living folk artist, Warren Kimble, whose stylized cows and Vermont scenes are familiar around the world. The **Kimble Gallery and Studio** is stocked with original works, prints, small furniture pieces, and more. From Route 7, take Route 73 east for just over a mile, going around a sharp curve and turning immediately right onto Country Club Road. The gallery and studio are in the large red barn. Open daily from July to mid-October, and weekdays the rest of the year; ☎ 247-3026.*

Brandon has in a sense become partners with its neighboring village to the south, Pittsford, a town that has focused on acquiring and dedicating land for public recreation areas and trails. The Green Mountain National Forest borders both towns, and its wilderness and recreation areas seem part of the local sense of place. Hiking and biking give way to Nordic skiing and snowshoeing, and there are always more natural features like geology and wildlife to observe and investigate.

Pittsford's latest addition to both history and natural history is the **New England Maple Museum** on Route 1 (☎ 483-9414). It only closes in January and February, although early spring and late autumn provoke shorter hours; call to be sure. There are murals and artifacts as well as live demonstrations from candy making to wood bucket construction.

■ Proctor

A detour off Route 7 onto Route 3 takes only four miles to reach Proctor, where a museum and a castle stand. To reach the museum take a left through the marble bridge (yes, marble!) and bear right to the **Vermont Marble Exhibit** (☎ 459-3311, ext. 435). Here are the roots of the commercial success of this region: Marble was discovered and quarried commercially in 1784, and the Vermont Marble Company formed in 1870. The museum has a gallery of bas-reliefs of American Presidents, a geological display, and there's a movie, as well as a chance to view the marble-shaping process inside the factory. Open months are mid-May to mid-October.

DID YOU KNOW?

Marble quarried around Proctor and Danby was used in the US Supreme Court building, as well as the Lincoln Memorial.

The **Wilson Castle** (☎ 773-3284) is also open seasonally, and is great fun to visit. It's a 32-room stone château on 115 acres, with its façade set with English brick and marble, and the furnishings a lush mix of Far Eastern and European antiquities. Oriental rugs and Chinese scrolls complement museum pieces. In addition to three floors to tour, with Swiss Guards and guides on hand, the grounds are attractive. See the carriage house and the aviary, especially the Indian peacocks.

■ Rutland

Downtown Rutland is a "city on the move" under the direction of the Rutland Partnership. Shops and restaurants in turn-of-the-century buildings, arcades, plenty of parking, and a lively sense of art, music, and general enthusiasm for life make the downtown area a lot of fun. You do have to drive through some less exciting sections to get there – a long strip of commercial development to the north of the city, and a ring of predictable malls to the south – but it's well worth the effort. The downtown commercial blocks vary in architectural style from Italianate to Neo-Classical Revival to Art Deco, and there are wide sidewalks and some nice views, especially of the larger and more historic churches in town. There's a May-to-November farmer's market, and even a free shuttle bus.

Entering Rutland from the north is the least confusing way to understand its layout. Route 7 cuts down the center of the city. Route 4 goes across at a right angle to Route 9, and its west branch, headed downtown, is called Business Route 4 (BR4). South of the city is the missing part of westbound Route 4, skirting the downtown entirely.

As you enter from the north on Route 7, the highway becomes North Main Street. The District Ranger office for the Green Mountain National Forest is on your right and very noticeable; across the road is the **Rutland Region Chamber of Commerce** (☎ 775-0831) at 256 North Main Street. It's open year-round. Stops at both will get you piles of information. If you miss these two stops and it's summer or fall, ahead of you is a Chamber of Commerce information booth where Route 4 comes from the east to meet Route 7. This is called the **Main Street Park;** the kiosk will be on your right. There are Sunday evening band concerts here in the summertime.

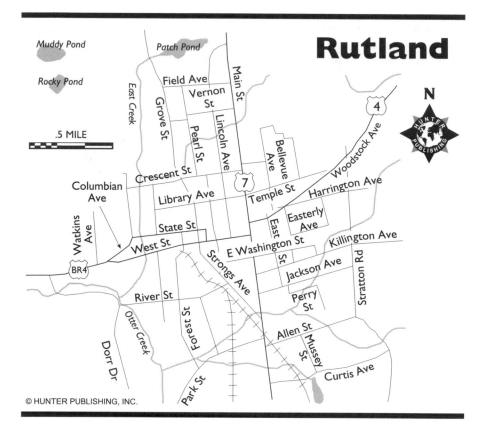

AUTHOR TIP

Do buy the $2 walking tour booklet from the visitors' center or other downtown location, which entitles you to a free guided walking tour, "Views Through Time," around the historic downtown area from mid-July to mid-October. Tours start at 10 a.m., six days a week, and begin and end at the visitors' center at Main Street Park.

Strolling without a guide, a don't-miss spot is the **Old Burial Grounds** on Main Street, near North Street. If you're exploring on your own, a nice place to start is right here. Stroll down Main Street and take the next right turn onto Business Route 4, otherwise known West Street. You are into the downtown district. Don't go past the post office, but turn left onto **Merchants Row.** This street, along with Center and West streets, has some of the best shops, as well as a nice assortment of eateries.

When you walk up Center Street away from Merchants Row, you pass the courthouse and then the library. The **Historical Society Museum** (☎ 775-2006) is at 101 Center Street, open Mondays and Saturdays. Keep going up Center Street. Up ahead is a left turn onto Main Street that takes you to the door of the **Chaffee Art Gallery** (☎ 775-0356). Open year-round (closed Tuesdays) in this turn-of-the century mansion, the museum changes its exhibits monthly, with special events and arts and crafts programs. A block south of the gallery is a great bookshop, **Charles E. Tuttle and Company** (28 South Main Street, ☎ 773-8930). Used book fanciers call it heaven: 40,000 used and rare books. Tuttle's has also published Oriental art books. The shop opened in 1938, after a century of family bookselling, and hours are Monday through Friday 9 to 5, Saturday 9 to 4.

South of the city on Route 7 are the fairgrounds, where the city hosts a week-long **Vermont State Fair** during Labor Day week each year. Agricultural exhibits, a giant midway, pari-mutuel harness racing, and nightly entertainment make the week exciting.

Saving Route 4 east (the way to the ski slopes) for later, follow Route 7 just south of town to Route 4 west; the second exit is Castleton, a college town and gateway to a handsome lake resort area.

■ Castleton & Lake Bomoseen

The little town of Castleton has played great roles in Vermont history: Here, Ethan Allen and Seth Warner planned the audacious capture of Fort Ticonderoga during the American Revolution, and nearby in Hubbardton Colonel Warner's militia fought a rear-guard action, the only military battle of the Revolution played out on Vermont soil. The town showcases its Greek Revival houses, and is the home of **Castleton State College** (☎ 468-5611). Note the slate roofs; Castleton once had 23 slate quarries.

Less than a mile west on Route 4A is Route 30, which heads north along the shore of **Lake Bomoseen.** Drive slowly through this time-honored summer haven and through the village of Bomoseen; when you've come five miles from Route 4A there's a left turn to the larger of the two state parks here, **Lake Bomoseen State Park** (☎ 265-4242). It has a lovely swimming beach and wildlife refuge, as well as plenty of summer and winter recreation facilities.

To reach neighboring **Half Moon State Park** (☎ 273-2848) you'll need to drive past the lake and through Hubbardton, then make two left turns to come down toward the west shore of Bomoseen. Half Moon Pond access is from Black Pond Road; the park offers much the same facilities as Bomoseen (and has canoe rentals), but is much more secluded, without a boat launch or picnic area, and may be less crowded on summer days.

The lake's fame in the 1930s came from a summer home on Neshobe Island, owned by essay-writer Alexander Woollcott, who entertained Harpo Marx and Dorothy Canfield Fisher, each capable of scandalizing onlookers in different merry (and often nude) fashion. The lake has another great claim to fame – in 1830, Julio T. Buel was eating lunch in his boat, and accidentally dropped his spoon into the water. When he looked into the clear water and saw a fish lunge at the sinking spoon, the idea of taking fish with a spoon lure was born; even today, the J.T. Buel Company makes fishing lures.

■ Hubbardton & Orwell

Interested in American Revolutionary War history? Are you a battlefield browser? **Hubbardton's battle site** is remarkably well preserved. The State of Vermont's visitor center portrays it well, too. There's a good diorama of the 1777 rear-guard battle by Seth Warner's Green Mountain Boys militia against the British. Then a quiet walk up to the crest of the hill lets you look out over the terrain, easily spotting the strategic points of the action. Although this battle was brief, it helped lead to British General Burgoyne's eventual defeat two months later at the Battle of Saratoga. The site is open from late May to mid-October; reach it from Route 4A by taking Exit 5 and heading seven miles north. If you're on the east shore of Lake Bomoseen, take the right fork at the north end of the lake and follow the curve around for six miles to Hubbardton.

When you've gazed at the battlefield long enough, start north, staying to the left at the fork, and reach Route 30 again in six miles; turn right and go six miles to Sudbury, then left on Route 73 for another four miles to reach Orwell. Here is **Mount Independence**, another state historic site. The peninsula juts into Lake Champlain and held an extensive Revolutionary War complex, with a floating bridge across the mouth of the lake to link it to Fort Ticonderoga. Designed for 12,000 soldiers in 1776, it was one of the largest forts in North America. Winter manpower fell to 2,500, who suffered greatly in the fierce cold and storms. As a result the complex was captured in July 1777 by the British, while the Continental Army made its escape and prepared for its later successful action at Hubbardton. A visitor center displays many of the site artifacts and explores how important land- and lake-based action were during the Revolutionary War. There's also a privately owned cruise boat, the *Carillon*, that will take you to **Fort Ticonderoga**, for a tour of a 1½-hour tour (☎ 897-5331). Walking trails in the historic park give another kind of feel for the terrain. Lest you suffer the pains of winter soldiering, the site is open only from late May to mid-October.

Other towns to explore around Lake Bomoseen are **Benson,** the scene of many early religious revivals and spiritual awakenings; and **Fair Haven,** a town on the Underground Railroad in the 19th century. Our touring description returns to Rutland on Route 4 and heads east, entering the resort approach to the ski slopes of Pico and Killington and the wilder acreage of the Green Mountain National Forest.

■ Route 4 East From Rutland

The rise of Route 4 from Rutland toward the ski areas to the east is quick and busy. An amazing assortment of shops, eateries, and lodgings hugs the roadsides. The **Norman Rockwell Museum** (☎ 773-6095, open daily) commemorates the painter's career with a great collection of his magazine covers that feature so many residents of nearby Arlington, Vermont. You can spot the museum by looking for the Taco Bell – the museum comes next, on the right-hand side. You'll barely notice passing the town of Mendon among all the roadside commerce.

Eight miles from Rutland is **Pico Peak** (☎ 775-4346 or 800-225-7426), the smaller of the two ski areas on this route. Described as "Vermont's friendly mountain," it is the little brother in a new partnership with Killington; trails connecting the two ski areas are in progress. A single pass will give winter sports access to both resorts. In summertime Pico's alpine slide and scenic chairlift give visitors a sense of flight and speed.

Another three miles on Route 4 and you're at the intersection with Route 100. The town here was called **Sherburne Center** for several decades, but now has returned to **Killington**, the name of the ski area that puts it on the map. At the shopping complex is a summer information booth for the **Killington-Pico Area Association** (☎ 775-7070). A right turn onto Killington Road leads, in five gradually rising miles, to the **Killington Base Lodge**, where ski adventures start in winter and where the summer and fall **Merrell Hiking Center** has taken residence. In snow-free weather, Killington offers mountain-biking adventures on 50 miles of trails with lift access to the summit.

As a ski resort, Killington is Vermont's biggest, with six interconnected mountains, 170 trails, 23 lifts, and over 1,000 skiable acres. **Killington Peak** is the highest, elevation 4,241 feet at the summit. There's enough resort room to have both the largest novice terrain in the state and also the most expert trails, with 45 black diamond and 10 double diamond trails. Snowboarding facilities are also on hand. See *On Snow & Ice*, page 195, for more details.

■ Pittsfield

From Sherburne Center, where Route 4 meets Route 100, Vermont's most scenic highway heads north through a series of small towns that offer access deep into the **Green Mountain National Forest**. The next 44 miles are picturesque and forested with green slopes in summer, flaming ones in early autumn, and dramatic snowy peaks in winter.

Along Route 100, the small enclave of Pittsfield holds a town office, library, and fire department, as well as the **Pittsfield National Fish Hatchery** (Furnace Road, ☎ 483-6618), where the Fish and Wildlife Service raises landlocked salmon and lake trout.

Just north of Pittsfield, where Route 107 intersects, there's a national forest barrier-free site called **Peavine,** with a wildlife viewing site, canoeing, fishing, and picnic area.

■ Rochester

Some 19 miles north from Sherburne Center is the left turn for Route 73, which climbs through a high pass in the Green Mountains. This is the way to **Mount Horrid**, one of the rock-cliffed ridges where peregrine falcons have made a successful comeback from near extinction in the state. There's a dramatic beaver pond close to Route 73 at Mount Horrid, where moose often browse. The Long Trail crosses northward nearby. Hiking and skiing trails run up over Gillespie Peak, Romance Mountain, and Hogback Mountain; this region is Moosalamoo, a national forest recreation area. Also accessed from Route 73 are the Chittenden Brook Recreation Area and the Brandon Brook Recreation Area. The forest has several interpretive sites along Route 73.

Just north of Route 73, the Green Mountain National Forest has a district office on the right; not only are there brochures, maps, and wise ranger advice here, but exhibits give a feeling for some of the region's wildlife and for the pressing ecological and environmental issues of the wilderness and recreation areas.

As a small town at the base of so much wild glory, Rochester has become a diverse community. Its picturesque village green and good restaurants are joined by art and craft and antique shops and a great bike shop that also supports Nordic ski adventures. A small publisher, Inner Traditions, brings forth alternative healing arts, spiritual history and philosophy books from this peaceful locale.

One mile north of Rochester is a national forest picnic area established by the local Lions Club, which helps with the White River restoration effort. Another mile brings you to the **River Bend** site, with canoeing and hiking. And at the three-mile point is the **Eaton Mill** site, a wildlife viewing location.

■ Hancock

This is also a "base town" for access into the Green Mountain National Forest, this time over Middlebury Gap on Route 125. The Texas Falls Recreation Area and the Middlebury College Snow Bowl (a small and refreshing ski resort) have access from Route 125. As it crosses the gap the road enters Robert Frost country at the Bread Loaf Campus of Middlebury College.

Hancock has the feel of a lumbering and mill town grown up; the Old Hancock Hotel is now filled with a bakery and gift shop and also offers overnight accommodations. Country inns begin to line the roadsides of Route 100 from here north.

Half a mile north of town on the right is the **Hancock Overlook,** a national forest interpretive site.

■ Granville

Two woodworking businesses vie for attention in Granville, and shopping can be great fun. Otherwise, the town is noteworthy mainly because the **Granville Gulf** begins just beyond it: a six-mile wilderness sliced by Route 100. Watch on the left for **Moss Glen Falls,** a great photo stop and a good climb. The headwaters of the Mad River are also along here, a mile before you reach Warren, and a roadside rest stop lets you admire them at leisure.

■ Warren

Just before you reach Warren, the Lincoln Gap Road cuts off to the left. This steep and narrow drive heads to a pass at an elevation of 2,424 feet, which runs beneath the peak of **Mount Abraham**. The Long Trail cuts across the road at the trailhead for Mount Abraham, too; there's a footpath up to the top of the 4,052-foot peak, and for one of higher peaks in the state it's a relatively easy climb because you start from such a height. The Lincoln Gap Road continues downhill toward Bristol. For this tour, instead, come back down to Route 100. Just ahead is the right turn onto an unpaved road into the village of Warren.

When you cross the 1880 covered bridge, take the left turn and stop at the **Warren Country Store.** This former stagecoach inn now features French bread, fine wines, and deli salads, as well as the daily and Sunday editions of *The New York Times*. It is the heart of Warren, pumping energy into the art gallery, antique shop, and pottery studio, among other small businesses. East Warren is reached by taking the turn at the bandstand in Warren, heading up the hill and curving to the left. Great views of the mountains are found on this high road as it works its way steadily north, passing along the way the Warren Airport, where you can enjoy a glider ride for two just as reasonably as for one. The road descends into Waitsfield; between them, Warren and Waitsfield are the local support towns for the mammoth ski resort in the mountains above, Sugarbush, which now includes five peaks and a wide variety of recreation options, from hiking and mountain biking and fishing to skiing, Nordic skiing, and off-the-trail winter touring by ski or snowshoe.

Sugarbush Ski Area

The access road to Sugarbush comes from Route 100, between Warren and Waitsfield. Don't take the high back road between the towns, but stay instead on the highway. **Clearwater Sports,** the area's canoe trekking expert, is on the left. So is Sugarbush. Although there may be 6,000 skiers here at any given time in the winter, there's little crowding on the valley roads – Sugarbush was the first of the eastern ski resorts to explore lodging at the foot of the lifts, and it worked brilliantly. The ski village is up on the mountain, and free shuttle buses transport resort guests down to the nightlife of Waitsfield.

Sugarbush is not just a winter resort: mountain biking and a partnership with a hiking boot company have made its summer events lively and well attended, into the glorious fall foliage season. The mountain lifts barely pause for a break in the "mud season" part of spring before rising again to take hikers and cyclists to the peaks.

The five Nordic ski centers in this region also double as bike trail networks in snow-free seasons. And the Long Trail hits some its most dramatic moments along the high peaks here, making this the heart of the state's adventure terrain.

■ Waitsfield

Who would think a little Vermont town in a picturesque river valley would be famous for its pizza? But it's true. Two nationally noted pizza companies are both here – along with a panoply of international cuisine, fine clothing, and galleries. There are also computer consultants, architects, and environmental instructors. A premier bike shop sponsors races, a canoe manufacturer encourages voyaging, and the fishing is supreme. And all this without feeling like a city! This section of Waitsfield is now called Irasville; the more walkable part of town is the picturesque older village half a mile to the north, where there's an 1833 covered bridge over the Mad River (which has an unpredictable flow with wild surges during spring snowmelt). The towering mountains punctuate each day's moods and weather speculations.

Route 17 meets Route 100 in Waitsfield. The road access to "**Sugarbush North,**" the trail network on Mount Ellen and Inverness Peak, is from Route 17, although a quad lift across the intervening wild slopes connects the two regions of the resort also. Route 17 rises to Appalachian Gap, elevation 2,356 feet, part of a local biking challenge competition. It continues toward Bristol and in the far distance Lake Champlain.

Festival lovers should note that Sugarbush hosts the **Ben & Jerry's One World One Heart Festival** in late June, with two days of music, craft booths, and food (especially ice cream!). Check the date with the **Chamber of Commerce** (☎ 496-3409). There's also a **summer bluegrass festival** at Mad River Glen (for dates, ☎ 496-3551).

North of Waitsfield, Route 100 soon arrives at **Waterbury**, home of Ben & Jerry's Ice Cream and of many state offices. Here, the scenic route crosses Interstate 89 and continues to the next major ski resort area at Stowe, then proceeds through increasingly rural landscape toward the Québec border. We investigate this region in *The Capitol District, Stowe & North*.

Adventures

■ On Foot

Bristol

 Bristol is a side trip from Route 7 that offers two interesting hiking areas. To reach Bristol, take Route 7 south from Vergennes for four miles and turn left onto Route 17, which approaches Bristol in another four miles. To the right, the **Bristol Cliffs Wilderness** can be glimpsed. This is Vermont's smallest wilderness area, 3,740 acres, and there are no paths in it; the access path and any other old trails quickly end. It's a map and compass exploration, with deer, black bears, beavers, and grouse (locally called partridge) sharing the space. To find the trail in, drive through Bristol (taking note of the casual eateries and great bookstore!) and look for the right turn to West Lincoln, about two miles out of town. There's a wilderness sign in West Lincoln to direct you onto York Hill Road for 1.7 miles to a 10-car parking area. The footpath enters the wilderness, then disappears. You should have at least the map provided by the Green Mountain National Forest (Middlebury Ranger District, Route 7, RD4, Box 1260, Middlebury, VT 05753; ☎ 388-4362); better yet is adding a USGS topological map. The cliffs, where Native Americans probably gathered quartzite for arrowheads and other tools, are at the western side of the wilderness area. Tramping through the untamed terrain brings you out at the top of the cliffs, where there is a good view of the Champlain Valley from 1,500 feet. The cliffs are the most visited part of this wilderness, so if you like seclusion, explore instead the two small ponds, Gilmore and North.

> CAUTION
>
> *The National Forest Forest Service advises that climbing the Bristol Cliffs can be extremely dangerous. If you go onto the rock slopes remember that Vermont rock tends to be weathered and more likely to give way, and that search and rescue in wilderness areas is your own financial responsibility – know your skill level and respect it!*

The other good Bristol hike is known locally as **The Ledges**. Take the roads back to town and just before (north of where) the shops begin, take

Central Vermont

the right turn, which is Mountain Street but may have no sign. Up ahead you can see the next right onto Mountain Terrace, which does have a sign; go to the end of Mountain Terrace and park. The trail begins just past the barrier. There's a good description of landmarks in the Green Mountain Club's *Day Hiker's Guide to Vermont*; mostly you need to know to turn left when you reach the large water tank serving as the town reservoir, and to expect a steep climb that's well worth while for the serene valley-wide vista at the top. The entire trail is only a mile long, and your descent takes much less time!

WATCHABLE

WILDLIFE

Keep an eye out for woodpeckers here; the small black and white ones are the hairy and the downy, but you may be lucky enough to spot the large pileated with its bright red crest and wide wing span.

Westward view from the Bristol Ledges.

Ripton & Bread Loaf

From Bristol, rather than go all the way back to Route 7, turn south on Route 116 and go about five miles to an unpaved road on the left marked with a US Forest Service sign – this is the turn for the **Abbey Pond Trail.** When the road forks (immediately), go right; it's 0.4 mile to the parking area, where you need to be well off the road to let gravel trucks go by. The trail goes straight ahead and right away you reach a series of cascades, or small waterfalls. The hike is about two miles, up but not very steeply, to the secluded woods pond. If you can get there early enough in the morning, bring field glasses for birdwatching. By the way, this trail is often wet underfoot!

Route 116 continues to East Middlebury, where it connects you with Route 125 east, your entry into the Green Mountains and Robert Frost country. Bring along some of his poems to look for connections, or stop at the **Robert Frost Interpretive Trail** on Route 125 about two miles past the mountain village of Ripton; here, some of Frost's poems are displayed on plaques along a mile-long easy pathway that's been designed to be barrier-free for handicapped access.

Just past the Robert Frost trailhead, there's a fork where Route 125 bears right. If you bear left instead, you'll find a trailhead for the **Skylight Pond Trail,** but this area is seeing too much use according to the Green Mountain Club, which maintains the Long Trail (Vermont's end-to-end hiking trail) and its spurs; do the area a favor and pick another hike. A different way to reach the Long Trail is to stay on Route 125 and pass by the Bread Loaf Campus of Middlebury College; the Long Trail crosses the road two miles past the campus, where the Middlebury College Snow Bowl ski area takes advantage of the terrain. If you choose to hike the **Long Trail** northward, you'll tramp over Burnt Hill, Kirby Peak, Boyce Mountain, and then arrive at Skylight Pond and the Skyline Shelter (fee) just beyond. This is a nice 5.6-mile sample of the Long Trail, going through the southern part of the **Breadloaf Wilderness,** and you'll feel you've had a taste of what the end-to-enders enjoy. For additional challenge, at the 0.4 mile point, where there's a junction, take the right-hand trail another 0.4 mile to Silent Cliff, where good views make up for the challenge of a difficult climb of 400 feet change in elevation.

The next recreation area along Route 125 is Texas Falls, which we view instead from the Hancock approach later in this section.

Seven miles south of Middlebury (or three miles from East Middlebury) on Route 7 is the well-marked left turn for Lake Dunmore. There's a fish hatchery to visit here, and after a mile there's a major "four corners," where the right-hand road goes down the west shore of the lake. The **Moosalamoo Recreation Area** is on the east shore, so ignore the right turn and go straight ahead past Kampersville (oh all right, stop for an ice cream or some hot fried food first). Get out your copy of the *Day Hiker's Guide to Vermont* for the most detailed trail descriptions. You can also get maps from the Middlebury Ranger District of the Green Mountain National Forest (RR4, Box 1260, Middlebury, VT 05753; ☎ 388-6688; located on Route 7 south of Middlebury, across from Rosie's Restaurant).

The first stop is the **Branbury State Park Nature Trail,** a pleasant one-third-mile introduction to the natural history of the area. Park at the state park campground and picnic area and pick up information from the natu-

Central Vermont

ralists on duty during the camping season. From the camping area, look for the blue-blazed **Falls of Lana Trail** to get you started into Moosalamoo. It's half a mile to the Falls of Lana picnic area, and a trail junction just past there will connect you with the **Rattlesnake Cliffs Trail** (which in turn leads to the Oak Ridge, Moosalamoo, and North Branch trails) to your left. If you bear right with the Falls of Lana Trail instead, you meet the **Silver Lake Trail** in another 0.2 mile. The Falls of Lana are a short distance downstream, where Sucker Brook has carved a deep gorge in the rock. Either continue down to the highway on the Falls of Lana Trail, wrapping up a 1.2-mile scenic walk, or else charge onto Silver Brook Trail and head for the Silver Lake dam, the lake itself, and the rocky slopes of Chandler Ridge. The far side of Silver Lake, the east shore, has a mountain-biking trail along it, part of the network of bike trails in the heart of Moosalamoo.

Two cautions about the maps of Moosalamoo: One, the forest roads marked so neatly in brown are wonderful summer and fall routes into the recreation area, but don't count on them being plowed in winter! Two, in winter there are specially designated ski and snowmobile trails that are groomed for these sports; it's a lot easier for the skiers if hikers, with their hole-punching boots, stay on the other trails instead.

Forest Road 32 runs north and south through the center of Moosalamoo, from Ripton in the north to Goshen in the south, and is a good access to the ski trails now in the heart of Moosalamoo. There's parking and camping at the center of the recreation area near a trailhead for Mt. Moosalamoo.

MOOSALAMOO HISTORY

By now you're probably curious about the name Moosalamoo: it's an Abenaki word meaning "the moose departs," or maybe "he trails the moose." The band of Abenaki in this region was called the Mississquoi, and was displaced by European settlers in the early 1700s. Brandon and Middlebury Gaps were travel ways though the mountains for the nomadic tribe. Artifacts found locally indicate Moosalamoo was an Abenaki winter encampment site, and their dugout canoes were found in Silver Lake (carbon dating sets them at over 300 years old). Also near the north end of Silver Lake are traces of a grand hotel that once stood there; signs of old tow ropes from early ski trails can be spotted.

Pittsford

There's a 32-acre walking trail network in this small town, created in what was once abandoned pasture. It's accessible year-round and has nice vistas as well as a wide variety of trees, mosses, and plumed marsh grasses. At the north edge of town as you enter from Route 7 there's a left turn onto Plains Road, where the Pittsford Municipal Offices are; pick up a trail map here (☎ 483-2931). If you like, enter the trail network behind the offices, or go back to Route 7 and drive south past the church and village green; when you see the Lothrop School and the Pittsford Historical Society Museum on the right, take the next left onto Furnace Road. The main entrance to the trails is on the left, a half-mile from Route 7.

Rutland

Didn't expect the city to have hiking opportunities? Actually, there are two chances to start in Rutland and have a great hike. One is with **Highlander Hiking** (☎ 800-429-8268), which will take you by courtesy van to the nearby mountains; the guided hikes are on weekdays, graded for novice to experienced, and require 24 hours notice. The other connection in town is through the **Great Outdoors Travel Adventure Company,** located along with a specialized sporting goods store at 219 Woodstock Avenue. Owner Bob Harbish and outfitter Chuck Wagonheim put together bike tours, ski trips, in-line skate camps, performance ski camps, fly-fishing clinics and schools, and archery and ultimate adventure camps. Stop at the store and find out whether they have any activities planned that you'd like to join, or call ahead (☎ 800-345-5182; e-mail cortina1@ aol.com; visit their Web site at: www.genghis.com/cortinainn/html/hiking-biking-htm).

Green Mountain Rock Climbing Center at 223 Woodstock Avenue (☎ 773-3343, e-mail gmrcc@aol.com) has over 8,000 square feet of climbing surface with 26-foot-high textured climbing walls, complete with wild murals. Guides will also take you on outdoor climbing adventures by arrangement. Classes, workshops, and rentals come at attractive prices.

Orwell

When you visit the American Revolution battlefield at Hubbardton and the archaeological site and visitor center at the old military complex at Mount Independence in Orwell, you can also take advantage of scenic hiking trails at **Mount Independence.** There's the 2.5-mile **Orange Trail** that crosses the high point of the mountain and goes out to the shoreline and back; the short **Red Trail** (0.6 mile) allows hikers to catch views of Mt. Defiance and Fort Ticonderoga; and the **White Trail** (0.8 mile) to the east side of the area.

Lake Bomoseen State Park

For a pleasant ramble, especially with kids, try the nature trails at this state park, open year-round, although certainly less accessible in winter. See touring directions (page 171) also to **Half Moon Pond State Park** nearby, where another two miles of nature trails add to what you might want to share with excited youngsters. Bring field glasses and teach the kids to approach Half Moon Pond quietly; you may spot some unusual waterfowl.

For less structured wildlife explorations, try the **Orwell Pond Wildlife Management Area** to the north, and the **Blueberry Hill Wildlife Management Area** east of the town of Castleton; don't expect paths, and prepare for wet feet, but also for a sense of peace.

Pico Peak & The Long Trail

Heading up Route 4 from Rutland, the landmarks tend to be shops and restaurants. For instance, after Sweatertown USA on the right comes the Killington-Pico Motor Lodge, and across the road from there is Turnpike Road (aka Elbow Road). Take this road to the lane on the left, which is the trailhead for the blue-blazed **Canty Trail.** If you like steep and rocky, this one's a delight. It takes 2.4 miles to reach the summit of Blue Ridge Mountain, a good workout. For more views, hike down to the rocky outcrop southwest of the main summit.

The next landmark on Route 4 is Churchill's Restaurant, about seven miles up from Rutland, on the right-hand side. To get to the luxurious **Cortina Inn**, which has walking trails among its gardens and some trail connections toward the higher hiking terrain, when you spot Churchill's move into the center lane immediately for a right turn. And if you reach the entrance to Pico Ski and Summer Resort on the right, you've overshot the Cortina.

The alpine slide at **Pico Ski and Summer Resort** (☎ 775-4346 or 800-898-PICO) is the resort's big summer and fall attraction, but the ski trails also offer good hiking to the peak at 3,957 feet. The **Long Trail** also comes close to the summit. Pick it up where it hits Route 4, but be careful to choose the well-marked white blazes, not the side trails. The 10-mile round trip on the Long Trail from Route 4 over Pico Peak to Killington, the state's second highest mountaintop, offers spectacular panoramic views of three mountain ranges: the Greens, the Taconics, and the Adirondacks. You can take a short spur over to the resort (open mid-June to mid-October for hikers) at Killington Peak for hot food and more great views from the tower. The chairlift can give you an easy trip down to the Killington base lodge during these months, too.

For a very organized and well-supported approach to the trails on and around Killington, visit the **Killington Hiking Center** at the Base Lodge of the resort (☎ 422-6776). Open from late June through mid-October, the center provides maps and optional guides to the trail system; a staff naturalist offers interpretive hikes enriched with topography, geology, and plant and animal knowledge. There are also special interest tours, such as birdwatching, wildflowers, photography, and geology; call for dates and details. Boots and backpacks can be rented; this is a great way to try out hiking boot styles. Child care is available on summer weekdays, with reservations required in advance.

A popular day hike from Route 4 in Sherburne Pass is to take the Long Trail north instead, to Deer Leap in the **Gifford Woods State Park;** however, the Green Mountain Club cautions that this trail is seeing too much use and the ecosystems along it are suffering. You can do something positive for this frail alpine environment by picking a different hike.

Pittsfield

At the north end of the village green, on the left if you're heading away from Killington on Route 100, is the Pittsfield Inn. The inn's activity center, **Escape Routes** (PO Box 685, Pittsfield, VT 05762; ☎ 746-8942; e-mail escapert@vermontel.com), provides guided and self-guided hiking tours, with trail maps and navigational challenges. Programs start in March and end in October; inn owner Tom Yennerell describes them as "easy strolls on well-worn paths as well as early and late winter assaults on 4,000-foot peaks" – take your pick!

Rochester

The ranger station for the **Green Mountain National Forest**, three miles north of where Route 73 meets Route 100, has a wealth of hiking trail maps and advice on everything from water safety to wildlife photography.

From the ranger station, backtrack three miles south on Route 100 and turn onto Route 73, driving up into the mountains. It is 9.5 miles to the top of **Brandon Gap,** where there is a parking area on the left. The trail here is actually the **Long Trail**, and there are two good hikes, one north, one south. Heading north first there's a half-mile climb to the summit of **Mount Horrid.** It's a difficult, steep route, but the views extend over the Lake Champlain Valley.

WATCHABLE

WILDLIFE

From March to August in some years, the cliffs here are closed to protect nesting peregrine falcons. Bring your field glasses and watch for these birds of prey, just reestablishing after facing extinction in Vermont. Watch the beaver ponds, especially early in the day, for browsing moose (but don't get too close to a moose, ever!).

Taking the Long Trail south from Route 100 for one mile, an easy walk through the woods, brings you to **Sunrise Shelter.** From a clearing along the way there's a view of the Great Cliff of Mount Horrid.

When you come back down Route 73 toward Rochester, watch for FR45, a little more than three miles down from Brandon Gap. Turn right (south) on the forest road, reaching a trailhead parking lot in half a mile. This is the **Chittenden Brook Trail,** which parallels the waterway and intersects the Long Trail at 3.7 miles. It's a challenging stretch; if you go all the way to the Long Trail and back, expect it to take five hours. The wetlands you walk around is a good spot for wildlife viewing; approach quietly and stay still for a while.

Hancock

Leave Route 100 by taking Route 125 west, up toward Middlebury Gap. After 3.1 miles you'll find a right turn into the **Texas Falls Recreation Area.** Across the road from the first parking area are the Texas Falls. Look for the rustic footbridge, where a nature trail meanders along the brook and picnic area. To get to the upper section of the nature trail, bear right before crossing the paved road. The trail circles back to the falls, 1.2 miles total.

A two-mile easy ramble on the **Hancock Branch Trail** follows an old logging road, passing through various stages of forest succession and showing you a wide variety of plantlife and birds to note. (Did you bring your bird list from the Rochester ranger station with you?) To get here, drive into the recreation area and past the picnic spot, parking near the gate.

Granville

As you head north from Hancock along Route 100, the mountains to the left of you are part of the **Breadloaf Wilderness**. This is Vermont's largest designated wilderness area, covering over 21,000 acres, and includes the state's own "Presidential" range, Mounts Wilson, Roosevelt, Cleveland, and Grant. The **Long Trail** runs the length of this wilderness, more than 17 miles passing over 17 major peaks. The highest point in the wilderness is Bread Loaf Mountain, 3,835 feet, from which the area takes its name.

The best access into Breadloaf Wilderness is traditionally from the Long Trail, either from Lincoln Gap southward or from Middlebury Gap northward. But you can also enter the heart of the wilderness from Granville on FR55, which leads to the Clark Brook Trail; the forest road is closed in winter.

WILDERNESS AREAS

Wilderness areas in national forests are Congressionally designated as defined in the Wilderness Act of 1964: "an area where the earth and its community of life are untrammeled by man, where man himself is a visitor who does not remain." The Forest Service encourages hikers to dress in subdued colors and blend into the surroundings, and keep voices low, for their own quiet pleasure and to help others appreciate the wilderness without too much human distraction. Camping and fires (from dead and downed wood only) are permitted, but with as little trace as possible, which means digging a shallow fire pit and then, after dowsing your fire, replacing the sod to erase signs of your stay.

You are on your own in wilderness areas, and need to be a good judge of your own skills and gear before going too far off the beaten trails. That said, though, the Forest Service does encourage bushwhacking; nobody is going to tell you to stay on the path. (But if you overreach and need search and rescue service, you'll be responsible for the cost.)

WATCHABLE

WILDLIFE

There are both black bears and moose in this wilderness, as well as deer, foxes, squirrels, raccoons, and abundant birdlife. Remember that although the bears and moose are shy, if you approach too close they get defensive and are unpredictable; keep your distance. Also remember that an animal that looks sick or behaves oddly, such as approaching a human, may have rabies; you don't want to take the chance of a bite or scratch, so again, keep that distance and let your eyes or camera do the approaching.

Watch for the brown and white FR55 sign for the left turn from Route 100, not even a mile north of Granville village. It's two miles along FR55 to the **Clark Brook Trailhead**. This is a three-mile hike that goes along the stream, crosses two bridges (after the second you're in the wilderness), and ascends to the Long Trail. The Forest Service doesn't offer ratings of wilderness trails, "in keeping with the wilderness ethic of self discovery" – check a topographical map if you're unsure of your ability to make the whole climb (but going back is easy enough). When you reach the Long Trail, do leave time for a northward hike on it for another 0.4 mile to the top of **Mount Roosevelt,** which offers a deeply satisfying view of the Upper White River Valley.

Central Vermont

Warren

As Route 100 enters Warren, so does the **Lincoln Gap Road:** it's on the left side, well marked, the old familiar route to the gap's pass-through at 2,424 feet. The road asks a lot of a car, and in the snowy season it closes at the top; you must use a lower, longer road to reach Bristol or Middlebury. In summertime, as the world turns green and blue and explodes with birdsong, the Gap Road is irresistible. It is also an entryway to the Green Mountain National Forest, especially to Mount Abraham.

So on a summer or glorious autumn day, drive the five miles up to the top of Lincoln Gap and find a place to park. Here, the **Long Trail** crosses the road, and your options are to go north or south. South takes you into the Breadloaf Wilderness; it's about three miles of tough hiking to Mount Grant from here. But for a vista, just hike 0.6 mile south and find the right-hand turn, a short trail that takes you to a good view south over the Champlain Valley.

A difficult trail with a 1,500-foot climb in elevation is the trip north on the Long Trail from Lincoln Gap to Mount Abraham, peak elevation 4,052 feet. Two miles north on the Long Trail is Battell Shelter, with bunk space for eight people. There's a small spring 100 feet to the east, likely to be safer than most because it's up above the beaver level, but not above the humans, so decide for yourself whether to indulge. Continue another 0.8 mile up the Long Trail (steep) to get to the panoramic summit view. Expect the round trip to take about five hours.

Sugarbush Resort

Sugarbush Resort includes six interconnected mountain peaks and 4,500 acres of terrain. The resort has teamed up with a crafter of mountain hiking footwear, Dolomite, and with the National Forest Service to create a trekking center. There are guided ecological treks, as well as more difficult adventures that meet the Long Trail and head for the mountain peaks. Contact Sugarbush at PO Box 350, Access Road, Warren, VT 05674-9500 (☎ 583-3333 or 800-53SUGAR). Lift service allows you to ride up and walk down, or vice versa, if you want a change of pace.

A list of more hikes here can be obtained from the **Sugarbush Chamber of Commerce**, which is on Route 100 just south of the village of Waitsfield (PO Box 173, Waitsfield, VT 05673; ☎ 496-3409 or 800-82-VISIT).

Waitsfield

Although there's a trail leading to Burnt Rock Mountain from the North Fayston Road, the Green Mountain Club warns that this area is getting overused; do the mountain a favor and pick a different hike.

Hiking in the Green Mountains is part of the inn-to-inn tours that **Hiking Holidays of Bristol** assembles (☎ 453-4816 or 800-537-3850, e-mail info@VBT.com). The vacation packages are pre-planned, but are also available in custom or private versions. This is a luxurious way to relax into your escape from routine.

If you are more interested in staying off the beaten track, but don't want to do the planning yourself, **Adventure Guides of Vermont** (☎ 425-6211 or 800-425-TRIP) might be the outdoor service for you. These guides arc determined to find out-of-the-way places where you can focus on, say, rock climbing, or birding, or bushwhacking, or wildlife photography. Based in North Ferrisburgh, north of Vergennes, AGVT offers year-round programs and a chance to design your own tour, from a morning bird walk to a week-long excursion. The group of guides also has experience in team-building programs, and offers courses in back-country first aid, survival, and search and rescue.

Country Inns Along the Trail presents a blend of serious hiking (eight to 10 miles a day, sometimes steep) with the intimacy of small country inns from the bygone era of horse-drawn carriages. This specialized touring service focuses on the Long Trail and its most lovely surroundings, and has matched day trips with inn-keepers who like personal contact with their guests and create comfortable retreats at the end of the day. The service is based in Brandon (RR3, Box 3115, Brandon, VT 05733, ☎ 247-3300, Web site www.inntoinn.com) and the inns extend from Marble Inn of Dorset north to the Siebeness in the foothills of Mt. Mansfield, near Stowe. Meals, trail familiarization, and car shuttle are included. This is a lovely way to have the independence of self-guided hiking along the Long Trail, with the support of experienced hikers and the comforts of charming inns.

■ On Horseback

The University of Vermont **Morgan Horse Farm** just outside Middlebury (see *Touring*) may be one reason that horse lovers are drawn to this region; the other is clearly the terrain, rolling and verdant, perfect for horse barns and for riding and carriage pulling.

The Firefly Ranch in Bristol (PO Box 152, Bristol, VT 05443; ☎ 453-2223) is a small inn that offers trail riding for its guests on country roads and on trails in the foothills.

Eight miles west of Middlebury on Route 125 is the small town of Bridport, where **Mazza Horse Service** offers guided trail ride lessons (RD1, Box 200, Hemenway Road, Bridport, VT 05734-9709; ☎ 758-9240). Deb and

Frank Mazza provide a warm-up in the ring, then guide small groups onto trails through the woods, beside the Lemon Fair River, and on quiet country roads; riders may be beginners to advanced, and seated English or Western.

Chittenden, at the edge of the Green Mountain National Forest, can be reached from either Pittsford or Rutland. Here the **Mountain Top Inn** (Chittenden, VT 05737; ☎ 800-445-2100), a luxurious resort, offers riding vacation clinics in summer and fall, with a focus on either dressage and evening, or hunter/jumper. The inn also provides riding vacations with hour-long or half-day rides and provides specialized group instruction in English, Western, dressage, jumping, and introductory polo. Bring your own mount if you like!

If you're in the Killington/Rutland area, call ahead to **Mountain View Ranch** (Letitia and John Sisters, Danby, ☎ 293-5837), to find out whether trail rides will be available during your visit.

South of Rutland, in Castleton, **Horse Amour** on Eaton Hill Road offers equestrian options (☎ 468-2200), and **Pond Hill Ranch** (☎ 468-2449) provides pony rides as well as scenic mountain trail rides, plus a professional rodeo on summer Saturday nights.

Another inn offering trail rides is the **Mad River Inn** of Waitsfield (☎ 496-7900), located on Route 10B north of the center of town. So do the **Waitsfield Inn** (Route 100, 496-3979), the **West Hill House** (Warren, ☎ 496-7162), and the **Millbrook Inn & Restaurant** (Route 17, Waitsfield, ☎ 496-2405).

Working closely with the Waitsfield and Warren inns is **Vermont Icelandic Horse Farm of Waitsfield.** The farm breeds and sells these sturdy, graceful horses whose tireless and efficient movement keeps them steady either on summer trails or in winter snow. Qualified European instructors give lessons. Inn-to-inn treks of two or six days are offered here, as well as full- and half-day rides on the four- and five-gaited horses. Reservations are necessary; call or write (☎ 496-7141, PO Box 577, Waitsfield, VT 05673).

Sugarbush Resort (Warren, ☎ 583-3333 or 800-53SUGAR) includes horseback riding among its snow-free seasonal activities. This resort also uses Icelandic horses, and provides lessons as well as guided trail rides.

In Waitsfield the Meg Hilly-Anderson School of Horsemanship is at **Dana Hill Stable** (☎ 496-6251), where lessons and trail rides can be arranged. Also in Waitsfield, **Kenyon's Farm** hosts part of the Vermont Summer Festival of equestrian events; get in touch at ☎ 496-4878. Nearby in Morestown on Route 100 is **Navajo Farm** (☎ 496-3656), which also offers trail rides and instruction.

■ On Wheels

Road Biking

The farmscape to the west of the **Green Mountains** is perfect for road touring, gently rolling and winding along brooks and small rivers. Avoid the heavy traffic on Routes 7 (through Middlebury and Rutland) and 22A (close to the shore of Lake Champlain). The valley portions of Routes 125 and 73 are nice traveling, as are Routes 116 and 30 in the north-south direction. If you're in Middlebury, try swinging onto Route 23, maybe making a side trip to the University of Vermont Morgan Horse Farm, and continuing toward Vergennes. When you reach Route 17, take the unpaved road north for a rising plateau that gives some nice views before arriving at Vergennes itself. From Vergennes, a nearly parallel road will return you through Weybridge to Middlebury. Trip planning as well as bike service in Middlebury can be found at the **Bike and Ski Touring Center** (74 Main Street, ☎ 388-6666).

Bristol is the home of **Vermont Bicycle Touring**. John Freidin, who founded this original country inn bicycling vacation business, is the author of *25 Bicycle Tours in Vermont*. It pays to profit from his years of touring experience; the book lays out great tours, mostly a day long but some take two days. The tour he suggests starting from Bristol is one that loops through Monkton and Starksboro, passing **Vermont Bicycle Touring** on the way (Monkton Road, Bristol, ☎ 453-4811). Do at least find VBT for yourself and, if you take this bike tour, be sure to stop at **Robert Compton's pottery studio** (on Route 16; ☎ 453-3778) to see the outdoor kilns and working pottery run by Compton and Christine Homer.

Freidin's book also offers a good tour that runs from **Brandon**, north of Rutland, across the rolling farmlands to Orwell where Mount Independence is, and then on the Shorewell Ferry from Larrabees Point over to New York State to visit Fort Ticonderoga. Another option for the battlefield buff is to visit both Orwell (Mount Independence) and the Hubbardton battlefield on the same day, including a stop at secluded Half Moon Pond State Park for lunch and a swim.

Another great biking tour is the 12-mile loop around **Lake Dunmore**, just south of **Middlebury** off Route 7. Take Route 53 east from Route 7 and, if you've arrived by car, park at Kampersville (do stop at the desk and get the okay). Circle the lake clockwise, starting with Route 53 and passing trailheads for hiking trails, reaching the southern end and continuing south to Fernville to include Fern Lake in your loop. Then head north on West Shore Road, Rodgers Road (briefly), and then West Shore Road again, to return to Route 53. The total loop is 12 miles on paved and gravel roads. Bring a swimsuit! If you're on a mountain bike and want an extra challenge, connect with the Moosalamoo trails (described later in this section) and head to Silver Lake and the Green Mountain National Forest.

Remember **Country Inns Along the Trail**, the group of fine small inns positioned to make life easy for hikers on the Long Trail? They also offer self-guided bicycling vacations, mostly starting and ending at the Churchill House in Brandon. Tours come in two basic varieties: along the gentle short hills of the Champlain Valley, or through the challenging passes of the Green Mountains. Get in touch and discuss your preferences (RR3, Box 3115, Brandon, VT 05733; ☎ 247-3300). Either way, you'll be spending nights in cozy inns where the innkeepers fuss to feed you well and make you comfortable before the next morning's ride. Luggage shuttle is also available; so is rental equipment.

Mountain Biking

Mountain bikers will exult in the trail system that the Green Mountain National Forest has laid out in the **Moosalamoo** region. Start from the west shore of Lake Dunmore at the parking area for the Silver Lake Trail on Route 53. Look at a Moosalamoo map before you start; your goal is to get to the far side of the lake and meet up with Forest Road 27. Head southeast on FR27 until it crosses the main north-south forest road of Moosalamoo, FR32. Drop south on FR32 to the right turn onto FR243, and connect with the **Minnie Baker Trail.** You can either bike down the Minnie Baker to Route 53 and back up the east shore of the lake to where you started, or choose the **Leicester Hollow Trail,** another designated mountain bike route, to get back to Silver Lake. The plus of the **Leicester Hollow Trail** is the chance to look for old cellar holes and other evidence of the 19th-century community that once thrived here.

Admittedly, this trail network is just a start on bike access to the Green Mountain National Forest, wherein there are few other bike routes. Only the forest roads and town highways are open to mountain biking now, but the GMNF is working on their next master plan, and by 2005 there will be greatly expanded access for mountain bikers to most of the recreation areas now set up for hikers and skiers.

Catch up with guided mountain biking at the **Cortina Inn and Resort** on Route 4 between Rutland and Killington (☎ 773-3333 or 800-451-6108, www.cortinainn.com). There are day tours as well as explore-it-yourself rentals. See page 203 for information about accommodations at the inn.

Rutland has four more bike shops: **Green Mountain Schwinn Cyclery** (133 Strongs Avenue, ☎ 775-0869); **Marble City Bicycles** (1 Scale Avenue, ☎ 747-1471); **Mountain Tread-n-Shred** (150½ Woodstock Avenue, ☎ 747-7080); and **Sports Peddler** (158 North Main Street, ☎ 775-0101).

Killington caught mountain bike fever some time ago and now has a complete mountain bike center with standard and high-performance rentals, as well as a repair and accessory shop. Guided trail rides, instruction sessions, lift access so you can take the easy way up and savor the excitement of coming down, without being worn out ahead of time – the mountain resort has gone all out. The lift is open weekends in the early season and then daily from mid-June to mid-October; call to check exact dates (☎ 422-6232 or 800-621-MTNS, Web site www.killington.com).

BIKE RACES AND EVENTS

■ July: **Beauty and the Beast Mountain Bike Weekend**, at Killington, the biggest NORBA-sanctioned mountain bike race and festival in the East. Includes cross-country, dual slalom, and short track derby. ☎ 800-621-MTNS.

■ August: **Thunder and Lightning**, at Killington, sixth stop on the Nike ACG New England Mountain Bike Championship series. For both avid racers and recreational cyclists. ☎ 800-621-MTNS.

■ August: **Apple Country Century** (road), riding 25, 50, or 100 miles, starts in Brandon. ☎ 247-3300.

■ September (Labor Day Weekend): **Killington Stage Race** (road), at Killington, one of America's largest stage races. ☎ 800-621-MTNS.

Great Escapes: Road & Mountain Resources

When you head north from **Killington** along Route 100, maybe the state's most scenic highway, the traffic can be heavy, especially during foliage season (late September). Get to Pittsfield at the north side of the village green, where the Pittsfield Inn has established its **Escape Routes** (☎ 746-8943), and you can relax. Escape Routes offers guided and self-guided tours from May to mid-October, sending mountain bikers on gentle grass-covered abandoned roads past long-gone settlements deep in the forest, or along steep single tracks plummeting down mountainsides, according to the rider's preference.

If you're still pedaling Route 100 in **Rochester** (and the river view from the bike is so good that it's hard to resist, despite the cars), make sure to stop at the Rochester Café, an area tradition complete with soda fountain. Rochester also has **Green Mountain Bikes** (☎ 767-4464), where you can get repairs, rent a mountain bike that's been specially geared, or tune in to outback guide service. The shop describes itself as "specializing in mountain bikes and dramatic repairs."

Of course, Route 100 north is eventually going to take you out of the lonely and lovely wild river valley villages and into populated territory again.

Central Vermont

Let's suppose you're pedaling north on Route 100 and you're coming into Warren, the first of the two support towns for the massive Sugarbush Resort. You can stay on Route 100 and have pleasant pedaling, with some traffic ahead in the half-mile of shops in Irasville (the southern village of Waitsfield), or you can take the back road north and really work those calves and thighs. To take this hilly side trip, in Warren, take the right turn toward East Warren, go through the covered bridge, and arrive at the Warren General Store, where French bread, fine wines, and delicatessen goodies will make a great lunch to eat on the spot or carry a little further. Then take the turn by the bandstand and head uphill, a challenging but do-able back road first toward East Warren and then on to Waitsfield. It's eight miles total, and some of it is really steep, but the sense of being entirely surrounded by the mountains is outstanding. Besides, you have the chance to detour to the Warren Airport and take a glider ride or just relax as you eat that lunch you toted up.

Another plus of this back road is the **Blueberry Lake Cross Country Center** in East Warren (☎ 496-6687), a mountain bike trail center in the snow-free seasons. Call ahead to be sure the snow is really gone and the mud has receded far enough.

You'll have to stay with Route 100 if you're headed for Sugarbush – but maybe at this point you'll be in the car, with the bike behind you. The main access to Sugarbush is a left (westward) turn from Route 100, and you're looking for the **Sugarbush Mountain Bike Center** (☎ 800-53SUGAR). There's a full-service bike shop, and the resort offers you "gentle cruisers, knarly descents, or a back road that provides spectacular mountain views." So take it! There are lift-serviced trails that let you start up high without being exhausted and cruise downward at your own pace over the un-snowy ski trails. Look for the Terrain Garden, the dual slalom course, and the "moto park," too.

The back road from Warren reaches Waitsfield and Route 100 a little north of Route 73, so if you want to visit the **Mad River Bike Shop** (Routes 100 & 17, Waitsfield, ☎ 496-9500) and you've taken the back way you'll have to go down the main highway south a mile or so. But it's worth the trip: this shop is dedicated to making the Mad River Valley the most exciting biking in the East, complete with a century ride with sag wagon; a road race or two mountain bike camps for teens; and the Mad King Challenge, a grueling set of mountain passes to ride. The shop also offers guided and custom tours as well as rentals. Mountain bikers might want to check out the advanced clinics and all-terrain park at **Madbush Falls Country Motel** (PO Box 457, Waitsfield, VT 05673, ☎ 496-5557).

■ On Water

Rivers To Run

Many of the rivers in this region are too small or too shallow for good paddling. The best choices are:

- The **Lemon Fair River** from Shoreham Center near Lake Champlain, to where it meets the Otter Creek 18 miles later, but watch the small dams in the first section. Consult the Appalachian Mountain Club (AMC) *River Guide* and then walk the questionable parts, since the river was last surveyed for the guide in 1983.

- **Otter Creek** from Proctor to the Threemile Bridge near the mouth of the Middlebury River, 32 miles later. This is passable at all water levels and the scenery is lovely, mostly farmlands.

- The **White River** from Granville to Stockbridge, a 14.5-mile stretch of quickwater with a few short rapids. Make sure to walk the area a half-mile after the VT73 bridge if you're not paddling with a companion who already knows this area.

- For dramatic spring whitewater, the **Mad River** from Warren to Waitsfield, about 7.5 miles of April adventure with ledges and chutes. Stop at **Clearwater Sports** (Route 100 between Warren and Waitsfield in Irasville, ☎ 496-2708) to get information and cautions, and do walk the run before you paddle. Cold-water canoeing is risky enough; get familiar with the water before you're in the middle of it. While you're in town, visit the **Mad River Canoe Company** showroom about a tenth of a mile south (☎ 496-3127), behind the Grand Union.

Flatwater Paddling & Sailing

The lakes large enough for good sailing here are **Dunmore** and **Bomoseen**. On the west shore of Bomoseen in Hydeville is **Duda's Water Sports** (☎ 265-3432) renting fishing boats, water skiing equipment, and paddleboats. There are also boat rentals at the state parks at Bomoseen and Half Moon Pond for campers.

Fishing

The **White River** is now home to Atlantic salmon parrs (young salmon), in the exciting return of this fish to Vermont's rivers. Please be sure to release any you have caught; the Green Mountain National Forest ranger offices have a leaflet on telling the brown trout and salmon apart.

Central Vermont

Stream fishing is especially good on the east side of the **Green Mountain National Forest,** in the area served by the Rochester ranger district. Pick up the district listing of streams at the ranger office on Route 100, three miles north of where Route 73 comes down from Brandon Gap. Expect to be fly-fishing for rainbow and brook trout.

The terrain west of **Middlebury** and **Rutland** is scattered with small ponds and lakes. Almost all can be accessed for paddling and fishing. If you're looking for rainbow trout, though, narrow in on Lake Dunmore, Chittenden Reservoir, Glen Lake, Half Moon Pond (in Half Moon Pond State Park), Kent Pond, Silver Lake (in Moosalamoo), Star Lake, and Sunset Lake (near Hortonia). The most common lake fish are yellow perch, bass, chain pickerel, and bullhead.

The Cortina Inn and Resort (☎ 733-3333), near Killington, is the home of **Stream and Brook Fly Fishing**, a guide service and casting school.

BASS FISHING IN THE LAKES

Word from the Rutland area is that these are great days for bass fishing, maybe the best yet. Largemouth bass, found mostly in weed-choked quiet waters, feed on minnows, frogs, and crayfish; you can use these for bait, or use nightcrawlers or surface lures and plugs. Try for early morning or just before dark. Smallmouth bass, on the other hand, prefer gravelly or rocky shorelines and respond best to minnows and nightcrawlers. **Lake Bomoseen**, accessed from the West Shore Road in Castleton, has arguably the best bass fishing of Vermont's inland lakes (notice that leaves out Champlain). For largemouth bass try the north end; smallmouths are along the shorelines of the main part of the lake and, when the water gets really warm in mid-summer, look for them along the weed lines in water about 20 feet deep. Shoreline angling is also possible from Bomoseen

Lake Hortonia in Hubbardton breeds largemouth bass as big as eight pounds, and you'll also run into northern pike in the weeds there. Northern pike also grow huge (would you believe 30 pounds?) at **Glen Lake** in West Castleton, where largemouth bass and rainbows compete. Remember to get this year's license and limits information at a local general store or town clerk's office (or from Vermont Department of Fish and Wildlife, ☎ 800-VERMONT).

ACCESSIBILITY NOTE: *Lake Bomoseen has a wheelchair-accessible fishing platform at the Kehoe access area.*

FISHING GUIDES & OUTFITTERS

If you're yearning to learn to fly-fish (or ready for some polish and someone else's tricks of the trade), there are a number of guides and outfitters available. Justin Rogers, at **Three Forks Fly-fisher** in East Middlebury (☎ 388-6575), gives instruction and guiding in the Green Mountain National Forest for beginners or intermediates, with choices like group or private instruction, and day trips. *The Vermont Traveler's Guidebook* (from the Vermont Chamber of Commerce; pick it up at any state rest area, or contact the chamber by e-mail at VT.Chamber@InternetMCI.com) lists some in Bomoseen, Rutland, Vergennes, and Waitsfield. Also, there's an Orvis-endorsed outfitter in Killington: **Vermont Bound Outfitters** (HCR34, Box 28, Killington, VT 05751, ☎ 773-0736 or 800-639-3167), with guided tours, a full Orvis shop, and fly-fishing school.

Swimming

Looking to get into the water for a good swim? Lakes **Dunmore** and **Bomoseen** each have nice beaches. State parks with swimming are **Half Moon Pond** (near Bomoseen), **Branbury** (Brandon), **D.A.R.** (Vergennes), and there's a pond at **Mt. Philo State Park** (North Ferrisburgh). Another swimming option is in Rutland, at the south end of town: a seven-acre pond called **Eddy Pond**, at the end of Curtis Avenue, which meets Route 7 south of the state fairgrounds. The **White River** will do for a quick splash as you wade in the shallows, and the **Mad River** has good swimming holes, easy to find on your own or ask at the sports shops.

■ On Snow & Ice

Downhill Skiing

There are two major downhill ski resorts in this region: Killington, which is now connected with little brother slope Pico, and Sugarbush. An unusual arrangement is found at Mad River Glen, a smaller slope entirely owned by cooperative (mostly skiing) investors and maintained as much wilder, with all natural snow and a single lift. Middlebury College also operates a smaller slope, the Snow Bowl, where racers train and there's plenty of space to move (and short lift lines).

Killington (☎ 800-533-8843, Routes 4 and 100 at Sherburne Center) is the largest ski resort in the east, with six interconnected mountains, over 1,000 skiable acres, and 170 trails with 23 lifts. The highest peak is Killington, a vertical drop of 3,150 feet. There's even the *Skyeship*, a heated lift with built-in sound system! The terrain allows for lots of novice room and many expert trails: 45 black diamond and 10 double diamond. The mogul slope is especially steep, and the Juggernaut Trail is 10 miles long, a national record. There's a lot of slopeside lodging, and free shuttle service to the Killington Road. Snowmaking coverage is 69%, because the natural snow season is so good, from early October in many years until early June (snow conditions: ☎ 422-3261). Snowboard access is resort-wide.

KID-FRIENDLY

Killington's children's programs are outstanding, and there is an entire slope devoted to families.

Pico Peak Ski & Summer Resort (Route 4, two miles west of Killington; ☎ 775-4345 for snow conditions, ☎ 775-4346 for lodging) joined Killington in late 1996 as an American Skiing Company Resort, with immediate plans for trails connecting the two resorts. It's small when compared to Killington: a vertical drop of 1,967 feet, 40 trails, nine lifts, and great snowmaking coverage of 95%.

Sugarbush (Warren, ☎ 800-53SUGAR or 583-3333), with access from Route 100 in the Mad River Valley, has 4,500 acres spread over six peaks. About 432 acres is skiable terrain, and between the main complex (Lincoln, Castlerock, Gadd, and North Lynx Peaks) and what's been called Sugarbush North (Mt. Glen Ellen and Inverness) there's a wild remote basin around Slide Brook, open to guided tours only, on skis, snowboards,

Ski racers taking a break.

and snowshoes. The main resort slopes put together 112 trails, including 35 black diamonds; there are 18 lifts. Mt. Ellen has the highest summit, 4,135 feet, with a vertical drop of 2,600 feet. More pluses: a tree skiing region for intermediates (Eden), a terrain park with halfpipe for dedicated snowboarders (access to all the rest of the trails too), and a family adventureland with snow sculptures. The kids' section gives complimentary beepers to parents! Sugarbush developed one of the earliest American slopeside lodging resorts, and the choices are wide, from condos to inns to bed and breakfasts, each with its own character and charm. A free shuttle links the lodging with the pleasures of the town. A February tradition at the resort is an ultimate board and band event, with tabletops of all sizes, halfpipes, transfers, big-air jumps, and quarterpipe by day, and a rock competition by night.

*Among the special programs offered at Sugarbush is one by the **Vermont Adaptive Ski and Sports Association,** which provides instruction and equipment for physically challenged skiers (☎ 583-4283).*

WINTER CARNIVAL IN THE MAD RIVER VALLEY

There's always snow in the Mad River Valley in January and February (and earlier, and later), and the wild exultation of hitting the slopes has expanded into a spectacular winter carnival. It's usually held the first week of February; check this year's dates at ☎ 496-3409 or 800-82-VISIT, Web site www.hows.com/thevalley/carnival). Expect sled dog races, a sleigh rally, the famous international progressive dinner, snowboard competitions, snowshoe races, snowmobile events, and of course skiing like mad on all the peaks of nearby Sugarbush. The grand finale includes snow sculptures, live music, a bonfire, and food. A romantic end to the week can be a parade of lights at nightfall as skiers carry torches and weave down the slopes. Keep your eyes open for international celebrities and sports figures having a midwinter great time.

The **Middlebury College Snow Bowl** (☎ 388-4356) is on Route 125, reached either from the Middlebury side or from Hancock on Route 100. It's a small outfit: skiing and snowboarding on 14 trails, with six covered by snowmaking, and three lifts. But that includes more than 12 miles of skiable surface, challenging expert trails, and a snowboard park. Pluses are short lift lines, lower fees and food prices, a full-service rental shop, and a strong professional ski school with a racing program geared to keep the college hotly competitive.

If your passion is the sport rather than the resort, and you lean toward natural snow cover, telemark skiing, or ski racing, **Mad River Glen** should be on your list (Route 17, Waitsfield, ☎ 496-3551 or 800-850-6742; snow reports from out of state, ☎ 496-2001, and from Vermont phones, 800-696-2001). It's the only US ski area owned by a cooperative of loyal skiers, dedicated to preserving the forest and mountain ecosystems of Stark Mountain and staying independent. Of the Glen's 42 trails, 18 are black diamond. Four lifts service the peaks and connect with parking areas. The expert terrain here is legendary ("where the real skiers go"), and you can ride the nation's last surviving single chairlift. There's just one base lodge, rustic and friendly; this is a place for families to enjoy, for friends to bond, and for new friendships to be made. The Glen is not shaped for snowboarding; instead, your visit is a pure ski experience.

Cross-Country Skiing

Nordic skiing just plain belongs in these mountains: it's the best way to get out into the woods and fields once the snow arrives, see the vistas remade, savor the weather and the wildlife. There are numerous Nordic ski centers, many around country inns, and the national forest trails are a winter-long ungroomed but lovely cross-country ski network. You can ski cross-country in local parks like **Pittsford's Recreation Area**; take advantage of **Green Mountain National Forest** trail networks and forest roads; and stay at inns where groomed trails lead from the doorway. Moosalamoo even grooms miles of the trails; the **Chittenden Brook Recreation Area**, off Route 73 near Rochester, is entirely open to winter skiing and snowshoeing and can be a good wildlife investigation site even in winter, when tracks are so much easier to spot. Near Middlebury, try going up Route 125 to the **Wilkinson Trail System,** reached from FR32 south of Route 125 – a trail map is available from the Middlebury Ranger District (RD4, Box 1260, Middlebury, VT 05752; ☎ 388-4362).

Remember the inn-to-inn programs coordinated with the Long Trail for hiking and biking? In winter the focus is on the **Catamount Trail** instead, Vermont's end-to-end mountain Nordic ski trail that meanders from (paid) touring centers to parks and forests and back roads. The trail is conveniently mapped in 26 daytrip sections; order your copy of the *Catamount Trail Guidebook* from the Catamount Trail Association (PO Box 1235, Burlington, VT 05402; ☎ 864-5794). In central Vermont, the **Country Inns Along the Trail** (RD3, Box 3115, Brandon, VT 05733; ☎ 247-3300) have organized an inn-to-inn self-guided ski program, which they customize and support with a luggage shuttle.

Inns offering their own or adjoining cross-country ski touring centers are **Blueberry Hill** (Goshen, 50 km groomed trails and connecting into Moosalamoo, ☎ 800-448-0707); **Churchill House Inn,** on Route 73 in Brandon (☎ 247-3078, Web site at www.pbpub.com/inntoinn), has 20 km of groomed trails and connects with Moosalamoo; and **Mountain Top Inn** in Chittenden, (☎ 483-3211 or 800-445-2100; snow conditions, 483-6089) at Chittenden Reservoir, a full cross-country ski resort with over 100 km of groomed trails, which connect to the Green Mountain National Forest.

From Middlebury, a trip up Route 125 shows that the Bread Loaf Campus of Middlebury College hosts **Rikert's Ski Touring Center** (☎ 388-2759), with 42 km of groomed trails for both classical and skating techniques and a friendly ski shop with rentals.

If you're in Killington and ready to ski Nordic instead of alpine, try the **Mountain Meadows Cross Country Ski Resort** on Thundering Brook Road (one-eighth of a mile east of the Killington Road, ☎ 775-1010 and 800-370-4567), where 60 km of trails are supported by a base lodge, ski shop, and snowmaking system.

Up Route 100 in Pittsfield, at the Pittsfield Inn, **Escape Routes** (☎ 746-8943, e-mail escapert@vermontel.com) sets up self-guided and guided tours by either Nordic skis or snowshoes, customized for ability and stamina; ski rentals are available.

In Rochester, be sure to stop at the Green Mountain National Forest district ranger office (☎ 767-4261) on Route 100 just south of town. Request the cross-country ski maps for the Hancock Branch Trail, Texas Falls Recreation Area, Pine Brook Trail, Brandon Gap Trail, and Austin Brook Trail, and take a look at potential forest road skiing near Granville and Hancock as well.

When you reach the Warren-Waitsfield area, there are three cross-country centers, plus the **Sugarbush Nordic Center** at the resort (☎ 583-2605), with 25 km of groomed trails, 10 km groomed for skating, and access to back-country guided touring. There are: **Blueberry Lake Cross Country Ski Center** (East Warren, 25 km, ☎ 496-6687), **Ole's Cross-Country Center** (Warren, 42 km, ☎ 496-3430), and the **Inn at the Round Barn Farm** (East Warren Road, Waitsfield, 30 km, ☎ 496-2276). There's also the **Skatium,** for ice skaters, in the Irasville part of Waitsfield: look for Mad River Canoe, and the Skatium is on the loop road that goes back toward the Grand Union.

SNOWSHOERS TAKE NOTE: *Information on the snowshoe supporting inns and snowshoe rental locations of the Mad River Valley can be obtained by calling 888-HIKESNOW.*

Other Winter Sports

Ride in a sleigh when you stay at the **Pittsfield Inn** (Pittsfield, ☎ 746-8943), at the **Mountain Top Inn** (Chittenden, ☎ 483-2311 or 800-445-2100), or the **Lareau Farm Country Inn** (Waitsfield, ☎ 496-4949). Mountain Top and Cortina Inn also have skating. There are two skating ponds in Killington, at the **Fall Brook Fitness Center** on Sunrise Mountain (☎ 422-7896) and at **Summit Pond** (☎ 422-4476). The Cortina Inn also rents snowmobiles.

ADVENTURES IN SNOWMOBILING

Either you love it or you hate it – that's the bottom line. If you think a wild ride through the snow with a gasoline-powered engine under you is your kind of adventure, get in touch with **Killington Snowmobile Tours** on Route 4 at the foot of the Killington Access Road (☎ 422-2121). KST gets you cruising through the Calvin Coolidge Memorial Forest on new machines at speeds up to 50 mph, taking you deep into the wilderness for spectacular scenery. Owner/guide Howard Smith encourages riders of all skill levels to try out the tours.

■ In The Air

Looking for a different view of the Mad River Valley – or of yourself? **Sugarbush Soaring** (☎ 496-2290 or 800-881-SOAR) at the Warren Airport, offers scenic glider tours and sailplane instructional programs in one of the East's prime spots for riding thermal and ridge waves.

Flight instruction, ground school, scenic tours, and aircraft rentals are all available at **Middlebury Flight School** at 25 Airport Road in Middlebury (☎ 388-0733, Web site www.middlebury.net/midflight). The crew also offers an unusual option for aircraft owners: come in for a vacation, and get your annual aircraft inspection and needed repairs done at the same time. By road, find the airport from Route 7, three miles south of Middlebury. Turn east (left) onto Cady Road and go 1.2 miles to the intersection with Route 116 and the airport entrance. Byron and Shirley Danforth, who operate the flight school, will enthusiastically show you classic Vermont villages and rolling farmland from a fresh perspective.

Eco-Travel & Cultural Excursions

Just a few miles from Lake Champlain, and reached by Route 22A from Vergennes, is the small town of Bridport, where **Blue Slate Farm** offers a unique "hands-on" dairy farming visit. Harold and Shirley Girard milk 110 cows and take care of 140 more head of young stock, two miniature donkeys, four horses, four ducks, and three pigs. When you sign up for their farm experience (☎ 758-2577 or 758-2267), you may participate in such daily activities as milking the cows, feeding and caring for the calves (and maybe help deliver one!), and preparing land for planting and harvesting. The Girards, whose farm has been family-run for four generations, will also discuss with you the complexities of dairy nutrition, genetics, and herd health, and will get into dairy issues like American agricultural policy, milk pricing, and Vermont's rural economy. Wear practical clothes and have fun!

In Killington, **Vermont Ecology Tours,** located at the Glazebrook Center on the Killington Road (PO Box 210, Killington, VT 05751, ☎ 800-368-6161; e-mail ecotrvt@vermontel.com), offers wildlife viewing and discovery trips like breakfasting with the birds – say, red-tailed hawks, warblers, woodpeckers. Guided rambles in the Green Mountain National Forest may include picking berries, looking for endangered peregrine falcons, or searching for moose and beavers. There are evening programs too. Trips include mini-coach transport, binoculars (adult and child size), rain gear, field guides, and more.

At Killington Peak, the **High Country Touring Center** offers alpine "skicology" tours with a naturalist (☎ 422-6776).

If you are looking for a team-building or stress-management-in-the-outdoors experience for a group, **North American Wellness Adventures** (☎ 496-4850) in Waitsfield plans adventure sports and wellness education programs.

Where To Stay

■ North of Middlebury

There are plenty of bed-and-breakfast homes along Routes 7, 22A, 116, and the east-west Route 125 and 73 in the area around Middlebury and to the north and west. At Lake Champlain on the edge of Vergennes the **Basin Harbor Club** (☎ 475-2311 or 800-622-4000, $$$-$$$$) offers lakeside cottages and country inn rooms to go with its 700 acres of resort activities. In the town of Vergennes, the **Emersons' Bed & Breakfast** (82 Main Street, ☎ 877-3293, $$) is in the midst of the historic district; there is also a motel, the **Skyview** (☎ 877-3410, $$), on Route 7 just north of Vergennes in Ferrisburgh. Bristol's **Firefly Ranch** (☎ 453 2223, $$-$$$) offers trail rides, fly-fishing in the New Haven River, and hiking on the Long Trail. **Mary's at Baldwin Creek** (four miles north of town on Route 116, ☎ 453-2432, $$-$$$) is a small bed and breakfast in a historic farmhouse, with exquisite and unusual dining.

> **INN-TO-INN TOURS:** *Country Inns Along the Trail makes life easy for hikers, cyclists, and Nordic skiers headed along either the Long Trail or the Catamount Trail. Contact the group at RR3, Box 3115, Brandon, VT 05733 (☎ 247-3300). Included in this collaborative are inns from Lincoln, which is near Bristol, to Killington, as well as farther south to Dorset and north to Stowe. The pluses for travelers include hosts familiar with the trails and adventure opportunities, and a network for reservations that smoothes out the problems of finding lodging in peak seasons.*

■ Middlebury

The area's most traditional lodging is the **Middlebury Inn** (14 Courthouse Square, ☎ 388-4961 or 800-842-4666, 75 rooms, $$-$$$$). Enjoy afternoon tea in the restored and lovely parlor, and other meals at the inn's restaurant. Frank, Jane, and Ty Emanuel even offer a newsletter so that guests (past and future) can keep up with changes or get to know corners of the inn better, like the Federal-style Porter Mansion that serves as a quiet retreat and annex to the inn. Locate the room with the hidden dumb-waiter, find the original kitchen cooking fireplace and oven hearth, or get the details about recent restoration. The Middlebury Inn also provides an itinerary for antique shopping in the region, as well as special packages for romance or mystery. Check the Web site, www.middleburyinn.com.

ACCOMMODATIONS LISTINGS: *Middle-bury's bed-and-breakfast homes keep multiply-ing; check with the **Addison County Chamber of Commerce** at 2 Court Street (☎ 388-7951) in the history-laden Gamaliel Painter house for an updated listing.*

Suggested bed and breakfasts include the **Swift House Inn and Café** (Route 7 and Stewart Lane, ☎ 388-9925, $$-$$$$); **Linens & Lace Bed & Breakfast** (29 Seminary Street, ☎ 388-0832, $$-$$$), which has after-noon tea and welcomes children; and **Middlebury Bed & Breakfast** (☎ 388-4851, $$-$$$). Outside town is the **Brookside Meadows Coun-try Bed & Breakfast** (☎ 388-6429, call for directions, $$-$$$). The **Sugar House Motel** (☎ 388-2770 or 800-SUGARHOUSE, $$) is just north of town on Route 7.

■ Brandon

This friendly town halfway between Middlebury and Rutland is perfect for access to the Long Trail, and Linda and Richard Daybell see many hikers at their **Churchill House Inn**. But with biking, fishing, cross-country skiing (from the doorstep), and horseback riding also nearby, it draws guests with numerous interests. The inn dates back to 1872 and offers both breakfast and a four-course candlelight dinner. Children are wel-come. The address is 3128 Forest Dale Road, which is Route 73 here (☎ 247-3078, Web site www.churchillhouseinn.com, $$).

■ Rutland

Much of the luxurious lodging for the Rutland area is on Route 4 en route to and in Killington. So are many of the bed and breakfast homes and small inns. But in town the **Inn at Rutland** (☎ 773-0575 or 800-808-0575, 70 Main Street, $$-$$$$) is a distinctive restored Victorian mansion with 10 guest rooms and rocking chairs on the porch. The **Phelps House** (19 North Street, ☎ 775-4620 or 800-775-4620, $$) is an unusual bed and breakfast, a Frank Lloyd Wright house next to the city playground (four tennis courts); innkeeper Betty Phelps makes dolls and has a stunning col-lection. Motels close to downtown are the **Royal Motel** (☎ 773-9176, $$)

and **Jen's Motel** (☎ 773-9480, pets welcome, $). There are also modern comfortable lodgings with **Howard Johnson** (☎ 775-4303 or 800-446-4656, $$), **Comfort Inn** (☎ 228-5150, $$), **Hogge Penny Inn** (☎ 773-3200 and 800-828-3334, $$), and **Holiday Inn** (☎ 775-1911 or 800-462-4810, $$-$$$).

■ Orwell

While you investigate Revolutionary War history in this area, you can enjoy a stately mansion that underwent a grand transformation from its 1789 farmhouse roots. The inn is **Historic Brookside Farms**, now listed on the National Register of Historical Places. In 1843, architect James Lamb turned it into a Neo-Classical Greek Revival beauty with shimmering white Ionic columns. Inside there's a grand salon, a library, gallery dining room, den with games and, of course an assortment of gracious rooms and suites for guests. Reserve well ahead for this four-season retreat with its 300-acre estate and working farmland, which includes animals, maple syrup production, homegrown vegetables and herbs, and fresh farm eggs. The inn is on Route 22A (☎ 948-2727, $$-$$$).

AUTHOR TIP

Historic Brookside Farms is a wonderful place for gatherings and grand celebrations, as the inn can provide space for a party of up to 250 people.

■ Killington

Killington's resort has very reasonable slopeside lodging at **Killington Resort Villages** (☎ 422-3101 or 800-343-0762, on the Killington Road, $$). On the same road is the **Inn of the Six Mountains** (☎ 422-4302 or 800-228-4676, $$-$$$$), a four-season resort with hiking spa and indoor and outdoor pools. There are also two local companies, **Killington Accommodations** (☎ 800-535-8938 or 422-2220) and **Wise Vacation Rentals** (☎ 773-4202 or 800-642-1147), which provide listings of homes and condominiums for vacation rentals. **Pico** has its own resort hotel, with slopeside condominium lodging (☎ 775-1927 or 800-225-7426).

For more elegant lodging, there's the **Cortina Inn** (☎ 773-3333 or 800-451-6108, Web site www.cortinainn.com, $$$-$$$$) on Route 4, with its landscaped acreage, fresh flowers in the rooms, and afternoon tea. The Cortina's recreation programs are coordinated with Great Outdoors Adventure Tours. **The Vermont Inn** (☎ 775-0708 or 800-541-7795, e-mail VTINN@aol.com, Web site www.vermontinn.com, $-$$), an 1840 country inn on six acres, offers a swimming pool and tennis courts as well as sauna.

Hikers and cross-country skiers have long appreciated the **Inn at Long Trail,** on Route 4 (☎ 775-7181 or 800-325-2540, Web site www.innatlongtrail.com, $$-$$$$). It is small, and sympathetic to travelers who arrive on foot or other non-automobile conveyance. The inn has its own pub and is strategically located next to the Long and Appalachian Trails.

■ Pittsfield

The 1835 **Pittsfield Inn** (☎ 746-8943, e-mail ESCAPERT@Vermontel. com, $$) at the north end of the village green offers an unusual treat: horse-drawn tours narrated by local historians. Rooms are comfortable and homey, and the inn's adventure program, Escape Routes, connects guests with guided and self-guided outdoor action.

Fleur de Lis Lodge (☎ 746-8949, open winters only, includes weekend stay of two nights plus breakfast, $$), **Stonewood Inn** (☎ 746-8881, $), and **Swiss Farm Lodge** (☎ 746-8341 or 800-245-5126, $) are all on Route 100, and an easy few miles from Killington as well as from the back-country opportunities of the Green Mountain National Forest.

■ Rochester

Try an 1890 mountain-top retreat with panoramic views: the **Harvey's Mountain View Inn**, which offers pet lodging on the premises (☎ 767-4273, $-$$). Or enjoy a family dairy farm where you can visit the barn and watch milking at **Liberty Hill Farm** (☎ 767-3926, $$). Both arrange sleigh rides.

■ Waitsfield, Warren & Sugarbush

Lodging comes in three forms here: country inns, of which some are very elegant and others more like ski lodges (but all expect skiers in the winter and hikers and bikers in summer), bed-and-breakfast homes, and condominiums.

*The **Sugarbush Chamber of Commerce** (☎ 496-3409 or 800-82VISIT, Web site www. madriver.com/lodging/) will help with information and reservations.*

Some of the popular bed-and-breakfast homes are **Hamilton House**, an English country house (☎ 583-1066 or 800-760-1066, $$$-$$$$); the **Inn at the Round Barn Farm**, which has its own trails (☎ 800-326-7038, $$$-$$$$); **Lareau Farm Country Inn**, an 1832 restored Greek Revival farmhouse offering sleigh rides (☎ 496-4949 or 800-833-0766, $$-$$$); **Mad River Inn**, riverside, with trails (☎ 496-7900 or 800-832-8278, $$-$$$); **Sugartree** (☎ 583-3211 or 800-666-8907, $$), the **Waitsfield Inn**, an 1825 inn filled with antiques (☎ 800-758-3801, $$-$$$); the **Weathertop Lodge**, which has a fitness center (☎ 496-8826 or 800-800-3625, $-$$); and **West Hill House**, with original art and a guest pantry (☎ 496-7162 or

800-898-1427, $$). Also note the **Hyde Away Inn**, with a restaurant and tavern on the premises (☎ 496-2322 or 800-777-HYDE, $$-$$$); the Colonial-style **Honeysuckle Inn** (☎ 496-3268 or 800-526-2753, $); and the **Millbrook Inn**, with a romantic restaurant (☎ 496-2405 or 800-477-2809, $-$$).

There's a motel, the **Madbush Farms Country Motel** (☎ 496-5557, $$), and a motor inn, the **Wait Farm** (☎ 496-2033 or 800-887-2828, $-$$).

Lodges include the **Sugarlodge** at Sugarbush (☎ 583-3300 or 800-982-3465, $), and the **Powderhound Lodge** (☎ 496-5100 or 800-548-4022, $$-$$$). At Sugarbush Resort, try the **Sugarbush Inn** (☎ 583-2301, $$), or let the resort (☎ 800-53SUGAR or 583-3333) set up the condominium or country inn lodging of your choice.

> *A Special Note: Just as Mad River Glen is the ski area of independent skiers, shunning both snow grooming and publicity, there's a ski lodge that has been a traditional "Glenner" place. It's the **Inn at the Mad River Barn** (☎ 496-3310 or 800-631-0466, $-$$), where oak furniture, old skis, heads of moose and bears, and the pub's enormous stone fireplace are part of the ambiance, along with staff members who are skiers themselves. The inn has trails and is of special interest to snowshoers.*

Central Vermont

■ Camping

Private campgrounds in this region include the following. In Vergennes, **Hillcrest Campground & Cottages,** on Otter Creek (☎ 475-2343). In Bristol, **Elephant Mountain Camping Area,** Route 116, 50 sites (☎ 453-3123). The Lake Dunmore area has **Kampersville,** which has 210 year-round accessible sites (☎ 352-4501 and 388-2661). Middlebury has **Rivers Bend Campground** (☎ 388-9092), with 57 sites near the Dog Team Tavern. In Brandon, there is the **Country Village Campground,** 41 sites (☎ 247-3333), and **Smoke Rise Family Campground,** 50 sites (☎ 247-6472). The **Lake Bomoseen Campground** on Route 30 has 99 sites (☎ 273-2061), and the **Killington Campground** at Alpenhof Lodge has 10 (☎ 422-9787). In Rochester, there is **Mountain Trails,** with 25 sites (☎ 767-3352).

State parks offering campsites are: Vergennes, **Button Bay State Park** (☎ 475-2377) and **D.A.R State Park** (☎ 759-2354); North Ferrisburgh, **Mt. Philo State Park** (☎ 425-2390); Brandon, **Branbury State Park** (☎ 247-5925); at Lake Bomoseen, **Lake Bomoseen State Park** (☎ 265-4242) and, to the northwest of the lake, **Half Moon Pond State Park** (☎ 273-2848); and Killington, **Gifford Woods State Park** (☎ 775-5354).

There's also primitive camping in the **Green Mountain National Forest**.

> *Remember that overuse can quickly devastate ecological systems and damage wilderness areas, so practice the skills of camping without leaving a trace behind.*

Where To Eat

■ Bristol

Breakfast at the **Main Street Diner** (☎ 453-4394), lunch at **Cubber's** (☎ 453-2400) for pizza, and dinner at the **Flying Fish** (no phone) with Caribbean food, reggae music, beer on tap, and a pool table – this is country comfort, all within the two-block span of Bristol's Main Street. For an elegant treat, go out to Sunday brunch or to lunch or dinner Tuesday through Saturday at **Mary's at Baldwin Creek** (four miles north of town on Route 116, ☎ 453-2432) and sample truly creative New England cuisine.

■ Middlebury

You'd need to stay at least a week to sample all the good food in this college town, ranging from Mexican casual at **Amigos** (☎ 388-3624) to the soda fountain at **Calvi's** (☎ 388-9038) and Italian meals at **Angela's** (by the Cannon Green, ☎ 388-0002). Three special favorites are outside town: the **1796 House Restaurant** on Route 7 in New Haven (☎ 453-4699), the **Dog Team Tavern** three miles north of town off Route 7 (☎ 388-7651, traditional New England fare), and the **Waybury Inn** in East Middlebury on Route 125 (☎ 388-4015), a historic hostelry. Also try **Woody's Restaurant** (☎ 388-4182) at 5 Bakery Lane in town for international cuisine, with a view of Otter Creek from the unique three-story dining room.

Microbrewery fanciers will want to stop on Exchange Street to visit **Otter Creek Brewing** (☎ 388-0727 or 800-473-0727); there are self-guided tours during weekday production, and guided tours on the weekends – do call to find out the hours.

■ Rutland

There are plenty of casual business and family dining opportunities in town, although most fine cuisine is up Route 4 in Killington. The **South Station** (☎ 775-1736) serves steak, seafood, and pasta at Trolley Square, 170 South Main Street. There's the **Weathervane Restaurant** (seafood, ☎ 773-0382) at 124 Woodstock Avenue, and **Sirloin Saloon** (☎ 773-7900).

For a really good lunch with fresh, tasty hot meals and sandwiches, not to mention the coffee roasted and ground there, try the **Coffee Exchange** (☎ 775-3337) at the corner of Center Street and Merchants Row; next door is the **Wine Room,** an evening aspect of the same business, with wines by the glass and live jazz on most weekends and some weeknights (☎ 747-7199).

The **Back Home Café** at 21 Center Street (☎ 775-9313) is a good local lunch stop with fresh-baked goodies; it has a breakfast partner called **Clem's Country Kitchen** (call the café for information).

KID-FRIENDLY

*Traveling with kids? Take them to the **Seward Family Restaurant and Ice Cream** (☎ 773-2738) at 224 North Main Street in Rutland.*

■ Killington

Zola's Grille (☎ 773-3333) at the Cortina Inn on Route 4 serves a menu of Northern Italian, French bistro, and Mediterranean delights, in a stylish and comfortable atmosphere.

Hemingway's Restaurant (Route 4, ☎ 422-3886) offers a gracious evening by the fire or in the old-world romance of the stone wine cellar, or under a vaulted ceiling. Fresh Atlantic seafoods and Vermont game birds are on the menu, as well as vegetarian specialties.

A long-time Killington tradition is **Casey's Caboose** (☎ 422-3795) on the Killington Road, a warm traditional steak and seafood restaurant.

Get into the playful vacation mood at **Outback Pizza** on Killington Road (☎ 422-9885, open year-round), where there's live acoustic music on most evenings, locally brewed beer and, of course, pizzas in traditional and outrageous varieties, like the Botcha Galoo (sausage, pepperoni, mozzarella, cheddar, asiago, and oregano), or the Vermonter BLT (need we say more?). The **Santa Fe Steakhouse** (☎ 422-2124) is also popular, at the Mountain Inn at the top of Killington Road, with its spread of American Southwest appetizers and entrées and a wide selection of microbrews and wines. Look for the Kokopelli figures on the front lawn. Open for both breakfast and dinner.

WHAT'S HOT: *The **Pickle Barrel** is Killington's hottest nightclub. Expect to see reggae and rock bands, including headliners like Ziggy Marley, Phish, and the Mighty Mighty Bosstones (☎ 422-3035, on the Killington Road).*

Central Vermont

■ Rochester

Tradition demands a breakfast at the **Rochester Café** (☎ 767-4302), for apple maple sausage, corned beef hash, and hot oatmeal with maple syrup. Lunch and dinner are served, too; the kids will enjoy the old-time soda fountain.

■ Waitsfield, Warren & Sugarbush

Dining in this resort area is more casual than elegant in style, although the food may be exquisite. A favorite "elegant barn" is the **Common Man Restaurant** at the Sugarbush Resort (☎ 583-2800), where the superb French cuisine garners much praise. **Giorgio's Café** at the Tucker Hill Lodge on Route 17 in Waitsfield (☎ 496-3983) serves Italian cuisine in a romantic atmosphere. **Jay's** (Mad River Green Shopping Center, ☎ 496-8282) has a more casual Italian ambiance; **Miguel's Stowe-Away** (☎ 583-3858) is the place for Mexican fare.

For a local delight, visit the **Bridge Street Bakery** in Warren (☎ 496-0077), where you can savor fresh soups and vegetable stews and specialty breads before indulging in the award-winning desserts. Chocolate lovers: **Royal Chocolates of Vermont** has its shop in the Irasville Common, on Route 100 just south of the village of Waitsfield (☎ 496-2144).

The Lake Champlain Valley

This is a region of spectacular sunsets, exuberant festivals, thriving arts. The land is rolling and gentle, perfect for long-distance walking, biking, and Nordic skiing. Water birds flock to its refuges; divers investigate its underwater world of mystery and ecosystems. Lake Champlain has been called the "Sixth Great Lake," and it gives Vermont its west coast and its deepest waters. It is 120 miles long, 12 miles across at its widest, a perfect lake to sail,

as it has been for two centuries of American history. Is there a Lake Champlain monster, Champ, as he's nicknamed? Who knows? But there are fish and loons and islands and cliffs, so that canoeing and kayak touring on the long lake are challenging and rewarding. In winter the ice freezes so thickly that fishing shanties form a village of structures on the lake, and skaters and hikers delight in the wide open spaces. To the west across the lake are the Adirondack Mountains of New York, massive and ancient. To the east are the high ski peaks of the Green Mountains; the snow that blows over the city of Burlington in January is headed for those peaks, a comfortable drive from the city of 40,000.

The waterfront of Lake Champlain was a harbor for lumber export when the nation was young, then lumber import by the mid-1800s. The ports along this shore played major roles in the War of 1812. Later, runaway slaves desperate for Canadian freedom traveled the Underground Railway along the lake, and hidden chambers and tunnels in old buildings remind today's visitors of those embattled years.

Now the Lake Champlain Valley is Vermont's serene farmland and its busiest commercial region. **Burlington** is the hub of the recreational playground that has developed. To the north there are large islands that form an idyllic summer and fall escape. To the south the beaches and state parks encourage boaters to make multi-day trips, spending their nights on shore and their days among the waves.

The Lake Champlain Valley

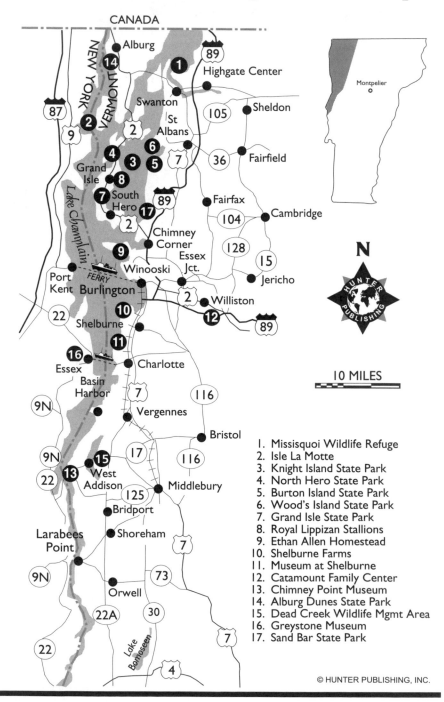

1. Missisquoi Wildlife Refuge
2. Isle La Motte
3. Knight Island State Park
4. North Hero State Park
5. Burton Island State Park
6. Wood's Island State Park
7. Grand Isle State Park
8. Royal Lippizan Stallions
9. Ethan Allen Homestead
10. Shelburne Farms
11. Museum at Shelburne
12. Catamount Family Center
13. Chimney Point Museum
14. Alburg Dunes State Park
15. Dead Creek Wildlife Mgmt Area
16. Greystone Museum
17. Sand Bar State Park

© HUNTER PUBLISHING, INC.

Getting Here & Getting Around

■ Burlington Area

If you fly into Vermont, you'll arrive at Burlington, the state's largest city and centerpiece of the Lake Champlain Valley. (Don't expect it to be really large, though; the shopping district can be easily explored on foot.) You can also arrive by boat across Lake Champlain from the New York side, or by car, probably the most familiar. The most direct road route is via **Interstate 89**, which, at its southern end, branches off from Interstate 91. Canadian visitors often come down Interstate 89. The older route, slower and more cluttered with shops and sights, is **Route 7**. Driving Route 7 north from Bennington is a charming way to approach the state's "coastal" area, and there are many smaller roads off Route 7 that head west for the two to 10 miles it'll take to reach the shore of Lake Champlain. Summer and fall foliage travelers have crawled through the traffic and slower pace of Route 7 and made the most of it as an entry to rural life. My own preference is to use the interstate to get here, then take the slower roads for enjoyment. From the east, if you're visiting Montpelier, **Route 2** goes nearly into Burlington, then trickles northward through the small town of Chimney Corner, and out onto the Lake Champlain Islands, passing through South Hero, Grand Isle, and Alburg at the Canadian border.

A NOTE FOR ARRIVALS BY HIGHWAY

Many a visitor has a first look at the Burlington area offerings at a rest area on Interstate 89, and the pair closest to the city, just south of Exit 13, are operated by the Lake Champlain Regional Chamber of Commerce (see below). There are generous racks full of information, and often there are staff members on hand to help pick out adventures or lodgings or sort out road directions. The buildings at these two rest areas are seriously outdated: designed to serve 35,000 visitors a year, now they serve well over 300,000. Groundbreaking for new structures is underway, so relief is in sight. Keep an eye out for construction. The rest areas also offer FM radio updates on local events and places to tour (tune in FM 89.7 while in the parking lots of each building).

The Lake Champlain Valley

NEW AIR ROUTE: *As this book goes to press, a new airline, to be called **jetBlue**, is announcing plans for economy service between Burlington and New York. With the freshly expanded and renovated Burlington International Airport as an anchor, the route may be a big success. The airport includes three car rental agencies, as well as taxi service into Burlington.*

It seems there ought to be an easy connection from the New York State Thruway, but you'll have to leave the northern connector of this road and take back roads through the little towns of the Hudson River Valley and Lake Champlain area to the ferry docks at Fort Ticonderoga, Crown Point, Essex, or Plattsburgh (south to north), or go all the way up to the bridge at Rouses Point that takes you into Alburg by the Canada border. Although none of these routes are quick, all are picturesque.

■ Lake Champlain

The Vermont shore of Lake Champlain begins in the south with the quiet bluffs and sandy spits that were once focal points of the Revolutionary War and the French and Indian Wars. From Chimney Point in the south, through Basin Harbor with its lovely resort, to tiny Charlotte and bustling Shelburne, the shoreline area is perfect for long strolls and especially for spectacular sunsets. Burlington is the center of the shoreline, and offers its own waterfront park as well as thriving marinas.

North of Burlington, Lake Champlain is divided by **Grand Isle**, also part of Vermont, and by the spit of land where Alburg hangs south from the Canada border. The easternmost shore along this stretch is relatively undeveloped, and much of it has already been preserved as bird and wildlife sanctuaries as well as campgrounds. The very northernmost 10 miles is more built up along the east shore, a residue of the days when being a border town to Canada meant being endlessly busy, but farmlands surround the town centers. Use Route 7 all the way north and south along the lake for access to these regions, taking the smaller secondary roads to actually connect with the quiet shoreline itself.

Railroad travel to and through the Lake Champlain Valley is in flux at the moment, with passage between Burlington and Rutland newly restored, and connections to Montreal possible through Alburg to Burlington with **Amtrak** trains. These also connect Burlington to New York and Washington, DC, once daily. There is no direct train connection with Boston or the coast of Maine. Amtrak (☎ 800-RAIL-USA) can give you current schedules and rates, which continue to be modest and include a free ride for children ages two to 15 to Vermont destinations (up to two children per adult passenger).

Touring

■ Burlington

Burlington is the center of this fertile strip of land and activity, and we tour outward from it, north and then south. You can arrive in Burlington by air at the state's only major airport, in South Burlington; or you can come by train on the *Sugarbush Vermont Express* during the summer (say, from Middlebury) or the Amtrak *Vermonter* year-round. Most people arrive by car, having traveled Interstate 89 either across the state from the east, or down from Canada. Before the interstates, many cars came to Burlington from the Northway of New York State, crossing the Hudson and heading north on Route 22A; this is still the major highway of the coast south of Burlington.

Queen City – that's Burlington's nickname. A walking tour of its waterfront and downtown starts with a visit to the **Lake Champlain Regional Chamber of Commerce** at 60 Main Street, which you can reach by taking Exit 14W from Interstate 89 and going right past the University of Vermont campus, through the downtown restaurant area, and nearly to the waterfront. There are 4,000 parking spaces in town, so pick one and take your bearings.

The road you've just come down, Main Street, is the main east-west road in the city. College Street is one block north; Pearl Street, two long city blocks past College, is already in a residential district, so you can see that the downtown area is modest and compact. From the Chamber of Commerce it's a short walk to the waterfront; stroll down Main Street, make the right turn onto Battery Street, and then the next left on College takes you right down to the "floating" **Community Boathouse** (☎ 865-3377), built on a recycled barge and endowed with a restaurant as well as the service center for the city marina. Here you can rent a sailboat or dock space, and you can take a lesson in sailing, sculling, swimming, scuba diving, or kayaking. Stand on the railed promenade of the boathouse and take a good look at the lake; you'll want to come back at sunset, when the colors over the water and mountains are extravagant. In front of you are three shipwrecks, open to the scuba diving community as an underwater preserve (check with the Vermont Division for Historic Preservation for access and recommendations, ☎ 457-2022); there are two more in the area, off the shores of Colchester and Vergennes.

Turn and look back at the city from the boathouse. To your right is the **Lake Champlain Basin Science Center** (open weekends 12:30 p.m. to 4:30 p.m., ☎ 864-1848; schools use it during the week), and beyond it the **Vermont Railway Depot**. Just down the waterfront from the Depot are the **Cornerstone and Wing Buildings**, home to some of the newest shops. The landing that sticks out into the lake immediately past those buildings is where the **Lake Champlain Cruises** dock, and at the shore end of the landing is the **Lake Champlain Aquarium** (open daily 11 to 5 from May to Labor Day; call for additional hours and for the rules for the associated international fishing derbies, ☎ 862-7777). To your right is **Waterfront Park**; a nine-mile bike path winds through the 11-acre park, perfect for cycle wheels or in-line skates. There are summer concerts in the park on Thursday evenings, and often weekend events. Beyond the north end of the park, off North Avenue, is the **Ethan Allen Homestead**, where the land once owned by Vermont's Revolutionary War hero is now a public park and the farmhouse has been restored to provide hands-on history (open mid-May to mid-October and by appointment in other seasons; call for hours, ☎ 865-4556).

To see the shopping focus of the city, walk up College Street five blocks and turn left to enter the **Church Street Marketplace**. This pedestrian mall has some 165 shops, cafés, and restaurants; sidewalk musicians and puppeteers take occasional advantage of the wonderful space. An information kiosk offers event listings and directions. The state craft center, **Frog Hollow** (☎ 863-6458) is at 85 Church Street. At the north end is the indoor **Burlington Square Mall**.

Head back to College Street and, if you're still in the mood for walking, go a half-mile uphill to the **University of Vermont**. Otherwise, you can take the free shuttle that goes up and down this road every 10 minutes from 11 a.m. to 6 p.m., and every 20 minutes from 6 to 9 p.m. The university's green spaces (white in winter) make for a good stroll. To find the city's art museum, turn left on University Place and then right on Colchester Avenue. The **Robert Hull Fleming Museum** (closed Mondays; ☎ 656-0750) is at 61 Colchester Avenue and houses extensive collections of American paintings as well as Native American artifacts and Oriental, pre-Columbian, and European art and archaeology.

Walk back toward the waterfront on Main Street to look over the eateries, galleries, and especially the music shops. The **Flynn Theater** (☎ 863-5966) is at 153 Main Street and presents great performers year-round. Another popular stop, off Main Street, is the **Church and Maple Glass Studio** (☎ 863-3880) at 225 Church Street, an open studio where you can watch molten glass being shaped and blown.

AUTHOR TIP

*Hikers, campers, and snowshoers can find used (and new) gear at the **Outdoor Gear Exchange**, 131 Main Street (☎ 860-0190).*

Other city locations to keep in mind are **St. Paul's Cathedral** (☎ 864-0471) at Cherry and Pearl Streets, where there's a free classical music series all winter and spring on Thursdays from noon to 1 p.m.; the **Union Station Gallery** (☎ 864-1557) at the foot of Main Street, housing a public gallery and several artists' studios; and the city's two major sports equipment shops, the **Ski Rack** (which also is into bikes in snow-free seasons,

Burlington Area

N

WINOOSKI

Mallet's Bay
1 mile

Elmwood Ave

127

Manhattan Drive

Park St

Archibald

North St

N Champlain St

N Winooski

S Winooski

N Union

Pearl St

Main St

King St

Maple St

S Prospect St

Lakeside Ave

Pine St

Shelburne Rd

Flynn Ave

Ledge Rd

Industrial Pkwy

Home Ave

Swift St

Winooski River

Mallets Bay Ave

W. Spring

Grove St

East Ave

Spear St

Dorset St

Kennedy Dr

Hinesburg Rd

Lime Kiln Rd

Airport Pkwy

White St

Williston Rd

15

2

7

2

89

89

189

116

Burlington Int'l Airport

Lake Champlain

BURLINGTON

SOUTH BURLINGTON

1 MILE

© HUNTER PUBLISHING, INC.

☎ 658-3313), on Main Street not far from the waterfront; and the **Down-hill Edge**, the ski and snowboard shop a few doors farther down Main Street.

Burlington's biggest festivals are the **Lake Champlain Balloon Festival** at the end of May, **Discover Jazz** (five days in June), and **First Night** (New Year's Eve performances), but the Chamber of Commerce (☎ 863-3489) can give you listings that show weekend entertainment year-round.

The smaller cities (or large towns) of Shelburne, South Burlington, Williston, Essex Junction, Winooski, and Colchester form a residential and commercial ring around Burlington. At the north edge of this ring is Mallett's Bay, a water-lover's haven. In the surrounding towns are several attractions associated with the cultural and college-town atmosphere of the

Queen City: in **Essex Junction** is the **Discovery Museum** (☎ 878-8687, open year-round but closed Mondays), a hands-on science and nature museum for kids; in **South Burlington** there are several large sports and recreation equipment shops, bookstores, and good eateries; and in **Shelburne**, three unusual museums provide excitement for both kids and adults – Shelburne Museum, Shelburne Farms, and Justin Morgan Memorial Museum (see *Shelburne* for details).

■ St. Albans

Only 28 miles north of Burlington, St. Albans is in an entirely different world, one of small-town life that focuses around a town common, Taylor Green. There are shops on one side of the green and a small mall north of town, but the town feels rural and family-focused, and is surrounded by successful dairy farms. The 1850s railroad days are close at hand, in the monumental buildings on the east side of the green, including the **Franklin County Museum** (open summer and early fall afternoons; ☎ 527-7933), with its apothecary shop and costume collections, and in history-based events like **St. Albans Days**, held in late September with a Civil War encampment on the green and often a mock skirmish that sends the roar of cannons through the town. St. Albans was once raided by Confederate forces from Canada in an attempt to tip the financial balance of the Civil War.

To the west of town on St. Albans Bay there are two state parks, **Burton Island** and **Kill Kare**, and access to a third, **Wood's Island**. To the north of St. Albans, just beyond the town of Swanton on Route 78, is the **Missisquoi National Wildlife Refuge**, full of quiet wonders and well worth walking through. Then Route 78 takes you over a narrow bridge to **Grand Isle County**, Vermont's very rural version of Cape Cod.

■ Lake Champlain Islands

This is Grand Isle County. Everyone calls it the Champlain Islands, although the most northern section, Alburg, is actually a peninsula from the Canadian mainland. Never mind the technicalities: you get to any part of these "islands" by crossing a bridge or by taking a boat over the sometimes choppy waves of Lake Champlain.

When you travel to Alburg on Route 78 by bridge from Swanton (northwest of St. Albans), you quickly run into Route 2, which then travels south through the islands. Alburg has some homey eateries and good boat care at a pair of marinas. From the southern end of the peninsula you can cross a bridge heading west to **Isle La Motte**, where the Edmundite Fathers and Brothers care for **St. Anne's Shrine**. There are Eucharistic celebrations offered here daily and Sunday during the summer and fall; grottos and a Way of the Cross encourage quiet prayer or meditation. Nearby is a statue of Samuel de Champlain, for whom the lake was named, and who is believed to have landed here in 1609.

ISLE LA MOTTE'S ARCHAEOLOGICAL TREASURES

When you are on Isle La Motte, you are standing on top of a 1,000-acre **fossil reef** that once lay south of the equator and migrated here with the continent. Along the West Shore Road you can see some exposed portions of the reef, but much of it is on private land. To find out this year's public spots to look at the fossils, stop at the **Champlain Islands Chamber of Commerce** on Route 2 in North Hero (☎ 372-5683). Also ask for directions to the **Fisk Quarry**, where black marble used to emerge under the hands of local quarrymen. Since nature reclaimed the site, it has become a peaceful wetland and wildlife habitat. Tranquil and timeless, it's the perfect place to use your wildflower guide to the max. Bring along binoculars for birding, too.

A return to Alburg by bridge takes you to another bridge, this time to **North Hero**, where there's a state park on the north shore. North Hero is the summer home of the **Royal Lippizan Stallions**. Before and after their shows on Thursday and Friday you can meet both horses and riders (☎ 372-5683; call for hours and season dates). Route 2 then heads south through Grand Isle (**Knight Point State Park** and an island that's a separate, very small state park, **Knight Island**). The southernmost isle in the chain is **South Hero**, home of the 1783 **Hyde Log Cabin**, believed to be the oldest log cabin in the country and now a state historic site open July 4 through Labor Day (Thursday through Monday, 10 a.m. to 4 p.m.). From South Hero another bridge leads to the mainland, arriving at the **Sand Bar Wildlife Area** just outside Milton; Interstate 89 and the return to Burlington are just a few miles down Route 2.

The islands are nearly flat, perfect territory for road biking. Resorts, inns, and restaurants are scattered along the shorelines, and marinas cater to anglers as well as pleasure boaters. Although some restaurants have weekend hours in the winter, many of the facilities close after apple harvest season. You might want to schedule a trip to the orchards here in late September or during the blossoming weeks in late May or early June.

THE TWO HEROES

Curious about the island names? The story is that the brothers Ira and Ethan Allen modestly named the island "The Two Heroes" after themselves and, with Gov. Thomas Chittenden, the Allens parceled out the land to their Revolutionary War militia, the Green Mountain Boys.

■ Shelburne

South of Burlington by only 10 miles, Shelburne thrives along Route 7. You can get here by train on the *Sugarbush Vermont Express* from Burlington or Middlebury, or by car down the often congested Route 7 (stay away during the rush hour entirely). A thicket of malls, large stores, and restaurants of all sorts has grown up around Route 7 between the city and the town. The area's main supplier of rock and ice-climbing equipment, **Climb High** (☎ 985-5055) is on Route 7. Shelburne Bay is dedicated to small boats.

The town has three wonderful museums. The first and largest is **Shelburne Farms** (☎ 985-8686), a grand agricultural estate of more than 1,000 acres, with walking trails and a working farm, complete with cheese-making and a children's farmyard. There are magnificent 18th-century buildings and furnishings, a stunning view of the lake, and a thoughtful environmental education center. Shelburne Farms is open daily from late May to mid-October.

The **Vermont Mozart Festival** performs in summer here, as does the **Vermont Symphony**. From Burlington, take Route 7. Four miles after you pass Interstate 89, take the right turn onto Bay Road. It leads down to the harbor. If you miss this turn, you can also get there from the center of Shelburne by taking the right onto Harbor Road; there are plenty of signs.

Shelburne Museum, farther down Route 7, creates a working history of Vermont's 18th and 19th centuries, with 35 exhibit buildings on 100 acres. Climb the gangway of the *Ticonderoga*, the last steam-powered side-wheeler of its type in the country; watch a blacksmith strike sparks at the forge, see candles being made, and marvel at the variety of carriages and sleighs that horses have pulled. This is one

The Round Barn at the Shelburne Museum.

of the largest collections of Americana in the country, and so much of it is active and hands-on that it's a good place for a family to spend an entire day. It's open daily from 10 to 5 in summer and during foliage season (☎ 985-3346).

*The **Owl Cottage** at the Shelburne Museum is designed for hands-on projects like stenciling, making paper hats or checkerboards, or trying to churn butter. For a list of this week's projects, call ☎ 985-3346, ext. 397, or check the Web site, www. Shelburnemuseum.org.*

Next door to the Shelburne Museum is the **Justin Morgan Memorial Museum**, dedicated to the breeder of the Morgan horse and, of course, to his horse, Figure. There are also glimpses into life with the First Vermont Cavalry and at the first National Morgan Horse Show. This museum is open year-round (☎ 985-8665).

The center of Shelburne is a historic district, focused around a green along Route 7. The **Shelburne Inn** is here, established in 1796. Look for the **Vermont Teddy Bear Company** as you leave the village to the south on Route 7; there's a tour here for collectors, kids, and bear appreciators (☎ 985-3001; shop open daily, but call for tour hours).

■ Charlotte

Five miles south of the Shelburne Museum is the right turn to Charlotte, a pleasant shoreline village where a ferry makes a 20-minute crossing of Lake Champlain to Essex, NY. The Town Hall serves as a community museum. If you stay on Route 7, immediately past the Charlotte turn on your right is the **Vermont Wildflower Farm** (☎ 425-3500), six acres of flowery fields and forest glades. Pathways are marked with notes on herbal histories and legends. Plan to visit between May 1 and mid-October.

Charlotte's bookstore, the **Flying Pig**, has traditionally called itself a children's bookstore, but now also carries great vacation reading and a wide selection of travel guides and books of local and regional interest. Owners Elizabeth Bluemle and Josie Leavitt love to talk about books and welcome e-mail (FlyingPig@aol.com). The shop address is 86 Ferry Road; it's actually just off Route 7 at the turn for Charlotte (☎ 425-2600).

KID-FRIENDLY

*The **Flying Pig** bookstore is a great spot to bring the kids on a rainy day, to select from books, games, and puzzles. The shop also offers special events, including readings for adults and book parties for kids.*

Also in Charlotte is a blueberry farm, **Pelkey's U-Pick Blueberries**, where you can pick your own sweet fruit in late July and August (follow the signs from the center of the village). There's an **apple orchard** nearby for autumn gleaning.

The Lake Champlain Valley

Adventure Across The Lake

For less than $4 round trip, you can take a 20-minute ferry ride from Charlotte across the waters of Lake Champlain to the New York "coastal" hamlet of **Essex**, a village full of 18th- and 19th-century homes and buildings, gift and antique shops, and marinas. It's easy to explore on foot, so there's a perfect excuse to leave the car in the free parking area on the Vermont side of the lake and take off for a day excursion. The ferry operates daily from April 1 to mid-October, and sometimes in winter (☎ 802-864-9804); you don't need a reservation at all. If you really want to bring your car, you'll still pay less than $25 round trip, including all your passengers.

From the ferry landing, walk up into town, turn left on **Main Street**, and find the town office a block down the road on the right, with its rack full of information (and sparkling clean public bathroom). Be sure to pick up the guide to the town's architecture, which includes Federal Greek Revival, Carpenter Gothic, Italianate, and French Second Empire styles. **Greystone**, an 1853 cut-stone Greek Revival mansion with scenic grounds, opens its museum displays on weekends from the end of May to mid-October and daily in July and August, from noon to 5 (admission; ☎ 518-963-8058, Web site www.essexny.net).

Greystone Museum in Essex, New York.

The gift shops and antique and book shops are obvious within the first few minutes of strolling around, and so are the snack spots like the **Essex Ice Cream Shop** (☎ 518-963-7951), **Essex Provisions** with sandwiches and breakfasts (☎ 518-963-7136), and the **Sunburst Tea Garden** (☎ 518-963-7482), which serves only afternoon tea, sometimes only on weekends. The spots for a more hearty meal are on the waterfront: the comfortable **Old**

Dock House Restaurant and Marina (☎ 518-963-4232) is next to the ferry landing. **Jimmy's Lakeside** is at the Essex Shipyard Marina and serves only dinner (☎ 518-963-7993), doing a nice job with diverse cuisine in its tiny dining room.

Sailors and anglers will appreciate their options along the waterfront: There's the well established **Essex Shipyard Marina** (☎ 518-963-7700), nearby **Essex Boatworks** with its fine wooden boats and repair (☎ 518-963-8840), and the **Essex Marina and Ship's Store** (☎ 518-963-7222). The town has been serving boats and their owners since the early 1700s; the first ferry service here dated to 1730.

Kayaking, canoeing, cycling, or camping out? Contact **High Peak Touring**, the local outfitting guide service, which rents and sells gear for all these activities (☎ 518-963-7028). You can also sign up for a sea kayaking course, or get a shuttle to take you onto the nearby Boquet (bo-KETT) River. Better yet, try the combined bike and boat tour for a day-long adventure.

> **AUTHOR TIP**
>
> *If you get caught up in the fun of this village and want to stay overnight, the **Essex Inn** on Main Street offers cozy accommodations (also open to the public for lunch and dinner), including a full breakfast (☎ 518-963-8821; e-mail theessexinn@hotmail.com; $$-$$$). A bit quieter but no less scenic is the **Stonehouse Bed & Breakfast** at Church and Elm Streets (☎ 518-963-7713; $$-$$$).*

The village offers a **Maritime Festival** and its traditional **Essex Day** in August, as well as celebrations on **Fourth of July** and during the **Christmas season**. Contact the helpful staff at the **Essex Town Hall** (☎ 518-963-4287) for this year's dates. They can also give you an update on a nearby nature preserve and campground that's still in progress but open for some use, **Noblewood Park**. It's on Route 22 along the Boquet River and offers a beach, walking trails, and a canoe launch. Primitive tent sites are available by reservation through the **Willsboro Town Hall** (that's in the next town inland; ☎ 518-963-8668).

■ Basin Harbor

The **Lake Champlain Maritime Museum** (☎ 475-2022) not only has small watercraft and a reproduction gunboat to clamber over, but it hosts boatbuilders in working shops and more than two dozen summer workshops on making your own boats and related skills. You could learn the techniques of lapstrake canoe construction as you actually build one; set to work making your own kayak; carve a canoe paddle with Native American techniques; or explore blacksmithing, hands-on, at the forge. There's a

The Lake Champlain Valley

nautical archaeology center, and there are stories of the lake and its rich history, including Revolutionary War gunboats. Picnic at the lakeside between events and exhibits.

Just north of the museum is **Kingsland Bay State Park**; south of the museum is the **Basin Harbor Club** (☎ 475-2311 or 800-622-4000), a resort where the harbormaster rents out canoes, rowboats, small outboards, and windsurfers.

Basin Harbor is reached from Vergennes; take Route 7 to Vergennes and then follow the signs to the west.

■ West Addison

Some 9,500 years ago, Native Americans regularly camped around **Chimney Point**, the portion of West Addison that forms the southern edge of Lake Champlain. Their campsites and artifacts left many clues to the way of life dependent on fishing and hunting. By 1000 BC the Woodland culture was taking over and the area became part of a trade route; eventually the Woodland people, ancestors of today's Abenaki ("People of the Dawn") tribe, began to farm this valley. The **museum** at Chimney Point (☎ 759-2412) exhibits artifacts from these cultures as well as from the French Canadians, who then settled at Chimney Point. From Route 7, switch in Vergennes to Route 22A and then in Addison to Route 17 west to the shoreline, or from Basin Harbor follow the coast road 12 miles south to the state historic site, which is open seasonally; call for hours.

By 1765 there were people of British background trying to settle in the area, building log cabins along the lake. For a fascinating look into the lives of one of the first of these families in Addison, John Strong's family, stop at the **Strong House**, just north of the Chimney Point historic site, in the D.A.R. (Daughters of the American Revolution) State Park. Find out what Mrs. Strong did when a Native American raiding party approached her home by canoe, and how her sons had to search for her and the baby some time later after the settlement was burned by another raiding party. The surrounding state park has recreation facilities on Lake Champlain.

The **Dead Creek Wildlife Management Area** is just east of West Addison village; this is a perfect spot for canoe exploration and birding.

Adventures

■ On Foot

Burlington

The entire city of Burlington is very walkable, with the uphill roads calling for brisk action, and the cross streets going through friendly neighborhoods. **Battery Park** lures wanderers to the shore, too. For the great ankle strengthening of shoreline walking, try **North Beach City Park** at the north end of town, reached by leaving the downtown area on North Avenue and making a right turn on Institute Road. There are also plenty of walking paths at **Red Rocks Park**, the southernmost of the shoreline parks; from Shelburne Road take Queen City Park Road, which is just south of the ramp to Interstate 89; turn left on Central Avenue.

Williston

Head east of town on Route 2 to Williston for more of a stretch. To get to the **Catamount Family Center** (☎ 879-6001) take Route 2 to the left turn onto North Williston Road, then right onto Gov. Chittenden Road. The center is on the right. There is summer running and hiking on the trails, as well as an orienteering course, interpretive (nature) trails, and special events. Keep an eye out for mountain bikers! Nearby at 1079 Williston Road is the 100-acre training location of **Pine Ridge Adventure Center** (☎ 434-5294), where adventure programs begin with community building and skills development on site before traveling to wilderness areas of New England, New York, and Canada. The adventure center also offers ropes courses and team-building exercises on site; the center is part of Pine Ridge School, an independent high school for students with learning disabilities, but it serves a wider community of individuals and groups seeking personal challenge and enhanced team spirit.

Camel's Hump, with its distinctive double-bump silhouette, is easily visible from Burlington and Williston. Its alpine summit has vulnerable plants and rapidly eroding soil and trails. Unfortunately, it is being hiked by far too many pairs of feet for its terrain, so I am not giving directions for its trails. If you're determined to go to a high spot nearby, try **Mt. Mansfield** (from Stowe or from Smugglers' Notch), which has been better protected or, better yet, go farther afield to a less traveled mountain like **Jay Peak**, **Mt. Abraham** or **Ascutney**, and feel good about giving the land a much needed break.

Swanton

An unusual wetlands walk is found at the **Missisquoi National Wildlife Refuge,** north of Swanton on a peninsula jutting into Lake Champlain.

Although the trails cover only two miles altogether, there are wildlife checklists and observation points, and blueberry picking is allowed off Tabor Road during July and August. Wear boots and a hat and bring a compass and bug repellent! Check in with the refuge manager when you arrive.

GUIDED WALKING TOURS: *If you'd like a guided walk, Kate Ketchum at* **The Road Less Taken** *(☎ 865-5123) puts together day tours ranging from a historic Montpelier/Barre trip to museums and trails around Jericho to a Vermont Islands ramble.*

ROCK CLIMBING

Rock climbers, attention please! Get in shape and practice new skills just a few miles out of town at **Petra Cliffs Climbing Center** (formerly Burlington Rock Gym) in Essex, with more than 6,000 square feet of climbing surface and 30 ropes, plus a bouldering cave, and outdoor guiding. Call for directions (☎ 657-3872 or 860-2894, Web site www.petracliffs.com).

Climbers will also want to schedule a visit to **Climb High** (☎ 985-5055) at 1861 Shelburne Road (Route 7) in Shelburne, the area's chief supplier of climbing and ski mountaineering gear. This is also a good place to pick up terrain maps and guidebooks.

■ On Horseback

A trip north to Georgia, off Exit 18 from Interstate 18, takes you to the **Georgia Stables** (☎ 524-3395 or 893-7268), where there are scenic riding trails through the woods and families are made welcome. Sleigh and hay rides are also available.

■ On Wheels

Road Biking

Burlington's nine-mile **recreation path** is designed with road bikers in mind, and the lake views are truly special; try to be there at sunset for a real treat. The Boathouse by Waterfront Park is the usual access point, where there's parking. Three other bike trails are available. One is the **South Burlington Recreation Path** (eight miles), which you can pick up at either Red Rocks Park or Oakledge Park (both are south of the downtown area, along the shoreline). The second is the two-mile **Essex Transportation Path**, starting from Route 15 just east of the Essex Junction police station. The third, the **Shelburne Bike Path**, is two miles long and graveled, running from the boat mooring area off Bay Road to the Shelburne Point Road; motivated cyclists can then ride on Shelburne Point Road all the way to the marina.

A locally interesting road route for views across the lake is to start from South Burlington High School and ride south for six miles on Dorset Street, then make the right turn onto Irish Hill Road and again onto Spear Street for another view; a right onto Swift brings you back to Dorset for the return trip. If you're up for a longer ride, try the route from the University of Vermont along Spear Street to East Charlotte and back, about 20 miles round trip.

For road biking south of Burlington, keep in mind that Route 22A, like Route 7, gets very crowded with car traffic on summer and autumn days. Stick to the smaller roads along the shore, which are really more fun anyway.

AUTHOR TIP

*To get you quickly out of Burlington, **Bike & Ride** (☎ 864-CCTA) offers buses with bike racks; there's no extra charge for the bikes, and the routes go to Shelburne, Malletts Bay, and Essex and Williston.*

The **Lake Champlain Islands** are a biker's holiday site: flat to rolling, with good curves along the paved roads and a handful of nice straight unpaved roads. Use the triple loop given in John Freidin's book *25 Bicycle Tours in Vermont*, or create your own. Freidin also offers a nice loop between St. Albans and Swanton. **St. Albans** is a nice town for biking, with gentle climbs and a 27-mile Rail Trail to pedal. Check in at **North Star Cyclery** on South Main Street (☎ 524-2049) for directions to the trail.

NEW BIKEWAYS IN PROGRESS

How about being able to ride 350 miles around Lake Champlain? If that sounds daunting, consider the possibilities of 24 interpretive bike loops connected with the waterfront, offering insight into natural, cultural, and historical resources of the region as well as connecting with campsites and other recreation options. It's all happening now, and you can get an update from the **Lake Champlain Bikeways** clearinghouse, c/o Lake Champlain Visitor Center, RR1 Box 220, Crown Point, NY 12928 (Web site www.lakeplacid.com/bikeways). You can also check on Burlington area trails through the **Lake Champlain Regional Chamber of Commerce** (☎ 802-863-3489, Web site www.vermont.org). There is already a 10-mile path to tour Burlington, and a number of other trails are in place on the other side of the lake.

The Lake Champlain Valley

Mountain Biking

The **Catamount Family Center** is in Williston. Take Route 2 east of Burlington to the light at the North Williston Road, turn left, then after a mile right on the Gov. Chittenden Road; the center is on your right; ☎ 879-6001. It offers mountain bikers 48 miles of trails, with some hills and a good mix of terrain plus views. There are races on Monday evenings at 6 p.m.. Bike rentals are available.

P.O.M.G. Bike Tours of Vermont (☎ 888-635-BIKE), centered in Winooski, puts together camping bike tours that challenge and refresh. Gourmet camp cuisine makes it all the sweeter. Each tour has multiple departure dates; send for the listing of this year's destinations. (What's P.O.M.G.? Glad you asked – Peace Of Mind Guaranteed.)

■ On Water

Canoeing & Kayaking

 Canoeing in this region focuses on the **Winooski River**, from Richmond to Essex Junction and from the Champlain Mill to Lake Champlain. There's also flatwater canoeing on **Lake Iroquois** in Williston, **Indian Brook Pond** in Essex, **Arrowhead Mountain Lake** in Milton (best at the north end), and **Shelburne Pond** (1½ miles west of Route 116 on Pond Road; it's about 2½ miles long, the wildlife is interesting, and the water snakes are not poisonous!).

You can get an intense look into wetlands, waterfowl life, and ecosystems by paddling through the 6,338-acre **Missisquoi National Wildlife Refuge**, reached from Route 78, two miles northwest of Swanton. Stop at the refuge manager's office for a map; launch sites vary by season. Where there are "Closed Area" signs, breeding birds or vulnerable habitat is being protected. There are miles of quiet creek boating, as well as lake boating around the shores of this peninsula in Lake Champlain.

WATCHABLE WILDLIFE

Be sure to bring field glasses and maybe a bird book to the Missisquoi National Wildlife Refuge so you'll know which unusual birds you're spotting.

CANOE & KAYAK OUTFITTERS

Paddlers who are ready to try Lake Champlain can do themselves a favor by first visiting **Canoe Imports** at 370 Dorset Street, a half-mile south of Burlington's University Mall in South Burlington (☎ 651-8760 or 800-985-2992, Web site www.canoeimports. com). From Route 2 (Williston Road) it's .75 mile. Owner Bob Schumacher can help with a review of equipment, weather, and where to go for all skill levels of paddling. Canoe Imports deals with and repairs canoes, touring and sea kayaks, whitewater paddling, and Sunfish sailboats. Maps and guidebooks are on hand, as well as accessories.

Canoe Imports' Bob Schumacher emphasizes that water temperature is the biggest risk factor on Lake Champlain. Falling into 50° water without the proper clothing and equipment is life-threatening.

Other resources for paddling Lake Champlain are the **Vermont Paddlers Club** (Rich Larsen, VPC Membership Chairman, 11 Discovery Road, Essex Junction VT 05452; ☎ 878-6828), with canoe and kayak whitewater training, a summer and fall schedule of trips, and conservation efforts; and the **Champlain Kayak Club** (c/o Bob & Barb Schumacher, 2064 Shelburne Road, Shelburne, VT 05482). A Lake Champlain Paddlers Trail is in progress, to encourage multi-day trips on the lake with shoreline camping.

Sea-kayaking trips can be arranged through Kevin Rose at **PaddleWays** (89 Caroline Street, Burlington, ☎ 660-8606; www.paddleways.com), with three-hour sunset paddles for about $5 per person (minimum six people per trip), inn-to-inn paddles that run three to five days, as well as excursions to the Champlain Islands. And **Back of Beyond**, an adventure outfitter and guide service, provides canoes and kayaks for rent, as well as special adventure tours and women's programs (☎ 860-9500 or 800-841-3354).

LESSONS & TOURS: *If you're ready for lessons or for a guided tour with the kinks already worked out, **True North Kayak Tours** on Lake Champlain (☎ 860-1910) has a line-up of classes and trips. So does **PaddleWays** (contact information above). Paddleways now offers inn-to-inn sea kayaking tours, an exciting new twist. Also contact the **International Sailing School** in Colchester (☎ 864-9065).*

The Lake Champlain Valley

Boating

This is the prime adventure mode of the Lake Champlain Valley. Marinas along the shore rent boats, offer guides, and put together fishing trips. At the **Community Boathouse** in Burlington (☎ 865-3377) there are rentals of sailboats, rowboats, and rowing shells; there are charter vessels and bareboats; and there are courses in boating safety, sailing, sculling, swimming, scuba diving (introductory), and kayaking. **Winds of Ireland** (☎ 863-5090) at the Boathouse offers sailing cruises during the day and at sunset, as well as Sea Doos, sailboat, and inflatable rentals. Also from the Boathouse the *Spirit of Ethan Allen II* departs on scenic, sunset, and moonlight cruises, as well as special trips for the Green Mountain Follies, mystery dinner theater, and captain's dinner cruises (☎ 862-8300). **Champ Charters** (☎ 777-0940 or 372-4730) also leaves the Boathouse for fishing cruises – lake trout, landlocked salmon, and brown and steelhead trout. At Slip 30 there's **Captain Lou Vallee's water limo** for cruises and lessons in boat handling, with some lake history and snorkeling thrown in (☎ 351-0291). At the King Street Dock just south of the Boathouse you'll find **Lake Champlain Cruise & Charter** (☎ 864-9804), a steamboat company that provides historic cruises along with tales of battles, legends, and shipwrecks, plus a telescope to search for the lake's fabulous monster, "Champ." The King Street Dock is also where the ferry to Port Kent NY, leaves three times a day all summer and during foliage (call for times, ☎ 864-9804).

Sailing has always been a favorite sport on Lake Champlain, and a local team recently garnered a gold medal at an international Olympics competition. To get into the spirit of wings over the water, try a sailing cruise on the sloop *Friend Ship*, with Captain Mike LaVecchia. Cruises last two hours, include at least one lighthouse, and cost about $25 (children 12 and under $15); half-day and full-day sails can also be arranged. Reserve well in advance, especially for the September and October weeks of fall foliage: **Whistling Man Schooner Company**, Burlington Community Boathouse, PO Box 1811, Burlington, VT 05402 (☎ 862-7245, Web site www. whistlingman.com).

Marinas in Burlington include the **Community Boathouse** (☎ 865-3377), the **Ferry Dock Marina** (☎ 864-9804), and the **City Dock Marina** (☎ 862-7200).

In the Champlain Islands, boats are so much a part of life that the state park rangers will transport you over the water to your campsite on Knight Island! There are marinas at City Bay on North Hero (**Hero's Welcome**, ☎ 372-4161; on the Bridge Road, **Dunham's Sea Ray**, ☎ 372-5131); at Alburg (**The Boatsmith**, ☎ 796-3686); Grand Isle (**Tudhope Sailing Center & Marina**, ☎ 372-5320); and at South Hero (**Apple Tree Bay Resort**, ☎ 372-5398). Hero's Welcome also offers kayak and canoe rentals. **Sea Trek Charters** (☎ 372-5391) has a 25-foot Baha cruiser fully equipped for trout and salmon fishing cruises. **Pirate Charters** (☎ 372-8357) also offers fishing cruises. The ferry from Grand Isle to Plattsburgh, NY runs year-round (☎ 864-9804).

Shelburne has the **Shelburne Shipyard** (☎ 985-3326), and the resort at Basin Harbor offers free dockage and mooring to restaurant and museum visitors (**Basin Harbor Club**, ☎ 475-2022). Addison also has a marina, **Champlain Bridge Marina** (☎ 800-SAY-AHOY). All the way down to where the lake is almost a river, at Chipman Point, reached from Orwell, is one more deepwater dock: **Chipman Point Marina** (☎ 948-2288).

Windsurfing

Windsurfers head for **Lake Iroquois** in Williston – unless they're going for the big lake, **Champlain**, where a good windsurfing launch is Oakledge Park, south of the downtown area.

Fishing

Planning to fish the big lake? Visit **Schirmer's Fly Shop** at 34 Mills Avenue in South Burlington (☎ 863-6105) for gear, maps, and general outfitting. **The Vermont Department of Fish and Wildlife** (111 West Street, Essex Junction, VT 05452; ☎ 878-1564) puts out a *Lake Champlain Fishing Guide* with 16 detailed fishing charts, and tips on the lake's gamefish, from trout to bass to pickerel and more. It's available at most local Chamber of Commerce offices too.

Captain Jim LeClair's **Lake Champlain Charters** (☎ 879-3680) is especially oriented toward fishing, and leaves from Perkins Pier in Colchester, just south of the ferry dock. Another fishing charter is **Fish N Rigg** with Captain Bill Gregorek (Charlotte, ☎ 425-3574).

Paul and Nancy Boileau offer **Champ Charters** (☎ 864-3790, Web site http://enhanced-design.com/champ) on their *Champ IV*, with home port at the Burlington Boathouse next to the *Spirit of Ethan Allen II*. Or check out **Sure Strike Charters** with Rich Greenough at the Perkins Pier (☎ 878-5074, Web site www.fishvermont.com).

FISHING LAKE CHAMPLAIN

"Jaw-dropping fantastic" is one description for the angling on this sixth Great Lake. Both smallmouth and largemouth bass are abundant, with plenty weighing three to four pounds. The lake is also abundantly stocked with brown trout, lake trout, salmon, and steelhead. (A tip for steelhead angling: experience the late March run at Lewis Creek in North Ferrisburgh for a good chance at this variety of rainbow trout. Egg sacks, egg imitations, night crawlers, and nymphs played along the bottom are all effective.) The landlocked Atlantic salmon are especially challenging to catch. Restoration of the big gamefish has been so successful that there is even hope for restoration of the lake sturgeon, a giant fish that was plentiful in the days of Samuel de Champlain (say, 1607); the fish don't reach spawning age until they are 12 to 20 years old, so this is a very long-term project.

There are smaller pleasures here, too. The daily limit for yellow perch on lake Champlain is 75 fish or 30 pounds, whichever is greater; yellow perch can number 50, or 25 pounds; and crappie have a limit of 25. That'll keep you busy even if you don't leave the shore.

For advance information on the sport, contact some of the local groups: Braden Fleming at the Central Vermont Chapter of **Trout Unlimited** (☎ 878-5859); Larry Greene for the **Lake Champlain Walleye Association** (☎ 928-3336); Jim Edelman at the **Bass Anglers Sportsman Society** (☎ 893-6571); and the **Lake Champlain Sportfishing Association**, the newest local association (PO Box 52, Essex, VT 05453).

Pick up maps through **West Marine** at 861 Williston Road (in the Staples Plaza next to Interstate 91; ☎ 865-8064).

Diving

Scuba diving is just catching on here in a big way as technology improves and shops to service the sport grow. At its deepest, Lake Champlain goes to 400 feet, and extreme divers have now plumbed it to about 265 feet. But most pleasure divers will focus on, say, the shipwrecks already marked out by the Vermont Division of Historic Preservation, which should be contacted for maps and guidelines (☎ 457-2022). The wrecks are the Horse Farm, the Coal Barge, and the *General Butler* off the Burlington shore, the *Phoenix* by Colchester, and the Diamond Island Stone Boat at Vergennes. They are marked with Coast Guard-approved buoys and are open to the scuba diving community. You can also get maps of the Lake Champlain dive and historic sites from **Dive Research, Inc.** (PO Box 817, Williston VT 05495; ☎ 985-8863). Supporting equipment suppliers include **Victory Sports** in Colchester (☎ 862-0963) and the **Waterfront Diving Center** on Battery Street in Burlington (☎ 865-2771 or 800-283-SCUBA).

Swimming

If you're just going into the water for a swim, the choices are wide. Head north of downtown Burlington to **North Beach City Park** (from North Avenue take Institute Road west to the beach), with its sandy beach half a mile long and great views of the lake and mountains. Just north of this beach is the one at **Leddy Park**. South of the downtown region is **Oakledge Park**, a rockier beach. The next park south is **Red Rocks**, with its dramatic views from the 70-foot cliffs, but also with a beach at the southern end of the park.

Outside Burlington, there is a small beach at **Bayside Park** on Mallets Bay to the north. Milton offers a very large and lovely beach at **Sand Bar State Park**, by the southern connection to the Lake Champlain Islands.

■ On Snow & Ice

Downhill & Cross-Country Skiing

The closest downhill skiing to Burlington is out in Bolton Valley or at the small tow-rope slope at Cochran's in Richmond. But there's a thriving Nordic ski center just out of town: the **Catamount Family Center** in Williston (take Route 2 east from Burlington to the North Williston Road, turning left and going a mile to a right turn onto the Gov. Chittenden Road; the center is on the right; ☎ 879-6001). With 64 miles of groomed trails and an 850-foot skating oval, the center stays busy once the snow flies. Activities also include ice skating, snowshoeing, sledding, weekly races, and cutting your own Christmas tree! Rentals and lessons are available.

In St. Albans there's a 27-mile **Rail Trail** for Nordic skiing, and at **Aldis Hill Park** there's still an old-fashioned rope tow for skiing, as well as sledding, hiking, and snowboarding. Snowmobile trails come right to town.

The trails at the **Missisquoi National Wildlife Refuge**, two miles north of Swanton on Route 78, are open to cross-country skiers; see *Eco-Travel* below for details.

Other Winter Sports

Lake Champlain in winter does freeze, and the ice is thick enough to support **ice fishing** shacks and you can even drive on it sometimes. But there are always thin places, and your best bet is to stick with places where others are already moving around. Breaking through ice into cold water is usually a deadly experience. On the other hand, there's a party mood on the ice once it's thick enough, and you'd hate to miss out. Remember, ice fishing requires a Vermont fishing license.

Sleigh rides at **Shelburne Farms** (☎ 985-8442) are offered daily during the Christmas-to-New Year's break and on weekends for the rest of the snow season.

Some **skaters** like lake ice and flock to Lake Champlain; others prefer the closer quarters and more controlled surface of a rink, and there are two good ones in this region: in Burlington at **Leddy Park** (☎ 864-0123, rentals available), and in St. Albans at the **Collins-Perley Sports Center** (☎ 527-1202; be sure to call ahead to find out which hours are open skating periods, as this rink is used by hockey teams).

■ In The Air

 Paragliding, a cross between parachuting and hang gliding, is the least expensive and simplest form of flying you can try. With gear that weighs only 20-25 pounds, and a takeoff from a small hill in a good wind, an inflated canopy shaped like an aircraft wing can support you on a flight of five or 10 minutes. More expert flights in the Green Mountains can last several hours. In Burlington, **Parafly Paragliding** offers ground school near the waterfront and short flights at Cobble Hill in nearby Milton, where flyers can start with their toes just a few feet off the ground and learn skills like glider inspection, self-launch, turns, and landing. Lessons begin as soon as the snow melts; call Rick Sharp and Ruth Masters at ☎ 800-PARAFLY.

Vermont Skydiving Adventures (☎ 759-3483) on Route 17 in West Addison invites you to make an appointment for a tandem, static line, or accelerated free-fall jump, jumping the same day as your lesson; they are open Tuesday to Sunday in the snow-free weather, from 9 a.m. to sunset.

The **Lake Champlain Balloon Festival** takes place at the Champlain Valley Fairgrounds, on Route 15 in Essex Junction, usually around Memorial Day. Some 50 hot-air balloons arrive, and there are rides, skydivers, games and exhibits. Count on fireworks if the weather is good. For details, contact the Lake Champlain Balloon Festival, PO Box 83, Underhill Center VT 05490; ☎ 899-2993.

AUTHOR TIP

*Flying in or out of Burlington International Airport? Take time to go upstairs and follow the arrows to the **Observation Tower**. At the foot of the narrow stairs is a small waiting area where volunteers, usually retired area residents, often linger to talk about airport history. They'll tell you the stories behind the many photos displayed around the facility, and then you can climb up the steep stairway to watch planes taking off from the two modest runways. The observation tower was once the control tower; the new one is out to your left from the wide glass window. If you're there early in the morning you might see the Air National Guard on maneuvers with its fighter planes. Observation tower hours are a bit irregular (mostly daytime, but not every day of the week), and there's no phone, so fit this in around other adventures.*

Eco-Travel & Cultural Excursions

Long-time environmental educator **Michele Patenaude** is a natural history guide based in the Lake Champlain Islands. Her specialty is birdwatching, and she has monitored osprey breeding for the Vermont Department of Fish and Wildlife. Call to discuss group walks, workshops, and tours (☎ 372-4864, e-mail SouthHero@ aol.com).

Give yourself the gift of a visit to the **Missisquoi National Wildlife Refuge**, on Route 78 two miles northwest of Swanton. In this 6,338-acre refuge of woods, wetlands, and the river delta are migratory songbirds, waterfowl, birds of prey, resident mammals and more. You may see a family of white-tailed deer across the creek from you, or watch a flock of Canada geese take off in spring or fall. The refuge is open year-round, and can be toured either on foot or by boat (or both). In winter you can explore it on Nordic skis. Just check in with the refuge manager when you arrive and pick up maps, trail guides, and wildlife checklists. In July and August you can pick blueberries, too. If you visit in spring or summer, be sure to bring insect repellent; you'll also need boots, a hat, and sunscreen, as well as a compass if you go picking berries.

Take Route 78 west across the water from Swanton, keep going west to Alburg (watch for turns), and discover a 608-acre parcel of sand dunes and the longest south-facing beach in the state, newly available to the public in **Alburg Dunes State Park**. This is a "work in progress" just added to state lands in 1996. Another brand-new access to Lake Champlain is at **Malletts Bay**, just north of Burlington, where the state is still deciding how to use 290 acres of freshly available undeveloped land.

South of Burlington there's another wildlife management area, **Dead Creek** (named for the way the water backs up from Lake Champlain), between the Vergennes area and Addison. It's best visited by canoe on the navigable creek of some 10 miles, among 2,814 acres of refuge. Check in at the area headquarters on Route 17 one mile west of Addison (or by mail from Dead Creek WMA, RFD1, Box 130, Vergennes VT 05491) to get an up-to-date map and any cautions about nesting birds. The map shows a road parallel to Route 17 where you can put a canoe into the creek, just west of the bridge. Spring and fall, when migratory birds come through, are especially good times to visit this refuge.

The Lake Champlain Valley

WATCHABLE

WILDLIFE

*If you're not planning to get into the water, the recent addition of a shelter on Route 17 has created a **wildlife viewing area** perfect for folks on foot or driving by. Pull into the parking area, which is about 1.5 miles west of Route 22A, on Route 17. You'll find large display panels that help you identify the geese and hawks in front of you, and the location is perfect for viewing the huge flocks of snow geese that stop here each autumn. During October there are as many as 20,000 snow geese here at one time. Bring field glasses and a camera. The sight of those wide-winged creatures lifting up against the backdrop of green hills is unbeatable.*

Where To Stay

■ Burlington

The **Radisson** (☎ 800-333-3333, $$-$$$) is Burlington's waterfront hotel, on Battery Street with views of Lake Champlain's spectacular sunsets and the mountains in the distance. It has 255 guest rooms and several dining choices. Located next to the Church Street Marketplace, it's perfect for downtown shopping and theater-going. The city's other large hotel is the **Sheraton Burlington Hotel and Conference Center** (☎ 865-6600, $$-$$$$), on the Williston Road (Route 2) between the city and the airport. The Sheraton has 310 rooms and a restaurant and pub with weekend entertainment.

Almost every major hotel chain has lodgings in Burlington, mostly along the Williston Road (Route 2) leading east out of the city, along Route 7 south (the Shelburne Road), and in nearby Winooski and Essex. The **Inn at Essex** (☎ 878-1100 or 800-727-4295, $$$-$$$$) has fireplaces in 30 of its rooms; its restaurants are operated by the New England Culinary Institute and serve fine cuisine, allowing the inn to proclaim "over 118 chefs and students at your service."

Dozens of small inns and bed-and-breakfast homes are available; the Lake Champlain Chamber of Commerce (☎ 863-3489) offers a *Bed & Breakfast Guide*, or you can stop by the Chamber office at 60 Main Street and browse through the racks of lodging brochures. Two that are a little different are **288 Maple Street** (☎ 863-2033, $$-$$$), an elegant Grand Victorian home in the heart of the city's historic hill section, with a view of the lake and mountains; and **Willow Pond Farm Bed & Breakfast** (☎ 985-8505, $$) at 20 Cheesefactory Lane in South Burlington, where the 200 acres of pasture, woods, and meadows provide hiking, cross-country skiing, and strolling through the gardens.

DOG LOVERS: *Those staying in the area may wish to contact* **Doggie Daycare** *(on Route 2 to the west of the airport;* ☎ *860-1144). They provide fun and games as well as overnight boarding for your canine companion.*

■ Essex

Since the interstate highway system linked Vermont's major cities, Route 15 out of the Burlington area has mellowed into a quiet rural road. Pick it up from Exit 15 of Interstate 89 (the northern Burlington exit, marked for Winooski and Essex Junction), and head east through the congested area of Essex Junction's shopping district, then enjoy the shift to wide open vistas as you emerge in Essex itself. Watch for the right turn onto Essex Way for one of the state's large and elegant hostelries, the **Inn at Essex**. This 97-room hotel is enjoys the presence of the New England Culinary Institute in its kitchens, and dining is an endless adventure. For fall foliage season, reserve months ahead; at other times, getting a room is easier (☎ 878-1100 or 800-727-4295, www.innatessex.com, $$$-$$$$).

■ Hinesburg & Richmond

There are two very special and very different lodgings less than 12 miles southeast of Burlington. In the bustling small town of Richmond is the **Richmond Victorian Inn B&B**, 191 Main Street (Route 2), where you can walk to nearby shops and enjoy baked treats at Daily Bread, a town tradition that's half bakery, half coffee shop. Gail M. Clark is your host at the inn. Since she loves to canoe and to ski, both downhill and cross-country, she'll encourage you to sample the area's opportunities. She also provides transportation to and from the Long Trail for hikers ($$-$$$; ☎ 434-4410 or 888-242-3362; Web site http://together.net/~gailclar).

By the Old Mill Stream, on the Richmond Road in Hinesburg, isn't in town at all. It sits on six acres with a cascading waterfall in the backyard. Michelle and Steve Fischer will give you directions to the 1867 Colonial and pamper you with breakfast treats like pumpkin gingerbread waffles or lemon-blueberry pancakes. "Well-behaved" children are welcome; so are anglers, who can expect to talk fish with Steve, an avid fly-fisherman who'll share of his favorite some spots to try your cast. The inn is open all year ($$; ☎ 482-3613, e-mail stream@together.net).

■ Lake Champlain Islands

Keep in mind that accommodations and restaurants on the islands cut way back after Columbus Day. Always call ahead. The tried and true favorites are **Ruthcliffe Lodge** (☎ 928-3200, $$) on Isle La Motte, and **Shore Acres** (☎ 372-8722, $$) at North Hero; both have the feel of

The Lake Champlain Valley

oceanfront resorts, with beach space and wide skies. Another friendly inn overlooking Lake Champlain is the **Terry Lodge** on West Shore Road in Isle La Motte, where Cherle and Matt Bean provide both a lodge and a tiny motel; breakfast and dinner are served to guests (☎ 928-3264, $$-$$$$). The **West Shore Cabins** on Route 2 in North Hero provide a no-frills location to enjoy the spectacular sunsets (☎ 372-8832, $$).

The town of Alburg is north of the islands, on a spit of mainland hanging down from Canada that is still part of the United States. Here is the **Thomas Mott Bed & Breakfast**, hosted by Patrick J. Schallert, an amateur radio operator and former wine importer and distributor. In his 1838 farmhouse he offers cozy amenities like quilts, and up-to-date graces like ceiling fans and a game room. Canoeing, fishing, and cross-country skiing are all handy; the property has a dock extending into the lake. A full breakfast is served (Blue Rock Road, Alburg, ☎ 796-3736 or 800-348-0843, Web site www.virtualcities.com/ons/vt/a/vta3502.htm, $$).

> **ACCOMMODATIONS ASSISTANCE:** *Summer rentals around Lake Champlain can be arranged through* **Island Property Management** *(☎ 372-5436). Also, the* **Lake Champlain Islands Chamber of Commerce** *(☎ 372-5683) maintains a Web site with information; visit www.champlainislands.com.*

■ Charlotte & Shelburne

Although it is a bed and breakfast in a modern building, the **Inn at Charlotte** (☎ 425-2934 or 800-425-2934, $$-$$$) still qualifies for the description "elegant, charming, and tranquil." Breakfasts here are unusual and delicious.

In Shelburne, fine lodging is found at the **Inn at Shelburne Farms** (☎ 985-8498, $$-$$$) from May to mid-October. Local bed and breakfasts include **Best Friends** (☎ 985-8185, $$), **Elliot House** (☎ 985-1412, $$-$$$), and the **Shelburne Bed & Breakfast** (☎ 985-2410, $$).

For a small informal motel that caters especially to families, try the **Dutch Mill Motel**, with its relaxed restaurant and adjacent campsites. Pets are allowed (although they must be on a leash) and kids are very welcome. There are two pools, a play area, horseshoe pits, laundry facilities, and more (2056 Shelburne Road, Shelburne, ☎ 985-3568; for camping, ☎ 985-2540, $-$$).

■ Basin Harbor

The **Basin Harbor Club** is an energetic resort with a touch of lakeshore elegance that dates back to 1886. Activities focus on the lake and there is a lot of attention paid to families. The resort has its own marina and 3,200-foot airstrip, as well as a world-class golf course. Nature trails wind through the 700 acres, and there is evening entertainment. (Basin Harbor Road, ☎ 475-2311 or 800-622-4000, e-mail res@bh-on-lc.com, Web site www.basinharbor.com, $$$$.)

■ St. Albans & Swanton

There is a **Comfort Inn** at St. Albans (☎ 524-3300, $$), with 63 rooms and suites. For country comfort try **Reminisce Bed & Breakfast** on the Lake Road, in an 1830s farmhouse next to a working dairy farm (☎ 524-3907, $-$$).

In West Swanton there's **High Winds Bed & Breakfast** (☎ 868-2521, $$) in an 1800s farmhouse. Or, go a mile and a half north of town on Route 7 to **Country Essence Bed & Breakfast** (☎ 868-4247, $$), bordering the Missisquoi National Wildlife Refuge.

■ Camping

The city of Burlington provides camping at North Beach Park, on the shores of Lake Champlain in 45 acres of woods and beach. **North Beach Campground** (☎ 862-0942) has 16 RV sites, 15 trailer sites, and 67 tent sites, as well as a beach bath house and full-service snack bar. Enter the nine-mile Burlington Bike Path from the park. Boat rentals and charters are nearby. A way of life different from any other campground in Vermont is found at **Lone Pine** (☎ 878-5447) on the Bay Road in Colchester. There are daily events at the rec hall, and weekends often bring shows, dances, and meals like corn roasts or barbecues. Folks driving RVs here will appreciate the RV resort in South Hero, **Apple Tree Bay Resort**, offering nightly activities, pool, beach, playground, marina, and nine-hole golf course (PO Box 183, South Hero, VT 05486-0183, ☎ 372-5398).

The state parks in this region offer some of the best camping. Two are on the St. Albans side of St. Albans Bay: **Burton Island** (☎ 524-6353) and the remote 125-acre island campground of **Wood's Island** (☎ 524-6353) are reached only through Burton Island State Park by private boat. **Knight Island**, another remote island campground, is closer to North Hero and has only seven campsites on the 200-acre island; contact Burton Island for reservations and the schedule of boat rides out to the island. On the Lake Champlain Islands, the state park campgrounds are at **Grand Isle State Park** (☎ 372-4300) and **North Hero State Park** (☎ 372-8727).

Where To Eat

■ Burlington

Dining out in this city is a full-time occupation. Two of the best loved places for fine dining are on the Shelburne Road (Route 7) in South Burlington: **Pauline's** (☎ 862-1081), with seafood, game birds, veal, duckling, and locally grown and produced foods blended into elegant regional cuisine; and **Perry's Fish House** (☎ 862-1300), accompanying the salmon, catfish, oysters, mussels, trout and more with Vermont-grown produce for delicious dining. And in nearby Essex (just a little farther up Route 15), turn right onto Essex Way for an elegant meal at the **Inn at Essex**, a major hotel, where dining is provided by the New England Culinary Institute (70 Essex Way, ☎ 878-1100).

Zap your tastebuds with the many varieties of Asian feasts available at the **Five Spice Café** (☎ 864-4045) on Church Street, or with Tex-Mex specialties at **Coyote's Café** (☎ 865-3632), also on Church Street. The **Daily Planet** (☎ 862-9647) on Center Street off the Church Street Marketplace is a traditional meeting place for local businesspeople and writers. So is **Carbur's** (☎ 862-4206) on St. Paul Street across from City Hall Park, with its 16-page menu and famous French onion soup. Also on St. Paul Street is the **Trattoria Delia** (☎ 864-5253) for fresh pastas, local fish and game, and fresh-baked breads. **Sweetwaters** (☎ 864-9800) in the Church Street Marketplace is a European-style bistro with outdoor café. Breakfast at **Henry's Diner** (☎ 862-9010, 155 Bank Street around the corner from the Marketplace) is a Burlington tradition too.

For exquisite baked goods and excellent coffees and teas, try **Mirabelle's** (198 Main Street, ☎ 658-3074; or at the waterfront in the Wing Building, ☎ 658-1466). Chocolate fanciers will want to stop at **Lake Champlain Chocolates** (☎ 864-1807) on Pine Street. Microbrewery tasters can find the **Magic Hat Brewing Company** (☎ 658-2739) at 180 Flynn Avenue and take a tour on Wednesday through Saturday afternoons.

> **TIP:** *To get acquainted with all the regional brews of the state, attend the **Brewers' Festival** at Burlington's Waterfront Park, usually held on a weekend in mid-June, (contact Vermont Brewers Association, ☎ 244-6828, Web site www. tastebeer.together.com). There are ales and pilsners to sample, as well as unusual beverages like "hard" lemonade, plus tidbits of drinking history from the Ethan Allen Homestead and some great local performers.*

When you're counting pennies (or trying to feed teenagers), **Paradise Burritos** is good to know about. Walk downstairs from the sidewalk of the Church Street Marketplace to 88 Church Street (☎ 660-3603, open Monday through Saturday, 11:30 a.m. to 9 p.m.). There are bounteous buffet lunches for about $5 each at the **Orchid Garden** in South Burlington, found by returning to Interstate 91 and crossing it on Main Street, which then becomes Williston Road. Turn right on Dorset Street, pass Barnes & Noble on your left, and watch for the little "Blue Mall," also on the left. Orchid Garden (☎ 658-3626) is behind the roadside bed and bath shops. You'll see University Mall on the other side of Dorset Street, where you can get a mall-type quick meal or snack if you're feeling the urge.

Burlington Nightlife

Nightlife in Burlington is lively year-round, and there's always music. The town's nickname is Queen City, a good description. Start at **Leunig's** at 115 Church Street (☎ 862-5306) for dinner and a glass of wine, whether indoors or at a sidewalk table, and make the most of the live music, jazz, or cabaret, on Tuesdays through Thursdays. On the weekends the club scene is hopping: there's **Nectar's** (188 Main Street, ☎ 658-4771), where the group Phish got its start, and upstairs from Nectar's at **Club Metronome** (☎ 865-4563); the rock-riddled and funky **242 Main** (at 242 Main Street, of course, ☎ 862-2244); and **Vermont Pub & Brewery** at 144 College Street (☎ 865-0500).

In Williston, the next town north and barely separate from Burlington, **Higher Ground** (1 Main Street, ☎ 654-8888) hosts many a headline performer; recent ones included Tom Rush and Dr. John, as well as top reggae, jazz, and rock shows. For the full range of evening entertainment, pick up a free copy of *Seven Days* when you get to town, or check the club listing at www.bigheavyworld.com. Don't forget to check who's playing at the **Flynn Theater** (☎ 86-FLYNN), downtown, where solo performers, big ensembles, and nationally known acts arrive regularly.

On Friday and Saturday nights, **The Comedy Zone** at the Radisson Hotel (60 Battery Street, ☎ 658-6500) showcases nationally known comedians. There are usually two shows. Take in dinner at the hotel's **Seasons on the Lake** award-winning restaurant to make a full evening of it (ask about dinner-and-show packages).

■ Winooski

Perhaps the most interesting view out a restaurant window is at the **Waterworks** (☎ 655-2044) at the Champlain Mill in Winooski: you look right into the waters of the Winooski River, and especially in spring the surge and force are magnificent to watch. **Libby's Blue Line Diner** (☎ 655-0343), with its friendly atmosphere and home-cooked food, is just a short way up Winooski's Main Street, which becomes Roosevelt Highway.

■ Essex Junction

A stop at the **Lincoln Inn** (☎ 878-3309), a century-old landmark at the town's five corners intersection, lets you sample the restaurant's "good old American basics," like the open-faced steak sandwich, as well as Greek specialties and reliably delicious desserts.

■ Lake Champlain Islands

Keep in mind that restaurants and attractions on the islands cut way back after Columbus Day. Always call ahead. Do stop in the summer or early fall at **Ruthcliffe Lodge** (☎ 928-3200) on Isle La Motte and **Shore Acres** (☎ 372-8722) at North Hero; both serve excellent meals. **Hero's Welcome** (☎ 372-4161) in North Hero makes good sandwiches and has its own bakery and café.

■ Basin Harbor

Dine in classic American style at the **Basin Harbor Club** (☎ 475-2311 or 800-622-4000), where you can choose among three restaurants: the Main Dining Room, the casual Red Mill, and the Ranger Room, situated between the golf course and the swimming pool.

The Capital District, Stowe & North

The capital district of Vermont is full of small colleges, winding rivers, and carefully preserved small towns built from red brick, white clapboard, and granite. Farms and maple sugaring sheds surround these pockets of country homes and small businesses. Only around Barre, the state's granite-carving center, has industry made a scar on the landscape – and it is a fascinating scar. The capital city itself, **Montpelier**, has fewer than 9,000 residents and is the smallest state capital in the nation, although its wide variety of cafés and bookshops emphasize diversity.

IN THIS CHAPTER
■ **Montpelier**
■ **Middlesex**
■ **Barre**
■ **Plainfield & Marshfield**
■ **Cabot**
■ **Northfield**
■ **Williamstown**
■ **Bolton Valley**
■ **Waterbury**
■ **Stowe**
■ **Jeffersonville**
■ **Smugglers' Notch**

Getting Here & Getting Around

Tucked into the valley of the Winooski River, **Montpelier** is at the crossroads of Interstate 89, Route 2 (Vermont's familiar old east-west route and still the road to Maine), and the very rural north-south Route 12. Most people arrive for the first time from Interstate 89, having left Interstate 91 an hour behind. If you've been touring the Mad River Valley you'll come up on Route 100B to either the interstate or Route 2 east; from the Northeast Kingdom you'll come to town on Route 2; and from neighboring Barre, the twin city to Montpelier; the connecting road is Route 302, better known locally as the Barre-Montpelier Road.

From the capital city, the interstate heads toward **Burlington**, but first passes through **Waterbury**, now full of state offices, as well as recreation providers who send canoes out onto the river, hikers up toward Mount Mansfield and Camel's Hump, and skiers into Stowe. Route 100 connects Waterbury with Stowe, and this stretch of the little two-lane road is one of the most heavily traveled in Vermont, especially in autumn and when the

The Capital District

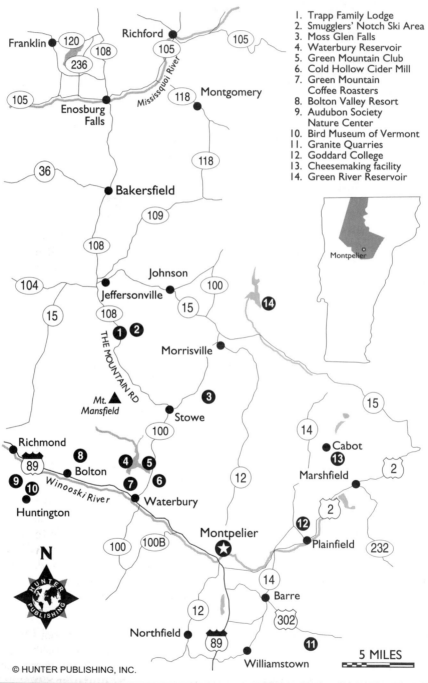

1. Trapp Family Lodge
2. Smugglers' Notch Ski Area
3. Moss Glen Falls
4. Waterbury Reservoir
5. Green Mountain Club
6. Cold Hollow Cider Mill
7. Green Mountain
   Coffee Roasters
8. Bolton Valley Resort
9. Audubon Society
   Nature Center
10. Bird Museum of Vermont
11. Granite Quarries
12. Goddard College
13. Cheesemaking facility
14. Green River Reservoir

Franklin
120
108
236
105
Enosburg Falls
Richford
105
105
Mississquoi River
118 Montgomery
118
36
Bakersfield
109
108
Montpelier
104
Johnson
100
15
15
108
Jeffersonville
THE MOUNTAIN RD
Mt. Mansfield
Morrisville
Stowe
100
14
Richmond
89
Bolton
Winooski River
Huntington
Waterbury
100
100B
N
Montpelier
12
14
Barre
302
Northfield
89
Williamstown
15
14
Cabot
13
Marshfield
2
12
2
12
Plainfield
232
11

5 MILES

© HUNTER PUBLISHING, INC.

snow is thick and powdery. Stowe has a distinctly European feel, perhaps first drawn from the Trapp Family Lodge; this elegant inn and touring center was founded by Maria von Trapp, whose American fame came from the movie, *The Sound of Music*.

Small towns scatter outward from Montpelier and Stowe: to the northeast, the traditionally toured towns of **Cabot** and **Calais** (pronounced *KA-liss*); to the northwest the ski resort town of **Jeffersonville**, home to Smugglers' Notch; and due north, a spread of mountain and valley towns in the **Green Mountains**, with covered bridges along the Lamoille and Trout Rivers and a scenic dairying region just south of the Canadian border.

Touring

■ Montpelier

Wherever you've come from, slow down as you enter Montpelier. The little city's streets are busy, and at rush hours the traffic is heavy but steady. There's plenty of parking in lots positioned off State Street and Main Street, the two main roads, which cross at the center of the shopping district. Parallel to Main Street is Elm Street, and the town's information kiosk is where Elm comes into State – a block south of Main Street and three blocks north of the small white capitol building with its golden dome. The information kiosk is a good place to start touring the town, which is so small that it's a pleasure to walk.

Start by walking up State Street to the busy shopping intersection of Main and State. Notice that all the town's main intersections have push-buttons for pedestrians to cross the road; the traffic from all directions will stop for everyone to cross at once. Close to this corner is the town's coffee shop, a bakery operated by the New England Culinary Institute, a Ben & Jerry's Ice Cream shop, a fine crafts shop, and two bookstores. Across Main Street, East State Street continues to Vermont College, where you'll find the **T. W. Wood Gallery and Arts Center** (☎ 828-8743).

Cross Main Street and head west past Burlington Bagels toward a lovely church and the **Kellogg-Hubbard Library**, where the reading room is so well stocked with periodicals and newspapers that you may want to linger. Then come back on the other side of Main Street to check the **New England Culinary Institute's** two teaching restaurants, side by side. Turn down narrow Langdon Street to find another bookshop and the area's best known eatery, the **Horn of the Moon Café**, which puts out a well-loved vegetarian cookbook.

Cross the river and turn left to return to Main Street for a walk south, into the state buildings district. Just past the post office is the Capitol Theatre, followed by the narrow driveway to the Thrush Tavern. Then comes the Pavilion Building, where the **Vermont Historical Society** (☎ 828-2291)

Montpelier

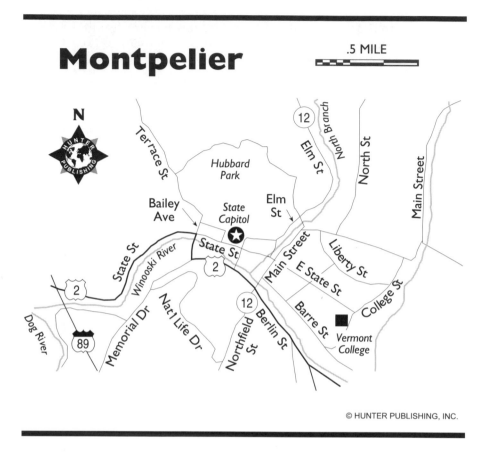

.5 MILE

© HUNTER PUBLISHING, INC.

has a great museum and research library that includes genealogical materials. Vermont's colorful history is portrayed here in costumes, furnishings, handbills, games, and curiosities, as well as maps, photographs, and stories. The Supreme Court building follows.

Next on the right side of State Street is the **Vermont State House**, built from blocks of Barre granite with a gold-leaf dome and topped by a gold-leaf statue of Ceres, the Roman goddess of agriculture. On the steps is a marble statue of Vermont's Revolutionary War hero, Ethan Allen, who led the Green Mountain Boys. Both sculptures are by Larkin Mead. Guided tours of the State House are given on weekdays and Saturdays from June through October, or you can step inside to pick up a brochure and look around on your own. Be sure to look at the flags that led Vermont's famous Civil War troops, hard fighters who turned the tide of a few battles, especially the one at Cedar Creek; in the State House the Cedar Creek Room celebrates this victory and the courage and stamina involved.

SEASONAL EVENTS IN MONTPELIER

Montpelier glows in autumn, with scarlet and gold fall foliage amidst the bustle of a small city getting back into gear. Peak foliage color is generally the first two weeks of October, and there are celebrations in and around the city. Plan to go to a church supper, maybe ham and baked beans with home-baked pies. The **Central Vermont Chamber of Commerce** (☎ 229-5711, Web site www.central-vt.com) can give you advance information, or check the bulletin board at **Ben & Jerry's**, the famous ice cream shop at the intersection of State and Main streets. Here you can also find the skinny on foot races and bike events, as well as at **Onion River Sports**, 20 Langdon Street (☎ 229-9409). Get to know the streets and historic buildings better with a **Capital Walking Tour**, starting at 134 State Street in front of the tourist information center on any Saturday morning at 10 a.m. (adults $3.50, kids free; other tour times by arrangement). Contact Margot George of the Montpelier Heritage Group for information (☎ 229-4842).

Winter in this little city is the perfect time for **gallery hopping** – there are seven galleries in town, including the **T. W. Wood Gallery and Arts Center** on the Vermont College campus (☎ 828-8743). An **evening art stroll** is offered once the weather settles down (☎ 229-2766). Look for holiday exhibits and events, as well as craft sales at the churches in early December. **Hubbard Park** offers outdoor events for skiers and snowshoers and, of course sledding (locally called sliding). On New Year's Eve, the city has its own **First Night** celebration, with performances and events all afternoon and evening, and fireworks at midnight.

In spring the town warms up, to kids especially, with a **Rotten Sneakers Contest** in March and a **Kite Flying Contest** in May. There's also an **Easter egg hunt**, free to those 12 years and under, at Hubbard Park on the Saturday before Easter (for all these events, more information can be obtained from the Recreation Department at ☎ 223-5141).

Summer is Montpelier's prime festival season, starting with the **Onion River Arts Council Street Dance** in June (☎ 229-9408) and the Recreation Department's **Water Carnival** (☎ 223-5141). This are performances ranging from Shakespeare to David Budbill (Vermont's wry-tongued playwright) by **Lost Nation Theater**, which performs at City Hall on Main Street (☎ 229-0492, Web site www.lostnationtheater.org). In July the **Onion River Arts Council** (☎ 229-9408) sponsors the **Vermont Philharmonic Concert**, and in August a **family circus**. To really get acquainted with the heart of Montpelier, bring your lawn chairs or blankets to the State House lawn on Wednesday evenings, where the free **band concerts** bring out the town.

Beyond the State House are more state office buildings, including the home of *Vermont Life*, where classic photographs of Vermont and articles on its past and present have built a loyal community of appreciators.

If you're up for a long walk, keep going past the state buildings and turn right onto Bailey Avenue, then take the second left onto Clarendon Drive, and find the right turn into Hubbard Park. Among its 180 acres of hills and trails is a 50-foot stone tower that will give you a 360° view of the city.

Later, you might want to drive along Main Street eastward toward Route 2 and turn left onto Barre Street, to visit the **Hunger Mountain Food Co-op**. Here you will see the former granite worksheds that have mostly become homes to other small industries. Also by the river, on Main Street itself, is the little **Savoy Theater**, showplace of foreign and classic films.

■ Barre

Barre is even more of a "Main Street" town than Montpelier. Slightly larger than the capital, its heart has been the granite carving that drew both industry and great artists in stone to the town and nearby villages. Almost all of the shops are on Main Street, which is also Route 302; the sec-

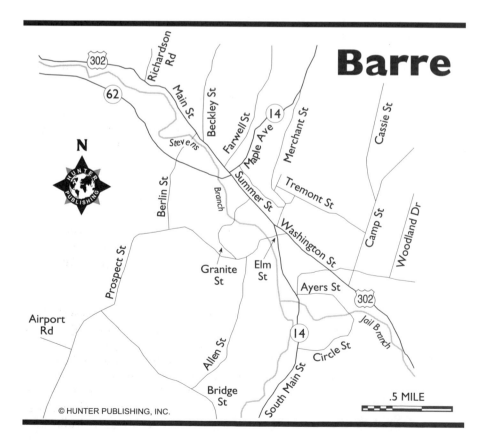

tion of Route 302 that connects Barre to Montpelier (the Barre-Montpelier Road) is crammed with eateries and lodgings, as well as department stores and more. Performing arts in town are housed in the newly reconstructed **Barre Opera House**. Where Routes 14 and 62 meet Main Street is the vest-pocket-size **Dente Park**. Here, a statue of a granite carver stands for the town's pride in its ethnic diversity – stonecutters and craftsmen swarmed here from Scotland, Eastern Europe, Italy, and French Canada, as well as England, Germany, Spain, Scandinavia, and the Middle East. Most came in the granite heyday of 1880-1910.

DID YOU KNOW?

Barre and the surrounding towns still provide a third of the nation's granite memorials, and the area nurtures stone-carving talent and art.

Mt. Hope Cemetery, just north of town on Route 14, includes wonderful marking stones, mausoleums, and ornate monuments. The carvers' striking classic and modern designs adorn not only the graves of others but also their own. The cemetery is really an outdoor art gallery. Another showcase is at **Vermont Granite Works**, 891 North Main Street (☎ 476-0699), between Barre and Montpelier.

■ The Granite Quarries

Today most granite quarrying and carving takes place southeast of Barre in the little towns along Routes 302 and 110. The long barns in which the granite is carved are called granite sheds. The quarries are marked, not only by the scars in the rock bed, but by the tall gantry posts with their anchored cables that spread like the tops of giant carousels, each one covering a city block or more, for the pulleys and hoists to strain against as they lift the massive granite blocks.

CAUTION

Rock climbers, please note: The granite quarries are not safe to explore on foot. Not only are there tons of rock in unstable positions, but some unexploded dynamite charges may linger. Consider the quarries extremely dangerous, despite their fascination and beauty.

Touring is best at the **Rock of Ages** quarries (☎ 476-3119), where there is a visitors' center and guided and self-guided tours (May through October). Route 14 heads there from town, going into South Barre, where you will see signs for the quarry across the road from the interstate highway access. Take the left turn uphill and follow signs to the visitors' center. The granite vein runs deep into the earth, eight to 10 miles deep, but the actual quarries can reach down only about 450 feet into the vein. This is because the top of a "hole in the ground" has to be quite wide to keep the walls from collapsing inward. The main quarry now in use is already 50 acres in "ground level" size, just to be able to reach down to that 450-foot depth. Although there were once more than 70 quarries here, they are now consolidated into six, and from June to mid-October a shuttle tour runs among the working sites. You can also visit the quarry's manufacturing division on weekdays year-round; get directions at the main office.

■ Plainfield, Marshfield & Cabot

From Montpelier, Route 2 north passes through several interesting small towns. At East Montpelier, watch the turn so that you don't accidentally end up on Route 14 (many do!). Plainfield, home of **Goddard College**, is just three miles farther. Goddard was widely noted for its experimental learning programs in the 1970s and for the politically active Bread and Puppet Theater, which was based there for several years. Today, the college maintains an active liberal arts program with innovative masters degree options. Although Plainfield is a small village, the college influence nourishes a bookstore and some special eateries nearby.

Marshfield is a long eight miles past Plainfield along the winding riverbanks of the Winooski. When you get there, note **Rainbow Sweets**, the heavenly bakery on the right; take the unpaved road next to Rainbow Sweets for half a mile and go a short distance up either fork in the road to see a spectacular, but little-known, **waterfall** – one of the longest in the state.

From Marshfield, Route 215 heads north to Cabot, home of Vermont's best known cheese maker. Cabot is especially famous for its cheddars; at the visitor's center (☎ 563-2231) on Route 215 you can see the cheeses being made, watch a short film, and sample to your heart's content. The center is closed Sundays and for the month of January; children are very welcome on the tour.

VERMONT HERITAGE WEEKEND

What happens when the state's most famous cheddar cheese maker and the Vermont Historical Society team up their energy? In 1999 the first **Vermont Heritage Weekend** took place, and was such a big winner that it is likely to be an annual event. Dates will be in mid-June, and although the Cabot Creamery is the center of the whirl of events, they also take place at 35 local historical society museums, meeting rooms, and collections throughout central and northeastern Vermont. Check this year's commitment at ☎ 888-TRY-CABOT. Among the treats: entertainment, tours, agricultural demonstrations, archeological insight, cultural demonstrations, and of course food, food, food!

For a very pleasant drive, go back down Route 215 less than a mile and take the Bathfield Road (also called the Cabot Road as you get farther along it) to Woodbury, passing a lovely old church and cemetery and arriving in the picturesque village on Route 14. To the north on Route 14 is Greenwood Lake; to the south, as you head back toward Montpelier, is **Woodbury Lake** (aka Sabin Pond), a summer haven for swimmers and boaters.

■ Northfield & Williamstown

If you choose to tour south of Montpelier, be sure to include a stop in Northfield to see the **military museum at Norwich University**, a private academy of about a thousand cadets. The town also has a classic July 4th parade.

Williamstown is on Route 14, reached by heading south from Barre or by taking the same exit from Interstate 89 as you would for Northfield, Exit 5, but heading east on Route 64. It has two unusual museums: **Knight's Spider Web Farm** (just off Route 14 on Cliff Place, ☎ 433-5568), and the **Weathered Barn Doll Museum** (from Route 64 turn at the school signs and go past the elementary school to the left onto Flint, then take a right onto George Rd.; ☎ 433-5502). Both are open in summer and through foliage season.

■ Waterbury

When the state offices overflowed from Montpelier to neighboring Waterbury, occupying the red brick buildings that were once used by the state hospital for the mentally ill, they brought new flavor to this town, which has always been the southern hub of the year-round Stowe resort. The downtown stores include eateries and modest shops. Near the railroad is the headquarters of **Green Mountain Coffee Roasters**. You can visit their company store in Waterbury Center, farther north. When you drive up Route 100 toward Waterbury Center, though, you're entering a region that supports adventure year-round, from fishing and canoeing, to hiking the great peaks of Mount Mansfield and Camel's Hump, to skiing, snowshoeing, skating, and snowboarding.

From Interstate 89, take Route 100 north and head toward Waterbury Center. A mile up the road is the region's most tasty adventure: **Ben & Jerry's Ice Cream** (☎ 244-5641 to reserve a tour; 244-TOUR for the hotline; or online at www.benjerry.com). Factory tours let you taste and have fun, and a movie tells the story of the boyhood buddies who founded the company in a Burlington garage and saw it grow to international proportions. Ben & Jerry's has a strong environmental and social action commitment; the tour deals with this as well.

Farther up Route 100 is a shop shared by Green Mountain Chocolate Company and Cabot Cheese (its annex store). **Green Mountain Chocolate Company** (☎ 244-1139) is the creation of a former White House pastry chef, Albert Kumin; there are 40 coffees from Green Mountain Coffee Roasters, and even a drive-through shop to accompany the chocolates, cakes, fudge, and cookies. You may also see the chef's chocolate sculptures and catch a chocolate-making demonstration.

Three miles north of Interstate 89, on the right, is the **Cold Hollow Cider Mill** (☎ 800-3-APPLES or 244-8771), where year-round demonstrations of cider-making include free samples.

If you're an avid hiker and lover of the Green Mountains, or on your way to becoming one, go just one mile farther up Route 100 and turn left into the parking lot of the **Green Mountain Club** (☎ 244-7037). This organization created the Long Trail, Vermont's hiking route through the mountain peaks, and it maintains the trail with the help of dedicated volunteers. A small bookshop offers a good selection on hiking here and in other regions of Vermont and New England, plus climbing, biking, canoeing, and winter sports. Catch up on the latest trail news and chat with other lovers of the mountains.

■ Stowe

Stowe is a four-season resort, a town caught up in the hundred different ways to savor life and especially life on **Mount Mansfield**, the true host of the town. Here, visitors explore high-altitude ecosystems, find recreation, and enjoy spectacular views.

LOCAL LORE

Native American folklore said a tired giant once lay down here with his face turned toward the sky. He lies there still, in the Green Mountains of Stowe: the forehead, nose, lips, and chin are at the top of Mount Mansfield, and the prominent chin is the highest point in Vermont, at 4,393 feet elevation.

Hikers were certainly becoming familiar with the mountain long before skiers; the first recorded descent of the mountain was in 1914 by Nathaniel Goodrich, a librarian from Dartmouth College. Today the mountain's slopes form two ski areas: **Stowe** to the east, and **Smugglers' Notch** to the west. Ski trails link them on a high ridge that gets battered by winter storms.

Over 40,000 people a year are visiting the summer face of the peak and its frail alpine ecosystem. The Green Mountain Club, caretakers for nearly a century of the high peaks and wilderness, urges walkers in the snow-free seasons to "do the rock walk" – walk only on the rocks, not the plants.

Route 100 from Waterbury rolls another smooth 10 miles north to reach the center of Stowe. Despite all the visitors, Stowe looks like a small town, neatly caught in the valley alongside the Little River, old-timey and quaint.

But when you make the west turn in the middle of town onto Route 108, which is the resort access road, you see where all the development has happened. The **Mountain Road**, as it's locally called, is lined with posh ski shops, art galleries, restaurants, and lodgings. Then there are the ski sheds and snowboard and mountain bike stores, where the decor is less important than the high-quality merchandise. There's a **recreation path** alongside the Mountain Road, a 5½-mile paved walkway that winds back and forth over the waters of the West Branch and is open to walkers, Nordic skiers, cyclists, and runners. There are four bike shops along the way.

You can easily tour the historic village on foot, browsing in craft shops, art galleries, and a great bookstore. The first tenth of a mile of Route 108 is part of this collection of attractive businesses. After that, though, you need to be on wheels, whether by car on the Mountain Road or by bicycle on the rec path; the village entrance to this path is behind the Community Church on Main Street (Route 100), where there's parking. By the way, across from the church is School Street; the **Helen Day Art Center** (☎ 253-8358) is three blocks down School Street and is open daily (except summer Mondays and winter Sundays and Mondays) with exciting exhibits of regional art and artists, and plenty of lectures, classes, and other special programs.

As you ascend the Mountain Road, crossing roads to note are the Luce Hill Road on the left, from which you can make the second left onto Trapp Hill Road to find the famous **Trapp Family Lodge**; higher up, the Edson Hill Road on the right, leading to a cross-country ski touring center and riding stables; and the Mountain Toll Road on the left, the beginning of the resort at the top of the mountain, a very driveable paved road to the summit in warm weather. Just beyond the toll road is the entrance to Smugglers' Notch State Park on the right. Don't let the name confuse you: both ski areas are in the park, and it really is **Mount Mansfield** you're about to visit on this side, to your left. The Mount Mansfield base lodge is just ahead on the left. To reach the Long Trail over the peaks you need to drive farther into the Notch itself, a 2,162-foot-elevation mountain pass that is most definitely closed once the snows arrive. In summer there's an alpine slide in the Notch; an **in-line skate park** is located near the Mansfield base lodge.

■ Jeffersonville

When the mountain is richly green or flaming in autumn's gold and scarlet, the drive over Route 108 through Smugglers' Notch (cows were being smuggled from Canada when the name was given!) is a breathtaking (and car-brake-challenging) way to reach Jeffersonville, the base town for Smugglers' Notch ski and resort area. In winter, the long way around is the only way: up Route 100 from Stowe nine miles to Morrisville (well, there is a little short cut on a back road to Hyde Park), then along Route 15, four miles to Johnson and nine more to Jeffersonville. Route 108 on the Jeffersonville side of the mountain ridge is less crowded, and has some nice eateries. The terrain around Smugglers' Notch is severe enough to be a training ground for rock and ice climbing and for military wilderness troops. Luckily, your car won't have to suffer; the roads are excellent.

Smugglers' Notch includes three peaks: Madonna, Sterling, and Morse. In winter it's a stunning ski resort. In summer the resort offers road touring, as well as hikes, guided walks, birders' breakfasts, canoeing connections, and fly-fishing.

■ Morrisville

If you took the winter route around to Jeffersonville and the Smugglers' Notch resort, you already discovered Morrisville, with its small and cheerful downtown section. This pleasant town has assorted shops as well as the **Noyes House Museum**, full of artifacts and architecture from the Federal and Victorian eras. It's an 18-room brick house at number 1 Main Street on Route 100, across from the police station. Don't miss the 1800 pitcher and Toby jug collection. Hours are afternoons from June to September or by appointment (☎ 888-7617).

Morrisville's biggest recreation asset is **Green River Reservoir**, a wild three-mile-long lake to the northwest, where canoes and kayaks can easily lose themselves among the islands and waterways. Moose, loons (one of Vermont's rare birds), and beavers flourish, and the wild area is so large that human use doesn't seem to have overly disturbed the residents yet.

■ Johnson & North

Between Morrisville and Jeffersonville is Johnson, with a woolen mill, good eateries, and assorted shops. The **Johnson Woolen Mills** opens its factory store Monday through Saturday for most of the year, and Sundays in the fall; in April and May the hours are shortened (☎ 635-2271). This is where you can get those great red-and-black-plaid wool jackets that oldtimers wear in the woods, as well as rugged sweaters and Hudson Bay Company point blankets (the "points" are marks that indicate how many beaver pelts would have been required to trade for each blanket in 1779). Nearby **East Johnson** on Route 100 has a gallery shop for **Vermont Rug Makers** (☎ 635-2434, Web site www.vermontrugmakers.com), where a traditional New England craft is transformed into up-to-date explosions of color and texture.

From Johnson, Route 100 heads north; a turn onto Route 118 in **Eden** enters a placid, rural landscape of wetlands and dairy farms, covered bridges and small pockets of history, home to deer, moose, raccoons and hawks. This landscape continues to the Canadian border towns of **Richford** and **West Berkshire**. From Richford a trip back south on Route 108 visits other agriculturally oriented towns: Enosburg Falls, Bakersfield, and back to Jeffersonville.

■ Bolton, Richmond & Huntington

A third ski resort lies on the side of the high mountains: **Bolton Valley Resort**, most easily reached from the Interstate 89 (Exit 11) at Waterbury and then taking Route 2 northwest, parallel to the limited-access interstate, for another 10 miles. This ski area is the closest to Burlington, and draws a good winter crowd from that area.

The next exit of Interstate 89, Exit 10, is at Richmond. If you'd like to step back an era in skiing history, the little ski area here, **Cochran's** (see *On Snow & Ice*, page 262), has a pair of rope tows and is a good place to take children.

Five miles south of Richmond is Huntington, where the **Green Mountain Audubon Society Nature Center** (☎ 434-3068) has a 230-acre preserve with year-round trails, and where the **Bird Museum of Vermont** (☎ 434-2167) with its carvings of over 200 species by naturalist Bob Spear makes an interesting summer stop.

Adventures

■ On Foot

Middlesex

The **Middlesex Trail** is a few miles north of Montpelier and leads to a view of the Green Mountain peaks, from Killington in the south to Whiteface Mountain in the north. In the distance you can see the White Mountains of New Hampshire, and closer, to the north, the Northeast Kingdom mountains of Burke and Bald Mountain. Start in Montpelier at the information kiosk. Turn onto Elm Street and follow it as it becomes Route 12 north. About 7.5 miles from town, as you drive alongside the Wrightsville Dam Recreation Area, take a left onto Shady Rill Road. Go through the cluster of houses that's called Shady Rill and keep going 2.2 miles; when you reach a "four-corners," take the right onto the Hill Road (Worcester Road). You'll go over a one-lane bridge, pass a right turn, and make the left at 0.7 mile from the four-corners onto North Bear Swamp Road. Stay on this road 2.2 miles to where you see a large house on the right with a windmill in the front yard; look for the logging road that goes straight ahead where the main road bears left, and park at the junction. The blue-blazed trail starts on the logging road, although you won't see blazes until you've gone through the fields into the woods. You'll start to climb gradually, and will pass a side path on the right at 0.8 mile.

Still following along the old road, the trail gets steeper and meets the **White Rock Trail** (white blazes) which comes in from the left at 1.6 miles. Swing to the right with the trail, noting a rock spur at 2½ miles, where you can take a side trip about 125 feet to an overlook. Go back to the trail and keep climbing, skirting the ledges; the trail will come to an apparent dead end at 2½ miles, but look around: it goes sharply left up onto a ledge. You are now climbing to the south summit of Mt. Hunger, and you meet the Waterbury and Worcester Trails here. Look closely at your own return path before you move up to the summit and enjoy the vista. The one-way trip is 2.8 miles.

Check the Green Mountain Club's (GMC) *Day Hiker's Guide to Vermont* for the trail to **Spruce Mountain**, which is reached from Route 302, east of East Barre; it's a 2.2-mile (one-way) ascent to the summit.

Two other summit hikes of about two miles (one-way) each are the **Elmore Mountain Trail** near Morrisville, and the **Mount Norris Trail** in Eden. Check the *Day Hiker's Guide* for trailhead and landmarks.

Stowe

When you get to Stowe, you'll want to climb **Mount Mansfield** for the "peak experience" of going up Vermont's highest mountain. To pick your approach to Mount Mansfield, get a copy of the *Long Trail Guide* and match the route to your level of skill.

Please keep in mind the fragility of the rare alpine plants, and try to step only on rocks; whenever you hike above the tree line it's a good idea to stay strictly on the trail, to preserve the land. The wear from 40,000 pairs of feet each year at the top of Mansfield is tragic; your help matters.

If you'd rather take it easy for the day, you can go up the Toll Road by car, a 4½-mile road with steep hairpin turns that can be exciting; there's a parking area at the top. Or you can go up in the eight-passenger gondola to the base station that's just under the "chin," the high peak of the mountain. The gondola runs from mid-June to early October. From the station at the top you can scramble up the steep trail for 0.3 mile to the summit ridge and the Long Trail, where you'll turn north (right) and go another 0.4 mile to the actual summit. Remember the rock walk and step on the rocks, not the plants! You can get dinner at Cliff House while you're up there. But if you're ready to hike in, the easiest route is from where the Long Trail meets Route 108 in Smugglers' Notch, 8.2 miles from Route 100. You'll need decent hiking boots even for this trail. Some of the more challenging routes in the *Long Trail Guide* actually involve ladders and squeezing through rock crevices – not much fun for backpackers!

The hike from **Smugglers' Notch to Sterling Pond** will give you another taste of the Long Trail, this time heading north. Your connection with the southbound Long Trail was at 8.2 miles from Route 100; this time, continue on into the Notch and look for a large parking lot on the left, with an information booth. Across from the parking lot find the white-blazed Long Trail and climb the steep rock steps. At 1.1 miles the trail meets a ski trail connecting the Spruce Peak and Smugglers' Notch ski areas and joins the ski trail to drop down and cross the **Sterling Pond Outlet Trail**. It's only another 0.2 mile to Sterling Pond and the associated hikers' shelter. At the pond, if you stay to the left you'll find a good overlook above the next chairlift.

HIKING EQUIPMENT & TOURS: *Speaking of hiking boots, if you didn't happen to bring any, or can't stand the ones you brought, there's another option: rent a pair.* **Pinnacle Ski & Sports** *(☎ 253-7222), at the foot of Mount Mansfield on the Mountain Road in Stowe, includes a Tecnica Hiking Center, and offers guided tours for hiking and natural history. Another shop with a stock of boots (Alpina) is* **Lamoille Mountain Guides & Topnotch Bike Rentals** *(4000 Mountain Road, ☎ 253-6433).*

Summer is the traditional time for a waterfall trek, but try it in the spring when the water is high for an exciting sense of the power of hydro. In the Stowe area, there's a quick hike less than half a mile long that leads to **Moss Glen Falls** (same name as the one in Granville Gulf, but not as high). From the center of Stowe at the intersection of Routes 100 and 108, take Route 100 north for 3.1 miles and turn right onto Randolph Road. At the next fork, 0.4 mile down Randolph Road, take the right onto Moss Glen Fall Road, which comes to another fork. Leave the paved road on the right, while you take the old road that goes straight ahead; park the car here at the turnoff. Follow the old road into the field and watch for where the trail angles off to the right into the woods; you can hear the falls already. A short, steep climb takes you to the lookout, with the bowl of the falls below you.

ROCK CLIMBING

Rock climbers, ice climbers, and mountaineers in training will find great opportunities for adventure climbing in the rock walls and ledges of **Smugglers' Notch**. Even the military brings its wilderness troops here for training. Two nearby guide and adventure training groups will help you get started: **Peak Concepts** (PO Box 338, Jeffersonville, VT 05464; ☎ 644-5385) offers a wide range of year-round courses in mountaineering, at both local and international locations. Also included are programs in Nordic and telemark skiing, self-rescue, and instructor training. **Green Mountain Guides** (PO Box 421, Jeffersonville, VT 05464, ☎ 644-8131) offers ice and mountaineering courses in the Notch, plus a wilderness first responder course (specialized first-aid course for rescuers). If you're headed for the cliffs, a challenging course will get you prepared.

AUTHOR TIP

*When you hike this region you have a terrific resource just down the road from Stowe, at the **Green Mountain Club** on Route 100 (☎ 244-7037): guidebooks, maps, brochures, and camaraderie.*

Bolton Valley

For a good ramble on guided or self-guided nature trails, head for **Bolton Valley Resort** (☎ 434-2131 or 800-451-3220), with 32 miles of marked trails. A pair of the endangered peregrine falcons is nesting on Bone Mountain within the resort; do the birds a favor and stay well away, but take along your field glasses to admire their soaring from a distance.

HIKING GUIDES

■ If you like experienced companionship on your hikes, guide Jeffery Kaiser specializes in taking hikers and campers along the trails and less traveled parts of this region. Reach him at **Ricker Mountain Guide Service** (PO Box 510, Moretown, VT 05660, ☎ 496-4077).

■ **Outdoor Adventure of Vermont** is centered in Montpelier, although their year-round hiking and winter skiing expeditions range from the Montpelier region and the peaks of northern Vermont to backcountry Quebec and Utah. For a look at the options in fully guided tours (with nights at country inns or in tents and cabins), check their Web page at www6.pair.com/oavt. You can also contact them by e-mail at hleyshon@plainfield.bypass.com, or ☎ 223-4172 or 800-639-9208.

Waterbury

Not all of the Mount Mansfield area is for death-defying climbers. The Little River block of the **Mount Mansfield State Forest** comprises several thousand acres around the Waterbury Reservoir. From Waterbury, take Route 2 west for about 1½ miles and look for the road to the Little River Campground on your right. It's a 3½-mile road in to the campground, but instead, drive just 1.7 miles to park at the Waterbury parking area. The **Little River Trail** starts here, and goes on to meet the **North CCC Loop**, the **Stevenson Brook Trail**, and others, totaling more than 12 miles. Little River Trail has orange diamond markers with some blue paint blazes. You can try to follow the trails just by watching for blazes, but the tangle is pretty fierce, and using the GMC's *Day Hiker's Guide* with close attention to landmarks and distances will help keep you headed in the right direction.

■ Travel With Horses Or Llamas

There are two riding stables in Stowe (**Edson Hill Riding Stables**, ☎ 253-8954, and **Topnotch Riding Stables**, ☎ 253-8585). Another is across from the Smugglers' Notch Resort (**Vermont Horse Park**, ☎ 644-5347). Expect trail rides, carriage rides, and winter sleigh rides.

Bolton Valley Resort provides trail rides every morning and afternoon, summers only (☎ 434-5329).

Enjoy family experiences with dignified, curious llamas, who carry the packs (and the food!) along the trails of the Green Mountains, departing from the village at Smugglers' Notch. Day treks, half-day treks, and sunset rambles are popular from summer through the foliage season. These guides adapt well to families with small children, too. Contact Geoff and Lindsay Chandler, **Northern Llama Co.**, RR1, Box 544, Waterville, VT 05492; ☎ 644-2257).

■ On Wheels

Road Biking

If you're ready for some out-of-town travel, get out your copy of John Freidin's *25 Bicycle Tours in Vermont*. Freidin founded Vermont Bicycle Tours, and he has great suggestions. The route he proposes from **Stowe to Morrisville** and back is a mellow 20-mile loop using a pair of roads parallel to Route 100, the Stagecoach Road and the Randolph Road. Watch for hot-air balloonists overhead, as well as gliders and small planes. Stagecoach Road offers long views of Mount Mansfield and the surrounding peaks; so does the Randolph Road on the way back to Stowe.

A very challenging road ride, 42 miles with one heck of a mountain in the middle, is the **Stowe to Smugglers' Notch loop**. From Stowe, go north on Route 100 and pick up the Stagecoach Road through Morristown to Hyde Park (11 miles). Using Route 15, bike through Johnson (nice eateries!) to Jeffersonville. Take a good rest now if you need it, then pedal up the seven miles of Route 108 to Smugglers' Notch and descend to Stowe; watch out, the first part of the descent is very steep.

BIG WHEELS OR SMALL ONES: *What size wheels do you want – bicycle, or in-line skate? Stowe offers opportunities for both. The recreation path is paved and handy. There's an in-line skate park at the top of the Mountain Road and there are at least four bike shops along the rec path to rent or repair what you have. And there's always the hardware store in Stowe village. AJ's Mountain Bikes (☎ 253-4593 or 800-226-6257, on the Mountain Road) will rent you either a bike or in-line skates.*

As you head north of Stowe, roads are less traveled and more appealing for biking. From Jeffersonville, there's a good loop with five covered bridges and a nice assortment of wetlands, pastures with cows and sometimes white-tailed deer, and gentler vistas. From Jeffersonville, go north on Route 108 less than half a mile to the junction with Route 109, and turn right onto this winding road along the Lamoille River. Stay with Route 109 through Waterville (five miles), Belvidere Center (six more miles), and the four-mile stretch to Route 118 (that's 15 miles so far). Bear right onto Route 118, enjoy Long Pond on your left, watch for signs of beaver, and then note that you're crossing the Long Trail. You come down into the village of Eden (you've now gone seven miles along Route 118), where the general store has tasty baked goods. Head south on Route 100, and after four miles take the right-hand cutoff, which is Route 100C, to see two more covered bridges in the five miles before you reach Johnson. A right on Route 15 brings you back to Jeffersonville in another nine miles (40 miles total).

GUIDED BIKE TOURS

Ready for a guided tour in different territory? **Majic Mountain Cycling** (☎ 496-2614), based in Moretown, offers multi-day rides on back roads, through the Lake Champlain Valley, or across New England. They even have a special tour for family riding. Check out the 70-mile foliage ride through central Vermont!

Mountain Biking

There are several good mountain bike rides described in the *Map & Guide to Stowe and the Mt. Mansfield Region* (Huntington Graphics), which you can buy at the Green Mountain Club's office on Route 100, about six miles south of Stowe. All use town roads or the recreation path in Stowe. If you want off-road biking, talk with the bike shop staff about whether any of the Nordic ski touring centers have yet opened their trails to summer use: **AJ's Mountain Bikes** (☎ 253-4593), **Action Outfitters** (☎ 253-7975), the **Mountain Bike Shop** (☎ 253-7919), **Stowe Mountain Sports** (☎ 253-4896), and **Lamoille Mountain Guides & Topnotch Bike Rentals** (☎ 253-6433). All are on the Mountain Road.

Mountain biking in Bolton gets a boost from the **Bolton Valley Resort** (☎ 434-2131 or 800-451-3220), where 30 km of old logging roads and single-track rides have been marked out. Bike rentals and trail maps are available; start at the lodge and head for the summit at 3,200 feet.

■ On Water

Rivers To Run

For canoe rentals, lake and river shuttle trips, a complete paddle shop, and some talk about the water, the place to go is **Umiak Outdoor Outfitters** (☎ 253-2317), on Route 100 in Stowe's "lower" (southern) village. There are also boat rentals at the **Fly Rod Shop**, about 2.6 miles up the Mountain Road in Stowe (☎ 253-7346 or 800-5-FLYROD, Web site www.flyrodshop.com).

The **Lamoille River** is the prime paddling river in this region; it flows for some 80 miles across Vermont, ending at Lake Champlain. There's a basic seven-mile stretch for a relaxed paddle if you drive north from Stowe through Johnson on Route 15, then bear right onto Hogback Road. Go another 1½ miles down Hogback to the put-in; the take-out is half a mile below the covered bridge in Cambridge.

Another playful quickwater paddle on the Lamoille is from **Hyde Park to Johnson**. Put in just below Cady's Falls Dam and take out just above the Dog's Head eight miles later; watch for a gravel pit on the right to spot the take-out on the left.

The stretch of the Lamoille from **Morrisville to Fairfax Falls** makes a more ambitious day of it, just over 34 miles. You need to scout the rapids carefully; they are Class IV at Ithiel Falls in high water. Use the *Appalachian Mountain Club River Guide to New Hampshire and Vermont* for a first survey, and then either walk the river or take your first run with someone who has already paddled it very recently.

From its start in Cabot, the **Winooski River** winds about 90 miles through about every kind of terrain the state offers, from mountains and forests to wetlands, farms, and even cities. Any river this scenic gets paddled often, which is not so great if you're looking for solitude, but terrific in terms of established access. A good half-day run starts just below the Middlesex Dam, where there's a put-in, to Waterbury, where you can choose among take-outs at the Route 2 bridge at River Road, the bridge and Winooski Street, or the recreation field at the far end of Waterbury. **Vermont Pack & Paddle Outfitters** (☎ 496-7225) in Waitsfield will help with route planning as well as rentals and shuttles. So will **Clearwater Sports**, also in Waitsfield on Route 100 (☎ 496-2708).

If you're headed north, all the way up near the Canadian border is a great paddling river for skilled canoeists – the **Missisquoi**. Expert paddlers can even request water releases. Study the *River Guide* before you head north so you know what you've got ahead (we're talking Class III rapids, a difficult ledge, and four portages between East Richford and Highgate Falls, one of which is a half-mile long). Check on water releases before you put in (Ray Gonda at Boise Cascade, ☎ 862-6164).

Vermont is a good place to try out the special skills of creek paddling. In the Johnson area, the **Gihon River** gives an interesting run. Plan on narrow banks and shallow water.

Smugglers' Notch Canoe Touring in Jeffersonville (☎ 644-8321 or 888-937-6266) puts together Lamoille River trips with shuttle service and all gear; they'll also equip you for fishing if you like, and for overnight camping. Weekend packages and options with kayaks or tubes are available too.

Flatwater Paddling

Two reservoirs in this region offer good flatwater boating: the **Waterbury Reservoir** and the **Green River Reservoir.** To reach Waterbury Reservoir, head from Waterbury Center south on Route 100 to the Old River Road, take a right turn, then go to the end of the road for the boat ramp. Or you can go farther south to Route 2 and turn right (west), looking for the Little River Road in less than two miles on the right. Again, go to the end of the road and find the boat ramp. Waterbury Reservoir gives you about four miles of open water and is surrounded by good hiking trails. To reach Green River Reservoir from Morrisville, take Route 15A out to Route 15 and start east; take the first left turn, which goes to the little hamlet of Garfield, where the road jogs right and immediately left again, for a total of about seven miles to the reservoir. This is a wild and unspoiled lake, where loons nest, beavers slap their tales, and moose tramp through the wooded hillsides. Take plenty of bug repellent; there is primitive camping allowed, as well as picnicking, but no motorboats.

Fishing

"Good fishing" is an understatement; the trout in these rivers draw anglers, and there's excellent ice fishing on the lakes too. In Stowe check in at the **Fly Rod Shop** on the Mountain Road (☎ 253-7346 or 800-FLY ROD, Web site www.flyrodshop.com). Also in Stowe is **Fly Fish Vermont** on

South Main Street (☎ 253-3964), where you can swap stories and buy or rent equipment. You can get your fishing license here if you haven't already got one, as well as maps and information on conditions. The Fly Rod Shop has fly-fishing courses and also fly-tying. Fly Fish Vermont offers casting clinics, instructional tours, and drift boat trips; on the lakes they get you going on float tubes fly-fishing for brookies.

Fishing rivers are the **Lamoille** (rainbow and brown trout), the **Brewster** (in Jeffersonville, stocked with trout), the **Little River** (just west of Waterbury), and the **Winooski** below Bolton Falls Dam. In Montpelier, walk east of town to the **Dog River** and angle for brown and rainbow trout. Up north on the **Mississquoi** there are plenty of fishing accesses for the abundant trout. Remember this river takes longer to warm up; spring doesn't come until the end of May.

For flatwater fishing, make sure you try **Green River** (see page 260). **Lake Eden** on Route 100 near Eden Mills has some nice rainbows. Ice fishing is prime at **Lake Elmore**, reached from Morrisville by taking Route 12 southeast about five miles to Elmore State Park. For ice fishing gear like power and hand augers, rods, lures, jigs, and live bait (as well as other wilderness sports gear), try **Water 'N Woods** (21 Portland Street, Morrisville, VT 05661; ☎ 888-7101). Another lesser-known fishing spot is **Lake Carmi**, at the state park northwest of Enosburgh Falls, up by the Canadian border. Boats can be rented at the park; look for smallmouth bass as well as northern pike and perch.

Finally, for a taste of really rich lake angling for trout, consider **Beaver Lake Trout Club** (☎ 888-3746) outside Morrisville near Green River Reservoir. The club has a 14-acre private lake stocked with 14,000 trout, open daily, no license needed, and no limit. Boats are rented, or fish from the shore. There's a bait and tackle shop too. No more than 30 anglers are allowed at any given time.

GUIDED FISHING TRIPS: *Other angling guides in this area are listed in the* Vermont Guides Directory, Angler's Edition, *which you can get (free) from the Vermont Department of Fish and Wildlife (103 South Main Street, Waterbury, VT 05676; ☎ 241-3700). One to mention in particular is* **Uncle Jammer's Guide Service**, *about 15 miles from Jeffersonville (RR1, Box 6910, Underhill, VT 05489; ☎ 899-5019 or 800-805-6495), where both fly-fishing and ice fishing are high in priority.*

Swimming

Swimmers can take advantage of the beaches at **Elmore State Park** (four miles southeast of Montpelier on Route 12) or **Little River State Park**

(Waterbury, 1½ miles west of Route 100 on Route 2). There's a beach at Lake Eden with a fee to swim there. For an adventurous afternoon, try the **Devil's Potholes** in Bolton. Park 0.2 miles up the access road to the Bolton Valley Resort and follow a well-worn path to the water. In Johnson there's a swimming hole at the **Lamoille River**, just above the village on Route 100C; look for the covered bridge. And from Jeffersonville go a half-mile south of the village on Route 108 for the left turn above the mill, followed by a right turn before the bridge. From the parking area, the path goes upstream to the polls and cascades. North of Montpelier on Route 12, **Wrightsville Beach** is ideal for family picnics; if you bring a canoe, you can work off your meal by exploring in the wetland areas and looking for herons and beavers.

KID-FRIENDLY

*For a summer afternoon when you want to just play and be silly, there's plenty of family fun at **Rumrunner's Hideaway** at Smugglers' Notch, in a 10-acre water recreation playground featuring wagon rides, fishing, boating, a water slide, and of course mountain views (☎ 800-451-8752 and www.smuggs.com).*

■ On Snow & Ice

 If you like life best when there are skis or a snowboard under your feet, welcome to the Northeast's best region. Not only is there the world-class ski resort at Stowe and its partner over at Smugglers' Notch, there are also six Nordic ski centers around Stowe, the smaller but adventurous alpine center at Bolton Valley Resort, a corner of ski history with a tow rope at the little Cochran's Ski Area, and easily a hundred miles of interconnecting groomed and wilderness cross-country trails around Mount Mansfield. Plus, you'll find that "ski" is both the language and the style of the area all winter (which runs from mid-October to at least mid-April!).

Downhill Skiing

Stowe offers a peak summit elevation of 4,393 feet and highest skiing elevation of 3,640 feet, with a vertical drop of 2,360 feet on its 480 skiable acres. Many of the trails are over a mile long, with the Toll Road extending 3.7 miles. A fourth of the trails are expert, including the traditional extreme skiing on the Front Four (Starr, Goat, Liftline, and National). The resort also offers off-piste skiing for experts who like risks, whether on skis or snowboards, challenging the steeps, chutes, and secret shots; a traverse connects the top of Stowe's Big Spruce with the Smugglers' Notch ski area on the other side of Spruce Peak, extending this wild area.

More than half the trails at Stowe are intermediate, and there is plenty of instruction for beginners, with some scenic gentle slopes carefully carved into the terrain. Besides the eight-person high-speed gondola, the lifts include a high-speed quad, eight double and triple chairs, and one poma. Snowmaking coverage is 73%.

Advance ticket sales are available, and Stowe has extensive and luxurious slopeside lodgings; ☎ 800-253-4SKI for both (on the Internet, www.stowe.com/smr).

AUTHOR TIP

SKIERS TAKE NOTE: *A specialty shop in Stowe that may help a lot of skiers is **Inner Bootworks** (☎ 253-6929), providing custom fitting to correct arch pain and cramping, numbness, ankle pressure and tenderness, heel slop, and cold feet, as well as poor edge control.*

Don't think **Smugglers' Notch** is less exciting just because its peak isn't as high as Stowe's; the vertical rise is actually greater (2,610 feet), the resort includes three big mountains (Morse, Sterling, and Madonna), and there are 60 trails. Smugglers' Notch has 5% double and triple diamond trails; its triple black diamond run at Freefall Woods, called the Black Hole, is the first and only one in the East.

Smugglers' specializes in diversity. For new skiers there's a Learning and Fun Park (lighted in the evenings), with all of Morse Mountain dedicated to new skiers and snowboarders. There are all-or-nothing runs like Pipeline Escape and Robin's Run; awesome bumps on Upper FIS and Smugglers' Alley; and smooth cruising on Garden Path and Rumrunner. The mountain also carves out traditional New England trails winding among the glades. Over 1,000 acres of wooded areas, glades, and between-trail regions are open to off-piste skiing and boarding.

The 55-acre Resort Village at Smugglers' also puts together winter activities like sleigh rides, cross-country skiing, and nearby horseback riding. There are parties, parades, and festivals. Smugglers' adds a petting zoo, a self-guided nature trail and night touring. You can reach Smugglers' at ☎ 644-8752 or 800-451-8752, e-mail smuggs@smuggs.com, Web site www.smuggs.com.

Bolton Valley Resort is a family ski resort with true slopeside access – no shuttles, just step out of the car and ski. It has recently changed hands, and has newly updated hotel-style and condo lodging. It is a lively spot, with 48 trails and six lifts, and 70% snowmaking coverage. This is the closest ski area to Burlington, just off I-89 (from Burlington use Exit 11 and take Route 2 to the access road; from Waterbury use Route 2). Night skiing and a kids' park add to its appeal. Bolton also has a special instructional program for skiers who want to switch to snowboards. ☎ 434-3444 for informations and reservations; ☎ 434-7669 for snow conditions.

The slopes at **Cochran's Ski Area** (☎ 434-2479) in Richmond are open all day on weekends and holiday weeks, plus afternoons on Tuesdays, Thursdays, and Fridays. If you've never skied from a tow rope, or want your kids to have this experience of early American skiing, this is the place to go. It's small, friendly, and very open to families. Many competitive skiers started here!

Cross-Country Skiing

The most famous Nordic ski center at Stowe is the **Trapp Family Ski Touring Center** (☎ 253-7311), founded by Maria Von Trapp whose story is known to many from the movie *The Sound of Music*. The Stowe resort offers the **Mount Mansfield Ski Touring Center** (☎ 253-3000). Nearby are also the **Topnotch Ski Touring Center** (25 km, ☎ 253-8585) and **Edson Hill Manor Ski Touring Center** (50 km, ☎ 253-8954). Smugglers' Notch resort has the **Smugglers' Notch Cross Country Center** (21 km, ☎ 644-8851); not far away is **Sterling Ridge Inn** (Jeffersonville, 15 km, ☎ 644-8265). All the Nordic centers in Stowe have easy ways to ski from one to the next. Over 130 miles of backcountry trails link Stowe, Bolton, Jeffersonville, Underhill, and Waterbury. The **Catamount Ski Trail**, Vermont's winter end-to-ender, also runs through the area (get the *Catamount Trail Guidebook*: Catamount Trail Association, PO Box 1235, Burlington, VT 05402; ☎ 864-5794). In Bolton is the **Bolton Valley Ski Touring Center** (☎ 434-2131, ext. 194), with 20 miles of groomed trails and 46 miles of marked outlying trails.

Other Winter Sports

Snowshoeing has gained popularity with recent new shoe designs; most ski shops (there are at least five in Stowe) now have them for purchase or rental. In Morrisville, **Water 'N Woods** (☎ 888-7101) offers rentals too, to go with their extensive line of outdoor equipment for winter (and more for summer).

Snowmobiling? Check with **Ride Vermont** in Williamstown (☎ 433-1208) for tours of the Notch, a hidden valley, and a country village. There's also **Nichols Snowmobile Rentals** in Stowe (☎ 253-7239).

Ice climbing is alive and well at Smugglers' Notch, but as someone who's not an expert I'm not even going to try to describe the variety of challenging routes. Instead, I suggest that you start with someone who already knows what they're doing here, as this is a very risky adventure. Meanwhile, there's now a guidebook, *The Local's Guide to Smugglers' Notch Ice*, published by The Duke of Jeffersonville, PO Box 487, Jeffersonville, VT 05454, and easily obtained by mail from Adventurous Traveler Bookstore (call for their catalog, ☎ 860-6776 or 800-282-3963, or order online at www. adventuroustraveler.com). Another way to enter this sport is through **Green Mountain Guides Climbing School** (Tim Kontos, Director/ Guide, PO Box 421, Jeffersonville, VT 05464, ☎ 644-8131, e-mail tkgmgcs @aol.com).

Resort lodging in this region generally includes **sleigh rides**, and so do many of the inns in winter; in Stowe you can also contact **Stowehof Inn** (☎ 253-9722) and **Charlie Horse Sleigh and Carriage Rides** at Topnotch Resort (☎ 253-2215).

■ In The Air

Ready for a **glider ride** and instruction? **Stowe Soaring** (☎ 888-7845) is six miles north of Stowe on Route 100.

Hot-air balloon trips are a specialty of **Ruth Ludwig** (☎ 333-4883), editor of *Ballooning Magazine*, who is often in the air around Stowe. She can accommodate up to three passengers.

Eco-Travel & Cultural Excursions

Jim Paige at **Green Mountain Outdoor Adventures** (☎ 229-4246) in Montpelier used to do all kinds of guide work, but has now narrowed his scope. He still offers wildlife photography sessions and special walks for birders.

Water 'N Woods in Morrisville (☎ 888-7101) stocks binoculars and monoculars for winter birdwatching.

The **Green Mountain Audubon Society Nature Center** (☎ 434-3068) in Huntington, five miles south of Richmond, has 230 acres of land, with trails and self-guided nature study. There are special programs for kids in the summer.

If you've been an advocate for land preservation and wildlife diversity, or would like to know more about these issues, visit the **Nature Conservancy of Vermont** (☎ 229-4425), which has an office at 27 State Street in Montpelier. The Nature Conservancy keeps most of its Vermont lands quietly private to protect the animals, plants, and intricate ecosystems there, but occasionally it'll send a naturalist-led field trip to some complex environment like the Maquam Bog in Swanton or the Chickering Bog in East Montpelier; you might consider becoming a member to support its efforts. The **Vermont Land Trust**, specifically geared to helping farm families conserve productive land for agriculture, also has its central office in Montpelier, at 8 Bailey Avenue (☎ 223-5234); visitors with questions and suggestions are welcome to stop in.

Ready to visit a farm? Pick up the listing of working farms interested in company, either from the **Stowe Area Association** or directly from the **Lamoille Valley Chamber of Commerce** (PO Box 445, Morrisville, VT

05661); there are llamas, cows, Christmas trees, maple sugaring to see, and a working horse ranch.

A traditional treat for Montpelier visitors is the **Morse Farm Sugar Shack**, three miles from the center of town. Take Main Street away from Route 2, across State Street, and in another two blocks the road swerves to the right around a small circle in front of a school, becoming County Road and climbing a hill. It bends to the left, passes a cemetery, and finally you'll see the farm well marked on the right (and there are plenty of signs). The best time to visit is in late March and early April, when the sap from the maple trees is being boiled into rich sticky syrup. But year-round there are folklife exhibits, a "woodshed theater," a maple trail to follow (learn the differences between the trees), and a gift shop, as well as delicious food-stuffs and even syrup samples to taste. The farm is open daily from 9 to 5, and in summer stays open until 8 p.m. (☎ 223-2740 or 800-242-2740, Web site www.morsefarm.com). The **Bragg Farm**, five miles out of town with signs on Route 14 north in East Montpelier, also offers a walk through the maple woods and a chance for tasting (☎ 223-5757).

 FOR DOG LOVERS: *It's hard to know where to list this, but for backpackers who've always wished their dogs would behave in the woods and want some training in canine wilderness companionship (or how to train a working dog), **Outdoor Adventure of Vermont** (Montpelier, ☎ 800-639-9208) has the course you've longed for.*

Cultural events in Montpelier, the state's capital, seem endless, from concerts to performances to lectures and classes. If you'll be in town in July, check the date for the **Midsummer Festival** and attend it for unusually fine folk and regional music, dancing and general fun. Stowe has a steady schedule of concerts too; the **Stowe Area Association** (☎ 253-7321 or 800-24-STOWE) in the center of town has listings. If you get north to Johnson, visit the **Vermont Studio Center** (☎ 635-2727), housed in assorted historic buildings, and the **Dibden Center for the Arts** (☎ 635-1386) at Johnson State College. In Hyde Park (between Morrisville and Johnson), the **Hyde Park Opera House** (☎ 888-4507) has been restored and the **Lamoille County Players** put on great summer shows there.

Where To Stay

■ Montpelier & Barre

Montpelier's **Capitol Plaza** (☎ 223-5252 or 800-274-5252, $$-$$$) has hosted its legislators since the 1930s. At 100 State Street, it is the obvious choice for government access while you stay, but it is also a comfortable center-city hotel, with its own restaurant and boutiques. Equally well known is the **Inn at Montpelier** (☎ 223-2727, $$-$$$), whose two buildings date back to the early 1800s and have been connected and added to since. Greek and Colonial Revival woodwork, fireplaces, and elegant staircases emphasize the mellow graciousness of this inn, which serves breakfast and a light gourmet dinner. An assortment of small inns and bed-and-breakfast homes, mostly in the center of town for easy walking, includes **Betsy's Bed & Breakfast** (☎ 229-0466, $$), the **Montpelier Guest Home** (☎ 229-0878, $-$$), **Gamble's Bed & Breakfast** (☎ 229-4810, $$), and **Raspberry Ledge Bed & Breakfast** (☎ 223-3903, no children or pets, $$).

Barre's lodgings cluster along the Barre-Montpelier Road and the South Barre approach to Interstate 89. There's a **Days Inn** by Interstate 89 (☎ 476-6678 or 800-325-2525, $$), along with the **Hollow Inn and Motel** (☎ 479-9313 or 800-998-9444, $$). On the Barre-Montpelier Road are the **Twin City Motel** (☎ 476-3104, $$), the **Vermonter Motel** (☎ 476-8541, $$), and the **Knoll Motel** (☎ 479-3648, $$). **LaGue Inns** (☎ 229-5766, $$) is between Barre and Berlin.

■ Waterbury & Stowe

South of Waterbury on Route 100 is the **Grünberg Haus B&B and Cabins** (☎ 244-7726 or 800-800-7760, Web site www.waterbury.org/grunberg, $$-$$$), with guest rooms in a hand-built Austrian chalet. In Waterbury at 18 North Main Street is the carefully restored **Old Stagecoach Inn** (☎ 244-5056, $-$$), an elegant small inn. Head over to Route 100 and start north to find the **Holiday Inn** (☎ 800-621-7822, $$), with its mountain views, restaurant and lounge, and outdoor heated pool.

Lodging in Stowe ranges from luxurious to practical; your best bet is to tour the town and the Mountain Road, then drop in at the **Stowe Area Association** in the center of town and look through brochures, letting the helpful staff assist you with reservations (☎ 253-7321 or 800-24-STOWE, Web site www.stowe.com). If you need to know where you're headed before you get to town, the **Stowe Resort** has luxurious slopeside lodgings ranging from the Inn at the Mountain to townhouses and condominiums (☎ 800-253-4SKI, $$$-$$$$). Another superb choice is **Topnotch at Stowe** (☎ 253-8585 or 800-451-8686, $$$-$$$$), a resort and spa with its own cross-country or hiking trails. **The Trapp Family Lodge** (☎ 253-8511 or 800-826-7000, $$-$$$$) offers a touch of Austria, and the **Green Mountain Inn** (☎ 253-7301 or 800-253-7302, Web site www.greenmountaininn.com, $$-$$$$) is an 1833 historic hotel. There are many small inns, like the **Siebeness** (☎ 253-8942 or 800-426-9001, $$-$$$$). Ask at the Area Association about ski lodges, too.

■ Cabot

The **Creamery Inn Bed & Breakfast** is in a rural two-acre setting not far from the Cabot Creamery, at Cabot and West Hill Roads. Hosts Dan and Judy Lloyd welcome guests to the 1835 Federal home. If you like animals (as your hosts do), you'll have fun here with the lambs, ducks, and shelties. Hike the back roads nearby, then settle in for a candlelight dinner (by advance reservation). A full breakfast is served each morning. Children are welcome (☎ 563-2819, $$).

■ Smugglers' Notch

The **Notch** has its own slopeside accommodations, from private rooms to efficiencies and studios (with fireplaces!) to multiple-bedroom condos; ask about multi-night discounts and special seasonal rates (☎ 644-8851 or 800-451-8752; Web site www.smuggs.com). For a different approach, Bette and Kelley Mann at **Mannsview Inn** at Smugglers' Notch offer classic New England bed and breakfast accommodations, including morning coffee or tea in your room (☎ 644-8321 or 800-937-MANN); this is also where you connect with Smugglers' Notch Canoe Touring, so there are canoe vacation packages as well as skiing ones.

AUTHOR TIP

For a nearby excursion from your Smugglers' Notch lodgings on a rainy day, keep in mind the **Boyden Valley Winery** *(☎ 644-8151) in Cambridge, offering tours year-round, Tuesday-Saturday, 10-5 (but less often in November and April).*

■ Camping

The state parks in this region have some of the best camping: **Elmore State Park** (at Lake Elmore, ☎ 888-2982); **Lake Carmi State Park** (north by the border in Enosburg Falls, ☎ 933-8383); **Little River State Park** (lots of hiking, Waterbury, ☎ 244-7103); **Smugglers' Notch State Park** (Stowe, on the Mountain Road, ☎ 253-4014); and **Underhill State Park** (Underhill Center, ☎ 899-3022).

For private campgrounds, check the many listings in the *Vermont Campground Guide* (Vermont Dept. of Forests, Parks, and Recreation, Division of State Parks, 103 South Main Street, Waterbury, VT 05671-0603; ☎ 241-3655). Note especially that there's one campground open year-round: **Gold Brook Campground** in Stowe (☎ 253-7683 or 800-483-7683).

For convenience in visiting the capital, it's hard to beat **Green Valley Campground** on Route 2 in East Montpelier, with river views that help make up for a lack of privacy. There's plenty of recreation at the campground, too, where Emile and Ginette Gosselin have been welcoming many of their campers for years in a row (☎ 223-6217 or 800-359-1899, e-mail GGosselin@aol.com).

Where To Eat

■ Montpelier

There are 22 cafés and restaurants in the center of Montpelier, and most of them are small and charming. The **Horn of the Moon Café** (☎ 223-2895) at 8 Langdon Street is famous for its organic vegetarian cuisine, and has published its own cookbook. The New England Culinary Institute operates both the **Main Street Grill and Bar** (118 Main Street, ☎ 223-3188) and its next-door neighbor the **Chef's Table** (☎ 229-2902), a sophisticated dining experience; across the street is a third NECI restaurant, **La Brioche Bakery & Café** (☎ 229-0443), serving breads and fine pastries.

Sarducci's (☎ 223-0229) at 3 Main Street offers good Italian food, and state legislators often dine here. The **Thrush Tavern** (☎ 223-2030) serves great burgers just north of the state buildings on State Street and has evening entertainment on Thursdays. And Mexican food is the ticket at **Julio's** (☎ 229-9348), upstairs at 44 Main Street. There are good quick lunches at the **Burlington Bagel Bakery** (☎ 223-0533) in the center of town.

A traditional capital city stop has been the **Lobster Pot Restaurant**, now located on the Barre-Montpelier Road (☎ 476-9900); also here is the **Wayside Restaurant & Bakery** (☎ 223-6611). Feed the kids at the fast food eateries on this route between Montpelier and Barre (Route 302). In Barre itself, **Soup 'N Greens** (☎ 479-9862) offers a tasty meal.

HIDDEN GEM

Follow the directions carefully to find a tiny gem of a restaurant, possibly the best Chinese one in Vermont and certainly the most unusual. Leave Montpelier by heading north on Route 2, and in about 1½ miles you'll come to the traffic light where Route 302 (known here as the Barre-Montpelier Road) heads east (right) toward Barre. Take this road and go 2.2 miles, crossing a railroad track. Look to your left immediately and find the Twin City Lanes & Games (a bowling alley and arcade). Pull into the parking lot and go to the far (eastern) edge of it, where on the small door of a separate building you'll see the sign for **A Single Pebble**. The restaurant's two gourmet cooks prepare fine Asian cuisine. It is open for dinner only, Tuesday through Saturday, 5-9 p.m. A reservation is usually necessary (☎ 476-9700).

Montpelier also has its own microbrewery, **Golden Dome Brewery**, on Pioneer Street (half a mile north of the center of town, off Route 2). This very small but authentic shop produces 10-barrel batches of handcrafted ales. There's a tasting room and a retail store; hours are Tuesday through Friday from noon to 6, Saturday from 11 to 5 (☎ 223-3290).

■ Waterbury & Stowe

Waterbury offers the **Crust and Cauldron Restaurant** (☎ 244-5111) next to the Amtrak Station for a good New England meal. **Arvad's** (☎ 244-8973), at 3 South Main Street near the center of town, is a café with ethnic cuisine. A mix of Indian and Mexican dishes in a unique setting gives the **Marsala Salsa Restaurant** (☎ 244-2250) on Stowe Street an unusual flair.

Stowe offers such a wide range of dining that there's an entire elegant menu book available at the Stowe Area Association office in the center of town (open 9 a.m. to 6 p.m.). Some of the most elegant dining is at the inns. The **Foxfire Inn and Restaurant**, 1½ miles north of town on Route 100, serves some of the finest Italian cuisine in Vermont. **Miguel's Stowe Away** (☎ 253-7574) is a popular Mexican restaurant and cantina. Breakfast at the **Gables Inn** (☎ 253-7730), a mile and a half up the Mountain Road, is a good choice, and there are sturdy, tasty lunches at **Food for Thought Natural Market** (☎ 253-4733) on Route 100, a mile south of the village. Stowe has a small winery shop, **L'Abeille** (☎ 253-2929), at 638 South Main Street in the Stoware Common; the specialty is mead, a honey wine. Microbrewery fanciers will want to visit **The Shed** (☎ 253-4364), a restaurant and brewery pub on the Mountain Road.

■ Smugglers' Notch & Jeffersonville

In Smugglers' Notch, start looking at restaurants right in the resort village, where there are three family-friendly choices and a bakery and pizzeria. On the slope down toward Jeffersonville are more options, ranging from continental cuisine to ethnic favorites. Fine French and New England dining describes the gourmet dinners at the **Windridge Farm Inn** (Main Street, Jeffersonville, ☎ 644-5556), which has its own bakery next door.

■ Morrisville, Johnson & North

No visit to Morrisville is complete without a meal at the **Charlmont** (☎ 888-4242) at the intersection of Routes 15 and 100, a lively overgrown diner with hearty meals.

One good reason for canoeing and hiking near Johnson is the chance to stop at the **Pie Safe** (☎ 635-7952), which calls itself "Gift & Gourmet." There are custom-built sandwiches, imported cheeses, freshly baked pies, of course, fudge, and Vermont epicurean treats. On Main Street, the **Plum and Main Restaurant** (☎ 635-7596) offers simply good food, and a generous Sunday brunch.

Although the ski resort at the Canadian border, **Jay Peak**, doesn't fall into this region, some of the restaurants patronized by the resort guests do. These are the ones in Montgomery Center, where you may find yourself touring if you head north to the Mississquoi River. In the village the **Inn on Trout River** (☎ 326-4391) serves entrées like baked rainbow trout in its formal dining room. The **Black Lantern Inn** (☎ 326-4507) offers continental cuisine served by candlelight in a pleasant old inn. There's a very unusual restaurant on the road that leads up into Hazen's Notch, Route 58: it's called **Zack's on the Rocks** (☎ 326-4500) and is probably worth a two-hour drive all by itself. The food is superb and the atmosphere romantic to the nth degree. Expect to wait for your table, even with a reservation (which you definitely need); also expect to spend hours there, savoring every mouthful and enjoying the offbeat elegance. Only dinner is served.

The Capital District

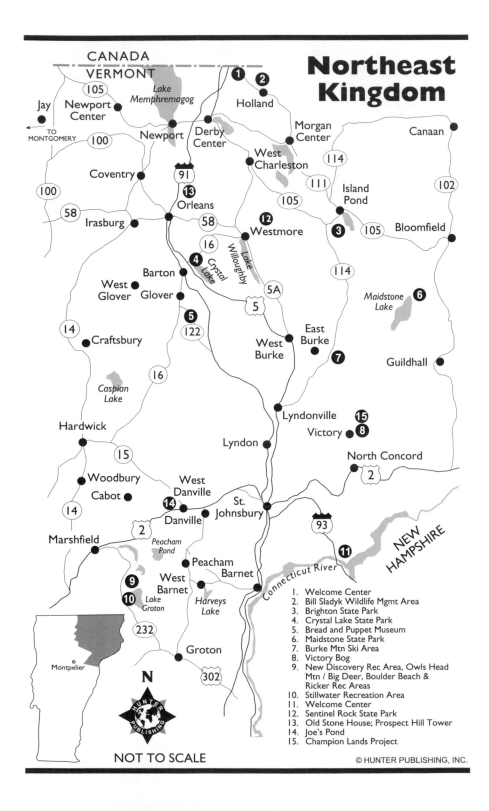

Northeast Kingdom

CANADA
VERMONT

Jay
TO MONTGOMERY
105
Newport Center
100
Newport
Coventry
91
100
58
Irasburg
13
Orleans
58
16
West Glover
Glover
Barton
4 Crystal Lake
14
Craftsbury
122
5
Caspian Lake
16
Hardwick
15
Woodbury
Cabot
14
Marshfield
2
West Danville
14 Danville
Peacham Pond
9
West Barnet
10 Lake Groton
Harveys Lake
232
Groton
302

Lake Memphremagog
Holland 1 2
Derby Center
West Charleston
Morgan Center
Canaan
114
111
Island Pond
102
105
3
105 Bloomfield
12 Westmore
Lake Willoughby
5A
5
114
Maidstone Lake
6
East Burke
7
West Burke
Guildhall
Lyndonville
15
Victory 8
North Concord
2
St. Johnsbury
93
NEW HAMPSHIRE
11
Peacham
Barnet
Connecticut River

Montpelier

N

NOT TO SCALE

1. Welcome Center
2. Bill Sladyk Wildlife Mgmt Area
3. Brighton State Park
4. Crystal Lake State Park
5. Bread and Puppet Museum
6. Maidstone State Park
7. Burke Mtn Ski Area
8. Victory Bog
9. New Discovery Rec Area, Owls Head Mtn / Big Deer, Boulder Beach & Ricker Rec Areas
10. Stillwater Recreation Area
11. Welcome Center
12. Sentinel Rock State Park
13. Old Stone House; Prospect Hill Tower
14. Joe's Pond
15. Champion Lands Project

© HUNTER PUBLISHING, INC.

The Northeast Kingdom

Secure and private between the Green Mountains to the west, the Connecticut River to the east, and Canada at the northern boundary, the Northeast Kingdom is the corner of Vermont best preserved, slowest to change, and least populated. There are actually town sites with no people in the far northeastern corner of the state; shy loons and peregrine falcons nest here, and if you spend a few days on the river roads in the spring you are almost sure to see a moose.

Hikers, skiers, and anglers know the Kingdom best. There are hilltops and forests to seek out where you may be the only human visitor that day. But there are also friendly villages, several large towns with welcoming shops and attractions, and a tradition of hospitality in guest homes, cottages, and small inns. It's a scrap of real frontier, where you'll get to stretch your sense of adventure.

Getting Here & Getting Around

A standard rural saying is "You can't get there from here," and it was true about the Northeast Kingdom until the 1970s, when Interstate 91 sliced its way northward. Now the Kingdom has three gateway towns. The largest (population about 7,600) is **St. Johnsbury**, where Interstate 91 enters the area from the south, Route 2 heads off to Maine, and Interstate 93 leaves for the White Mountains of New Hampshire. **Newport**, only six miles from the Canadian border, is the northern gateway, a small town with about 1,500 residents. And at the southwest edge of the Kingdom is the equally small town of **Hardwick**, once a granite-cutting center and now home to musicians and artists, cheesemakers and farmers.

Touring

■ St. Johnsbury

Once an industrial center with mills all along the Connecticut, Moose, and Passumpsic rivers, St. Johnsbury has gracious old homes and stately buildings that date from more than a century ago. Exit 20 from the interstate takes you north into town on Railroad Street. For touring, take the first left up the hill off South Main Street, to the most architecturally interesting section.

Because the Fairbanks family thrived here, producing the Fairbanks platform scale since 1830, the town is endowed with the **Fairbanks Museum and Planetarium**, founded in 1889 as a natural history and science museum with its own planetarium. Now the museum's trained meteorologists provide weather forecasts for much of Vermont. Virtually every kind of Northeast Kingdom mammal and bird is represented in the museum's collections of taxidermy and paintings. In summer, there's a learning center with live reptiles and small mammals. The museum is open year-

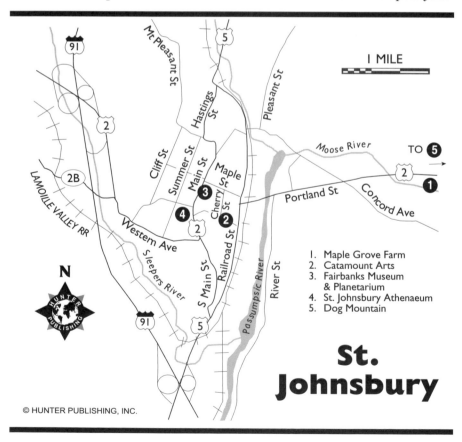

1. Maple Grove Farm
2. Catamount Arts
3. Fairbanks Museum & Planetarium
4. St. Johnsbury Athenaeum
5. Dog Mountain

St. Johnsbury

© HUNTER PUBLISHING, INC.

round, and planetarium shows are held at least every Saturday (call for show hours; ☎ 748-2372).

St. Johnsbury's other gem, just a block south of the museum on Main Street, is its **Athenaeum** (☎ 748-8291, open year-round, closed Sundays), the oldest art gallery in the country maintained in its original condition. With the Athenaeum's 19th-century paintings and sculpture is the town library. You can get a walking map here that identifies the many Main Street homes designed by architect Lambert Packard in the Richardson Romanesque style. Across the road is an information kiosk, open summers and during the fall foliage season. For information at other seasons, drive south on Main Street and bear to the right with Route 2; the Chamber of Commerce is half a mile farther on the left.

When you return to Main Street, find a parking space and walk around the **St. Johnsbury Academy,** a gem of a school with a campus that wraps around South Main Street. The independent school accepts most of the students of St. Johnsbury and a dozen surrounding towns, but also draws about 200 boarding students each year, many of whom are Asian, lending a pleasant note of ethnic diversity.

The town's two parallel business streets, Main Street and Railroad Street, are linked by east-west roads that are pretty steep. Do wander down Eastern Avenue from Main Street, though, to take a look inside the **Catamount Arts Building**, the town's music, theater, and dance showcase with its own small gallery. Just past Catamount Arts is the impressive **Masonic Hall**, followed by an interesting octagonal home that has served recently as a funeral home and a florist. You can see the Passumpsic River at the bottom of the hill, with the still-used railroad tracks alongside it. A bicycle path along the river is underway.

AUTHOR TIP

SHOPPING: *You can buy deer antlers or even the "rack" of a moose at **Moose River Lake & Lodge Store**, 69 Railroad Street in St. Johnsbury (☎ 748-2423). Vintage canoes, antiques, rustic camp furnishings, and Pendleton wool blankets also nestle in the many corners of the shop. Ask owners Ann and Bob Hoffman how the idea grew from Bob's "mountain man" shop concept and Ann's passion for art and architecture.*

Across the river to the east, where many of the Route 2 travelers are bound for Maine, are two landmarks where New England visitors have stopped each summer for generations: **Maple Grove Farms** (tours Monday through Friday except holidays, ☎ 748-5141), where maple sap is remade into maple syrup and leaf-shaped chunks of maple sugar candy, and the **Farmer's Daughter**, a classic old (unheated) barn of a shop for traditional tourist treasures like balsam-stuffed pillows and sweet treats.

The Northeast Kingdom

Stephen Huneck's Dog Mountain gallery and workshop.

While you're heading east on Route 2, just before you reach the Farmer's Daughter, on the left, note the turn for Spaulding Road. There is usually a sign at this corner to direct you to Stephen Huneck's gallery park, the whimsical **Dog Mountain**, 0.7 mile uphill on Spaulding Road and then left onto Parks Road. The cluster of buildings includes a workshop, gallery, and the chapel of St. Bernard, all dedicated to the loving relationship between people and their pets, mostly dogs but with a few things for cat-lovers. There are benches flanked by solemn carved black Labradors (or goldens if you prefer), full-size dog carvings to stand in your yard or by the front door, and playful notions described in numbered prints that portray the ultimate canine postures. The gallery is open from June through October (10 a.m. to 5 p.m.; Sunday 11 to 4), with other dates and times by appointment (☎ 748-2700, Web site www. huneck.com). Huneck's work is internationally known, and he has five other galleries across the country. This location is his home base, so he may even be around to meet or to talk with about a custom design.

■ Danville, Peacham & Barnet

To the west and southwest of St. Johnsbury are the small picturesque villages known so well from *Vermont Life* photographs over the years. There's Danville, where the American Society of Dowsers has its headquarters and where summer festivals flourish on the village green. Peacham has hillcrest homes and the friendly **Bayley Hazen Country Store**, which has settled into providing hearty soups and sandwiches, rich baked goods, local crafts and, of course, maple syrup. Call ahead to have a lunch made up for you (☎ 592-3630). The store is at the intersection a mile south of Peacham village, where the road to West Barnet connects.

Barnet has five village centers, each with a different character. **West Barnet** focuses on the summer haven of **Harvey's Lake** (also an ice-fishing spot). **Barnet Center** is a maple sugaring area and home to a picturesque old church and cemetery; and in Barnet village itself are two Tibetan Buddhist retreat centers, **Karme Choling** (☎ 633-2384, e-mail karmecholing@shambhala. org) and the **Milarepa Center** (☎ 633-4136).

Karme Choling is the larger of the two, founded in 1970 and focused on Buddhist and Shambhala teachings, with year-round courses and retreats, and festivals that draw hundreds of people. Milarepa shares the traditional lineage of the Dalai Lama, has Tibetan monks and nuns in residence from time to time, and offers small retreats and workshops. The two are on opposite sides of Barnet Mountain. Karme Choling is reached from the road between Barnet and Barnet Center, and Milarepa from Route 5 just north of Barnet village. The other two villages within Barnet are on the Passumpsic River: both **Passumpsic** and **McIndoe Falls** villages have small hydropower dams and nice picnic spots by the resulting waterfalls.

MEDITATIVE SHOPPING

With two Buddhist retreat centers in one village, Barnet portrays a fresh sense of New England's heritage of spiritual seeking that dates back to the Great Awakening, and even to the arrival of the Pilgrims. Just up School Street from the traditional general store is the brightly painted home of **Samadhi Cushions**, a Karme Choling offshoot that crafts mediation cushions in round and square shapes and bold colors. Open from 8 to 4 on weekdays, the small cushion showroom sometimes offers other enrichments for the thoughtful life, such as books and decorative items (☎ 633-4440 or 800-331-7751).

Neighboring Peacham, less eclectic spiritually with its simple **Congregational Church**, happens to have one of the finest church organs around, and local musicians whose talents are sophisticated enough to take full advantage of the deep rich sound. When you're in the area, check store bulletin boards to see who is performing there and when. Across the road and up the hill from the Peacham Congregational Church is a small **archaeological site** at a former blacksmith building, often open to the public; the **historical society collection** is a bit farther up the hill on the same side. Peacham residents enjoy local history so much that they've put together an annual event called the **Ghost Walk**, when residents costume themselves as noted Peacham characters of the past and converse with visitors, sharing anecdotes about the person and the time. This event, usually scheduled during the Fourth of July weekend, has often been held at the cemetery, hence the name "Ghost Walk." For details, ☎ 592-3432, e-mail senturia@connriver.net.

Barnet and Peacham, along with Marshfield, Walden, Cabot, Plainfield, Groton, and St. Johnsbury, also collaborate in the **Northeast Kingdom Fall Foliage Festival**, a 10-day series that usually begins during the last week of September and features history, country living, craft shows, and especially Vermont foods, with church suppers and local traditions like **West Barnet's European Coffee Hour** (ask about how the traditions

The Northeast Kingdom

arose in each village). For information, ☎ 563-2472, or check the Web site, www.vermontnekchamber.org.

These three small towns host an endless series of summer and fall events, from church suppers to fireworks. Details about the Fourth of July display at Joe's Pond are on page 294. Smaller and more intriguing is the **Fourth of July Gala** at Peacham, where local residents perform the roles of founding families buried in the cemetery (see the Ghost Walk, above), the old blacksmith shop shows off anvil work as well as a tiny archaeological "dig," and you can compete at horseshoes.

The old-time sport of horseshoes is also part of **Lake Harvey Day** in West Barnet, held on the third weekend of July at Harvey's Lake. Plan to swim at the beach, but bring warm clothes for the long evening, which begins with a chicken barbecue and ends with fireworks over the water.

And for one of the smallest and friendliest summer fairs, try the **Danville Fair** on the first weekend of August, where the rides are still fun for kids, the cotton candy is perfect, and the bingo tables and flower exhibits are traditional favorites; there's a wide variety of food, from salads to grilled items to ice cream, and the whole town gathers for the parade in the morning and the music in the evening (for this year's date contact the Danville Town Clerk at ☎ 684-3352).

Autumn foliage draws many visitors to the back roads and villages, and eight towns of the Northeast Kingdom collaborate for the eight-day **Northeast Kingdom Foliage Festival** during the last week of September. For a listing of the dozens of events and dinners, contact the Fall Festival Committee, PO Box 54, West Danville, VT 05873-0054 (Web site www.vermontnekchamber.org).

■ Lyndonville, Burke, LakeWilloughby

When you travel north from St. Johnsbury, the quickest route with the best long-distance vistas is Interstate 91, especially when it rises over Sheffield Heights, a 1,900-foot elevation that divides two watersheds, north-flowing rivers and south-flowing ones. (Howard Mosher's book and movie, *Where the Rivers Flow North*, is set in the part of the Kingdom north of this divide.)

But to connect with the road to East Burke, home of Burke Mountain, or to visit the Bread and Puppet Theater's home in Glover on Route 122, it's easier to take Route 5, the older "shadow" road that parallels the interstate. The large town north of St. Johnsbury is Lyndonville, a college town with both the elegance of more Lambert Packard designs and the rough-and-ready feel of country agricultural fairgrounds.

At the north end of Lyndonville, Route 5 continues north and soon sends a branch, Route 5A, to Lake Willoughby, a spectacular glacial gouge rimmed with cliffs and notable hikes. Peregrine falcons nest to the east of the lake. Hikers use the trails on Mount Pisgah, Mount Hor, and Wheeler Mountain, where the best climbs are.

Leaving Route 5's North Lyndonville intersection to the right, Route 114 heads northeast to East Burke, the ski and hiking resort at Burke Mountain, and the state park around it.

■ Barton & Glover

These two small towns are reached from Route 5 or Interstate 91 (Exit 25). If you take Route 5 from Lyndonville you'll pass lovely **Crystal Lake,** with its public beach and good small-boat sailing just before you pull into the center of Barton. Turn left onto Route 16; in half a mile you'll see the right turn to the county fairgrounds, used mainly in August for a big and merry agricultural fair. Interstate 91 is just ahead on Route 16; to the southwest of the interstate is **Sugarmill Farm Maple Museum** (☎ 525-3701, call for hours).

Another mile past the maple museum brings you to the village of Glover, where **Currier's** is an old-fashioned general store with baked goods, a meat counter (they'll butcher your wild game if needed), and all kinds of hardware and fishing gear. When you finish browsing, continue down Route 16 another mile to the left onto Route 122; the **Bread and Puppet Museum** (☎ 525-3031) is about a mile up the hill and houses hundreds of masks and giant puppets used by the noted political theater group in its international performances. You may hear about the noted Bread and Puppet Domestic Resurrection Circus, a local summer event, but this has been discontinued due to overgrown "counterculture" crowds. The theater group still offers modest performances on summer evenings to try out its show before going on the road. Check the local newspaper, *The Chronicle*, or ask at the museum.

AUTHOR TIP

*Have you ever wondered what lumberjacks looked like? Or how they could maneuver logs with pulp hooks, have at 'em with axes, and tear into them with two-man saws? If so, the event to see is the **Vermont Forestry Expo**, held at the Orleans County Fairgrounds by Route 5 in Barton on one of the last July weekends. For this year's date, call the forestry association at ☎ 533-9212.*

Outdoor bread ovens at Bread & Puppet, in Glover.

■ Westmore

This picture-perfect village lies on the west shore of Lake Willoughby and is a photographer's dream. Stop at **Bill and Billie's Lodge** at the center of "town" to rent a "boat with motor" and see whether there's a "housekeeping unit" available for the night. Half a mile south is the **Blue Anchor**, another home-grown cottage setup with a modest gift shop; another 1.3 miles south on Route 5A takes you to the trailhead for **Willoughby State Forest**. A waterfall cascades down the steep slope, 3.5 miles south of the village.

From the center of Westmore you can also visit a state park in the process of being born, so to speak. You'll find a small memorial park on the lakeshore, and across Route 5A is Hinton Hill Road. Take this steeply climbing side road exactly one mile and you'll find **Sentinel Rock** on your left. This glacial erratic overlooks both Lake Willoughby and the range of the Green Mountains. The distant peak with a double mound on top is Camel's Hump, the really large mountain to the north of it is Mt. Mansfield, and the one even farther north that looks like it has a tooth sticking to the top is Jay Peak (the "tooth" is the gondola top and ski lodge). Sentinel Rock and 365 acres around it are a gift from Windsor and Florence Wright, whose family owned the land from 1947. Soon there will be a sign that says "Sentinel Rock State Park," and maybe a few other gentle changes like paths to walk on – but the local dairy farmer is allowed to keep his Holsteins pasturing the fields.

Yes, the road past the new state park does "go somewhere": both forks pass over the ridge and down to Route 105 between East Charleston and Island Pond. The road is rough but really lovely, a perfect scenic drive toward the quietest part of the Northeast Kingdom (see Island Pond).

Sentinel Rock State Park, in Westmore.

■ Brownington

On its way north from Barton and Glover, Route 5 enters the manufacturing town of Orleans, best known as home to one of the plants building Ethan Allen furniture. Ethan Allen was one of Vermont's Revolutionary War-era patriots; his brother Ira had his name incorporated in the next village to the northwest, Irasburg. Orleans is also noted as the location to watch spawning rainbow trout leap upriver in mid-May. Ask in town for directions to the best viewing spot.

For a lovely drive on back roads and a chance to see a collection of Vermont historical artifacts in an unusual old school, take Route 58 east out of Orleans and in about a mile make the well-marked left turn onto the road to Brownington, another three miles north. When you reach the cluster of homes that represents the old village, there is a right turn, also well marked, onto Old Stone House Road, to the Old Stone House. Here is the school building erected by Alexander Twilight, perhaps the nation's first person of African heritage to be a college graduate and legislator. He was a teacher and minister, and the 30-room school he erected of granite blocks now houses the collection of the Orleans Historical Society. It's open Friday-Tuesday, 11 a.m.-5 p.m., in late May and June and in the fall; in July and August it is open daily (admission charged). Tours can be scheduled in advance (☎ 754-2022, http://homepages.together.net/~osh). Leave extra time to stroll around the historic neighborhood of homes and to climb the observatory tower on **Prospect Hill** (see *Eco-Travel*).

■ Island Pond

Beyond Burke, Route 114 goes on to Island Pond, the last group of shops and eateries before the wild lands of Essex County open up, with their noted deer and moose populations and internationally known snowmobile trail network. The French-Canadian influence is clear in Island Pond; listen for the lilt of Quebecois accents around town, and watch for the license plates that say *Je me souviens* – "I remember" – on many of the cars.

Taking Route 114 north out of Island Pond will lead you toward the border town of **Norton**, a quiet village where hunting, fishing, and forestry make up the fabric of life. Visit the small border station, then turn right on Route 114 to reach Canaan and the bridge into New Hampshire at West Stewartstown.

WATCHABLE

WILDLIFE

If you're hoping to see moose, Route 114 and Route 102 south, along the Connecticut River, offer frequent glimpses of the ungainly animals. Just remember that, unlike dogs and cats, moose seem to have no understanding of the danger of cars – they stay in the road even if you honk the horn or flash your headlights, and they may take either a car or a person as a personal challenge. Being charged at by an antlered male is a life-threatening situation. So is running into a moose by car, because the heavy animals generally break the windshield and crush the roof as they fall. The local bumper sticker says "Brake for Moose," and it's a good idea.

Some 26,000 acres of former paper company land around Island Pond, recently logged and therefore home to abundant deer, moose, and migrating birds, became part of the **Silvio O. Conte National Fish and Wildlife Refuge** in 1999. Trails and facilities are developing. Contact the refuge manager for permission to hike there (☎ 723-4398, Keith_Weaver@fws.gov; Web site www.fws.gov/r5soc).

CAUTION

Note that hunting is taken seriously in this region – if you're walking in the woods in October or November, wear blaze orange clothing (not white, which can look like the flash of a deer tail) or, better yet, delay your visit to the forest until a less challenging season.

If you choose not to go out to the quiet wooded area along the border, you can still take Route 114 north out of Island Pond but, when you are 2.5 miles out of town, turn left onto Route 111. This lovely road winds through Morgan Center and Morgan, among dairy farms and horse paddocks, and along the shoreline of **Seymour Lake**, and there are local housekeeping cottages, lodges, and guide services, not to mention the **Village Sportsman**, a home-based business by the lake where a local angler sells streamer flies to the trout seekers. The long public beach at Seymour is a special summer treat. Route 111 eventually reaches Derby (see *Newport* description), and brings you back to the world of fast food and gift shops.

■ Newport

Newport's charm is its position at the south end of **Lake Memphremagog** (pronounced Mem-fre-MAY-gog), a 30-mile international lake with excellent sailing and good swimming. In summer and fall, tour boats (☎ 334-6617), cruise the lake several times a day. In winter the lake is a busy thoroughfare for skaters and snowmobilers and the occasional ice boat. **Doug Nelson's elk farm** is in Derby Center (at the intersection of Routes 5 and 105). Best time to see the elk is at 4 p.m. feeding. Please stay behind the fences, and keep pets in the car. Among the other attractions are the fishing lakes to the southeast – **Salem**, **Seymour**, and **Echo**.

Newport's Princess *on Lake Memphremagog.*

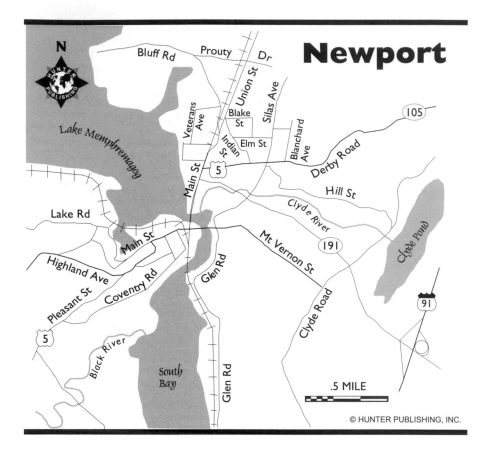

Newport

AUTHOR TIP

*If you like your touring organized by someone else, who also does all the driving, **Northeast Kingdom Tours** (☎ 334-8687 or 800-286-7344) is based in Newport and specializes in foliage touring as well as other regional packages.*

■ Jay

Newport's vista to the west is dominated by **Jay Peak**, with the lodge at the top giving an unmistakeable jagged tooth at the summit. Route 105 takes you out of Newport to the west, where you follow a well-marked set of turns on Routes 100, 101, and 242 to reach the village of Jay. Jay Peak, elevation 3,861 feet, is just west of the village. The **Long Trail** reaches the Canada border by crossing the ski slopes at Jay, and hikers celebrate completing their end-to-end Vermont trek; the northernmost piece of trail is also a great day hike. At Jay Peak and on the country roads beyond it are fine restaurants and plentiful lodging.

COVERED BRIDGE BONANZA

Take Route 242 to the west of Jay down the mountain to the river town of Montgomery Center and, to the right on Route 116, Montgomery, where seven covered bridges show what a busy rural center this once was. Two are next to Route 118: the Fuller or **Blackfalls Bridge** across Black Falls Creek, dating from 1890, and the 1863 Longley or **Harnois Bridge** over the Trout River. Travel south of Montgomery Center on Route 118 to the hamlet once called Hutchins, and find the **Hutchins Bridge** (1883) over the south branch of the Trout River, and the **Hectorsville Bridge** (also 1883) on the same river, but to the west side of Route 118. Other Montgomery covered bridges are **Hopkins** (1875), the **Comstock** (1883), and the **Creamery** (1883).

■ Hardwick, Greensboro & Craftsbury

There is a third gateway town into the Kingdom: Hardwick, where you enter this three-county region if you drive north on Route 14 from the center of the state. Although the match hasn't been friction-free, Hardwick residents have taken to hosting an **annual reggae fest** (☎ 985-8446) at the end of July, a lively music festival in an outdoor amphitheater. Hardwick's downtown district is a tiny arts oasis, and the **Craftsbury Chamber Players** perform here most Thursday evenings in the summer at the Hardwick Town Hall (the Hardwick Town Clerk will often be able to confirm this year's dates, ☎ 472-5971). Nearby are the retreat areas of Greensboro and Craftsbury, long-time picturesque summer havens and now Nordic ski centers. Craftsbury is especially lovely, with white homes and churches surrounding a wide green at Craftsbury Common, and back roads rising to small hill farms. Greensboro has been a summer home to many writers and public figures, notably author Wallace Stegner; the wide clear waters of **Caspian Lake** welcome boaters and anglers, as well as swimmers.

Adventures

■ On Foot

Groton State Forest

The largest wild region in the Kingdom is Groton State Forest. Its 25,000 acres of forest include miles of hiking trails and five campgrounds, each relating in a different way to the wild land around it. Black bears, deer, moose, grouse, mink, beavers, otters, fisher cats (a large weasel), loons, and great blue herons live at Groton State, and there are plenty of fish and even a pond devoted only to fly-fishing. **Peacham Bog Natural Area** (700 acres) contains one of the largest bogs in Vermont, with rare orchids and unusual birds. There's also a small mountain, **Owl's Head**, where the Civilian Conservation Corps in the 1930s built stone steps for hikers, to protect the alpine ecosystem around the trail.

Reach the park from either St. Johnsbury or Hardwick by heading for Route 2 and going eight miles past Danville to the well-marked Route 232 south. You'll want a trail and facility map, which you can pick up from the rangers at any of the campgrounds during summer and the early weeks of foliage season, or during winter and spring from the Department of Forests, Parks and Recreation (103 South Main Street, Waterbury, VT 05671-0603; ☎ 241-3655). At about two miles from Route 2 you arrive at the first campground, New Discovery, on your right; the trail to the left from Route 232 goes up toward Burnt Mountain and Marshfield Mountain, and may be restricted in early spring when peregrine falcons breed on the cliffs above Marshfield Pond. This is a really exciting comeback for a bird that had been driven to near-extinction by the combined forces of DDT and land development.

Park at New Discovery and hit the trails for Owl's Head Mountain, Little Deer Mountain, Big Deer Mountain, and around Osmore Pond. You can also hike from here to the **Nature Center** near Big Deer Campground, or take the trails to the east of Lake Groton and after four miles end up at **Boulder Beach** for a swim. The trail into Peacham Bog cuts off between the Nature Center and the beach. Trails are blazed; check with the rangers about recent changes from the maps and about moose activity.

A mature bull moose may reach 1,400 pounds. During early spring, they wander out to trails and roads as they graze, and can cause serious accidents. In the autumn rutting season moose may become dangerously aggressive. At other times, these eerily giant mammals stay mostly out of sight, although you'll find mounds of their scat (marble-sized and golden) where they've ranged among the marshlands looking for wet browse. The general rule is, don't approach or interrupt a moose's business and he (or she) won't bother yours.

Owl's Head is the most popular hike in the forest, especially on clear days when there's a view, so go early. For a good workout, select one of the steep, direct trails up the rocky north slope while skirting the scree and south-side cliffs. Owl's Head plants to notice include dwarf mountain laurel and an occasional crisp carpet of alpine lichens; large holes torn in this "rug" are where winter-starved deer have settled for second-best feeding.

When you reach the top of Owl's Head (plan on one to two hours, depending on whether you take trails or not), check your map to help identify the peaks. To the west are **Camel's Hump** and **Mount Mansfield**; to the northwest, with its jagged toothlike top, **Jay Peak**, which straddles the Canadian border; and to the east, on a clear day, the **Presidential Range** in New Hampshire.

WATCHABLE

WILDLIFE

Most clear days on Owl's Head you'll spot hawks sailing the thermoclines. With a basic bird guide, the broad-winged and red-shouldered hawks are easy to identify by silhouette and call. Golden eagles are sometimes seen too. Chickadees and bluejays in the tree canopy are a sure bet.

An alternate way of hiking the forest is to use the old railbed of the **Montpelier-Wells Railroad**, which runs some 14 miles through the forest. Check your map for turnoffs to the southwestern, wilder section of the forest, and to Kettle Pond, where there's a special group camping area on one shore and isolated campsites on the other that can best be reached by canoe. Avoid drinking water near the ponds, as beaver spread the human intestinal parasite *Giardia* in these lower waterways; instead, wait to sip from chill mountain springs higher up. If you bushwhack up the slopes, small caves are on hand for easy rain shelter; large ones should be investigated for black bear before you enter. The black bear is shy and mostly vegetarian, but protective of cubs. You may find yourself sharing a berry patch with one occasionally, and will certainly see evidence of bear and deer having rested in high grass. Watch for tree trunks scraped by bear claws at about head height. A sign of recent deer browsing is the blunt, square-clipped ends of maple twigs that would otherwise have ended in fat buds or fresh leaves.

CAUTION

Although there are no poisonous snakes this far north in Vermont, it's a good idea to check the ground for poison ivy before you perch or picnic. Remember the familiar "leaflets three, let it be" if you don't know the plant already.

Besides New Discovery, the Groton State campgrounds are **Stillwater** (at the heart of the forest), **Big Deer** (near the Nature Center), **Kettle Pond** (with its group camping area) and, at the south end of where Route 232 cuts through the forest, **Ricker Campground** on Ricker Pond.

A special feature of this forest is a fly-fishing lake with its own lodge and rental boats. On the shore of the lake (which is called **Noyes Lake**) is Seyon Lodge, where private and semiprivate sleeping quarters and hearty meals are provided. Make reservations well in advance, as the lodge fills quickly for its only open months, those of trout fly-fishing season. From

May to October, contact the Seyon Recreation Area, Groton, VT 05046, ☎ 584-3829; from November to April, contact the Park Regional Manager, Dept. of Forests, Parks and Recreation, 324 N. Main Street, Barre, VT 05641, ☎ 479-3241).

Victory Bog

The lack of views in this 5,000-acre preserve keep the trails from being crowded with hikers. On the other hand, if you've got your heart set on seeing a moose, have been keeping a bird checklist, or know your bog plants and orchids well, this wildlife management area is waiting for you. (It's heavily hunted during deer and moose seasons, though, so it's better to stay away for at least the month of November.)

AUTHOR TIP

Bear in mind that bogs are actually easiest to hike in winter, when the wetlands freeze; in May and June, be sure to apply plenty of insect repellent and wear a hat and boots.

Access to the preserve is from Route 2 at the North Concord intersection, which is about 10½ miles east of St. Johnsbury; watch for Copp's Store on the right. You want the left turn, marked Victory and Gallup Mills. From Route 2 it's 4½ miles up the gravel road to the first parking area on the left (there are two more farther north). Park here and walk across the road, looking for the wooden bridge through the trees just south of where you're standing. Cross the river on it and head either left (north) or right; you're on an old woods road. To the south, it passes a stream gauge that lets canoeists and naturalists keep an eye on water level. To the north, it heads toward the 25-acre boreal bog and wetlands of 1,800 acres. You should have a compass with you, as well as drinking water; the dark water is colored with tannin, which isn't a health problem, but the parasite *Giardia* in this and all beaver-inhabited waters can give humans a nasty intestinal infestation. Bring a camera so you won't be tempted to "collect" the rare plants in any other way than taking their pictures! Remember, if you do see a moose, keep your distance; in fall especially, moose are unpredictable and dangerous.

Lake Willoughby & Burke

There are many trails around this narrow and deep glacial lake, and they're all interesting. The local favorite is the hike up **Mount Pisgah** on the east side of the lake, where the steep cliffs make for dramatic views. Just as challenging and with more rocks that are climbable is the hike from Route 5A on the west side, up **Wheeler Mountain**. These trails are not especially well-blazed, as they are old and have seen some wear; bring your *Green Mountain Club Day Hiker's Guide to Vermont* and watch the landmarks closely. If you don't want much human company, use the trails early in the day, and stay away from this area on the most lovely summer and foliage season days, when they do get crowded.

A new trail system around **Burke Mountain** provides miles of hiking. For details, stop at East Burke Sports (☎ 626-3215 and the related Kingdom Trails Web site, www.kingdomtrails.org) in the village of East Burke.

Jay Peak

Jay Peak Resort opens its trails to summer hikers, and there are plenty of interesting rambles on this steep mountainside. The northernmost part of the **Long Trail** rises up Jay Peak and then North Jay Peak, before descending to the Canadian border, and makes several good day hikes. The Green Mountain Club puts out a *Long Trail Guide* that does a nice job of splitting the trailway into three hikes; see the guide for details. An easy climb is to head up Route 105 through North Troy (note the border crossing station) and continue for eight miles west; there's parking on your right. The Long Trail heads north with an easy climb up Carleton Mountain to a lookout, for a round trip of 2.4 miles; if you want to go farther, you can get some good ridge walking and a view north into Canada at Post 592, making a total round trip of 5.2 miles.

Don't cross that international border, or you will be expected to report to a customs station on your way back down. This is not a joke! The border is well monitored and, because drug smuggling continues, no one takes crossings lightly.

A different trek with more extensive views includes the summit of Jay Peak. From the village of Jay, go 5.1 miles west on Route 242 and park on the left. Head north on the Long Trail to the summit, 3,861 feet; the round trip is 3.4 miles and is a good stretch of those calf and shin muscles. Day hiking boots are suggested.

Island Pond, Maidstone & The Bill Sladyk Wildlife Management Area

Island Pond is the name of both the village and the lake at this scenic center in Essex County; the surrounding town is actually named Brighton, and the park on the lake is **Brighton State Park**. Brighton State Park has nature trails and a summer naturalist in residence (as well as campsites, swimming beach, rental boats) and is a good place for a summer ramble. So is **Maidstone State Park**; to reach it from Island Pond, take Route 105 southeast 16 miles to Bloomfield and then after another five miles south, make the right turn onto five more miles of unpaved road. The forest offers hiking trails around a large lake.

There's a 10,000-acre wildlife management area near the Canada border, reached from the village of Holland or from Route 114 north of Island

Pond. If you want wilderness hiking with few cut trails and a real demand that you manage your compass and map well, the **Bill Sladyk Wildlife Management Area** was meant for you. Do get a topographic map before heading in, and study the few trails marked in the *GMC's Day Hiker's Guide*. Again, don't fool around with the international border; because of drug traffic, it's serious business to get close to it or cross it, and the border is well monitored.

Runners' Camps

There are week-long camp sessions for runners at both the **Craftsbury Outdoor Center** (☎ 586-7767 or 800-729-7751) and **Lyndon State College** (John Holland, Green Mountain Running Camp, 1720 Baptist Church Road, Yorktown Heights, NY 10598; ☎ 914-962-5238). It's great to get pumping on those back-country roads and be able to soak your legs afterward in a cold mountain stream.

■ On Wheels

Road Biking

Although Essex County is relatively flat, there are few connecting roads. This means the best road biking in the Northeast Kingdom is actually around **Craftsbury** and in the circuit of **Barnet, Peacham, Danville, St. Johnsbury**; both of these loops are well described in John Freidin's *25 Bicycle Tours in Vermont*.

The roads that connect **East Charleston**, **Island Pond**, **Morgan Center**, and **Morgan** are perfect for road biking, with their gentle rolling curves, except for the presence of large logging trucks that may travel at a pretty high speed. Be aware of road traffic and use a biking rear-view mirror. These roads are so lovely that it's worth the effort to travel them, and back roads like **Five Mile Square** and **Ten Mile Square**, which run between and in East Charleston and Island Pond, get you away from the road traffic almost entirely.

Mountain Biking

For mountain biking, on the other hand, the entire Kingdom is a playground. Focus on two centers where there is good support for pedaling: the **Craftsbury Outdoor Center** (☎ 586-7767 or 800-729-7751, Web site www.craftsbury.com, e-mail crafts@sover.net) has trails and summer programs for mountain bikers, and the area around East Burke, including the ski trails at Burke Mountain, is very accessible with support from **East Burke Sports** (☎ 626-3215, seven days). Rentals can be found at both locations; East Burke Sports does repairs, as does the **Village Sports Shop** (☎ 626-8448) on Route 5 just south of Lyndonville's business center.

In Burke, the **Kingdom Trails Association**, spearheaded by the folks at East Burke Sports (☎ 626-3215), has put together 100 miles of interconnected trails for spring, summer, and fall, running along the ridgelines of East Burke with great long-distance views, and up through the ski area of Burke Mountain. A Victorian mansion and some lovely farms are along the routes, as well as fields and forests. Single-track trail abounds. A map detailing the trails and grading them (and also reserving one trail for hikers only) can be purchased at the sports shop in East Burke or by mail for $4 ($3 plus $1 handling) from Kingdom Trails Association, PO Box 204, East Burke, VT 05632.

Jay Peak (☎ 988-2611) offers aerial tram rides for experienced mountain bikers; the longest trail from the summit is five miles, and there's a network of lower mountain trails and a wooded trail network. The trail fee is modest and can include use of the resort's swimming pool all day.

One last, little-known trail: At **Groton State Forest**, the old railbed has been turned into a rec path with about 14 miles of pretty level pedaling through forest and over streams. Do explore the railroad ghost town of **Lanesboro** at the north edge of the state forest.

MORE MOUNTAIN BIKING TRAILS LIKELY

Some 133,000 acres of former logging land in Essex County, from Victory northward through East Haven and east to Bloomfield, have opened to public access. By 2002 there should be mountain biking on the rough gravel roads. Views are spectacular, and it wouldn't be hard to put together a "century" trail on the land. Keep in touch with the **Kingdom Trails Association** (PO Box 204, East Burke, VT 05832, ☎ 626-3215, www.kingdomtrails.org) to find out the latest status; this is also likely to be where you'll get a map of the trails as they emerge.

Vermont Mountain Bike Advocates (VMBA, PO Box 563, Waterbury, VT 05676, Web site www.vmba.org) also offers information on biking on state and private land; for updates on this particular region, called the Champion Lands Project after its former owner. There's also news at the **Vermont Land Trust** Web site (www.vlt.org).

■ On Water

Rivers To Run

 The Northeast Kingdom rivers have their best paddling at high water in spring, late April to early May, and that means you're going to be traveling in "snowmelt" that hasn't warmed up a lot. So here are some extra pointers for cold water paddling.

COLD WATER CANOE TIPS

■ Check the weather forecast and keep aware of changes as you go along the river. A sign of dropping temperature is ice starting to form on your paddle. You're going to start losing body heat fast.

■ Use a dry suit with fleece underwear, neoprene socks, even neoprene booties. Experiment with hand coverings. Gloves with rough palms work for some, but a thin polypropylene glove covered with a surgical glove can be a thinner combo better-suited to small hands.

■ Use the most buoyant PFD vest you've got; if you enter cold water you need all the help you can get.

■ Know your skill level, and then cut back one or two levels for cold water paddling. This is not a wise sport for nonswimmers or even poor swimmers; you need good self-rescue skills.

■ Eat more calories, both before and during the trip. Count on burning plenty of carbohydrates and fat to keep your internal temperature up. Lose weight some other day!

The **Connecticut River** has its source in four lakes in northern New Hampshire; by the time it reaches Vermont at the northern boundary, it's runnable but small and quiet from **Canaan to North Stratford**. **North Stratford to Guildhall** is a peaceful 25-mile run, and the next 20 miles to **South Lunenburg** is also a gentle paddle. There are nesting swallows along the banks that provide interesting distraction; their nests are hollows in the mud banks, and the numbers are amazing. Consult the *Appalachian Mountain Club River Guide to New Hampshire and Vermont* for how to handle the Class II rapids that follow, and the dams that begin at Gilman. The section from Gilman to East Ryegate is broken up by numerous small dams. The *River Guide* gives an overview; you should check all the portages and anywhere that an old dam has stood, for changes in this river happen often.

The **Passumpsic River** has even more dams per running foot, so to speak, but is runnable well after other rivers are too low. From Lyndonville to the Connecticut River there are six dams, and some challenging ledges. Central Vermont Public Service has put out a free book on canoeing the Passumpsic, available at local bookstores and the Chamber of Commerce in St. Johnsbury; it's chatty and fun to read, but snags, blowdowns, and degrading dams need to be checked right before you paddle.

The nicest part about paddling the **Moose River** is going quietly through the Victory Bog Wildlife Management Area. Save this paddle for when you're truly in the mood for natural history rather than water excitement; birdlife is rampant, and you may well share the river with a moose browsing to the side.

For a guided tour of the waters to the northwest, connect up with **Raven Ridge** in Enosburg (☎ 933-4616 or 888-933-4616, Web site www.together.net/~ravenrdg). The team of Chas Salmon and Olga Lermontov has been recognized as 1999 Vermont Guide of the Year and offers canoe and kayak rentals and customized outings, complete with shuttle service, guided fishing, and even animal tracking and photographic opportunities. The couple refers to their work as "opening doors to the Natural World for people of all ages and abilities."

Flatwater Paddling

Flatwater paddling in the Northeast Kingdom pairs up well with angling or birdwatching. Look for the smaller ponds like **Keyser** (near Peacham), **Ewell's** (between Peacham and Danville), and **Harvey's Lake** (West Barnet; **Harvey's Lake Cabins and Campgrounds**, ☎ 633-2213, rents rowboats and canoes). On these lakes you may see great blue herons and, in spring, loons and geese. **Lake Groton** is good for summer relaxation, although it's pretty well settled around the shores. **Crystal** has a wider expanse but less interesting shoreline.

Vermont Waterways (☎ 472-8271 or 800-492-8271), based in East Hardwick, provides weekend paddling tours on the Vermont rivers, kayaking weekends on Lake Champlain, and some walk-and-paddle combos.

Sailing & Windsurfing

Windsurfers usually head for **Willoughby**, although the steady breezes at **Harvey's** in West Barnet make it a good practice lake. Sailboats also do well at Willoughby, but the prevailing wind rarely changes and it's a long series of tacks back again.

Lake Memphremagog is a much better sailing lake, with a prevailing wind from the north, and the islands make it even more fun; some of the islands were used by smugglers in the past century, especially rum runners. Pick up a good lake map at the marina in Newport. Don't play around with the international border. If you do go across it, report in to Customs on shore, both on your way north and on the way back again. Although there's no real island camping on the lake, there are plenty of spots to anchor near shore for the night if you want to stay out longer. Remember that most sightings of the "sea monster" of the lake, nicknamed Memphre, have been along the wilder west shore! Quietly motoring this lake after dark is peaceful and lovely. There are boat rentals at **Newport Marine** (☎ 334-5911), and two marinas – the **city dock** (☎ 334-5726), where you can also board *Newport's Princess* (☎ 334-6617) for a cruise of the lake on a small paddlewheeler, and the **East Side Landing** (☎ 334-2340).

Boating on **Greensboro Lake** has a long history, and should be set up as a relaxing day with picnicking and plenty of time to spend; winds are not reliable. The **Highland Lodge** in Greensboro (☎ 533-2647) rents boats and

The Northeast Kingdom

has a nice beach from which to to launch. At the south end of **Crystal Lake** is another boat rental location (☎ 525-3904 or 525-4548).

A SPECIAL FOURTH OF JULY

What's the best way to watch fireworks on Independence Day? Maybe leaning back, well bundled up in your floatation vest plus a wool blanket, in a canoe or rowboat on **Joe's Pond** in West Danville. Joe's is really three small ponds joined by channels and surrounded by seasonal cottages (the traditional place to stay when you first arrive is Indian Joe Court, PO Box 126, West Danville 05873, ☎ 684-3430). Borrow or rent a boat and get out on the water on fireworks night for a sensation of falling stars cascading over you. Make sure you stay around until Sunday morning, too, in order to connect with the pontoon boat that carries Archie's Bakery goods around the shore. Your other goal for the weekend might be to see how many versions you can find locally of the story of "Injun" Joe and Molly. Joe was a Native American and Molly was his wife, and the tale dates back to about 1745. (You'll find Molly's Pond to the southeast, just down Route 2, a great photo spot and birding location.)

At the **Craftsbury Outdoor Center** (☎ 586-7767 or 800-729-7751, Web site www.craftsbury.com, e-mail crafts@sover.net) there are courses in canoeing, but there's also the specialized **Craftsbury Sculling Center**, with more than two decades of experience in individual and group coaching. Coached by Steve Wagner, head coach at Rutgers University, the program takes place on (and off) area lakes like the Hosmer Ponds, Great and Little. In winter the same group offers a rower's cross-training weekend in snow sports.

At **Brighton State Park** there are boat rentals at the park office. Most cottage rentals around Salem Lake include boats, too. In the town of Island Pond, **Mahoney's General Store** (☎ 723-6255) supplies sporting goods and, just west of town, **Northern Wildlife** (☎ 723-6659) rents canoes and sells fishing tackle and live bait.

Fishing

If you're angling in the Northeast Kingdom, you'll probably go for the trout streams and the big lakes like Willoughby and Memphremagog. Jim Keely offers **Memphremagog Bass Guide Service** (☎ 334-6862); David Benware at **Seymour Lake Lodge** guides fly-fishing on lakes, ponds, rivers, and streams (☎ 895-2752 or 800-207-2752); and at **Northeast Kingdom Outfitters** in Morgan (east of Newport) there are casting clinics and guided fly-fishing trips (☎ 895-4220).

Northeast Kingdom Outfitters guide Dave Smith will also help you take advantage of a new asset: the recent and remarkable return of salmon to the **Clyde River** in Newport. A power dam that blocked the Clyde a mile north of town for 40 years has been removed, and the big Atlantic salmon now accompany brook trout in the river. Fall is the best time to catch the salmon migration out of the nearby lake, say from mid-September to mid-October, between Lake Memphremagog and the old powerhouse. After October 1 the season is controlled for artificials only, catch and release, to protect the spawning fish. Keep up with changing regulations in the annual free book that you can pick up at local outfitters like **Wright's Sport Shop** in Newport (☎ 334-1674) or by calling the Department of Fish and Wildlife at ☎ 241-3700.

Fly-fishing addicts will especially appreciate the farther stretches of the Clyde River; look for Five Mile Square Road, which connects Route 105 and Route 114 between East Charleston and Island Pond, and find a perfect canoe access and parking area maintained by the state, at the Route 105 end of this back road. In spring especially, it's quiet except for the trill of the red-winged blackbirds all around.

In late April or early May the trout leap up the falls in **Orleans**; if you're in the area, it's a great sight and a traditional start to the season.

Don't miss out on the **Seyon Lodge** at **Noyes Pond** in Groton State Forest, where only fly-fishing is allowed on the pond (☎ 584-3829 from May to October; other times, ☎ 479-3241; also see *On Foot*).

Swimming

In summer, **Prouty Beach** in Newport has lifeguards; so do **Crystal Lake** in Barton and **Harvey's Lake** in West Barnet. There's a good beach at the north end of **Lake Willoughby. Seymour** and **Caspian** also have swimming beaches. The nice beach **Brighton State Park** doesn't get very crowded. For family swimming, the beach on the west shore of **Shadow Lake** in Glover is small and friendly.

Swimming holes abound on the small rivers. One of the nicest (but swim at your own risk) is **Adams Hole**, a local "drop in" on the Joe's Brook between Danville and East Barnet. Get directions locally to the Joe's Brook Road from Route 5; then head toward Danville and, when the pavement ends, watch for the pull-off about half a mile farther on the right-hand side.

■ Travel With Horses

For a trail ride that combines great horses with spectacular vistas, Neal and Cheryl Perry provide some of the nicest-tempered Morgans you'll ever find. The couple has a farm in Brownington – the **Perry Farm** – where they welcome riders of all abilities, and will customize trips through the fields and woods and along back roads. They also offer pony rides and, in winter, hayrides and sleighrides, including moonlight versions. The farm is a mile from Brownington's historic Old Stone House; call for directions. Reserve well in advance, especially during fall foliage season (☎ 754-2396). To add to the fun, you can stay with the Perrys for a "working" farm vacation and learn how to take care of the horses, fix the fences around the cow pastures, and generally have a great time in the country. Guests have a private apartment.

Debby and Denny Newland at **D-N-D Stables** say you don't need to call ahead, just come, on any day in June and July, for a guided hour-long trail ride. The Newlands also offer foliage rides, winter rides, and more, but reservations are important for those. D-N-D is on Route 114 north of East Burke; contact them at ☎ 626-8237. For these rides, as for all horse rides, bring along a hat, wear shoes with a heel and, in summer especially, apply insect repellent so that you won't be slapping at bugs instead of guiding your mount.

■ On Snow & Ice

Downhill Skiing

Two major ski resorts dominate the downhill recreation in the Northeast Kingdom: Burke and Jay. Both have the plus of short lift lines and plenty of space; both also offer tree skiing and a chance for extreme excitement (with signature of a waiver, of course!).

Burke's vertical drop of 2,000 feet is more than respectable, and its longest trail is 2.3 miles, also right up there. Although the mountain seems "out in the boonies," actual driving time from Interstate 91 is about half an hour. There are four lifts (a quad, a double, a J-bar and a poma) and 30 trails, including eight black diamond trails. About half the trails have snowmaking coverage (70% overall coverage). The resort went through an auction in late 2000 that broke up the parcels and brought in new ownership. Plans for the next ski season are uncertain; try the resort's old phone number (☎ 626-3305); if it's not available, try directory information. Chances are the slopes will reopen, as they are just too good to stay idle long.

Jay Peak has the air of a tiny international resort, and sits practically on the Canadian border. It claims to offer the longest, steepest, and snowiest glades and chutes in the East. The whole mountain is a terrain park in a way – snowboarders have full access to the 285 trail acres and over 100 acres of glades (16 glades). The vertical drop is a heady 2,153 feet, with 64 trails, glades, and chutes (longest trail is three miles), an aerial tramway to the summit, and six lifts, including a pair of T-bars. Snowmaking coverage is 80%. Accommodations include a slopeside hotel and condominiums and there are several inns nearby. The ski school includes kids' versions too. (☎ 988-2611 or 800-451-4449, snow conditions 988-9601, Web site www.jaypeakresort.com.)

Cross-Country Skiing

Both Jay and Burke offer cross-country trails. **Burke** has 40 miles of groomed trails (☎ 626-3305). **Jay** has 12 miles (☎ 988-2611). Less than two miles from the Burke Resort is the **Burke Cross Country Ski Area** (☎ 626-8338 or 800-786-8338), a separate center with about 50 miles of trails, mostly groomed for both classic and skating use. There's a ski shop and rentals, with lessons by appointment.

GUIDED SKI TOURS: *If you're looking for a private guide to the back-country in snow season, **Jesse Williams** (PO Box 51, Montgomery Village, VT 05470; ☎ 326-3201) offers tree skiing and boarding tours and multi-day adventures and instruction around Jay Peak.*

Specializing in Nordic skiing are the **Craftsbury Nordic Center** (☎ 586-7767 or 800-729-7751), with 53 miles of groomed trails, 93 miles total; **Hazen's Notch** in Montgomery Center near Jay (☎ 326-4708), which has 19 miles groomed, 28 miles total; **Highland Lodge** in Greensboro (☎ 533-2647), offering 25 miles groomed, 50 miles total; and **Heermansmith Farm Inn** between Irasburg and Coventry (☎ 754-8866), with six miles groomed, 19 miles total. Of these, only Heermansmith Farm doesn't offer a ski shop, rentals, and lessons (but go anyway for the wonderful peace at this little inn). As you can guess from the miles of trail, Craftsbury is really dedicated to the sport and its trails connect with other networks, offering village-to-village touring with return by shuttle bus. Snowshoeing is welcome at all the centers, and Craftsbury has weekend ski camps as well.

Don't forget the **Catamount Trail**, Vermont's end-to-end ski trail. It passes through the Craftsbury Nordic Center and then north through Lowell to Jay Peak. The trail guidebook is available from the Catamount Trail Association (PO Box 1235, Burlington, VT 05402; ☎ 864-5794). Of course, the state parks in this region are also open to Nordic skiers, but don't expect parking areas to be plowed.

Snowshoeing & Winter Hiking

The state parks, and especially those in the Northeast Kingdom, offer great winter hiking – and, once the snow gets deep enough, snowshoe trekking. Officially the parks are closed at this time of year, so you won't find support staff, or even bathrooms (but yes, there are usually outhouses open year-round). A good way to visit and to learn the ropes of winter hiking – for instance, that you try really hard not to get sweaty, a big difference from other seasons – is to join a **Green Mountain Club** adventure in the snowy months. Learn to pack for day and overnight treks, handle snowshoes skillfully, and take reasonable safety precautions. Have fun with a group interested in learning the same skills. And get a handle on the terrain, so if you come back later on your own (or, for safety's sake, with a few friends), you'll know where to go and how to get there. **Groton State Forest** is a wonderland in winter, the lowlands crisscrossed with animal tracks and the peaks silent and crystalline. There are even lean-to shelters. As usual, plan to cook over as small stove rather than to make fires – camping has changed with better understanding of forest preservation needs. Which brings me back to learning those skills: Get in touch with the GMC at the headquarters on Route 100 in Waterbury Center (☎ 244-7037).

Snowmobiling

Snowmobilers have a field day in the Northeast Kingdom. From early December to late April there's nearly always snowcover, especially in Essex County, which is why **Island Pond** has become the snowmobile capital of Vermont. The trails, maintained by the Vermont Association of Snow Travelers, also spread into surrounding towns and villages, threading through Danville, all of Barnet, over the wild lands around Burke, and past many a friendly country inn. Groton State Forest, like Maidstone and Brighton, is open to snowmobilers. However, the state Wildlife Management Areas restrict powered vehicles to specific maintained trails, especially to protect deer, which, if startled can easily exhaust themselves in deep snow and die.

More information about this celebrated winter sport is available from the **Brighton Snowmobile Club**, PO Box 400, Island Pond, VT 05846.

SNOWMOBILE RENTALS & GUIDED TOURS

In Island Pond, **Barnes Recreation** (☎ 723-6331) gives guided snowmobile tours of Vermont and Canada; feel free to bring your own machine.

To rent a snowmobile by the day, weekend, or week, contact **Kingdom Cat Corp.** in Island Pond at ☎ 723-9702; guided tours are also available here.

Other Winter Sports

For **sleigh rides**, head to the inns: the **Wildflower Inn** at Lyndonville (☎ 626-8310 or 800-627-8310) and **Rose Apple Acres Farm Bed & Breakfast** in North Troy (☎ 988-2503). In Albany at **Little Hosmer Farm** (☎ 755-6280) the rides in the two-horse box sleigh are followed by mulled cider and cookies.

Ice fishing is a way of life on **Lake Memphremagog** and on **Willoughby**; the smaller lakes of Salem, Seymour, and Harvey's also draw anglers for trout and smelt.

SOUTH OF ALASKA, SLED DOGS!

In late January, **Craftsbury Outdoor Center** often hosts **dog-sled racing** if the snow is good enough. It's a weekend event, from the "adopt a Musher" program to the races to the Sunday morning mushers' breakfast and awards. There are sled rides, too. For this year's date (and to check on snow conditions), call John Broadhead at the Center, ☎ 586-7767.

Interested in trying a dogsled yourself? Musher Keith Ballek at **Hardscrabble Tours** in Sheffield, off Interstate 91 north of Lyndonville, offers excursions as long as there's deep snow. Reservations are required (☎ 626-9895), and trips can take from a half-hour to a half-day. Ask about snowshoe hikes, too. Expect good conversation, and maybe a mug of hot chocolate when you're done.

Eco-Travel &
Cultural Excursions

A guided expedition can make a big difference in what wildlife you notice and name, as well as how you navigate the waters or woods. Traveling with resident biologist Will Staats of **Kingdom Guide Service** will reveal some of the secrets of **Victory Bog**, the serene glories of the **Nulhegan River Basin**, or the moose pastures and rugged summits of the mountains of **Essex County**. Staats puts together personalized one-on-one trips, for a full day or half-day, by canoe, on foot, or both. As a lifelong woodsman and professional biologist, he adds details about animal habits, plant life cycles, and ecology. Various fitness levels are accommodated (but no babies, please, in the canoes). The office is just west of the Gallup Mills "four corners" in Victory, but it's best to get in touch in advance (☎ 328-3057).

If you visited Sugarmill Farm Maple Museum in Barton (see *Touring*), you already know a lot about how the delicately scented sap of the maple tree gets boiled down 40-fold to become sticky, amber maple syrup. Close to Jay is the farming village of Westfield, and on Route 100 is **Couture's Maple Shop** (☎ 744-2733 or 800-845-2733), where Jacques and Pauline Couture invite you to sample their spring crop. They put in 4,000 tree taps each year. In addition to maple syrup, they make maple cream (heavenly on toast), granulated maple sugar, and a maple French dressing. Ask them about French-Canadian culture in this part of the Kingdom, too.

A VERY SPECIAL PLACE TO SEE THE FOLIAGE

In the 1890s, William Barstow Strong built an **observatory** in Brownington, a small village popular among Orleans County residents for its back roads and spectacular autumn foliage displays. Strong's structure was rebuilt by townspeople in 1976 as part of the national bicentennial, and rebuilt again for Brownington's own bicentennial in 1999. It's on Prospect Hill and is open from 8:30 a.m. to dusk daily to November 1 (information: ☎ 754-2022). To get there, from Interstate 91 take the Orleans exit (Exit 26) and turn east on Route 58. Go through the manufacturing town of Orleans and watch for the sign to Brownington (not Brownington Center), a left turn about a mile from the Interstate. The center of the village is three miles from Route 58, and Prospect Hill is on the left just past the cluster of homes.

Where To Stay

■ St. Johnsbury

The **Fairbanks Motor Inn** (☎ 748-5666, $$) is the newest in town, on Route 2 just west of Main Street; it's beautifully landscaped and has a heated swimming pool and putting green. The **Yankee Traveler Motel** (☎ 748-3156, $-$$) is also on Route 2 just east of Railroad Street, across town. There's also the **Holiday Motel** (☎ 748-8192, $-$$), across Hastings Street from the friendly local restaurant called the **Lincoln Inn**, which adjoins the **Maple Center Motel** (☎ 748-2393, $$); both are at the north end of town.

For truly elegant lodging (and dining), head out of town on Route 2 east and, after a mile, take the right turn onto Route 18; it's eight miles to Lower Waterford, a "white village," the local name for this picturesque village made up of white houses with green shutters, a New England classic collection. There you will find the **Rabbit Hill Inn** (☎ 748-5168 or 800-76BUNNY, $$$$), which enchants guests with sitting rooms, a library, pub, afternoon tea, and a hammock by the pond. Rabbit Hill has been repeatedly named one of America's 10 best inns; it's a 200-year-old country classic.

Looking for a compromise between in-town motels and elegant lodging? At Exit 1 from Interstate 93 (or reached from the center of St. Johnsbury by taking Route 2 east to meet the interstate highway) is a cozy Victorian home serving as a bed and breakfast: **Moonstruck Inn**. There are six rooms with private baths, and innkeeper Megan Fletcher enjoys providing a hearty Vermont breakfast (St. Johnsbury, ☎ 748-4661, $$).

■ Danville, Peacham, & Barnet

In West Danville, summer holidays start at **Indian Joe Court** (PO Box 126, West Danville 05873, ☎ 684-3430, $-$$) on the shore of Joe's Pond, easily located on Route 2. In the village of Danville, watch for signs to **Emergo Farm Bed & Breakfast** at 261 Webster Hill (☎ 684-2215 or 800-383-1185; e-mail emergo@together.net, $$), where antiques and family heirlooms add to the charm of the sitting room and two guestrooms at the farmhouse. Emergo Farm is great in winter too, with sledding on Webster Hill and nearby cross-country skiing. Or head east of Danville on Route 2 to Dole Hill, where **Sugar Ridge RV Village and Campground** recently opened (☎ 684-2550).

Barnet offers a pair of bed-and-breakfast homes, both on Route 5, which passes through the village of Barnet (there are four other villages within this spread-out town). The **Inn at Maplemont Farm** is an elegant turn-of-the century farmhouse filled with antiques, handmade quilts, and music boxes (☎ 230-1617 or 800-230-1617, $$-$$$), and is just south of the village. The **Old Homestead**, within walking distance north of the general store, is an 1850 Colonial that has been an inn since 1919. Innkeeper Gail Warnaar loves to bake (☎ 633-4016, $$-$$$). Both are close to the Connecticut River, so bring a canoe or kayak, or plan to bike along the rolling river-valley roads.

■ Lyndonville

A Federal period home in town offers five rooms for guests, at **Branch Brook Bed & Breakfast** (☎ 626-8316 or 800-572-7712, $$). Or you can go to the north end of town and take Route 114 to the first marked left turn up Darling Hill to the **Wildflower Inn** (☎ 626-8310 or 800-627-8310, Web site www.wildflowerinn.com, $$-$$$$), where the gardens and the view across Willoughby Gap would almost be enough alone, without the charming inn rooms and the scrumptious meals. A romantic cottage is perfect for honeymoons. Families are also welcome, and there's a small petting farm as well as heated pool, tennis courts, spa and sauna.

■ Burke

Right up on Burke Mountain is the **Old Cutter Inn** (☎ 626-5152 or 800-295-1943, $$), on the road from East Burke to the resort. This is a country farmhouse with lovely grounds and a heated pool; the adjoining restaurant is one of the area's finest, offering Swiss cuisine. In the village of East Burke near Bailey's Country Store (a general store with room after room of old-fashioned, tasty or lovely treats) is the **Village Inn of East Burke** (☎ 626-3161, e-mail villgin@together.net, $$).

The Inn at Mountain View Creamery was once the noted farm estate of hotel magnate Elmer A. Darling, the one for whom Darling Hill is named.

The red-brick creamery building has been transformed by innkeepers Marilyn and John Pastore into a 10-room inn furnished with antiques and handmade quilts. The gracious little restaurant, Darling's Country Bistro, offers chef-prepared specialties, and in gentle weather guests can dine on the patio, which has a stunning view of Burke Mountain. A full country breakfast is served. Access to Kingdom Trails for hiking, mountain biking, and cross-country skiing begins beyond the barns, with 440 acres of rolling hills. The Pastores put together regular outdoor programs with local ski-and-cycle-enthusiast John Worth to enrich use of the meadows and slopes and introduce beginners to new adventures. Sleigh rides and hayrides can be requested in advance. A special note: Early in December, guests at the inn can visit a Christmas tree farm and select their own fresh, fragrant tree to be cut and sent home with them, at a modest farm price. The inn also has facilities for group retreats and family reunions, and there will soon be a spa in one of the remodeled barns. Massage is already available by advance arrangement. Mailing address: Mountain View Creamery, Box 355, Darling Hill Road, East Burke, VT 05832. ☎ 626-9924; Web site www.innmtnview.com; $$-$$$$.

The Inn at Mountain View Creamery in Burke.

Around the area are bed and breakfasts and small inns such as the **Garrison Inn** (☎ 626-8329 or 800-773-1914, $$) and **Das German Haus** (☎ 626-8568, $$).

■ Barton & Glover

The bed-and-breakfast homes in Barton and Glover each offer a special activity: The **Anglin' B &B** (☎ 525-4548, Web site www.anglinbb.com, $$) is located on Crystal Lake, ready for you to drop in a line. **Our Village Inn B&B** (☎ 800-525-3380, e-mail ourvinn@sover.net, $$) has an antique shop in the barn. In West Glover, on Lake Parker, **Tranquillity Farm** (☎ 525-3646, $$) offers dedicated birding, complete with a guide if you like. And at the **Rodgers Country Inn** (☎ 525-6677 or 800-729-1704, $), where hospitality has been offered for many years in the 1840 farmhouse, there are small animals for petting and a dairy farm down the road. Snow travelers appreciate the **Pinecrest Motel & Cabins** (☎ 525-3472, $) on Route 5 north of Barton, directly on the snowmobile corridor trail maintained by VAST, the Vermont Association of Snow Travelers.

The nearby village of **Albany** is slowly opening its sleepy farming vistas to visitors, and there on Route 14 Jon and Kate Fletcher have opened their cozy Victorian home as the **Village House Inn & Restaurant**. There are eight guest rooms, each with private bath, and dinner is served with a flourish of fresh produce (☎ 755-6722, $$). A mile north of Albany village is **McCleary Brook Antiques and Gifts** (☎ 755-6344, www.collector-online/collect/booth-21.html), open weekends from 10 to 6 and by appointment.

ACCESSIBILITY NOTE: *The **Village House Inn** (see above) near Barton & Glover is fully handicapped accessible.*

■ Westmore

On the east shore of Lake Willoughby, actually in the small village of Westmore but only eight miles east of Barton village, is the **Willoughvale Inn** (☎ 525-4123 or 800-594-9102, $$-$$$), which has a superb restaurant adjoining the small cluster of rooms. The view from the front porch out over the lake is breathtaking, and the gardens are charming.

FOR GROUPS: *Go to the far (south) end of the lake to find **Cheney House**, a retreat center made available to groups through the Vermont Department of Forests, Parks, and Recreation. Talk with John Alexander, ☎ 334-0184 days and 723-6688 nights; or from September through April, speak to Bruce Amsden at ☎ 479-3241).*

■ Island Pond & East

Whether you're here for the winter snowmobiling or the summer fun on the lake, the **Lakefront Motel** offers practical vacation accommodations ranging from standard rooms to efficiencies to suites. There are boat rentals, too (Cross Street, ☎ 723-6507, $-$$).

Anglers, hunters, and dedicated hikers and botanists sometimes find their way east of Island Pond. Up in Canaan, **Jackson's Lodge & Log Cabin Village** provides a peaceful retreat at Lake Wallace (☎ 266-3360, $-$$). Averill, as far north as Canaan but a little to the west, is the home of **Quimby Country**, where the lodge and 20 cottages are the heart of a 700-acre family resort that provides meals, picnics, cookouts, and sports, as well as complimentary canoes and rowboats. Ask about special rates for spring fishing and fall foliage (☎ 822-5533, $-$$$).

■ Coventry

This little town just south of Newport on Route 14 has waterfalls, good fishing, and the very comfortable and peaceful inn at **Heermansmith Farm** (☎ 754-8866, $$). Jack and Louise Smith encourage a simple vacation of walks, fishing, a little Nordic skiing, some quiet conversation and reading, and plenty of good food and fine wines.

■ Derby & Newport

Derby Line, the northern village beyond Derby, right on the Canadian border, has the more picturesque selection of inns. The **Derby Village Inn Bed & Breakfast** is in an elegant Victorian village home (☎ 873-3604, Web site http://homepages.together.net/~dvibandb, $$); innkeepers are Catherine McCormick and Sheila Steplar. There's also the **Birchwood B&B** (☎ 873-9104, $$, ask about the canopy bed). On Main Street in Derby is the **Border Motel** (☎ 766-2088 or 800-280-1898, $), where there's a long tradition of evening entertainment, especially on weekends.

To the east of Derby, if you're fishing at Seymour Lake, the **Seymour Lake Lodge** (☎ 895-2752, $-$$) welcomes guests to its homey atmosphere, with guide Dave Benware at the breakfast table with you.

Newport has a handful of motels; a stop at the Newport Chamber of Commerce office on the "Causeway" (where the interstate meets the town's shopping plaza) will get you brochures from all of them and a reservation at the same time (or you can also call the Chamber for the same service, ☎ 334-7782). Some listings for cottages and rentals on Lakes Memphremagog, Seymour, and Salem are also found at the Chamber of Commerce.

■ Jay

If you're not staying at the slopeside lodging of the resort (☎ 800-451-4449), you can use the same number for free reservation services at the **Black Lantern Inn**, a restored 1803 stagecoach stop with a wonderful restaurant (☎ 326-4507 or 800-255-8661, $$-$$$), the **Schneehutte Inn**, with a German-American restaurant (☎ 988-4020, $$), the **Jay Village Inn**, a popular country inn with a casual lounge (☎ 988-2306 or 800-565-5641, $$), and the **Inn on Trout River**, a historic inn with superb dining (☎ 338-7049, $$-$$$). Jay also has a pair of ski lodges, the **Snowline** (☎ 988-2822 or 800-638-4661, $) and the **Woodshed** (☎ 988-4444 or 800-495-4445, $).

■ Craftsbury & Greensboro

Make the most of the old-fashioned elegance of these two summer havens by staying at inns where authors, artists, politicians and sincere vacation lovers have stayed for decades: the **Inn on the Common** in Craftsbury

Common (☎ 586-9619 or 800-521-2233, $$$), with its luxurious rooms and fabulous cuisine; the **Craftsbury Inn** in Craftsbury (☎ 586-2848 or 800-336-2848, $$$), an 1850 country inn with gourmet dining; and **Highland Lodge** in Greensboro (☎ 533-2647, e-mail Hlodge@connriver.net, $$$$), where 120 acres of woods, fields and beach accommodate hikers, Nordic skiers, boaters, and anglers.

If you're looking for an energizing vacation, the place to stay is the **Craftsbury Outdoor Center** (which in winter is the Nordic Center; ☎ 800-729-7751, $$), on 140 acres, with simple lodging and wonderful healthy food to go along with the many programs in hiking, running, sculling, mountain biking, Nordic skiing and snowshoeing.

Another Greensboro gem is the **Lakeview Inn & Café/Bakery** (call for directions, ☎ 533-2291, $$), in a restored historic home near Caspian Lake. The 12 guest rooms are filled with antiques and have private baths. Innkeepers Kathryn Unser and John Hunt offer a country breakfast in the sunny dining room or out on the porch, with its views of mountains and garden.

BICYCLISTS, TAKE NOTE: *The area around Lake View Inn is a good location for bicyclists, for whom the roads northward open out appealingly. Make sure to include both Craftsbury Common and the quieter village of East Craftsbury on your route.*

■ Camping

One of the nicest campgrounds in this region is in West Barnet: **Harvey's Lake Cabins and Campground**, with 53 sites (190 Campers Lane, Barnet, VT 05821, ☎ 633-2213, Web site www.harveyslakecabins.com). It's the only campground on the 350-acre lake. In addition to rowboat, canoe, and bike rentals, they offer group rates, retreats, and receptions. The campground was a 1999 *Yankee Magazine* "Editor's Pick of the Year."

Other private campgrounds, mostly open from mid-May to mid-October, are **Belview** (Barton, ☎ 525-3242), **Burke Mountain** (East Burke, ☎ 626-1204), **Char-Bo** (Derby, ☎ 766-8807), **Fireside** (Derby, ☎ 766-5109), **Idle Hours** (Hardwick, ☎ 472-6732), **Lakeside** (Island Pond, ☎ 723-6649 or 723-6331), **Moose River** (St. Johnsbury, ☎ 748-4334), **Mill Brook** (Westfield, ☎ 744-6673), **White Caps** (☎ 467-3345), and **Will-O-Wood** (Orleans, overlooking Lake Willoughby, ☎ 525-3575).

A new family campground in North Concord, **Breezy Meadows Campground**, offers a place to pause before exploring the bog country of Essex County. Sites are not especially private, but kids enjoy the large pool, basketball and volleyball courts, shuffleboard, horseshoes, and playground, and there are three miles of nature trails, as well as access to the Moose River for canoeing or fishing. Breezy Meadows is east of St. Johnsbury on Route 2. (Wendel Road, PO Box 326, Concord, VT 05824; ☎ 695-9949, off-season phone 603-788-3624; Web site www.gocampingamerica.com.)

Camping at **Brighton State Park** (☎ 723-4360) includes secluded spots on Spectacle Pond, and there are nature trails and a nature museum, as well as boating. Farther to the southeast is **Maidstone State Park** (☎ 676-3930), where there's a boat ramp and boat rentals.

Groton State Forest offers five campgrounds, ranging from busy lakeshore sites to more primitive locations. For a full description of the forest, see *On Foot*. Phone numbers for the campgrounds are: **New Discovery**, ☎ 584-3820; **Ricker Pond**, 584-3821; **Big Deer** and **Stillwater**, ☎ 584-3822. Group arrangements can be made, and there are lean-to shelters as an alternative to tenting. The fly-fishing retreat at **Seyon Ranch** (see *On Water*) is also part of this immense state forest. Rangers are on hand from May 15 to October 15, and there are many afternoon and evening programs, some featuring natural history, others offering local musicians and storytellers. For general information and maps, visit the Vermont State Parks Web site, www.cit.state.vt.us/anr/fpr/parks. You can also contact Stillwater Campground through Ranger Jim Dresser by e-mail, jdresser@plainfield.bypass.com (May 15-October 15). Reservations are strongly advised.

Where To Eat

■ St. Johnsbury

Northern Lights Book Shop and Café (☎ 748-4463), on Railroad Street, offers breakfast and lunch, with omelets, homemade soups, and good croissants. On Thursday and Friday evenings the café serves dinner also.

Anthony's Diner (☎ 748-3613), also on Railroad Street, is a St. Johnsbury tradition; ask for the Woodsman Burger. The **St. Jay Diner** (☎ 748-9751) on Route 5 north of town is noted for its hearty hot meals and tasty strawberry pie.

Head north on Railroad Street, out of the center of town, through one modest traffic light at Concord Avenue and to the next one, at a busy three-way intersection. On the right is an old creamery building, and tucked into one end of it is **Cucina Di Gerardo**, a modest-sized Italian restaurant with wonderful sauces and frequent indulgence in generous portions of seafood. The pasta dishes are best, and the volcano pizza is unusual and flavorful. Ask about the special pesto marinara sauce. Devora and Gerardo have plenty of "regulars" dining there, and on a weekend you'll definitely need a reservation (☎ 748-6772). By the way, the local **bagel shop** is at the far end of the same building, if you get one of those Saturday morning cravings.

For good pizza and hefty sandwiches, try **Tim's Deli** (☎ 748-3118) on Route 2 at the east edge of town, on the corner of Concord Avenue.

■ Lower Waterford

This "white village" is close to St. Johnsbury. Take Route 2 east of town to the intersection with Route 18, which reaches Lower Waterford in eight miles and brings you to the **Rabbit Hill Inn** (☎ 748-5168). The Northeast Kingdom's most elegant service and beautifully served cuisine is also delicious, with unusual sauces and intriguing combinations of fruit. Dessert is a feast in itself. Music often accompanies weekend dining.

■ Danville

When you get to the center of Danville on Route 2, turn north at the blinking light onto Hill Street; the **Creamery Restaurant** (☎ 684-3616) is a block down on the right and serves excellent food, with a constantly changing blackboard menu. Be sure to save room for the maple cream pie. A pub downstairs serves more casual cuisine on weekends.

■ Lyndonville

The **Miss Lyndonville Diner** (☎ 626-9890) is a sister to the Miss Vermont in St. Johnsbury, and offers a hearty breakfast, good burgers, and good old-fashioned puddings. North of the diner on Route 5, across the road, is **Trout River Brewing Company** (☎ 626-3984); the microbrewery offers half a dozen brews. Call for tour and tasting hours. Keep going north to the center of town and find **Holly Berry's** (☎ 626-3546) on the right, just before the T-junction. This little bakery is a local prize, serving meal-sized muffins and good coffee. It opens early: Monday-Friday, 5:30 am-2 pm; Saturday, 6-11 am.

On the main street of town, Depot Street, there are hearty vegetarian lunches cooked to individual preference at **Avery's Kitchen** (☎ 748-3587).

■ East Burke

In the center of town is the **River Garden Café** (☎ 626-3514), where the chef changes the blackboard menu daily, often including smoked salmon or poached fruit in the breakfast specials, and exquisite Italian entrées at dinner.

Across from the River Garden is **Bailey's & Burke** (☎ 626-9250), a general store with fresh pizza and sandwiches.

The Northeast Kingdom

Go up the Mountain Road toward the slopes of Burke Mountain and find the **Old Cutter Inn** (☎ 626-5152) for exquisite Swiss cuisine. Arrive hungry, and don't plan to do anything energetic afterward.

Take the road west out of the village, climbing slowly uphill to the left until you come to the Darling Hill Road (also reached from Lyndonville). Here is **Darling's** (☎ 626-9924), a fine restaurant at the Inn at Mountain View Creamery. Do make reservations.

■ Westmore

The **Willoughvale Inn** (☎ 525-4123 or 800-594-9102, Web site www. willoughvale.com) is only eight miles from the village of Barton; take Route 16 east to Lake Willoughby, turn down the East Shore Road (Route 5A) and the inn is on the left. The view over the narrow gouge of the lake is exhilarating, the gardens are charming, and the food is classic cuisine with a delicate hand on the fresh fish.

■ Newport

There are a wide variety of eateries in and around Newport, from pizza to German and Italian cuisine. The **East Side** (☎ 334-2340) offers family dining on the shore of Lake Memphremagog. The **Hidden Country Restaurant** (☎ 744-6149) in nearby Lowell serves mini-meals if you arrive early enough, and offers a good prime rib. During the summer the **Newport Country Club** (☎ 334-1634) is open to guests and provides pleasant dining.

■ Coventry

Heermansmith Farm Inn (☎ 754-8866; see *Where To Stay*) is open for dinner; call ahead to be sure there's room at the inn. The meals are excellent and the wine list unusually good.

■ Jay & Montgomery Center

For a sandwich or a backpacker's lunch, the **Jay Country Store** (☎ 988-4040) is a friendly place to stop. If you're looking for a more formal dinner, head over the mountain and down Route 242 to Montgomery Center, then north onto Route 118 to the **Black Lantern Inn** (☎ 326-4507 or 800-255-8661) for exquisite candlelight dining. The **Inn on Trout River** (☎ 326-4391 or 800-338-7049) is in Montgomery Village and also offers fine cuisine. For a sense of both romance and humor as well as superb dining, leave Montgomery on Route 58 and head eastward into Hazen's Notch. About a mile up the mountain is **Zack's on the Rocks** (☎ 326-4500), where the "brown paper" menu changes often and the chef, your host, creates an atmosphere of unusual joy in both the cuisine and the customers.

Roast duck, delicate salmon dishes, and chicken banana are among the entrées. Plan to stay all evening; reservations are necessary.

■ Greensboro

Driving to Greensboro for Sunday brunch at the **Highland Lodge** (☎ 533-2647) is a fine way to savor the weekend. Be sure to call for hours, which vary by season. Dinner is sumptuous, befitting an inn where most guests are busy all day either boating, hiking, or skiing cross country.

Later in the day, slip a few miles beyond Greensboro to East Hardwick, where **Perennial Pleasures Nursery** (☎ 472-5104) offers a "cream tea" in the tea garden. Reservations are requested.

Index